# Utah

# Utah

Christine Balaz
*with principal photography by the author*

FIRST EDITION

The Countryman Press ✳ Woodstock, Vermont

ISBN 978-0-88150-738-6

Cover photo © Micah May
All interior photos by Christine Balaz unless otherwise noted
Book design by Bodenweber Design
Page composition by PerfecType, Nashville, TN
Maps by Mapping Specialists Ltd., Madison, WI © 2009 The Countryman Press

Published by The Countryman Press, P.O. Box 748, Woodstock, Vermont 05091

Distributed by W. W. Norton & Company, Inc., 500 Fifth Avenue, New York, NY 10110

Printed in the United States of America

10 9 8 7 6 5 4 3 2 1

# EXPLORE WITH US!

Welcome to this first edition of *Utah: An Explorer's Guide*. As an imported resident of the state, I have used my insider's knowledge of its resources and drawn upon my experience as a newcomer to create a guide that would include all of the state's most famous offerings, as well as its lesser known but equally important assets. I compiled these listings with attention to variety of interest, price, region, and importance. If you discover that I have missed something that should have been included, please be in touch. My goal is to create the best guide possible, and though I've worked incredibly hard to do so, it is impossible to attain perfection alone.

## WHAT'S WHERE

This is a quick hits list. Be sure to browse these; it will only take a minute. Likely you'll come across many topics that may surprise you, or that address nagging concerns such as the grid system and liquor laws. These also may inspire you to check out various items that you hadn't previously been aware of.

## LODGING

Lodging in Utah varies wildly from city to city as well as town to town. Resort towns have many hotels, bed-and-breakfasts, vacation rentals, and the like. In these towns, I list lodgings with many subheadings. Other towns put their visitors up differently; though they may be very popular destinations, their lodging might be entirely composed of national-brand hotels. Though these establishments require no descriptions, they can be completely booked during peak season. In these situations, I give a laundry list of these establishments, so you have as many options as possible to conform to your traveler's points or personal biases, or to simply have a chance of finding a vacancy. The bottom line is that I want this guidebook to be as resourceful as possible, and its usefulness not limited by any kind of imposed format.

## RESTAURANTS

Restaurants have been divided into two rough categories: the more formal *Dining Out* and the more casual *Eating Out*. Casual does not necessarily mean lesser quality, but generally describes a less expensive, more informal atmosphere and a faster experience. When I categorize a restaurant as being more formal, I imagine a place fit for a slow-paced romantic or business dinner, complete with bottles of wine and attractive décor and plating.

## KEY TO SYMBOLS

- ✒ This symbol indicates an establishment, activity, or destination particularly well suited to the interests of children and families.
- 🐾 The paw print indicates a pet-friendly establishment, or a place where dogs are allowed to roam off-leash.

☙ This symbol indicates a restaurant, hotel, or any sort of attraction with especially good value.

☙ Where you see a leaf before an entry, you know it is an establishment that purchases wind power, has green architecture, or is otherwise environmentally friendly.

Suggestions are always appreciated. Please send them to Explorer's Guide Editor, The Countryman Press, P.O. Box 748, Woodstock, VT 05091.

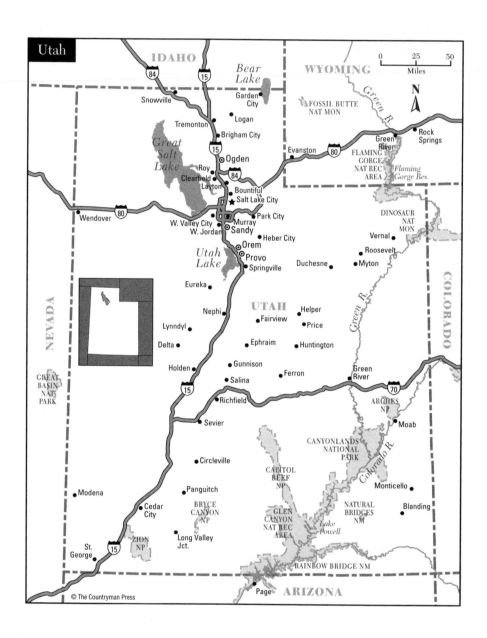

Utah

IDAHO

WYOMING

Bear Lake

0   25   50
Miles

N

Snowville

Garden City

FOSSIL BUTTE NAT MON

Green R.

Tremonton

Logan

Rock Springs

Brigham City

Green River

Great Salt Lake

Evanston

FLAMING GORGE NAT REC AREA

Flaming Gorge Res.

Ogden

Roy

Clearfield

Layton

Bountiful

Salt Lake City

DINOSAUR NAT MON

Wendover

W. Valley City

Park City

Vernal

Murray

Sandy

Roosevelt

W. Jordan

Heber City

Myton

NEVADA

Orem

Provo

Duchesne

COLORADO

Utah Lake

Springville

Eureka

UTAH

Helper

Nephi

Fairview

Price

Lynndyl

Ephraim

Huntington

Delta

Green R.

Holden

Gunnison

Ferron

GREAT BASIN NAT PARK

Salina

Green River

Richfield

70

ARCHES NP

Sevier

Moab

CANYONLANDS NATIONAL PARK

Circleville

CAPITOL REEF NP

Colorado R.

Modena

Panguitch

Monticello

Cedar City

BRYCE CANYON NP

NATURAL BRIDGES NM

Blanding

GLEN CANYON NAT REC AREA

Lake Powell

St. George

ZION NP

Long Valley Jct.

RAINBOW BRIDGE NM

© The Countryman Press

Page

ARIZONA

# CONTENTS

# LIST OF MAPS

# INTRODUCTION

Utah is one of the most misunderstood states and best-kept secrets in the nation. It is represented by such a huge collection of ideas, but most people choose to only consider a handful: Mormons and skiing, or perhaps red rocks and sandstone arches. In fact, Utah has all of these and much more, in scope and depth more substantial than most could imagine—even those who have spent their entire lives here.

I grew up in the Bridger Mountains near Bozeman, Montana, close enough to visit Utah, but not close enough to really understand it. I remember thinking Utah was a geographically perfect state with some serious hang-ups. I knew of its red deserts, huge mountains, vast wilderness, its genuine metropolis, and Great Salt Lake. I knew Utah had bigger mountains and more snow than any place around, great rock climbing, dozens of universities, lunar desertscapes, and professional sports teams. But I also heard strange rumors of its Mormon residents.

Utah indeed has it all; it has everything I thought it had: the mountains and the Mormons (called Latter-day Saints). I've lived in this state now for three years and have learned a lot. It turns out this religion is one of the state's best assets. It is what enabled these arid lands to be settled in the first place. It gives the area religious significance, and its history gives Utah vividness. Today, the creeds of the religion go a long way toward keeping the city streets clean and safe, even if only about two-fifths of Salt Lake City is Mormon.

Utah has one of the most diverse geographies that can be drawn into the borders of any single state. It has high plains, sculpted sandstone formations, lush green canyons, severe desert salt flats, and the sky-scraping Rocky Mountains. Spanning the middle latitudes of the United States and 2 vertical miles in elevation, it has a climate made-to-order. Southern Utah shares the same weather as Las Vegas; northern Utah experiences the same seasons as Wyoming and Idaho. Sunny valleys radiate with warmth, and mountain towns enjoy crisp air in the summer months. Salt Lake City enjoys moderate winters, while resorts only 30 minutes up-canyon are buried annually under 500 inches of the world's best snow.

It is of course true that Salt Lake City is home to the Church of Jesus Christ of Latter-day Saints. Mormonism is a keystone in Utah's fascinating and turbulent biography, and gives the region a special richness. However, it is hardly the only cultural dimension. Contrary to popular myths, this state is populated with a diverse collection of religions and heritages, all of which have arrived in this state by way of a most interesting journey. Utah is home to some of the Intermountain

West's oldest Catholic and Thai societies, historic mining and industrial communities, and Ute, Paiute, Shoshone, Dine, and Goshute tribes.

Besides all this, there are internationally ranked restaurants, dance troupes, professional symphonic orchestras, and a world-renowned independent film scene. The list goes on to include wineries, breweries (one of which, Salt Lake City's Red Rock Brewpub, just won Best Brew Pub in the nation), even an up-and-coming distillery, as well as popular outdoor concerts, mountain biking, and gallery strolls. Utah's geography and climate breed hoards of professional athletes, including Olympic ski racers and jumpers as well as extreme skiers and boarders, road cyclists, mountain bikers, rock climbers, and over-distance trail runners.

Unfortunately, most people outside of the Beehive State were raised on a diet of exaggerated rumors that Utah's population is all Mormon and believe the state is therefore strange and untrustworthy. Fortunately, I lucked out and was suckered in by the beauty and bounty of the state. Today, a resident of Salt Lake City, I am smugly grateful for the existence of that nasty, unappetizing rumor, as it has done wonders in keeping the state free from the exploitation that other similarly awesome places have suffered. And I am at once glad that I was brave enough to take a closer look. Though the falsified, fear-inspiring myths about Utah have slandered the state, they have also served to safeguard its rich urban and outdoor opportunities from overcrowding. These misunderstandings have kept accessibility high—and crime, expenses, and crowding low. Today other "brave" visitors can enjoy Utah's world-class opportunities without the inflated travel costs and tourist gridlock characteristic of other premium destinations.

Utah continues to become more widely accepted as an attractive place to visit and less feared as a hotbed of some spooky religion. The state is growing ever more mainstream and easy to digest. As Utah becomes a more comfortable place to visit and live, more people from more diverse backgrounds come to experience the state for themselves and leave their own mark. During your visit, you will be amazed by the outdoors and surprised by the quality of the amenities, and you'll feel intrigued by the state's unique heritage, yet comfortable among its people.

NOVEMBER WEATHER THREATENS NEAR A BOULDER FIELD ALONG THE GREEN RIVER SOUTH OF DINOSAUR NATIONAL MONUMENT

The last ice age, called the Wisconsin Glaciation, began roughly 70,000 years ago and ended just 10,000 years ago. It enacted major climactic changes around the world. It decreased temperatures and evaporation, and increased precipitation. In North America, all of these changes coalesced to fill the land-locked Great Basin with huge amounts of water. This resulted in much of present-day Utah being covered by a massive, ancient reservoir called Lake Bonneville. These early shores were more than 800 feet higher than those of the modern-day Utah Lake and Great Salt Lake. Bonneville's surface area was somewhere around 20,000 square miles, nearly one-quarter of the area of modern Utah. Enclosed in part by natural earthen dams prone to failure, this basin filled and refilled as many as 28 times. At the end of its final filling, the lake overflowed and breached an earthen dam at Red Rock Pass, Idaho. Evidence suggests that 1,000 cubic *miles* of water burst out of the lake over the course of a few weeks. Today, horizontal striations, visible along the foothills of the Wasatch, mark the bygone lakeshores.

As the Wisconsin Glaciation abated, ancient societies began to emerge in Utah. It is believed that people inhabited the region as early as 12,000 years ago. These were migratory tribes of Paleo-Indians, traveling through the region to hunt game, but vacating during the harsh winters. The first permanent derivatives of these earlier tribes were the Anasazi and Fremont, who planted Utah's first crops and raised animals for consumption. These peoples left behind evidence of their agriculture, artwork, basket-weaving, and tool-making, and were the ancestors of the Shoshone, Ute, Paiute, Bannock, and Gosiute tribes native to Utah when the first whites began to penetrate the region.

The first Europeans came to Utah in the 1700s, passing through the land nomadically as most had before them. These explorers, Catholic priests, and trappers were the first to document Utah's wild landscape. They lived as drifters, harvesting wild game and using rivers as throughways. Despite its plentiful land and wild beauty, Utah remained uninhabitable to most would-be European American residents because of its harshly dry climate and profound isolation from populated seacoast cities.

On July 24, 1847, Mormon pioneer Brigham Young and 148 followers crossed into this open landscape after a grueling 1,300-mile journey from Illinois. Upon arrival, Young declared modern-day Salt Lake City "The Place" that marked the end of a flight from persecution and the beginning of a religious boom. The Mormons, laden with dissident religious beliefs and misfit polygamist practices, were refugees from traditional American civilization. It was here they hid themselves from discrimination.

Tucked into a vast region formidably barren to Western civilization, they were safe from society's hounds, yet were faced with the especially ominous challenge of surviving the elements. Only the intrinsic industriousness and organization of their religion enabled the Mormons to overcome the region's lethal aridness with ingenious infrastructure. Even before federal bureaucracies, the Mormons were able to find, tame, and distribute the area's scarce water resources and thus convert its lands into a productive growing region. Since that time, the area has undergone a most rapid and expansive development.

With the water tapped and the foundations for civilization laid, other pioneers ventured to Utah to create lives for themselves on the shoulders of the Mormons.

Miners perched themselves high in the mountains of Park City, and in Big and Little Cottonwood canyons, exploiting the region's silver and other precious mineral ore. Ranchers and soldiers trickled into the Salt Lake Valley and lived uneasily alongside their Mormon neighbors. The Mormons, who otherwise would have been happily settled among themselves, continued to endure attacks from these "gentile" newcomers and even the United States government. Weary of harassment in their holy land, members of the Church of Jesus Christ of Latter-day Saints grew increasingly hostile toward outsiders. Non-Mormon "heathens" often lived tucked away up in the canyons, literally afraid for their lives. One relic from these tumultuous days is Ruth's Diner, a Salt Lake City establishment that was literally moved out of downtown and into a boxcar up Emigration Canyon. Today Ruth's Diner still serves their famous "mile-high" biscuits with every meal and showcases framed pictures of this early nonconformist, a pioneer in her own right.

Indeed, conflict yielded occasional violence between the two opposing groups. The years 1857–1858 brought the Utah War, a battle between Mormon settlers and the United States government for power in Utah. The Mormons had proposed an expansive sovereign nation called State of Deseret and had begun establishing outposts like Moab to establish rule over what today would be nearly all of the southwestern United States. President James Buchanan and the federal government forcibly removed Brigham Young from gubernatorial office. Though this action was received gracefully in northern Utah, there was movement for upheaval in the south. Some men even bragged they had enough wives to tamp out the United States Army. In the first year of the war, a reactionary massacre was staged by the Mormons to avenge the violent death of their slain apostle Parley Pratt. The result was the death of 137 innocent pioneers passing through Utah en route from Arkansas to California at Mormon Meadows, just north of present day St. George. Eventually the reality of the United States' overwhelming power subdued the flames of the Mormon resistance.

In 1896, the First Transcontinental Railroad was completed just 56 miles west of Ogden at Promontory Point, commemorated today by the Golden Spike National Historic Site. Utah Territory's newfound accessibility resulted in a population surge, and the United States began efforts to include Utah in the union. However, a fundamental barrier stood in the way of this naturalization: the polygamist practices of the Mormon religion could not be condoned. Conveniently, leaders of the Mormon Church experienced divine revelation in 1890 that instructed them to eliminate polygamy from mainstream LDS religious practices. While it did not completely end plural marriages, it did enable Utah to be admitted into the United States in 1896. Although separatist Fundamental Latter-day Saints still practice illegal polygamy across the western United States and in British Columbia to this day, the major branch of the Mormon religion has greatly normalized. To casual observers, it is indistinguishable from more common and understood sects of Christianity.

Today Utah's diversifying residents coexist in a symbiotic relationship, with cultures blending and a variety of religions flourishing. Since Utah's inception as a state, Mormons and non-Mormons alike have prospered. Currently, the Salt Lake region is blooming as a cultural, economic, and educational center. Twice a year thousands of merchants from around the nation gather at the Salt Palace Convention Center for the famous Outdoor Retailer Show. The Sundance Film Festival

DESPITE ITS FORMIDABLY TALL WALLS, DESOLATION CANYON WAS HOME TO SOME OF UTAH'S EARLY RANCHERS.

takes place in Park City each January and has spurred the uprising of filmmakers and societies around the valley. The University of Utah, Westminster College, Brigham Young University, and Utah Valley State College have a combined student total of 80,000. The Mormon religion is the fastest-growing religion in the world—and anyone can join a free, guided tour through Temple Square in downtown Salt Lake City, marvel at its atypical architecture, and learn history from a Mormon tour guide. As Mormonism has grown, so too has there been an influx of non-Mormons, diluting the LDS population within Salt Lake City to around 40 percent. What remains of yesteryear's Mormon dominance is a thought-provoking forum for the blending of cultures and dynamic self-discovery.

Utah's modern culture is purposeful and vibrant. It is represented by newcomers, converts into and out of different religions, businesspeople, students, musicians, professional athletes, and sixth-generation Brigham Young descendents—and most people span several of these categories in quite unexpected ways. Introspection, and reflection on this state's diverse heritage, is expressed through art, music, creative fashion, and even widespread tattooing. Although the Mormon, non-Mormon cohabitation is peaceful, this culture-counterculture phenomenon is a platform for contemplation and action. It is clear to see Utah's residents—the Jews, Mormons, Muslims, Christians, agnostics, atheists, outdoors enthusiasts, artists, students, vagrants, businesspeople, and immigrants—are deep in an identity search, visibly defining their conclusions through fashion and artistic expression.

## ITINERARY SUGGESTIONS

Utah is much too big to digest in one chunk. However, for especially popular amusements, I've listed some of the state's best. Though you likely won't have time to cover each of the items listed (and won't want to sprint from one end of the state to the other), this allows you to choose a handful of some of Utah's must-sees.

### SKIER'S DELIGHT

If you are a skier, then you've found the right place. In the United States, Utah is matched in snowfall only by Californian and Alaskan mountain ranges. But what

Utah has that these ranges usually don't is feet and feet of *light, dry* snow—"the greatest snow on earth."

The most obvious place to plan a ski vacation is Salt Lake City or Park City. **Park City,** just 30 minutes east of Salt Lake City, is home to Park City Mountain Resort, The Canyons Resort, and Deer Valley Resort. **Park City Mountain Resort** is the most notorious for its all-around, family-friendly terrain and accommodations. **The Canyons** is known for its utter vastness, lingering powder stashes, and excellent backcountry access. **Deer Valley** has its niche in absurdly attentive customer service—yes, it is true that they will put your boots on for you, even if you don't request it.

**Salt Lake City** is conveniently connected by I-215 to **Big Cottonwood Canyon** and **Little Cottonwood Canyon.** These two canyons have some of the country's best resorts and are within 25 to 35 minutes from downtown because of the well-designed beltway. BCC is home to Brighton and Solitude. **Brighton**'s specialty is its terrain parks and snowboarder-friendly turf. **Solitude**'s name says it all; though it is not a huge mountain, it has very good stashes of terrain and virtually no crowding. Little Cottonwood has, in my opinion, two of the state's best mountains, Alta and Snowbird. **Alta,** unlike Brighton, does not (and likely never will) allow snowboarders. It calls itself Alta Lift—it is very deliberately a ski area, not a resort. This ski area has excellent terrain and an old-school attitude. The best stashes are reached by traversing and hiking, and the name of the game here is hard skiing, not fashion. **Snowbird** is one of Utah's most hard-core mountains. Its bottom-to-top tram, 3,200 vertical feet, and very aggressive terrain make this the training and competition grounds for some of the nation's top extreme skiers.

Less famous are Ogden Valley's ski areas: Powder Mountain, Snowbasin, and Wolf Mountain. **Wolf Mountain** is a very small hill but is inexpensive and a perfect place for families and people new to skiing. **Powder Mountain** has the most skiable acreage of any mountain in the lower 48. **Snowbasin** has very good, Alta- or Snowbird-like terrain, but much less crowding. It is also a Sun Valley resort and has ridiculously luxurious facilities, but very reasonable (even inexpensive) prices.

## NATIONAL PARKS BUFF

Utah is one of the nation's richest states in terms of public lands and national parks. If you have never visited its parks, you should spend at least one day in the southern portion of the state. Begin in the southwestern corner of the state, at **Zion National Park.** If you are pressed for time, keep your visit to Zion Canyon only (bypassing the less-accessible Kolob Canyon). Travel through the park on UT 9, which will take you through the Zion–Mount Caramel tunnel, which is more than a mile long. Travel north along US 89, and then east on UT 12 to enter **Bryce Canyon National Park.** Park your car and hike a small section of the very flat Rim Trail, which overlooks the amphitheaters below.

As you continue northeast along UT 12, you will be passing through the northern portion of **Grand Staircase–Escalante National Monument.** This 1.9-million acre BLM land contains a rainbow of cliffs that rise over 6,000 feet from the Grand Canyon to Brian Head. If you have time, consider taking Hell's Backbone Road into Boulder, instead of UT 12. This remarkably exposed road was for a long time the only way to reach the town of Boulder. If you're hungry or tired, stop at the **Hell's Backbone Grill** or **Boulder Mountain Lodge,** both on the same property. (Call ahead for reservations; information is listed in "Boulder and Escalante" chapter of this book.)

Once replenished, travel north along UT 12, and east on UT 24 into the northern portion of **Capitol Reef National Park.** The **Waterpocket Fold** is this park's most predominant feature, an unmistakable sandstone uplift 100 miles long. Though **Canyonlands National Park** is physically the next closest park, it is slightly out of the way, as it is centered around the junction of Utah's two biggest rivers, the Green and Colorado. I suggest first going north to I-70, and then down into **Arches National Park.** Moab is the next stop along the way, where you can pick up sunscreen and head to **Canyonlands National Park** for some hiking.

## OFF THE BEATEN PATH: LESSER KNOWN AND JUST AS COOL

Utah, like any other state, is subject to stereotyping. People think of this state and picture Arches National Park, Temple Square, and Wasatch skiing. However, the state has many, many areas equally as splendid, but less exploited. If you like the national parks but don't want to mill about in a crowd, try checking out **Grand Staircase–Esclante National Monument** or **Goblin Valley State Park**. The Grand Staircase is an incredible geological phenomenon, created by a 10,000-foot-vertical uplift of many different types and colors of sandstone strata. Goblin Valley State Park has some of the state's most densely concentrated and bizarre-looking globular rock formations. On the way, drive over Hell's Backbone Road (north of Boulder), and eat at **Hell's Backbone Grill.**

If you like Moab's slot canyons, sandstone formations, and the like, try the **San Rafael Swell**. This region, bisected by I-70, has some of the state's best canyoneering, camping, and most remote recreational opportunities. If it's summertime and you need to escape the heat, don't drive to Montana; go just 90 minutes east of Salt Lake City to the Uintas. These mountains are the tallest range in the state and are 20–30 degrees cooler than the Salt Lake Valley at any given time. The incredibly scenic Mirror Lake Highway is the most popular means to access this region and is an 80-mile stretch of road that crosses the northwestern corner of the Uintas on its way from Kamas to Evanston, Wyoming.

## FAT-TIRE FREAKS

Moab is hands down the most famous mountain biking locale in Utah. Its slick rock was one of the nation's cornerstones in the development of the sport. And today its warm, dry climate, and very tourist-friendly nature, make this town an easy place to rent a bike and learn the sport—or the ultimate place to test your fitness and the you've already developed. The two most famous trails in the area are the Slickrock Trail and the White Rim Trail. The 12-mile, incredibly challenging **Slickrock Trail** is Moab's bread and butter, and sees more than 100,000 visitors each year. The **White Rim Trail** is a 103-mile loop and the ultimate multiday party trail. Though there is a respectable amount of elevation gain and loss, the journey is almost all on jeep roads and is usually completed over the course of three or four days.

The other place for some of the best biking in Utah is in **Park City.** Though not as famous, the riding is arguably better and much more diverse than in Moab. Many, many, many miles of trails exist here. One major center of riding is at the

Swaner Nature Preserve, in **Kimball Junction.** From here, many buffed-out single-track loops exist. Some are fairly short and moderate; others are long and more challenging. One feature of this area is its **Bob's Basin Downhill** course—a system of three different downhill trails with many jumps and fun features built into them. A pleasant and mild climb brings you back to the top for more laps. Also in Park City is the famous **8,000-foot trail** that traverses from Park City Mountain Resort all the way to The Canyons. **Deer Valley**'s downhill riding has a reputation for being among the best of its kind in North America.

## MORMON CURIOSITY

Whether Mormon or not, you almost certainly have some curiosity about this religion's history and infrastructure. **Salt Lake City** has the most obvious attractions. **Temple Square** is the site of dozens of landmarks, including the famous **Salt Lake Temple** and egg-shaped **Salt Lake Tabernacle.** It is within a short walk of the world's largest genealogical records collection, the **Family History Library,** and the **Global Headquarters** of the Church of Jesus Christ of Latter-day Saints.

Though Salt Lake City will always be the original home base, **Provo** has shouldered quite a crucial role in the church. Not only is it home to some very essential Mormon infrastructure, it has definitely replaced Salt Lake City as the church's more culturally and spiritually pure society. Here, the church-sponsored **Brigham Young University** is one of the more academically respected institutions in the nation, but it is also Mormonism's largest and most strict educational facility. The **Missionary Training Center,** also in Provo, is where the young men and women representing the church are educated before heading into the world on their infamous missions.

# WHAT'S WHERE IN UTAH

AIR TRANSPORTATION **Salt Lake International Airport (SLC)** (801-575-2400 or 800-595-2442; www.slc airport.com) is located just 10 minutes west of downtown Salt Lake City by way of I-80. This is a significant hub for 13 major airlines, including Delta. Numerous minor airlines operate shuttle services from this facility to smaller state airports. At 444 South River Road in St. George is the **St. George Municipal Airport (SGU)** (435-634-5822), the other primary airport in Utah. Small, public-use airports worth noting are **Bryce Canyon Airport (BCE), Cedar City Regional Airport (CDC),** servicing Delta and US Airlines, and **Canyonlands Field Airport (CNY)** in Moab, where Air Midwest (US Airways Express) offers service to Salt Lake City. In reality, the most practical air travel itinerary in Utah includes arriving at Salt Lake International Airport and utilizing the network of interstates crisscrossing the state, whose nexus is located in Salt Lake City.

ALCOHOL If you were to believe all the rumors about Utah's liquor culture, you would think that watery beer is the only alcohol around, and that it's only sold to members of exclusive "private clubs." While it is absolutely true that Utah enforces tighter restrictions on alcohol than most states, these laws are easily navigable.

Truthfully, much of Utah's beer is indeed limited to 3.2 percent alcohol by weight (which is the same as 4.0 percent alcohol by *volume,* as labeled by clever marketers). This "Utah" beer is available in grocery stores, gas stations, and the like. The alcohol content might appear sadly weak compared with national norms. However, many beers across the nation are measured in terms of ABV instead of ABW, making this content reduction less drastic than it seems—and many varieties of beer sold round the world, such as stouts and porters, do not have much greater alcohol content than these 3.2 (or 4.0) beers anyway. Some other beers like Belgians and IPAs are much more strongly affected. Happily, full-strength local and imported beers are available; you simply must purchase them in a state-operated liquor store, bar, or restaurant. In **Utah State Liquor Stores,** you will also find the state's inventory of wine and liquor available for in-container purchase; gas stations, grocery stores, and the like are not permitted to sell anything but low-alcohol beer.

**Private clubs** are, simply put, bars. They are social establishments with a liquor license where the main attraction (and source of revenue) is booze.

You can gain access to any club either by accompanying a member or by purchasing an inexpensive (four- or five-dollar) temporary membership. This will grant you and approximately seven guests access to this establishment for up to two weeks. Some restaurant-type establishments also are catalogued as private clubs, and the distinction is based on a ratio of liquor-to-food sales. This creates a problem for families, as no person under the age of 21 is allowed on the premises of such an establishment (unless there is a section distinctly partitioned from the bar side of the business, which is often the case).

A final thought: despite popular rumor, Utah technically has no **"dry counties,"** or counties that forbid the sale of alcohol. State law (Utah Code Section 32A-1-102) does not allow local jurisdictions to regulate alcohol in a fashion contradictory to state law. Therefore no county can officially ban the sale of alcohol, though it will certainly be difficult—if not impossible—to find alcohol in highly concentrated LDS settlements, particularly those set away from tourism and interstates. Also see *Package Stores*, below.

AREA CODES Utah currently has only two area codes: 801 and 435. **801** applies to Salt Lake City, Ogden, Provo, and Central Utah. The **435** area code covers the rest of the state. However, the 801 area code is expected to soon reach capacity, at which point the 385 area code will be added to the current 801 territory.

BICYCLING Utah has an abundance of opportunities for cycling—on roads, trails, and desert slickrock—and a perfectly sunny, dry climate to accompany this. Mountain bikers have perhaps the best situation in Utah, though road bikers have it pretty good as well.

In the northern region, a network of trails, particularly the **Bonneville Shoreline Trail System,** borders the Wasatch cities of Salt Lake City, Tooele, Provo, Logan, and the remainder of the Wasatch Front. However, it is generally thought that **Park City** has the best riding in northern half of Utah. At a higher elevation than the valleys below, Park City offers the best temperatures during the hot summer months. It has miles and miles of rolling and buffed single-track near **Kimball Junction,** and near town, linking its ski resorts. Road riding in the Wasatch is best in the spring and fall at lower elevations, where the paved canyons are tolerably cool. Up high, near **Kamas** and **Coalville,** and even **Logan,** unpopulated stretches run eastward toward Wyoming and remain much cooler than in lower valleys.

In the southern part of the state, Moab and St. George have abundant road and mountain cycling. **Moab** is world famous for its slickrock mountain biking but also has some cycling in the **La Sals**—even extensive trails like the famous and scenic 103-mile **White Rim Trail** and **Porcupine Rim Trail** that links all the way to Durango, Colorado. Though **St. George**'s riding is less famous, there is plenty of it in the vicinity, including in the nearby **Dixie National Forest.** Though riding is possible year-round, it's best done outside of the summer months.

For an amazing online statewide database of mountain biking trail descriptions, photographs, and even video, visit www.utahmountainbiking .com. For road rides, visit www.salt lakecycling.com. *Cycling Utah* (www .cyclingutah.com) is a statewide free magazine that, among other things, features riding events and lists retailers across Utah.

BIRDING The most famous bird-watching venue in the northern part of the state is Brigham City's **Bear River Migratory Bird Refuge** (435-734-6426; www.fws.gov/bearriver) and the nearby environs of the Great Salt Lake. Other bird-watching opportunities present themselves in the canyons of the Wasatch near Logan, Salt Lake City, the **Ouray National Wildlife Refuge** (435-545-2522; www.fws.gov/ouray) in Randlett, and along the **Provo River** (and US 189) from Park City to the Provo area. Farther south, the **Matheson Preserve** (435-259-4629) near Moab and along the Colorado River, and the 34,000-acre **Upper Beaver Dam Wash** (www.blm.gov/ut) in the far southwestern corner of the state, are other rich bird habitats.

BOATING Perhaps the most famous boating in Utah is at **Lake Powell,** in the southeast corner of the state. This massive reservoir is nearly 190 miles long and has several different access points. Other major reservoirs popular for boating are the **Flaming Gorge** in the northeast corner of the state, and the **Jordanelle, Deer Creek, Pineview, Strawberry,** and **Willard Bay** reservoirs in the vicinity of Salt Lake City and the general Wasatch/Uinta mountains area. **Utah Lake** and **Bear Lake** are two very sizable, natural lakes in the same vicinity and are the first- and second-largest freshwater lakes in the state.

River running is done all over the state, though it is concentrated in the eastern half of the state. The Green and Colorado rivers offer the most white-water mileage, although the Provo River is also popular for its Wasatch rapids. Big trips are usually done on the **Green River,** as it has many stretches of white water from the point where it enters the state, by way of **Lodore Canyon** and **Dinosaur National Monument,** to its confluence with the Colorado as it travels through Grey, Desolation (both whitewater), Labyrinth, and Stillwater (both very gentle) canyons. The Green pours into the **Colorado River** in the

SOARING MESAS TYPICAL OF THE CANYONLANDS' HIGHEST ROCK STRATA

Jonathan Echlin

center of Canyonlands National Park just south of Moab, and the two rivers form enormous rapids in **Cataract Canyon** before becoming quiet in the waters of Lake Powell. **Provo River,** as it runs through Heber Valley and Provo Canyon (along US 189), is the Wasatch Front's local place for river running. It is not nearly as big as the Green, but it is much more accessible. The **Ogden and Weber rivers** also offer some smaller, almost creek-style paddling just east of Ogden, where a play-boat park (the **Ogden Whitewater Park**) awaits kayakers on the Weber River in town. The best **flat water** canoeing is on the Green River as it flows through Labyrinth and Stillwater canyons (part of the Green River, above).

Visit **www.utahwhitewaterclub .org,** a Web site that offers important information for white water paddlers, including daily updated river flows and other in-state links. Another Web site, **www.paddling.net,** is a national link that has a Utah-specific database including trip reports, and links to guides and outfitters.

**BUS AND LIGHT-RAIL TRANS-PORTATION Greyhound Lines** (800-231-2222; www.greyhound.com) operates stops in Brigham City, Green River, Logan, Ogden, Provo, Richfield, Salt Lake City, St. George, and Tremonton, transporting passengers to Utah and shuttling them across the state. **Metro bus** transportation exists only in the populous Wasatch Front region and is operated by the **Utah Transit Authority** (801-743-3882 or 888-743-3882; www.rideuta.com). Downtown Salt Lake City enjoys a dense network of bus and light-rail routes, including bus service to nearby Big and Little Cottonwood canyons ski areas. Adjoining cities as far north as

Ogden and as far south as Provo see less extensive bus scheduling.

**CITIES AND TOWNS** Of Utah's 2.2 million residents, 1.5 million live along the western edge of the Wasatch Range, or **Wasatch Front.** Salt Lake City, at the center of this metropolis, is the most populous city in the state. Though Salt Lake City has only 200,000 people, that number is hardly representative, and many townships continue, uninterrupted, to form an elongated urban compact that reaches north beyond Ogden and south past Provo. Outside of this complex is a vast landscape dotted with several mid-sized outposts. For the most part, these are along I-15 and I-70. In the southwest corner of the state, the most sizable townships are **St. George** and **Cedar City;** in the center of the state, **Price;** to the southeast, **Green River** and **Moab;** and tucked in the mountains of northeast Utah, **Logan.**

**CLIMATE** For a state that spans 350 miles (5° latitude) from its northern border to its southern edge, and has more than 2 vertical miles difference in elevation, it is impossible to neatly generalize climate. What can be said is that Utah sees the sun around 250 days each year and has virtually no humidity. The little precipitation that does fall skillfully blankets the ski resorts by winter and gives life to the rivers and forests as summer rain without drowning the valleys. Spring and fall are exceptionally pleasant (though spring tends to be wetter than fall); summer is dry and very warm; winter is cold, but not frigid. The state's major mountain ranges, including the Wasatch, Uinta, and Henrys, rise dramatically out of the desert floor, raking precipitation out of passing winter storm fronts. The 1.5-mile vertical relief of the Wasatch Range places its resorts in a very elite group of ski areas that consistently average 500 inches of snowfall each year. Yet Salt Lake City, just 20 minutes below these ski resorts, receives an average of just more than 50 inches of snow each year. Summer heat can be avoided at elevation and in shady canyons, and winter dreariness can be escaped on the red sandstone of Moab.

COUNTIES Utah has 29 counties. Salt Lake County has more than 900,000 residents, and Utah County (home to Provo and Orem) has more than 400,000. By contrast, Daggett County (Utah's far northeastern corner) has only 921 residents, the fewest in the state. Most counties lay somewhere in between, with midsized and small townships scattered throughout. As dictated by state law, there are no dry counties in Utah that prohibit the sale of alcohol.

DIVING No one would guess it, but there are more than 30 diving sites across Utah. Some diving sites are merely lakes and rivers, but Utah is home to a few interesting sites as well. One such site is the **Bonneville Seabase** (9390 West Hwy. 138, Grantsville; 801-884-3874; www.sea base.net), a geothermal pool stocked with a wild array of exotic fish. Another is the **Homestead Crater** (700 North Homestead Dr., Midway; 435-654-1102; www.homestead-ut.com), a naturally formed, hourglass-shaped, 65-foot-deep, 96°F pool at the Homestead Resort. More information about Utah's diving locations, outfitters, and culture can be found at www.utah diving.com.

DRIVING AND THE GRID SYS-TEM Considering Utah's nearly 85,000

square miles, it is fortuitous that the state is crisscrossed with interstates and major highways. Running north–south through the state, and connecting Ogden, Salt Lake City, Provo, and St. George to Las Vegas, is **I-15. I-80** heads due east into the state from Nevada, passing by 100 miles of desert and the Bonneville Salt Flats before intersecting with Salt Lake City. This continues up into the Wasatch, though Park City, and joins with the short connector segment, **I-84,** before heading into Wyoming. **I-70** comes west into Utah from Denver and Grand Junction before dipping south and joining with I-15. A major diagonal cut-across from northern I-15 to I-70 is **US 6.** This is a major shortcut for those traveling the central portion of the state between Salt Lake City and Moab. Most of the interstate miles in the state are kept at a 75 mph speed limit, with the exception of 65 mph in urban compacts and major junctions. Other major state and U.S. highways are generally 65 mph.

A major object of curiosity—or dread—for Utah visitors is the **"grid system"** by which the streets are named and organized. Before attempting to navigate the streets of any sizeable town in Utah, you should familiarize yourself with this scheme that integrates Mormon practicality and the local landscape.

Utah's flat, unobstructed valleys (in which most Utah towns are settled) allow for the construction of extremely linear streets. These city roads have historically been designed to mimic a coordinate plane whose center is the major LDS temple in that town. To begin, imagine the streets as a graph whose origin, "(0,0)," is usually the Mormon temple. In Salt Lake City, this intersection occurs at the intersection of Main Street and South Temple.

Counting in either cardinal direction away from the temple, each street has a value 100 greater than the last. In Salt Lake City, Main Street runs north–south. The next street to the west is 100 West (a parallel, north–south running road), then 200 West, and so forth. Heading south, the street parallel to and south of South Temple (an east–west running road) is 100 South, then 200 South and so on.

Interpreting addresses adds one more level of complexity. To understand the address 753 East 700 South, you must recognize that 700 South is the street. This street is seven blocks south of the temple and runs east–west. The building of interest is on this street about 7.5 blocks east of the temple. Think of it as "(7.53, 7.00)."

To make things just a bit more confusing, some of these major blocks are interrupted by smaller, side streets. These have been added after the fact to fill the 200 yards between major streets. These also have their place within the grid system, but have names like 540 South and 725 East. Many streets, including these side streets, have dual names. Near Sugarhouse in Salt Lake City, 1100 East is also called Highland Street, and 2100 South is sometimes called Commonwealth Avenue. Most streets of this variety are signed with both numeric and out-of-the-box names.

EMERGENCY In case of emergency, dial 911. For information on regional hospitals and clinics, look in the *Medical Emergency* section of the relevant chapter of this book.

EVENTS The annually occurring events of each region are listed after the introduction to each chapter in this book and range from cultural activities to athletic happenings. Note the

dozens of summer concert series in the Park City, Salt Lake City, and Moab regions. Also, look for farmers' markets throughout the state during the summertime. During winter, the most famous ski resorts host international competitions, from the freeride competitions at Snowbird, to World Cup snowboarding at Park City, to World Cup skiing bumps and aerials competitions at Deer Valley.

FARMERS' MARKETS Because of the extensive sunshine and long growing seasons in Utah, farmers' markets exist here in abundance. Nearly every major town has its own, including Salt Lake City, Park City, Moab, St. George, Logan, Escalante, Provo, Zion, and dozens more. Complete listings can be found on the Web, and within this book in the *Special Events* section at the beginning of each chapter.

FISHING Whether you prefer fishing from a boat on a lake, ice fishing, or extracting river fish with flies, Utah can satisfy your tastes. The best fly-fishing spots in Utah are along the **Green River,** particularly near the **Flaming Gorge Dam,** and along the **Provo River** between Park City and Provo. As with any other state in the nation, a license is required to fish any waters. These permits are available from the **Utah Division of Wildlife Resources** (www.wildlife.utah.gov) and are sold at various locations across the state. Their Web site details all the regulations and gives current fishing reports. More concrete information is listed in the each chapter's recreation section.

GARDENS Though Utah's precipitation alone would not naturally support gardens, the warm climate and long growing season, coupled with irrigation, give life to many gardens across the state. Of these gardens, the expansive and meticulous **Gardens at Temple Square** (800-453-6027; www.visit templesquare.com) and botanically diverse **Red Butte Gardens** (801-581-4747; www.redbuttegarden.org), both in Salt Lake City, are some of the most impressive.

GAY & LESBIAN Most would not peg this Intermountain West state as being particularly gay-friendly; however, Utah (and metropolitan Salt Lake City in particular) is not nearly as barren as the state's consistently red politics would suggest. As with anywhere else in the nation, one must not expect to find queer support in rural and conservative communities. However, in the same way that Utah shocks outsiders with its Muslim, Chinese, and Catholic populations, so too does Salt Lake County surprise with a thriving queer community. While an outright presence remains somewhat underground, a strong network of nightclubs, events, and organizations connects the regional community.

State queer publications advertise an array of activities, online groups, parties, clubs, retreats, and gay-friendly businesses. The so-called **Marmalade District,** just southwest of the Capitol Building (west of the Avenues), is becoming recognized across the city as the representative of gay digs.

*Q Salt Lake* (www.qsaltlake.com) and *Pillar of the Gay, Lesbian, Bisexual, and Transgender Community* are two free publications found in newspaper stands, particularly in coffee shops. The *Little Lavender Book* (www.lavenderbook.com), an online directory, lists community resources, and gay-friendly establishments from bed-and-breakfasts to lawyers. The **Utah Pride Center** (www.utahpride page.org) has a Web site with a strong events section, including current

political activities, balls, and pride events.

GEOGRAPHY It is impossible to exaggerate the geographic diversity of Utah. In the western half of the state are the salt flats and lunar desertscapes characteristic of the unique **Great Basin.** The eastern half of the state is occupied by the high **Colorado Plateau,** cleaved by the **Green River** and lifted by the **San Rafael Swell.** The **Rocky Mountains** divide the state in half and are a north–south spine that separates these two distinct regions. Among the list of features throughout the state are red rock arches, sand dunes, alpine peaks and lakes, grasslands, and evergreen forests.

GOLF Utah has almost 120 golf courses, the majority of which are public and of very high quality. The highest concentration is around Wasatch Range, extending from Logan through Ogden, Salt Lake City, and into Provo. There is also a significant number of courses near St. George and Cedar City. Otherwise few dozen courses are scattered throughout the rest of the state. Golf courses are listed in this book according to their region.

GRID SYSTEM See *Driving*.

HIKING Even listed by region, there is much too much hiking in Utah to even summarize in this book. However, hiking is one of the most abundant, spectacular, and accessible activities in Utah. Each region's best hikes are included, with attention given to a range of difficulty. Naturally, the best and most abundant hiking is located in the major mountain ranges—in the Wasatch, approached from the east or west; the Oquirrs near Tooele; the Uintas east of Kamas and north of Duchesne; the Beaver Dam Mountains and Snow Canyon State Park near St. George; the various overlook, arch, tower, and canyon hikes near Moab; and in the slot canyons in the Grand Staircase–Escalante National Monument region of the state.

**HISTORICAL SITES** Utah's lands are abundant in both indigenous and European American landmarks and historical sites. Because of the harsh and dry climate of Utah, early residents tended to be nomadic. Evidence of cliff dwellers and early fur trappers along the Green and other rivers, as well as huts of nomadic sheep herders and old-time desert ranching hermits, are scattered across the state. The first group of people who were able to systematically tame and permanently inhabit Utah were the Latter-day Saints. Today many well-maintained historical sites and landmarks spread throughout the region pay tribute to various chapters of that religion's history. Other factions of Utah's past like the mining histories of Park City, Alta, and Brighton, and the industrial and rail histories of towns like Tremonton and the Golden Spike National Historic Site, have their own representative museums.

**HOT SPRINGS** With its powerful geologic shaping so visibly evident, it is no surprise that Utah has many hot springs. Most hot springs in Utah have not been advertised and developed, and likely never will be due to their remoteness. Each area is different from the next in temperature infrastructure, accessibility, and scenery. Pools near towns are maintained by community effort and frequented by locals—so be advised, if you are thinking about swimming in your birthday suit. Though many of the pools are located throughout the Wasatch Mountains, there are also less well-

known pools hidden throughout the southwestern portion of the state.

**INDIAN RESERVATIONS** Native Americans have lived in present-day Utah for around 12,000 years. Because of the changing seasons and inherent dryness of the region, almost all of these tribes were nomadic. These tribes included the Bannock, Goshute, Paiute, Navajo, Anasazi, and Shoshone. The exception to the rule was the Utes tribe, who established permanent residence on the shores of the freshwater Utah Lake. Today tribal lands occupy a small portion of the state, but they are grouped into five major reservations.

The largest reservation in the nation, the **Navajo Nation,** occupies lands in Arizona, New Mexico, and the far southeast corner of Utah. The largest reservation within Utah's borders, the **Uintah and Ouray Reservation,** has major holdings in the

THE CORAL PINK SAND DUNES STATE PARK NEAR KANAB HAS NEARLY 4,000 ACRES AND IS POPULAR AMONG CAMPERS AND ATV RIDERS.

Jonathan Echlin

northeast and east-central portion of the state, much of which is along the Green River. The **Goshute** and **Skull Valley reservations** are significantly smaller plots of land in the west-central side of the state. The **Paiute** tribe has lands scattered across the southwest corner of Utah. More information on these tribes can be found at www.indian.utah.gov.

**LIQUOR AND WINE** See *Package Stores.*

**MORMON INFLUENCE** If you are unfamiliar with Mormons, you have undoubtedly developed many preconceived ideas about what to expect to see with respect to this church. In fact, unless you are at the temple, Mormon influence will generally be unobvious, with a few exceptions. The trademark system of naming roads "100 South," "700 East," and so on is a ubiquitous Mormon institution. In fact, you probably have seen more Mormon missionaries at home and on your travels than you will see in Utah. Otherwise, the Mormon Church (called Church of Jesus Christ of Latter-day Saints) has a lexicon of recurring themes and names that may escape the untrained eye. The name Brigham Young, that of the early church president and leader of the first westward LDS trek, appears everywhere in this state. Parley Pratt, an early Mormon leader and poet, has left his stamp in many places as well.

Industriousness is one of the most-prized values in the Mormon religion. The beehive, the church's symbol for this concept, is found in many places around the state, including on highway signs and on business façades. The word *Deseret* refers to the Mormon domain—"State of Deseret" would have been the name of their own sovereign nation in western North America, had the U.S. government granted their many requests in the mid-1800s. *Pioneer* is used in Utah interchangeably with 19th-century Mormon pioneers. These pioneers were devout Mormons who risked their lives to trek across the country on foot, bringing nothing with them but what could fit into their famous handcarts. Finally, the California Gull (improperly, but commonly, called Seagull) is the Utah state bird because of its important role in Utah's early Mormon survival. A freak swarm of crickets descended upon the settlers' first crops, and it seemed these crops would be completely devoured. However, a huge wave of gulls swooped in and demolished the crickets.

**MOUNTAINS** That most of Utah is lifted, rifted, and folded by Rocky Mountains is one of the state's most significant and best assets. Of all the state's ranges, the **Wasatch Range** is probably the most famous. This dramatic range steeply rises 7,000 feet above the Great Salt Lake and the Salt Lake metropolitan area. An hour to the east, east of Kamas and north of Duchesne, is the **Uinta Range.** These mountains are one of North America's very few east–west running ranges and are the tallest range in the Utah. King's Peak, the tallest point in Utah at 13,528 feet, is in this range. Other distinct ranges are the **La Sals,** just southeast of Moab, and the imposingly tall and extremely lonesome **Henry Mountains** to the north of Lake Powell. Less famous, but equally beautiful ranges across the state are the **Oquirrhs** to the west of Salt Lake and Utah counties, the **Tushar Mountains** just east of Beaver, the **House** and **Confusion** ranges west of Delta, and the **Markagunt Plateau** and smaller ranges near St. George and Cedar City.

Where Utah isn't lifted into distinct

ranges is just as often rifted, split, and shorn into equally spectacular canyons and plateaus like the **San Rafael Swell** and **Glen Canyon,** as well as various cliff bands like the **Waterpocket Fold** of Capitol Reef National Park and multicolored crags of **Grand Staircase–Escalante National Monument.** Nearly all of Utah (aside from the Great Basin floor) is mountainous, so many dozens of ranges go unrecognized that would stand out in most other parts of the country.

**PACKAGE STORES** In Utah, state-owned liquor stores are the seller of booze, wine, and full-strength beer (outside of a restaurant). Though liquor and wine typically cost an average amount, full-strength beer is quite expensive—usually around $1.70–$2 per beer. Limited-alcohol beer (3.2 percent alcohol by weight/ 4.0 percent alcohol by volume) can be purchased at gas stations, grocery stores, and the like. The price on these beers is pretty close to the national average.

Liquor store hours vary, even within the same town. However, they are universally closed on voting days, holidays, and Sundays. In general, expect hours to be fairly limited. Most liquor stores close around 7 PM, though exceptional stores close at 11 PM. For locations and hours, visit the Web site www.alcbev .state.ut.us, or call the Salt Lake City Office (801-977-6800).

**PUBLIC LANDS** Utah has five complete national parks and has a total of 18 complete and shared national monuments, parks, recreation areas, and trails. **Arches National Park, Bryce Canyon National Park, Canyonlands National Park, Capitol Reef National Park,** and **Zion National Park** are all contained fully in the state. **Grand Staircase–Escalante National Monument, Natural**

Bridges National Monument, Glen Canyon National Recreation Area, Cedar Breaks National Monument, Dinosaur National Monument, Golden Spike National Historic Site, Hovenweep National Monument, Mormon Pioneer Historic Trail, Natural Bridges National Monument, Rainbow Bridge National Monument,** and **Timpanogos Cave National Monument** are some of the state's more famous, non-park playgrounds.

The **Bureau of Land Management** has stout workload in Utah. This agency alone manages 22.9 million acres, approximately 35,800 square miles. With the total land area in Utah at 84,900 square miles, this accounts for 42 percent of the state. These lands range from deep orange sandstone to high prairies, lunar salt flats, and remote mountain ranges. The BLM State Office (801-539-4001; www.ut .blm.gov) is located at 440 West 200 South, Suite 500, Salt Lake City.

Six national forests make up another enormous portion of Utah. **Dixie National Forest** (435-865-3700; www .fs.fed.us/r4/dixie) is the largest at almost 2 million acres (83,000 of which are wilderness acres). This forest is concentrated in the southwestern portion of the state, near Moab, Cedar City, and beyond. It extends from the far southwest corner of the state to the northern tip of Grand Staircase–Escalante National Monument, almost without pause. The **Manti-La Sal National Forest** (1.41 million acres; 435-637-2817; www.fs.fed.us/r4/ mantilasal) is located in the southeastern portion of the state, near Moab. **Fishlake National Forest** (435-896-9233; www.fs.fed.us/r4/fishlake), with 1.40 million acres, is just to the north of the Dixie National Forest. It is bounded to the west by I-15, roughly from Cedar City to Nephi, and stretches quite far to the east. This contains the Sevier and Wasatch plateaus. **Ashley National Forest** (435-789-1181; www.fs.fed.us/r4/ashley), with 1.38 million acres, is in the northeastern part of the state and presides over a huge share of the Uinta Range and the lands near the Uintah and Ouray Indian Reservation. **Wasatch-Cache National Forest** (801-466-6411; www.fs.fed.us/r4/wcnf), with 1.30 million acres, is one of the state's most famous and stretches from the far northern part of the state, down through Salt Lake City and Park City, and over to the Uintas. The **Uinta National Forest** (801-342-5100; www.fs.fed.us/r4/uinta) is the smallest of them all, with 880,000 acres, and is most concentrated in Heber Valley and the area just east of Nephi. These forests together make up another 8.4 million acres (13,000 square miles), or 15 percent of the state's land.

There are 42 state parks in Utah. These range in size and notoriety and include some real gems, such as **Snow Canyon State Park** (435-628-2255) in St. George, **Dead Horse Point State Park** (435-259-2614) near Canyonlands National Park and Moab, and **Goblin Valley State Park** (435-564-3633) in southeastern Utah, as well as

STREAKED NAVAJO SANDSTONE NEAR THE CONFLUENCE OF THE YAMPA AND GREEN RIVERS

historically and culturally important parks like **This is the Place State Park** (801-582-1847) in Salt Lake City and **Utah Field House of Natural History State Park Museum** (435-789-3799), 496 East Main Street, Vernal. More information can be obtained through the **Utah State Parks Office** (801-538-7220 or 877-887-2757; www.stateparks.utah.gov).

**PUBLICATIONS** *Salt Lake Tribune* (www.sltrib.com) and *Deseret News* (www.deseretnews.com) have most of Utah's daily goings-on covered and are the state's biggest newspapers. *Deseret News* is a Mormon operation; the *Tribune* is (for the most part) not. *St. George Spectrum* (www.thespectrum.com) attends to the southeastern corner of the state, and the *Moab Times* (www.moabtimes.com) represents the southeastern portion. *Salt Lake City Weekly* (www.slweekly.com) is a free, profusely distributed weekly, written largely to liberal youth, that has many good events listings regardless of your political persuasion or age. *In Utah This Week* (www.inthisweek.com) is an up-and-coming weekly with content parallel to *Salt Lake Weekly*. *Salt Lake Magazine* (www.saltlakemagazine.com) covers a lot of the higher-end events and concerns in the Wasatch Region and beyond, often featuring statewide "best-of" lists and great restaurants and lodging across the state.

**RAIL TRANSPORTATION** Amtrak (800-872-7245; www.amtrak.com) makes daily stops in Salt Lake City. The line also provides service to Ogden and Provo. In eastern and southeastern Utah, there is service to Helper and Green River. In southwestern Utah, there is a stop in Milford.

**ROAD REPORTS** Utah is no Montana or Alaska, but road conditions certainly can get hairy. Especially in the mountains, winter closures and hazards can present, even on the interstate. In and around the Wasatch Front, traffic can become congested during rush hour or construction projects. **Utah Department of Transportation** (801-965-4000; www.utdot.gov) operates a hotline and Web site with road conditions map. This Web site also has up-to-date information on construction projects and traffic, especially on I-15 in the Wasatch Front region and on I-80 between Park City and Salt Lake City.

**SCENIC BYWAYS** Of Utah's many fine points, its natural scenery is one of the best. In the northern part of the state, **Mirror Lake Highway** (UT 150) is one of the most aesthetic roads, traveling the northwestern portion of the Uinta Range from Kamas, through Bald Mountain Pass, and into Wyoming. In the Wasatch Range, **Little Cottonwood Canyon** (UT 210) is a scenic one-way road accessing Snowbird and Alta through a deep, U-shaped white granite canyon. Just to the south, the **Alpine Loop** travels through American Fork Canyon (UT 92), past the Sundance Resort (Alpine Loop Scenic Byway), underneath Mount Timpanogos, and down Provo Canyon (US 189). The **Burr Trail** (UT 1668, southeast of Boulder) is a 70-mile, mostly dirt road that tours Utah's remote canyons and desert between Canyonlands National Park and Lake Powell. Just 3 miles west of Boulder is the **Hell's Backbone Road** (Forest Service Road 153), a wild and curving ridge-top road that used to be Boulder's only connection to civilization. When in the Moab region, a trip into **Castle Valley** via UT 128 is recommended, as is a trip through **Indian Creek** via UT 211, the route to Canyonlands National Park's southern entrance.

Utah has 13 ski resorts, the healthy majority of which are truly world-class for terrain, "Greatest Snow on Earth," acreage, and vertical relief. Ten of these resorts are within an hour of Salt Lake International Airport, and many receive an average annual snowfall of more than 500 inches—snow that is much lighter than at any of the Sierra or Cascades resorts with the same statistics. **Beaver Mountain** (435-753-0921; www.skithebeav.com) is the farthest north, near Logan. In the Ogden Valley you'll find **Wolf Mountain** (801-745-3511; www.wolf mountaineden.com), **Snowbasin** (888-437-5488; www.snowbasin.com), and **Powder Mountain** (801-745-3772; www.powdermountain.net). Park City has **Park City Mountain Resort** (435-649-8111; www.parkcity mountain.com), **The Canyons Resort** (435-649-5400; www.thecanyons.com), and **Deer Valley Resort** (800-424-3337; www.deervalley.com). Salt Lake City has **Solitude** (801-532-4731; www.skisolitude.com) and **Brighton** (801-532-4731; www.brightonresort .com) in Big Cottonwood Canyon and **Alta** (801-359-1078; www.alta.com) and **Snowbird** (800-232-9542; www .snowbird.com) in Little Cottonwood Canyon. **Sundance Resort** (877-831-6224; www.sundanceresort.com) is just east of Provo. **Brian Head** (435-677-2035; www.brianhead.com) is Utah's southernmost resort, near Cedar City. Backcountry skiing is also rampant across the state, pending safe avalanche conditions. Utah's top-notch safety resource for this information is www.avalanche.org.

Cross-country skiing can be done on many, many wooded trails across the state, as well as at **Snowbasin** (888-437-5488; www.snowbasin.com) in Ogden Valley; **Utah Olympic Park** (435-658-4200; www.olyparks.com),

Zac Robinson

A SKIER WILL APPRECIATE THE SOFT
LANDING OF LITTLE COTTONWOOD
POWDER AT ALTA.

near The Canyons and in Park City; at
**White Pine Touring** (435-649-8710;
www.whitepinetouring.com) in Park
City; **Mountain Dell** in Parley's
Canyon between Park City and Salt
Lake City; at **Solitude** (801-532-4731;
www.skisolitude.com) in Big Cottonwood Canyon; **Alta** (801-359-1078;
www.alta.com) in Little Cottonwood
Canyon; at **Soldier Hollow** (877-831-
6224; www.sundanceresort.com);
**Homestead Resort** (www.homestead
resort.com) in Heber Valley; **Sundance Resort** (877-831-6224; www

.sundanceresort.com) east of Provo;
**Ruby's Inn** (www.rubysinn.com); and
**Brian Head** (435-677-2035; www
.brianhead.com) in the south.

TAXES Sales tax in Utah is generally
around 6.5 percent. Local taxes vary
due to such add-ons as transportation
tax and resort tax, which brings taxes in
Alta to 8.1 percent and 7.35 percent in
Park City. Other applicable taxes are a
meals and room tax, which are 5 and 3
percent, respectively. Liquor tax is
included in the purchase price of
booze and wine. Utah law dictates a
statewide price, and so a bottle of
booze at a resort liquor store must be
the same price as the same item in a
city.

TIME ZONE Utah abides by **Mountain Standard Time** and observes
Daylight Savings Time. Arizona, to the
south, does *not* observe Daylight Savings Time—so if you are traveling near
that state, say near Lake Powell, be
aware that cities in that state will be
operating in a different time zone half
of the year.

# Northern Wasatch

SALT LAKE CITY

PARK CITY

HEBER VALLEY

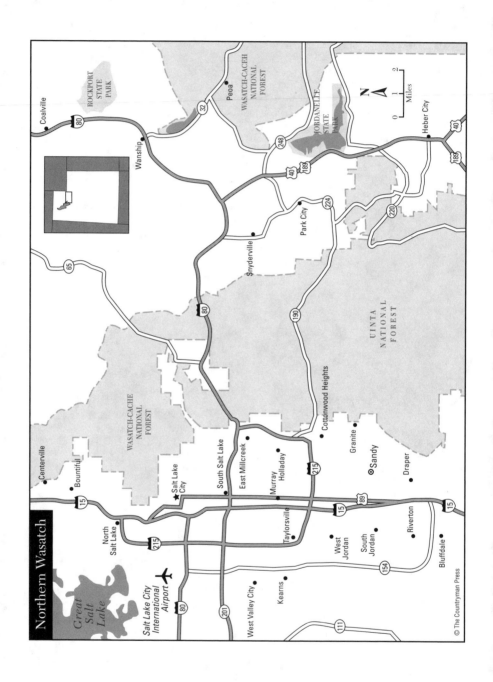

Northern Wasatch

Great Salt Lake

Salt Lake City International Airport

Coalville

ROCKPORT STATE PARK

Wanship

WASATCH-CACEH NATIONAL FOREST

Peoa

32

80

65

JORDANELLE STATE PARK

Heber City

40

189

40   183

248

224

Park City

Snyderville

80

190

UINTA NATIONAL FOREST

220

Centerville

Bountiful

North Salt Lake

215

15

WASATCH-CACHE NATIONAL FOREST

Salt Lake City

South Salt Lake

East Millcreek

Murray

Holladay

Cottonwood Heights

Granite

Sandy

Draper

215

89

15

Taylorsville

West Valley City

Kearns

West Jordan

South Jordan

154

Riverton

Bluffdale

15

201

80

111

N

0   1   2
Miles

© The Countryman Press

# NORTHERN WASATCH IN BRIEF

The Wasatch Region is arguably Utah's most famous region. Though it occupies just a small portion of the state, it contains nearly three-quarters of its population and represents much of its geologic diversity. Salt Lake City, the birthplace of modern Utah, is the cultural and historic center of the Mormon Church and the famous Temple Square. The 2002 Winter Olympics brought Salt Lake City into the global spotlight and gave it the chance to show off its party skills. Park City, just 30 minutes up Parley's Canyon from Salt Lake, has for decades been one of the Rocky Mountains' most famous resort destinations. Park City's resorts, The Canyons, Deer Valley, and Park City Mountain Resort, are regular hosts of World Cup Ski Racing and celebrity events. This resort town is the annual host of the world-famous Sundance Film Festival by winter and is a world-class mountain biking town by summer. Salt Lake International Airport is a major hub in the United States and is just five minutes west of downtown Salt Lake. The Cottonwood Canyons, just 20 minutes from downtown Salt Lake City, are home to Utah's most intimidating ski resorts, Alta and Snowbird.

Lesser known are Salt Lake City's extraordinary (and extraordinarily affordable) restaurants, free outdoor-concert series, and local film industry. Heber Valley, just south of Park City, shares the same wild beauty as the rest of the Wasatch towns, yet has vastly less crowding and is a perfect escape from the urban rush of its sisters. The Utah Symphony is led by conductor Keith Lockhart, who splits his time between Salt Lake City and the Boston Pops. Wasatch backcountry skiing is at least as good as in-bounds skiing and is many times more vast. Park City and Salt Lake City both enjoy remarkable amounts of outdoor concerts ranging from chamber music and reggae to rock, many of which are free.

In addition to the urban and outdoors perks, the area also is home to quieter towns whose agricultural background is palpable, and whose streets are still quiet. Heber City is one such town whose beautiful backdrop is relatively untouched by a cityscape. Yet the town has abundant opportunities for Nordic skiing, hiking, and excellent ranch-style lodging. The northern Wasatch Range as a whole has some of the nation's best mountain-bike trails, and a complementary dry climate. Between Salt Lake City (at around 4,500 feet above sea level) and Park City (about 1,700 feet higher), the biking season lasts quite a while. The same climactic customization works for golfing, hiking, and the like.

In fact, in a region with 8,000 feet of vertical relief, the climate can be made-to-order all year long. The lowest point around is the surface of the Great Salt Lake, at around 4,200 feet above sea level. The highest point is Mount Nebo at 11,928 feet. The sun bakes the arid valleys, and streams fed by plentiful snow pack refrigerate the numerous canyons. By winter, the resorts on the western front of the range receive an average greater than 500 yearly inches of snowfall, while Salt Lake Valley receives only 50 inches of snow annually. The lower valleys enjoy pleasant temperatures during spring and fall, while Park City and Heber Valley offer temperate reprieve during the heat of the summer.

Though the Wasatch Region has all of these perks and many more, some people are still wary of Utah because of its Mormon background. Almost universally, people who are afraid of Utah are operating on outdated information or urban legend. Salt Lake City is now significantly less than half Mormon. Some estimate that as few as 35 percent of its residents are active members of the church. Additionally, those who know the Mormons appreciate them for their family values, courteousness, and industriousness. Though some of Utah's liquor laws are indeed twisted by this faith, they are not much more strict than those of Massachusetts. Do not let the funky lingo and rumors of "private clubs" deter you. Most residents and visitors of Utah don't even notice the liquor laws; as there is so much to do outside, little time is left to spend inside a bar.

The truth about the area, with respect to Mormons, is this: the Mormons have undoubtedly shaped the region. They were the pioneering settlers and the very designers of the cities. They erected Salt Lake City as their mecca, yet are willing to share it with others. The Mormon religion, once outcast for its polygamist and other eccentric practices, has become much more mainstream in the last century. The Wasatch Region is bustling with music, excellent cuisine, and world-class outdoor recreation. Because of the shadow cast over Utah by myths about Mormonism, all of this is much, much more affordable than in comparable regions in Colorado and California.

## ✳ Weather

Climate in the Wasatch is probably about as varied as you could get in such a small sample of land. More than 1.5 miles of vertical relief does a lot to affect the temperature and precipitation averages from one place to another. Air at almost 12,000 feet above sea level will already be much cooler than that at 4,200 feet above sea level. Add wind and naturally elevated precipitation levels to the higher regions, and the difference is even more exaggerated. Cutting into the slopes of these mountains are streams, which carve, refrigerate, and irrigate cooler canyons. The foothills of the mountains serve as reflectors, which trap and reflect heat back into the valleys, warming them significantly during each season. Salt Lake City, parked in a bowl-shaped valley at relatively low elevation, is much warmer throughout the year than Park City and Heber, which are perched a few thousand feet higher in narrower valleys and do not experience the same sunbowl effect. By summer, the mountains are much cooler and pleasant than the basins below; by winter, the mountains squeeze 500 inches of snow from the clouds onto their slopes, while the valleys stay sunny and relatively temperate.

Park City's coolest daytime highs occur during December and January, at around 33°F; its warmest months are July and August, during which their average highs barely break into the 80s. Add about 3°F to Heber's high temperatures throughout the year. Salt Lake City's hottest months average around 90°F for the daytime highs. Its coolest months see average highs around 44°F. Expect the air temperature to drop severely each day with the setting sun, as there is usually very little humidity or cloud cover to retain heat.

Aside from the slopes, the region is arid. Salt Lake City proper averages 15.3 inches of precipitation each year. Park City receives about 21.4 inches, and Heber gets 16.9. Alta and Snowbird receive almost 39 inches, which translates to an average of 514 inches of snowfall annually.

## ✳ Special Events

*Early January:* **Huntsman Cup** (435-649-3991; www.nac1985.org), Park City Mountain Resort, Park City. This is one of the nation's most prestigious disabled ski races, which takes place around the beginning of the month each year.

*Third Week of January:* **Sundance Film Festival** (877-733-7829; www.sundance.org), mostly in Park City, but also in Salt Lake City and Ogden. This is the world's most famous and influential independent film festival. Park City, its hometown, is saturated each year with its concerts, parties, celebrities, and high intensity.

**Outdoor Retailer Trade Show** (www.outdoorretailer.com), Salt Palace Convention Center, Salt Lake City. The OR Show is a twice-yearly event that takes place at the Salt Palace Convention Center, on the western end of downtown. This event brings thousands and thousands of industry members, including some of the world's best climbers, kayakers, and other athletes who come to represent their sponsors. As there is such an influx, there is usually a large, exposition-style climbing competition, many associated parties, and concerts. January's show is not quite as large as August's, but it is still a very major event.

*January and into February:* **Utah Winter Games** (www.utahwintergames.org), statewide. This event offers a monthlong roster of competitions in Alpine and Nordic skiing, ski jumping, freestyle skiing, biathlon, snowboarding, luge, speed skating, and curling.

*January and February:* **FIS** (Fédération Internationale de Ski) **Freestyle World Cup** (Deer Valley Resort; 800-424-3337; www.deervalley.com) brings

**OUTFITTER SERVICES**

**Rocky Mountain Outfitters** (435-654-1655; www.rockymtnoutfitters.com) offers guided trips of almost any outdoor adventure you could want on your visit to Utah. Their office is in Heber City (just south of Park City), and they primarily service the central Wasatch Region (from Park City to Sundance and Provo). On their list of activities you'll find horseback riding, fly-fishing, snowmobiling, heli-skiing, wagon rides, and chuck-wagon dinners. They also offer horse and snowmobile rentals. Trip lengths vary, and certain services are restricted to specific locations. Call to inquire.

**High Country Rafting** (801-224-2500 in Provo or 435-649-7678 in Park City; www.highcountryrafting.com). A company based in Provo, High Country specializes in rafting, kayaking, and fly-fishing. In addition to these activities, the company also offers tubing and a ride on the Historic Heber Railroad as a means to reach the put-in for rafting trips.

bumps and aerialist skiers to Deer Valley's slopes. Many of the competitions take place at night and are accompanied by free concerts by national bands and consumption of delicious beer.

*Early March:* **Nordic Combined Junior Olympics** (435-658-4200; www .olyparks.com or www.skijumping central.com), Park City. One of Park City's unique assets is its set of Olympic-sized Nordic ski jumps, the biggest of which is the 120-meter jump. Watch the world's best juniors launch off these 2002 Winter Olympics jumps.

*Mid-March:* **U.S. Freeskiing Championships** (800-232-9542; www.snow bird.com), Snowbird Resort. This big mountain skiing competition is one of the wildest skiing competitions, and one of the most accessible to spectators. Each year the course changes, but the idea is the same: the best freestyle skiers from around the nation and world attempt to ski the most outlandish lines with as much speed, style, and air time as possible. A must-see event for ski enthusiasts.

**World Superpipe Championships** (435-649-8111; www.worldsuperpipe .com or www.parkcitymountain.com), Park City Mountain Resort, Park City. This is yet another of Utah's world-class ski competitions. This event takes place in the huge half- and quarter-pipes at PCMR. This brings some of the biggest names in pipe skiing and snowboarding to town during the second week of March. The town sees an influx of partying and people watching during this event.

**Spring Events Series at The Canyons** (435-649-5400; www.the canyons.com), The Canyons Resort, Park City. **The Slopestyle Competition** showcases some of the country's most talented freeskiers in the terrain park. **The Pond Skimming Contest,** if you've never seen one, involves skiers in ridiculous attire attempting to gain enough speed that they might ski across a cold—but not frozen—pond. This hilarity usually brings out the best in costumes, beer, and music. **The Spring Concert Series** also begins during this month.

*End of March:* **Red, White, and Snow Wine, Culinary, and Ski Festival** (435-200-0985; www.redwhiteand snow.org), across Park City. This festival is a citywide benefit for the National Ability Center, which provides adaptive outdoor sporting opportunities to the disabled.

*April:* **Semiannual LDS World Conference** (www.lds.org), Salt Lake City. This gathering brings a very noticeable influx of visitors to the downtown area. As one of Salt Lake City's major conferences, it is accompanied by many thousand participants, which make Temple Square and its environs hop during this time.

 **Salt Lake Bees AAA Baseball** (801-325-2273; www.slbees.com), Franklin Covey Stadium, 77 West 1300 South, Salt Lake City. This beloved sports team's season begins in April. Their home field is extremely pleasant and clean, and enjoys an uninterrupted view of the Wasatch Range—likely one of the best backdrops in the country. Home games that fall on "Thirsty" Thursdays can be enjoyed with $2.50 beers.

*Easter:*  **Snowbird Easter Sunrise Service and Easter Egg Hunt** (800-232-9542; www.snowbird.com), Snowbird Resort. This is a long-running, nondenominational local favorite for early risers. A 5:30 AM Tram to Hidden Peak kicks off a mountain-top Easter egg hunt and nondenominational sunrise service.

*Summerlong:* **The Farmers' Market at The Canyons** (435-649-5400; www

.thecanyons.com) takes place throughout the summer and begins in May,
weather permitting. The market is
active Wednesday 2–7 PM.

**Deer Valley** (435-655-3114; www
.ecclescenter.org) hosts **free outdoor
concerts** throughout the summer; the
Park City Performing Arts Foundation
sponsors these shows featuring local
artists. Also at Deer Valley is the **Deer
Valley Music Festiva**l (www
.deervalleymusicfestival.org), which
begins in June, weather permitting.
Musical genres vary from show to
show. Concerts take place at Deer Valley Resort's outdoor amphitheater.

**Downtown Farmers' Market** (www
.downtownslc.org), Pioneer Park, 300
South 300 West Salt Lake City. This
market showcases produce, local food
vendors, and artists, and kicks off in
early June and continues into October.
It takes place each Saturday, weather
permitting, at 8 AM and lasts into the
late morning/early afternoon.

**Gallivan Center Twilight Concert
Series** (801-535-6110; www.gallivan
events.com), Gallivan Center, 239
South Main St., Salt Lake City. This
series is one of the best parts about
summer in Salt Lake City. These
Thursday evening concerts begin in
July and usually run from 7 to 10 PM.
The location is a downtown outdoor
pavilion where beer can be purchased
and dancing takes place. Some of the
musicians are from around the world
and are world-famous, sometimes
Grammy-winning artists.

**Park City International Music Fes-
tival** (801-943-0169; www.pcmusic
festival.com), Park City and Salt Lake
City. This is yet another summer music
series that takes place in several different venues around town and features a
wide variety of styles.

**Park City International Jazz Festi-
val** (www.parkcityjazz.org), Park City.

At Deer Valley on Friday and Sunday,
and at The Canyons on Saturday, this
is yet another Wasatch summer concert series not to be overlooked.

☙ **Flying Ace All Stars Freestyle
Show** (www.utaholyparks.com) takes
place each Saturday at 1 PM between
the middle of June and end of August,
during which the Freestyle portion of
the U.S. Ski and Snowboard Team perform their tricks for 25 minutes, using
the Nordic jumps to loft them incredibly high above a landing pool.

*Mid-May:* **Dine O' Round** (www
.downtownslc.com or www.dineoround
.com), Salt Lake City downtown. This
is a rather under-the-radar opportunity
to try some of the best restaurants in
town for an exceedingly good price.
For two weeks around the middle of
May, a long list of participating restaurants create their own Dine O' Round
menus for a set price (either $15 or
$25, depending on the establishment
and number of courses). These meals
showcase the kitchens' best work,
often at more than a 50 percent
savings.

**The Great Salt Lake Bird Festival**
(801-451-3286; www.greatsaltlake
birdfest.com) takes place on Antelope
Island. The Great Salt Lake and Bear
River Migratory Bird Refuge is one of
the most important intermountain
avian stopovers and unique inland bird
habitats in the United States. The festival involves lectures, sea kayaking,
and bird-watching, and attracts people
from around the country.

**Utah Asian Festival** (South Towne
Exposition Center; 801-467-6060;
www.southtowneexpo.com), which
takes place in Sandy, just south of Salt
Lake City, observes Asian and Pacific
Island cultures.

**Saturday Freestyle Big Air Show**
(435-658-4206; www.olyparks.com),
Utah Olympic Park, Park City. This is a

Craig Bowden

ANTELOPE ISLAND, GREAT SALT LAKE

recurring Saturday event that begins in June and showcases some the nation's best aerialist skiers performing their tricks over a pool of water. Routine for these athletes, spectacular to see.

*End of May:* **The Salt Lake Century** (801-596-8430; www.cyclesaltlake century.com). Actually a 107-mile ride, this kicks off the road biking season. Around 2,000 participants cycle the valley, starting at the Salt Lake Fairgrounds and going north, visiting Antelope Island on the tour. The ride is extremely flat and, barring major wind or severe weather, is a very user-friendly ride for the distance.

*June:* **Salt Lake City Classic 5 & 10K Races** and **Salt Lake City Marathon and 5K** (801-412-6060; www.saltlakecitymarathon.com), **Park City Marathon** (www.pcmarathon .com), and **Wahsatch Steeplechase** trail run (www.wahsatchsteeplechase .com) comprise some of Utah's biggest running events and take place during the summer, before the hot months of July and August.

*Second Week of June:* **Pedalfest** (800-424-3337; www.deervalley.org), Deer Valley Resort, Park City. This is a

cycling rendezvous put on by the Intermountain Mountain Biking Cup that takes place on the world-famous mountain biking trails of Deer Valley.

*Third Week of June:* **Utah Arts Festival** (801-322-2428; www.uaf.org), Salt Lake Public Library Main Branch, 230 South 500 West, Salt Lake City. This festival is one of the most vibrant and popular in the city. It fills the expanses of Library Square, located amid the award-winning modern architecture of the Main Library.

*July:* ✍ **Days of '47** (801-521-2822; www.daysof47.com), statewide. This is a tradition that is unique to Utah. This includes Salt Lake City's oldest parade honoring early Utah Mormon Pioneers. A family-friendly event.

**Sundance Institute Outdoor Film Festival** (801-328-3456; www.sun dance.org), Park City Municipal Park, Park City. This is a much more low-key event than the actual Sundance Film Festival. Each week, one of the festival's best films is screened outdoors for viewing at no charge.

*End of July/Early August:* **Snowbird's Folk and Bluegrass and Rock and Blues Festival** (800-232-9542; www

.snowbird.com), Snowbird Resort. This is a big deal for music lovers in the Salt Lake area. The festival always features an impressive lineup of big-name musicians and takes place in the second weekend of July and at the end of the month.

*Early August:* **Kimball Arts Festival** (435-649-8882; www.kimball-art.org), Main St., Park City. Main Street is blockaded and completely inundated with hundreds of artists and their work, as well as thousands of spectators.

*Mid-August:* **Outdoor Retailer Trade Show** (www.outdoorretailer.com), Salt Palace Convention Center, Salt Lake City. This show happens twice a year in Salt Lake City. As described in the January portion of this events calendar, this event is major for this outdoorsy city. Summer temperatures allow for big events including parties and an exposition-style rock climbing competition. In 2007, this was held on the roof of the Shiloh Inn, downtown, on a portable climbing wall. Spectator tickets were sold out.

*Late August/Early September:* **Oktoberfest** (800-232-9542; www.snowbird.com), Snowbird Resort. Bavaria takes over the base area, with tents filled with folk bands and beer gardens. Show up during the day; nightfall brings a close to this party.

*Labor Day Weekend:* **Soldier Hollow Sheepdog Championships and Highland Games** (435-649-6619; www.soldierhollowclassic.com), Soldier Hollow, Midway. This is a huge event that brings participants from 14 countries and five continents. In addition to sheepherding competitions, there are many side attractions such as a flying dog competition, duck herding competition, and regional food and art sales.

*Early September:* **Dine O' Round** (www.downtownslc.com or www.dine oround.com), as described in the May section of this chapter's events calendar, is a two-week block toward the beginning of the month during which restaurants create a set Dine O' Round menu that invites people to sample their cuisine at a very low price.

**Wasatch Front 100-Mile Endurance Run** (www.wasatch100.com). Usually called the "Wasatch 100," this is a chance for elite endurance runners to traverse 100 miles of mountain trails with more than 25,000 feet of elevation gain and loss.

*Mid-September:* **World of Speed at the Bonneville Salt Flats** (801-485-2662; www.saltflats.com), Bonneville Speedway, west of Salt Lake City. This is an event you don't want to miss that takes place at the world's most famous speedway, where all the land speed records are set.

*Early October:* **Utah Brewers Festival** (www.gallivanevents.com or www.utahbrewersfest.com) takes place downtown at the Gallivan Center and brings together the state's biggest and best breweries. Despite the low alcohol content in many of Utah's beers, many of these breweries are recognized nationally.

*October:* **Semiannual LDS World Conference** (www.lds.org). As described in the April section of this events calendar, this conference sees its second resurrection during the month of October.

*November:* **Antelope Island Buffalo Roundup** (801-652-2043; www.utah.com/stateparks), Antelope Island State Park. This is a Western tradition enhanced by the surreal environment of the island and Great Salt Lake. During the round-up, onlookers can see the workings of a bison ranch and participate in the auction during which buffalo are purchased as whole units.

**Luge World Cup** (435-658-4200; www.olyparks.com), Utah Olympic Park, Park City. This takes place at one of very few luge facilities in North America during the last week of the month, lasting four days. (Watch for the Bobsled and Skeleton World Cup immediately following in early December.) Also, keep your eyes open for **World Cup ski races** and aerialist competitions in Park City beginning this month.

**Utah Jazz** (www.nba.com/jazz). This NBA team kicks off its season during this month. Home games are played at the EnergySolutions Arena (301 West South Temple; ticketing: 801-325-7328; www.energysolutionsarena.com) in Salt Lake City.

*Day After Thanksgiving:* ✿ **The Lighting of Temple Square Holiday Lights** (www.lds.org), Temple Square, Salt Lake City. This lighting kicks off the Christmas season beautifully. Thousands come to witness the event. Temple Square takes on a special aura during this time.

*Early December:* **Bobsled and Skeleton World Cup** (435-658-4200; www.olyparks.com), Utah Olympic Park, Park City. This event follows November's Luge World Cup and is a special opportunity in Utah; there are very few such facilities in the world.

**Celebrity Ski Fest** (800-424-3337; www.deervalley.com or www.dvski

fest.com), Deer Valley, Park City. This is one of Utah's stranger events, taking place at Deer Valley toward the beginning of the month. As expected, celebrities come to the area to ski and participate in fund-raising events. Great people watching.

*December:* **Mormon Tabernacle Choir Christmas Concert** (www .mormontabernaclechoir.org), Mormon Tabernacle, Temple Square, Salt Lake City. This is one of the world's finer traditional Christmas concerts. These repeating concerts take place during the middle of the month.

**Tchaikovsky's** *Nutcracker* is put on each year by Salt Lake City's Ballet West (801-323-6900; www.balletwest .org) in the historic **Capitol Theater,** 50 West 200 South, Salt Lake City.

*End of December:* **Deer Valley's Torchlight Parade** and The Canyons' **New Year's Eve Celebration** end the year in Park City with a bang on New Year's Eve.

✿ **Salt Lake City First Night** (www.downtownslc.org) is quite subdued when compared to that of many cities, but it nonetheless gives people a chance to stroll the streets and enjoy street vendors and musicians in the absence of cars. This event ends early and is very family-friendly.

# SALT LAKE CITY

Salt Lake City is Utah's largest city, was first to be founded, and is the capital. Though only 180,000 people technically reside within its borders, its effective population is more than 1.1 million. Taken together, the entire Wasatch Front metropolitan area, from Ogden down to Provo, has about 2.2 million people. This accounts for more than 80 percent of Utah's estimated 2.7 million. Though Salt Lake City has long had enough of a population to be genuinely urban, it has always maintained a distinctly suburban feel.

Salt Lake City's substantial population and simultaneous small-town feel often confuse people who don't know what to expect. But those who do know what to anticipate appreciate the city's funny duality. Salt Lake City indeed has a full supply of high-end metropolitan offerings: world-class restaurants, the Utah Symphony, a steady influx of performing arts, a proficient public transportation system, and a major airport. Yet the way Salt Lake City has been built, and the family values that many of its residents hold dear, keep this city something more like a small town.

In so many ways, this is one of the nation's most incomparable cities. Its heritage is predominantly Mormon. This will continue to define the city indefinitely—but not in the way most would expect. Though the city was founded by leaders of this religion, and its global headquarters are located here today, Salt Lake City's Mormon population was as little as 50 percent by 1890. Today estimates vary as to the city's actual Latter-day Saint population, but it would be reasonable to guess that somewhere around 35–45 percent of the residents here are members of the church. And because of sticky church "membership" rules, it would also be reasonable to guess that the actual population of active church members is much lower.

Even if outsiders were to know the population statistics, they would still not understand the full picture. Though Mormons have historically had a very negative rap, the religion is today fairly mainstream. Many of its beliefs and practices are indeed quite different than other sects of Christianity, but they are so in a very nonthreatening way. Some of the very basic values of the church are what gives Salt Lake City its best qualities today. Industriousness and work ethic yield clean, attractive streets. Family values go a long way to produce low crime rates. And in a way Mormons never directly intended, they have benefited the city by their very reputation: though this city has hands down one of the country's best climates, natural settings, and small-city economies, it also has one of the lowest relative costs of living in the country. The world's naive fear of this religion has preserved this

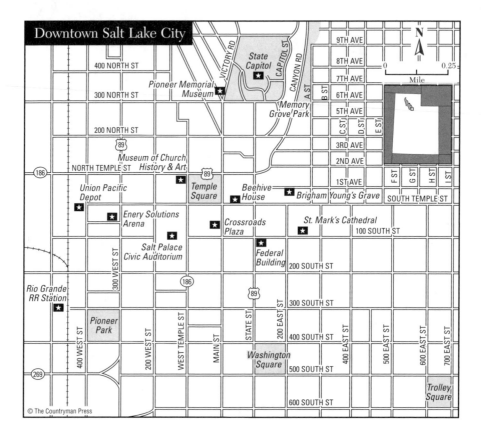

city and kept it safe from the utter exploitation and uncontrolled ballooning, which cities of similar geography and economy experience.

In 1848 by Brigham Young and 148 Mormon followers were the first to settle in Salt Lake City. These pioneers specifically chose this land for its harsh climate and extreme geographic isolation. Since the inception of their religion, they had been persecuted wherever they had lived. As no other party had been able to settle the Great Basin before, the Mormons knew they would be able practice their religion in peace. They considered this their holy land, and treated it as such. They put great care into designing a perfect city, and devoutly worked to be able to survive.

The first year in Utah was rough. After a deadly pedestrian trek to reach this place, the bedraggled pioneers faced a harsh winter with less-than-sufficient provisions. The following spring, fledgling crops were almost destroyed by a freak, apocalyptic swarm of crickets. But they were saved by a flock of California gulls that followed and ate the crickets. Today this is the state bird.

After the first year, the Mormons became solidly settled, and growth was exponential and rampant. Almost immediately, people of other backgrounds—miners, ranchers, rail workers—came to Utah on the shoulders of the Mormon's infrastructure, hoping to capitalize on its resources and wanting to settle among the area's natural beauty. But there never would be a total takeover by "outsiders," as the Mormons already carried a strong, unfavorable reputation across the country. But

there would be blending. The first transcontinental railroad was completed 22
years after the city's founding, 80 miles north of Salt Lake City, and another 10
years later, roughly half of the city was non-Mormon. And over the years, that percentage has fallen—but importantly, the Mormon religion has also become much
more conventional.

In the last few decades, this city and state have enjoyed slow, fairly steady
growth of economy and population. While the rest of the nation enjoyed the housing bubble, and then suffered its burst, Utah's housing market has sagely plodded
along, and Salt Lake City was considered the best city in the union to own a home
by *Forbes Magazine* in November 2007. Residents enjoys a clean city, beautiful
environs, relative seclusion, the perks of metropolis, but also a low cost of living,
clean streets, and low crime rates.

GUIDANCE ❧ **Downtown Alliance** (www.downtownslc.org). This organization's
Web site highlights some of the best events and current goings-on in Salt Lake
City, including the twice-yearly Dine O' Round, festivals, and concert series.

**Salt Lake Chamber of Commerce** (801-364-3631; www.saltlakechamber.org).
The chamber's Web site offers good advice on all points of living in or visiting the
city.

❧ **Salt Lake Convention & Visitors Bureau** (www.visitsaltlake.com) has three
branches: in the **Salt Lake International Airport** at the baggage claim areas in
Terminals 1 and 2, in the **Utah Office of Tourism** (801-538-1030) on 300 North
State Street, and inside the **Salt Palace Convention Center** (801-534-4900), 90
South West Temple.

**Utah Office of Tourism** (801-538-1030), 300 North State St., Salt Lake City.
Located in Salt Lake City, this office receives those arriving in Utah for the first
time and has information on the state as a whole. Located just beneath the capitol
building on Capitol Hill.

GETTING THERE *By car:* Salt Lake City is located at **Interstates 15** and **80.** It
is connected by I-15 to San Diego, Los Angeles, Las Vegas, St. George, and Provo
to the south—and to Idaho, Montana, and Alberta to the north. To the west, I-80
travels to San Francisco, Nevada, and the Bonneville Salt Flats. To the east it
reaches Park City and Wyoming before joining I-90 in Chicago. Also in the vicinity
are **I-84** and **I-70**, both east–west pipelines. I-84 brings travelers from Oregon,
Washington, and Boise into Utah, and merges with I-15 just an hour north of Salt
Lake City. I-70 comes into southern Utah from Denver. Be advised, Utah renumbered its freeway exits in 2005, rendering the exit numbers on old maps incorrect.

*By air:* **Salt Lake City International Airport** (801-575-2400 or 800-595-2442;
www.slcairport.com) is less than 10 minutes from downtown on I-80. It is a major
hub in the Intermountain West, particularly for Delta Airlines. It services 12 other
major airlines, including American, Continental, Frontier, JetBlue, Northwest, SkyWest, Southwest, and United, and provides puddle-jumper shuttle service to small
regional airports in St. George, Moab, and Provo.

*By bus:* **Greyhound Bus Lines** (801-355-9579 or 800-231-2222; www.greyhound
.com), 300 South 600 West. Greyhound has a station in Salt Lake City, as well as in
other Utah cities such as Moab, Provo, Ogden, St. George, and Green River.

*By train:* **Amtrak** (800-872-7245; www.amtrak.com), 340 South 600 West. Amtrak services Utah with stops in Salt Lake City, St. George, Provo, and Green River, with lines to Los Angeles and San Diego, San Francisco, Denver, Portland, Seattle, and Vancouver. Salt Lake City's station shares a location with the Greyhound bus station.

GETTING AROUND *By mass transit:* **Utah Transit Authority (UTA)** (801-377-7433; www.rideuta.com) has an ever-strengthening bus and rail service that heavily services the downtown and university districts, including a Free Ride Zone downtown. Service has expanded to beyond the immediate downtown vicinity, and now the Frontrunner, a high-speed commuter train, operates shuttles between Salt Lake City and Ogden.

*By car:* **Car rentals** in Salt Lake City are numerous and include **Alamo Rent A Car** (Salt Lake City International Airport; 801-575-2211; www.alamo.com); **Avis Rent A Car** (Salt Lake City International Airport, 801-575-2847; and in downtown Salt Lake City: 255 South West Temple, 801-359-2177; www.avis.com); **Budget Rent A Car** (Salt Lake City International Airport, 801-575-2500; and in downtown Salt Lake City: 750 South Main Street, 801-575-2500; www.budget.com); **Dollar Rent A Car** (Salt Lake City International Airport, 801-575-2580; www.dollar .com); **Enterprise Rent A Car** (Salt Lake City International Airport, 801-537-7433; and in downtown Salt Lake City: 843 South State Street, 801-534-1622; www.enterprise.com); **Hertz Rent A Car** (Salt Lake City International Airport, 801-575-2683; and in downtown Salt Lake City: 730 South West Temple, 801-596-2670; www.hertz.com); **National Car Rental** (Salt Lake City International Airport; 801-575-2277; www.nationalcar.com); **Rugged Rental** (Salt Lake City International Airport; 801-977-9111; www.ruggedrental.com); and **Thrifty Car Rental** (Salt Lake City International Airport, 801-265-6677; and in downtown Salt Lake City: Radisson Hotel, 215 West South Temple, 801-355-7368; www.thrifty.com).

For a little enlightenment on Utah's famous **grid system,** see the *Driving and the Grid System* section of the "What's Where in Utah" chapter of this book.

*By shuttle:* Ski shuttles are plentiful and useful in the region, and each has its own flavor. Due to popularity and demand, many can be booked, so a comprehensive list is useful. **All Resort Express** (801-575-6420; www.allresort.com) offers shared ride or limousine service; **Park City Transportation** (435-649-5466; www.park citytransportation.com) runs private and shared shuttles to any Utah ski resort; **Resort Transportation** (801-998-8443; www.utahskiguide.com) offers private shuttle rides only; **Xpress Shuttle** (800-397-0773; www.expressshuttle.com) gives the option of private and shared shuttles to the greater Salt Lake Area; **Yellow Express** (801-521-5027; www.yellowcabutah.com) is exclusively a private shuttle company.

*By cab:* Though there are multiple cab services in Salt Lake, it can be incredibly difficult to actually hail a cab, and no company seems to be necessarily more reliable than the next. Be prepared to wait for your cab, and be sure to call ahead on a busy evening. Cab Companies include **City Cab Company** (801-363-5550), which offers service in Salt Lake City and to ski areas; **Freshtraks** (801-228-1330 or 888-840-1330), a Salt Lake City taxi and ski-area cab service; **Murray Cab Company** (801-238-5704), a Salt Lake City taxi only; **Ute Cab** (801-359-7788), a city taxi only; and **Yellow Cab** (801-521-2100), a Salt Lake City and ski area service.

**HANDICAPPED RESOURCES Splore** (801-484-4128; www.splore.org) is based in Salt Lake City. It is a nonprofit organization whose mission is to provide the disabled with access to Utah's huge variety of outdoor sports, from hiking to skiing, rafting, and rock climbing. Call in advance for different trip options.

**MEDICAL EMERGENCY Alta View Hospital** (801-501-2600), 9660 South 1300 East, Sandy. This is the nearest hospital to the Cottonwood Canyons and has good access for injured skiers and mountain recreationalists.

**Cottonwood Hospital** (801-314-5300), 5770 South 300 East, Murray. This hospital is very near I-15, which gives it good access from within the suburbs of South Salt Lake.

**IHC Instacare** (801-464-7777), 2000 South 900 East, Salt Lake City. Many times you don't need an emergency room, but don't want to schedule an appointment. Salt Lake's Intermountain Health Care Clinic is clean, up-to-date, and speedy.

**LDS Hospital** (801-408-1100) Eighth Ave. and C St., Salt Lake City. LDS is located in the hilly neighborhood north of town called the Avenues. This has a good location for downtown visitors.

**Saint Mark's Hospital** (801-268-7111), 1200 East 3900 South, South Salt Lake. This is another resource south of downtown. It is in the heart of the suburbs between the interstate and the mountains.

**University Hospital** (801-581-2121), 50 North Medical Dr., University of Utah, Salt Lake City. This is in the far northeastern corner of downtown. It is near many of the bed-and-breakfasts of the area and is home to the Huntsman Cancer Institute.

**NEWSPAPERS** *The Salt Lake Tribune* (www.sltrib.com) and *Deseret News* (www.deseretnews.com) are the Wasatch Front's major daily papers. *Deseret News* reports from a Mormon perspective, and the *Salt Lake Tribune* does not for the most part.

*Salt Lake City Weekly* (www.slweekly.com) and *In Utah This Week* (www.inthisweek.com) are two free weekly publications that are widely distributed in coffee shops, restaurants, corner boxes, salons, and in bars. These have a younger, alternative readership, but the calendars cover events across the spectrum.

*Salt Lake Magazine* (www.saltlakemagazine.com) produces six issues annually and has a high-end readership, focusing for the most part on the Salt Lake and Park City areas.

## ✳ To See and Do

*❂* **Steiner Aquatic Center/Salt Lake City Sports Complex** (801-583-9713; www.recreation.slco.gov), 645 Guardsman Way, Salt Lake City. This massive, public fitness center has a number of different facilities, including weight lifting, an arena of treadmills and stationary bicycles, and sports courts. Its major features, though, are its Olympic ice sheets and its two Olympic-sized pools. There is a 25-meter indoor pool, and a 50-meter outdoor pool (open during summer only). The outdoor pool is one of the most scenic pools around, with outstanding, virtually uninterrupted views of the Wasatch Range in the background. $5 for an adult day pass, $4 for seniors ages 60 and up, $3.50 for children ages 13–15, $2.50 for children ages 4–12, and $1 for toddlers.

**MUSEUMS AND GALLERIES** ✇ **Clark Planetarium** (801-456-7827; www .clarkplanetarium.com), 110 South 400 West. Open Monday–Thursday 10:30–9, Friday–Saturday 10:30 AM–11 PM, and Sunday 10:30–8. In addition to the planetarium, another major attraction here is the **Hanson Dome Theater** and its **IMAX** presentations. A **free gallery** has more than a dozen exhibits from deep space, including photographs from the Hubble Telescope, a Marsscape and Moonscape, and an Earth Globe. Admission is free for exhibits, à la carte for shows.

✇ **Discovery Gateway** (801-456-5437; www.childmuseum.org), 444 West 100 South, Gateway Center. Open Tuesday–Thursday and Saturday 10–6, Monday and Friday 10–9, closed Sunday. Formerly the **Children's Museum of Utah,** this relocated and completely revamped children's museum is bright, clean, and full of stimulating, educational, and entertaining gadgets that make hands-on learning fun for kids and their parents. $8.50 for adults and children, free for ages one and under.

**Hellenic Cultural Museum** (801-328-9681; www.pahh.com), 279 South 300 West. Open 9–noon Wednesday, "for one hour after church services" on Sunday, and by appointment otherwise. A little-known fact: Salt Lake City has been home to one of the Intermountain West's biggest Greek and Greek Orthodox cultural centers since the early 1900s. A trip to this museum offers a glimpse at the lesser-known minority histories of Utah, and a departure from the more obvious Latter-day Saints tour. The **Holy Trinity Church,** built in 1905, has been considered the culture's home base from which religion, language, and Hellenic festivals operate. This community becomes particularly active in September during the annual Greek Festival. Free admission.

**Kennecott Copper Mine** (801-252-3234; www.kennecott.com), off the western end of 12800 South UT 111, Bingham Canyon (see Web site or call for exact directions). Visitors center open 8–8 daily. This mine is a bit southwest of the city but is quite a spectacle and worth the visit if you'd be impressed by a man-made hole 2 miles wide and nearly 1 mile deep. Not only is the mine incredibly large, but its mutant implements and vehicles are a must-see. This mine produces 150,000 tons of copper each day and draws nearly 200,000 visitors annually. $5 admission to visitors center.

**Salt Lake Art Center** (801-328-4201; www.slartcenter.org), 20 South West Temple. Open 11–6 Tuesday–Thursday and Saturday, 11–9 Friday, closed Sunday and Monday. The Salt Lake Art Center, an institution since the 1930s, has been a long-standing pillar of art education and appreciation. This center has three separate galleries, permanent collections, multiple performing arts halls, and a schedule of events and classes. Large spaces allow for the display of oversized sculptures and other works. Free admission.

↬ **Salt Lake Public Library** (801-524-8200; www.slcpl.lib.ut.us), 210 East 400 South. Open 9–9 Monday–Thursday, 9–6 Friday–Saturday, 1–5 Sunday. The main branch of the Salt Lake Library System is something to behold with its massive, open campus, sweeping lines, and green design. This building, with its award-winning, ultramodern architecture, is not only a beautiful place for reading, but a major community center. Every year it hosts the **Utah Arts Festival** (at the end of June; www.uaf.org) and is office space for groups like the **Salt Lake Film Society** (www.saltlakefilmsociety.org), a very active group that promotes films from around the globe with free screenings each week throughout the year. Inside and out, the layout integrates sunlight, gardens, glass, and raw and finished building materials to create this curving structure filled with function and aesthetic pleasure. A small **gallery on the fourth floor** showcases changing art exhibits; many other art pieces are on display on other floors, as well as in the entryway.

**Utah Museum of Fine Art** (801-581-7332; www.umfa.utah.edu), 410 Campus Center Dr., University of Utah. Open 10–5 Tuesday–Friday, 10–8 Wednesday, 11–5 Saturday–Sunday, closed Monday and holidays. This clean, modern facility has big rooms and small rooms alike, high and low ceilings—plenty of space adaptable to a variety of installations. These rooms host traveling exhibits and resident collections, including paintings and photographs whose subject is Utah's early state history. Artists range from local to national, and ages range from centuries old to contemporary. Be sure to get a parking voucher at the front desk in order to avoid a hassle or fee. $5 for adults, $3 for seniors, $3 for students (with ID) and youth, free for ages six and under.

✔ **Utah Museum of Natural History** (801-581-6927; www.umnh.utah.edu), 1390 East President's Circle, University of Utah. Open 9:30–5:30 Monday–Saturday, noon–5 Sunday. Utah's natural history is quite a story to behold. For example, all of Salt Lake Valley (and an area half as big as present-day Utah) used to be under the waters of ancient Lake Bonneville. Utah is certainly one of the most diverse geological regions in the world, as is easy to see—from the red sandstone arches of the south to the Wasatch Range dominating the Salt Lake City skyline. Sandstone, limestone, quartzite, conglomerate, and granite are all within 30 minutes' drive of downtown Salt Lake City alone. Paleontology digs across the state and ruins of Native American dwellings attest to a history of animal and human life in the state. This museum serves to educate its visitors in all of these arenas with reassembled dinosaur skeletons, displays, artifacts, and traveling exhibits. Children will enjoy the museum as well, for its fantastic scale and stimulating scope. Parking is tricky on campus, but limited free parking is in front of the museum. $6 for adults, $3.50 for seniors, $3.50 for youth ages 3–12, and free for children ages 3 and under.

DOWNTOWN SALT LAKE CITY FROM THE UNIVERSITY OF UTAH

Craig Bowden

## TEMPLE SQUARE AND NEARBY ATTRACTIONS

Temple Square is the oldest and, some would say, most important block in Salt Lake City. This is truly the center of the Mormon church; within a few block radius is the **Global Business Headquarters,** the genealogical records of the **Family History Museum,** the **Tabernacle,** and much more. Tours of the actual square are free and given year-round. Though outsiders are not allowed within the Temple itself, they are enthusiastically welcomed to explore the campus and this showpiece of Mormonism. Temple Square is readily noticeable by the limestone walls around its perimeter. Many more LDS attractions can also be found within a block or two outside of the actual square.

INSIDE THE SQUARE **Assembly Hall** was constructed in 1877 and is a Gothic-style structure characterized by stained glass and dramatic spires. Free concerts are held here each Friday and Saturday evening (with additional Tuesday and Wednesday evening concerts during the holiday season). Children under the age of eight are not admitted to concerts. Located on the southwest corner of the square.

**Seagull Monument.** Immediately in front of Assembly Hall, this bronze sculpture is dedicated to the "seagulls" (technically called California gulls) that are credited with saving the early pioneers from starvation. In 1848 an apocalyptic cloud of voracious crickets descended upon the Mormon settlers' first fledgling crops. The gulls arrived shortly after and ate these insects, saving the crops and earning their title as Utah's state bird. Many people believe incorrectly that the gull was declared the Utah state bird because the Mormons had thought they had arrived at the Pacific Ocean; in fact, they had specifically chosen the Great Salt Lake and Great Basin region as their relocation destination for its isolation so that they could be able to live in peace and escape persecution.

**Salt Lake Temple on Temple Square.** Center east on Temple Square. This massive structure was the first temple in Utah for which ground was broken. However, this was not the first opened, as it took more than 40 years to complete. Its size and immaculate construction are particularly impressive considering the extreme adversities Utah's early Mormons faced; simple survival was an enormous challenge in those first years. During the years of the Utah War (1857–1858), the construction was halted and the foundation hidden under soil so as not to attract any attention from the U.S. government. This neo-Gothic structure was constructed from massive blocks of granite (specifically quartz monzonite) quarried in part from Little Cottonwood Canyon, and covered from corner to corner with religious and astrological symbolism. The most visible symbol on the building, sitting atop the tallest (210-foot) tower, is a 12.5-foot-tall sculpture of the Angel Moroni covered in gold leaf and copper.

**Tabernacle on Temple Square.** West-central Temple Square, west of the

Temple. This is a unique structure with an oval-shaped dome roof that is entirely self-supported. Designed by Brigham Young and constructed from 1863 to 1875, the Tabernacle has an organ of 11,623 pipes. This building is made famous by its Mormon Tabernacle Choir, whose Christmas concerts are world-renowned. Currently it is under construction to better prepare it to withstand earthquakes. However, when the Tabernacle is not under construction, the choir can be heard every Sunday at 9:30 AM. **"Music and the Spoken Word,"** a live-broadcast Sunday-morning radio show, has been continuously airing the choir's Sunday-morning concerts since July 15, 1929.

**Temple Square Gardens,** Temple Square, North Temple–South Temple and Main St.–100 West St., consist of 250 beds (redesigned and replanted twice each year) containing more than 160,000 plants and nearly 800 varieties. Tours of the gardens are available and free. The tour guides discuss the gardens' place in LDS heritage and offer tips for home gardening. The gardens are lit the day after Thanksgiving for the Christmas season.

IMMEDIATE VICINITY These attractions begin nearest the northwest corner of Temple Square and are listed in counterclockwise order as they wrap around the outside of the square.

**Museum of Church History and Art** (801-240-4615; www.lds.org/church history/museum), 45 North West Temple St. Open Monday–Friday 9–9, Saturday and Sunday 10–7. This museum showcases historic and modern art and artifacts that illustrate important events and themes from the Book of Mormon and church history, including the treacherous and taxing pioneer handcart treks westward. Free admission.

**Family History Library** (801-240-2584 or 866-406-1830; www.familysearch.org or www.visittemplesquare.com), 35 North West Temple St. Open Monday 8–5, Tuesday–Saturday 8–9, closed Sunday. Family is one of the most sacred concepts in the Mormon faith; members of this church believe that they will spend eternity with their families. Not surprisingly, genealogy is quite a studied and well-kept body of knowledge. This museum, opened in 1985, is the largest of its kind in the world, with more than 2 billion names on record. Information extends to all of the continents and includes family trees as well as census, property, and cemetery records, and more. Free admission.

**Deuel Pioneer Log Home,** 31 North West Temple St. This cabin is one of only two remaining provisionary homes created by the first Mormons arriving in Utah in 1848. Facing a long winter and desperately low on energy and supplies, the Mormons constructed small homes like these in order to survive the harsh initial winter. This restored home is decorated with furniture and articles from the period.

**Brigham Young Monument,** South Temple and Main St., is a commemorative bronze monument cast in 1893 in honor of Brigham Young, leader of Utah's first

Mormon pioneers, early president of the Mormon church, and Utah Territory governor. The Native Americans and mountain men who lived in Utah upon Mormon arrival are also honored here.

**Joseph Smith Memorial Building,** 15 East South Temple, formerly **Hotel Utah,** is a bustling, multipurpose structure rich with function and religious art. There are bright and elaborate murals on the interior laden with religious significance. Also within the building you'll find a theater, reception halls, and two rooftop restaurants, **The Garden** (801-539-3170) and **The Roof** (801-539-1911). Though both serve delicious contemporary American cuisine, The Garden is a bit less formal and more inviting for a casual lunch or dinner experience. The Roof is more formal.

**Lion House,** 63 East South Temple. This home was commissioned in 1856 to serve as yet another private residence for early Mormon leader Brigham Young. The house's name comes from Young's nickname, "Lion of the Lord," and is marked by a stone lion on the front porch. Today it serves as a reception hall and houses a restaurant, **The Lion House Pantry** (801-539-3257). This restaurant is open to the public and serves meals based on recipes passed down through many generations of Young lineage.

**Beehive House,** 67 East South Temple, one block east of Temple Square. This house was completed in 1854 and was one of Brigham Young's numerous homes across Utah. This house, one of his best kept and most famous, was his primary residence during his early years as president of the Mormon church and governor of the Territory of Utah. Just above the front door of the house is a carved namesake beehive—the state symbol, adopted as such because of the Mormon advocacy of industriousness as a virtue. Free 30-minute guided tours.

**Eagle Gate,** corner of South Temple and State St., is the powerful symbol selected by Brigham Young to stand at the entrance of his historic City Creek Canyon home. Though this is not the original Eagle Gate, it is an enlarged and durable replica. Arches spanning 76 feet support a 2-ton eagle with 20-foot wingspan.

**LDS Church Office Building,** corner of State St. and North Temple. This is a respectably large office building northeast of Temple Square. Opened for business in 1972, this building has one central tower 28 stories tall with two flank-

GARDENS, PARKS & ZOOS **Brigham Young Historic Park** (see the *Temple Square and Nearby Atractions* sidebar in this chapter).

🐾 **Herman Frank's Park** (700 East 1300 South) is just on the other side of 700 East from Liberty Park (to its immediate east). Though not in Liberty Park itself, it is a designated off-leash park for dogs and thus a much better option for some. (In

ing structures adorned with massive maps of the earth. On the 26th floor there is an observation deck open to the public.

**Relief Society Building,** 76 North Main St. This building is the headquarters for the all-female LDS social works Relief Society that has been in constant existence since its Nauvoo, Illinois, 1842 founding. This building, finished in 1956, is one of the least historic structures of the LDS tour but is the home of one of the most historic institutions, offering a chance to learn about (or volunteer for) the society.

A BIT FARTHER **Mormon Pioneer Memorial Monument,** 140 East First Ave. This memorial was built in honor of the more than 6,000 Mormon pioneers who perished on their westward pilgrimage to Utah in the late 1840s and 1850s. Here are the gravesites of Brigham Young and historic Mormon poet Eliza Snow, whose works are used in many Mormon hymns.

**Social Hall Heritage Museum** (801-321-8745), 51 South State St. Open 10–9 Monday–Friday, 10–7 Saturday, closed Sunday. This museum commemorates the bygone pastimes of Utah's early Mormon residents. Artifacts, written stories, and illustrations explain these good times. Near Temple Square, this is worth a stop. Guided tours are available. Free admission.

**Daughters of Utah Pioneers Museum** (801-538-1050; www.dupinternational .org), 300 North Main St. Open 9–5 Monday–Saturday, 1–5 Sunday during the summer (closed Sunday in winter). The Daughters of Utah Pioneers is one of Utah's oldest and most active historical societies. This society is responsible in large part for the preservation and promotion of Mormon history and has opened many museums across the state. On display are photographs, furniture, and clothing, and paintings illustrating 19th-century frontier life. Handcarts, which seem banal, were pushed 1,300 miles by pioneers coming westward from Illinois (sometimes farther) as they relocated their families to Utah, fleeing persecution. Free admission; donations accepted.

**Brigham Young Historic Park,** State St. and Second Ave. This small park, just north of downtown, is located on land once farmed by Brigham Young and his family. City Creek flows through a waterwheel here, and free concerts are given on Tuesday and Friday evenings during the summer.

Liberty Park and most other Salt Lake City parks dogs must be on a leash at all times.)

 **Hogle Zoo** (801-582-1631; www.hoglezoo.org) 2600 East Sunnyside Ave., located at the mouth of Emigration Canyon (on the northeast side of town, just above the University of Utah campus), is a very popular family destination open all year long (with trimmed-back displays in winter). Thousands of mammals, reptiles, fish, snakes, insects, and spiders have been relocated from around the globe to live in this zoo. Kids love the miniature train that circles the campus.

**Jordan River Parkway** (801-533-4496; golf: 801-533-4527) is a very long park parallel to and west of I-15 alongside the Jordan River that flows from Utah Lake into the Great Salt Lake. Its many facilities include paddleboat and canoe marinas, **International Peace Gardens** (900 West and 900 South), picnic areas, a nine-hole golf course, and a somewhat discontinuous, paved trail system. (This trail system is under construction by a cooperative of many different cities along its length.)

**Liberty Park** (900–1300 South and 500–700 East). This large, rectangular park is one of Salt Lake City's oldest and most major, situated on the very land used for the former Pioneer Farm, owned in part by Brigham Young. This 110-acre space is visited today by many for its paved bike paths and wood-chip jogging paths, tennis and volleyball courts, swimming pool, and open spaces. Tall, old trees keep the park fairly well shaded.

**Memory Grove** (running north–south between 135 East North Temple and 130 East Bonneville Ave.). This is located beneath the mouth of City Creek Canyon (the northern apex of Bonneville Ave.) and above north of downtown. This recessed, shady park follows the length of, and is refrigerated by, City Creek. At the southern end of the park is a memorial for Utah soldiers who fought and died during the World Wars and Vietnam. The park has paths that extend uphill and to the north. These roughly paved bike- and pedestrian-friendly paths lead up to **City Creek Canyon** and the **Bonneville Shoreline Trail System** (as discussed in the *Biking* and *Hiking* sections of this chapter). A paved road runs for 5.7 miles up City Creek Canyon. (See the *Road Biking* section of this chapter) This is closed to motor vehicles and can be biked and walked on odd-numbered days without vehicular encounters. The road becomes a bit rougher in the top third. The entire road is closed to bikes on even-numbered days.

**Red Butte Garden and Arboretum** (801-581-4747; www.redbuttegarden.org), 300 Wakara Way, University of Utah, is tucked just northwest of the University of Utah, near the University Hospital and a massive business and research complex. Located just beneath the foothills and Bonneville Shoreline Trail System, these gardens have indoor and outdoor attractions, more than 200 plant species, educational seminars, and are open year-round. During the summer, the gardens attract headlining artists such as Emmylou Harris, John Hiatt, and Keb Mo for outdoor evening concerts (see their Web site for details).

**Sugarhouse Park** (2100 South–I-80 and 1300 East–1700 East) is another major park at the southeastern corner of the Sugarhouse neighborhood, popular for jogging, baseball, basketball, soccer, and sledding in winter. Few people know that this park was actually the home of the Utah State Prison until 1951, and the surrounding gentrified neighborhood was actually quite dingy until just a few decades ago. The park is accessed along its northern edge at 2100 South Street.

**Temple Square Gardens** (as discussed in the *Temple Square and Nearby Attractions* sidebar in this chapter) consist of more than 160,000 plants in over 250 beds; they are replanted completely twice each year.

✎ ✈ **Tracy Aviary** (801-596-8500; www.tracyaviary.org) is located on the southern end of the park and has more than 400 individual birds representing more than 130 species.

The **Chase Home** (801-533-5760) has been a center for musicians and dancers since its completion in 1853. Today the Chase Home houses the **Museum of Utah Folk Art,** where handicrafts and music are created. Also in the park is a pond (actually a holding reservoir for the mountain streams as they pour through town in underground culverts) with paddleboat rentals.

## ✳ Outdoor Activities

### BIKING

### *Mountain Biking*

Not only is Utah gifted with some of the nation's best mountains, their slopes are gifted with bike-perfect soil (not too sandy), a very long season (March through October in the Wasatch region; year-round in the south), and a huge number of trail systems that offer the full spectrum of difficulty and length. In Salt Lake City, the best biking seasons are spring and fall. Summer is usually much too warm, unless you plan to ride early in the morning. Winter covers the hills with snow and gives the air a bite. Salt Lake City cyclists often go up to **Park City** and **Kimball Junction** to ride during the summer, as Kimball Junction is just a little more than 20 minutes up Parley's Canyon, and Park City is only another 10 or 15 minutes farther. For information on those areas, see the "Park City" chapter. During colder months, **Moab** and **St. George** have a lot to offer; see those chapters for information on southern Utah's mountain biking. The Web site www .utahmountainbiking.com is a very comprehensive site listing rides per region of the state, illustrated with maps, explicit driving and riding directions, photographs, and even sometimes video. Most rides have at least a few variations, and so consulting a detailed resource such as this site is advised.

For more suggestions, call or visit the following:

**Utah Ski & Golf** (801-355-9088; www.utahskiandgolf.com), 134 West 600 South. A rental venue for mountain bikes. Road bike rentals are nonexistent.

---

✎ **Lagoon** (801-451-8000; www.lagoonpark.com), 375 Lagoon Dr., exit 322 on I-15, Farmington. Open seasonally. Just 17 miles north of Salt Lake City, Lagoon is Utah's full-sized amusement park, loved as much by teens and adults as by kids. During the summer, its water slides, pools, and splash rides help cut through Utah's heat. Amusement park rides include The Rocket, a 200-vertical-foot tower with rapid rise and freefall, the Jet Star Roller Coaster, which travels up to 45 miles per hour, and other more common creations, such as bumper cars and a tilt-a-whirl. The Sky Coaster is perhaps Lagoon's most intimidating ride; this enormous swing requires the customer to (willingly) step off a 143-foot platform whilst harnessed to the end of a 120-foot cable. $25.95 plus tax per person (more for select rides), $7 parking fee.

↪ **Wastatch Touring** (801-359-9361; www.wasatchtouring.com), 702 East 100 South. This a locally owned downtown shop that covers many sports, including mountain biking. Front suspension rentals are available here.

**Bonneville Shoreline.** This complex system has many access points and even more trails. From **City Creek Canyon** (at the northern apex of Bonneville Boulevard, and just above Memory Grove Park), you can catch the western end of this trail system. Some trails ride up into the canyon, but the easiest and least contrived riding is to the east, along the foothills. Another major access point is across the street from the **Hogle Zoo** (2600 East Sunnyside Ave., 800 South). From here you ride west on any number of trails. (Other access points are scattered between these two, throughout the Avenues neighborhood and University of Utah campus; consult with www.utahmountainbiking.com, or either of the bike shops listed above, for more information on these tricky access points.) These trailheads can seem confusing, as a high number of trails depart from each. However, the trails are quite intuitive to follow, and visibly popular trails generally lead to a good ride. One of the best parts of this trail system is the **Bobsled Trail,** a one-way, downhill-only trail. Just like a bobsled track, this trail has hugely banked turns and is incredibly fun for people with an intermediate or higher skill level. Bonneville Shoreline is generally south facing and lacks substantial vegetation, so sun exposure and temperatures run high here.

🐾 **Millcreek Canyon** is one of Salt Lake City's favorite multisport canyons, mountain biking included. However, it is also a dog-friendly, off-leash canyon. To resolve conflict, the Forest Service declared that every odd-numbered day is for off-leash dog access (mountain bikers are forbidden to ride on certain trails), and every even-numbered day is given to mountain bikers (dogs must be on leash). Not every trail falls under this rule, but the most popular do. The **Pipeline Trail** is a favorite for bikers. Park just a mile into the canyon at Rattlesnake Gulch, the first

A MOUNTAIN BIKER ON PARLEY'S PASS BETWEEN PARK CITY AND SALT LAKE CITY (RIGHT NEXT TO I-80, THOUGH YOU'D NEVER GUESS)

major parking lot on the north side of the road. From here, ride up the road to Burch Hollow trailhead, about 2.5 miles above the parking area. Poke into the woods on the north side of the road, and head back down the canyon, west along the flat Pipeline Trail (named after the old pipeline that used to carry water to SLC along this route). At the top of Rattlesnake Gulch, bomb down to your car, being very careful of pedestrians (and rattlesnakes) on this steep, steep trail. (Alternately, continue along the Pipeline Trail to the Salt Lake City overlook before returning to the top of Rattlesnake Gulch.) More biking at the very top of the canyon is possible on the multiple trails originating at the **Dog Lake Trailhead.** (The top of the road is closed between November and July.)

**The Wasatch Crest Trail,** whose SLC origin is on the shoulder of Guardsman Pass (via Big Cottonwood Canyon), is a great option as well. This ride has many variations, but the most popular requires a vehicle shuttle, which is worth it for the 20 miles of mostly downhill riding. Other large-scale linkups are possible, as Park City, the Canyons resort, and many trails are just over the ridge from Millcreek and the Cottonwood canyons.

## Road Biking

In Salt Lake City, road biking is best done a bit outside of the city center. For better or worse, most of the good rides are in canyons. These steep routes make for a great workout and a chance to escape traffic.

**Big Cottonwood Canyon** is a big ride. It is the longest straight-shot canyon ride in the vicinity of Salt Lake City and is also quite an ambitious climb. From the mouth, the ride is 14.7 miles to the top, with an average gradient of 7.8 percent. Do the math, and you'll calculate nearly a mile of elevation gain, 4,600 feet. The canyon itself is filled with the beautiful, if strange, geometry of its resident rock, quartzite. Despite its extreme statistics, it seems to ride easier than Little Cottonwood, as it is less exposed and offers fewer long lines of sight.

**City Creek Canyon,** to the north of and above Memory Grove Park (see *Gardens, Parks & Zoos*), is accessed by taking 11th Avenue west of the Avenues neighborhood and parking at the hairpin kink in 11th Avenue/Bonneville Boulevard. This ride is 5.7 miles each way. At an average grade of 7.3 percent, it gains nearly 1,500 feet. The road is open exclusively to bikers and pedestrians on odd-numbered days; conversely, it is open exclusively to motorists on even-numbered days (and is closed to cyclists). As of 2008, the asphalt in the upper portion of this ride needed some serious improvements but was still very rideable with caution.

**Emigration Canyon** is the city's easiest and quickest canyon to ride, with options for ride extension. It begins just east of the Hogle Zoo (2600 East Sunnyside Ave., 800 South) and heads straight east and up the canyon for a total of 7.8 miles at a 5 percent average grade. About 6 miles into the canyon, riders take a sharp right to follow the main road to Little Mountain Pass. Once you reach the obvious top, you can turn back or keep going down into East Canyon for 1 mile to a stop sign. This is another turnaround point. If you still want to keep going, head left and ride to the top of Big Mountain. You can even go past that, down to the town of Henefer via UT 65. If you were to do that, the round-trip ride would be about 85 miles with six legitimate climbs.

**Little Cottonwood Canyon** is a big ride, and perhaps the most severe in the Salt Lake region. The climb, from the mouth of the canyon to the top, is 8.2 miles long with an average grade of 9.2 percent. The road is often quite exposed to the sun as well as to traffic. The best time to ride, by far, is *very* early in the morning. During the hottest months of the summer, early morning temperatures are ideal, and you can finish the ride before traffic gets heavy. To give you an idea of scale, this ride's profile is almost identical to the famous Alpe D'Huez climb of France.

**BOATING** Boating in Utah is mostly done in the eastern and southern parts of the state. The numerous reservoirs in the Park City area are popular for flat water boating, and the **Green River,** running the eastern length of the state, is the most popular for canoeing and white-water boating, with the **Provo River** being a distant second. The freshwater **Utah Lake** near Provo and **Bear Lake** in north-eastern Utah are also popular. For information on these bodies of water, including guide services, see those sections of this book. Though the Great Salt Lake technically *can* be boated, most avoid it because of its strong briny smell, saline content, and insect population.

**Invert Sports** (801-830-8864; www.utahboatrental.com) rents all the necessary motorized gear, including Jet Skis and motorboats with appropriate trailers and vehicles for towing, if necessary, and accessory toys for waterskiing and wakeboarding. This company takes care of everything, including boat delivery and cleanup.

FISHING Salt Lake City itself does not have much fishing, rather much of the state's best fishing is found in the **Uinta Range** in mountain lakes, **east of Park City** on plateau reservoirs, or along the **Green and Provo rivers.** (See those sections of this book for information on those bodies of water.) **Destinations Inc. Fly Fishing** (801-816-0790; www.flyfishingdestinationsllc.com) and **Western Rivers Flyfisher** (800-545-4312; www.wrflyfisher.com) are two guide services based out of the Salt Lake City area that offer trips nearby and as far away as the Green River.

GOLF Because of its climate and open landscape, Utah has many excellent golf courses, a very high percentage of which are public. If you do not see a course that meets your needs listed below, visit the Web site www.utah.com/golf for a complete listing of courses in the state per region.

**Bonneville Golf Course** (801-583-9513), 954 Connor St. This 18-hole, par-72 course is located on the east bench of town, just north of where the Cottonwood Canyons spill into the valley. It offers pleasant views of the city below and mountains above, as well as 6,824 hilly yards and a driving range. This is one of the excellent public courses in the area. $27 for 18 holes, $15 for 9 holes.

**Forest Dale Golf Course** (801-483-5420), 2375 South 900 East. This nine-hole, par-36 course was originally the Salt Lake Country Club. Built in 1905, this is the oldest course in Utah. Though the course was largely redesigned in the late 1980s, many of the original greens still exist today. A large lake is a major obstacle on three of the holes. $12.

**Nibley Park Golf Course** (801-483-5418), 2780 South 700 East. This nine-hole, par-34, 2,895-yard course is completely flat and very central to downtown. Wide fairways are dotted enough with trees to lend the course seclusion from the surrounding city. The ninth hole is the best. $10.

**Mountain Dell Golf Course** (801-582-3812), exit 134 on I-80, Parley's Canyon. Mountain Dell, despite its location in Parley's Canyon, is a quiet course with beautiful natural surroundings. (I-80 shares this canyon but is far enough to the side that it does not pollute the course with noise.) Because of its canyon location, this golf course if very elongated and is known for its narrow, tree-lined fairways. Two separate courses here are 18 holes each, par 72 and 71, with 6,787 and 6,710 yards, respectively. $27.

**University of Utah Golf Course** (801-581-6511; www.utah.edu/campusrec), 102 Central Campus Dr., University of Utah. This nine-hole, par-33, hilly course is perched high on the bench and offers great views of the valley below. These bent fairways make up a total of 2,500 yards of playing space. $7.

**HIKING** Salt Lake City's hiking is quite plentiful. The hikes below are selected for accessibility, range of difficulty, unique views, and pet access. Most hikes in the area are along the length of Millcreek Canyon, and at the tops of Little and Big Cottonwood canyons. Some smaller canyons like Big Willow and Neff's have hikes as well. For more suggestions on hikes in the Wasatch, check www.fs.fed.us/r4/wcnf, or read the *Mountain Biking* section of this chapter.

**Bonneville Shoreline** (from the Hogle Zoo or City Creek; see *Mountain Biking*) is a very accessible trail system that sits on the northern shoulder of the town. Most trails in this system traverse more or less horizontally with a bit of rolling—great for running. Some trails head higher toward the mountain tops and are more suited to hiking. The western side of this system, near City Creek Canyon, has a few trails that head to the top of Big Mountain, while some of the trails in the middle and on the eastern side gain smaller mountains and ridgelines.

**☻ Millcreek Canyon Grandeur Peak,** exit 4 off I-215. Head east under the overpass, north one block, and then east toward the mountains on 3800 South. Trailhead is 3 miles past the mouth of the canyon at a picnic area labeled CHURCH FORK. The trail begins by heading up a fairly steep gulch. About one-third of the way up the trail, it breaks across a slope covered in scrub oak. Near the peak, it gains a shoulder with great views. The actual peak itself has excellent views of the surrounding mountains, as well as Salt Lake City below. The trail is 3.4 miles long and gains almost 2,300 feet to top out at 8,299 feet. As with all trails in Millcreek Canyon, dogs are allowed off-leash on odd-numbered days (and must be on-leash on even-numbered days).

**☻ Millcreek Rattlesnake Gulch to Pipeline Trail.** Drive to Millcreek Canyon, as for Grandeur Peak, above. The Pipeline trailhead is about 1 mile from the mouth of the canyon, at the first major parking lot on the left. This trail climbs for

TAKEN FROM A TALUS PILE ON THE NORTH SIDE OF LITTLE COTTONWOOD CANYON, ABOUT HALFWAY UP THE ROAD

only 0.75 mile through a steep, sheltered gulch to reach a T-intersection with the Pipeline Trail. This flat trail runs east–west through the canyon along the path of an old water pipeline. Head west toward Salt Lake City for a good overlook point in about 1.5 miles. This is an easy hike for the views. Dogs are allowed off-leash on odd-numbered days.

**Snowbird** has a number of hiking trails, most of which reach the top of Hidden Peak. During the summer, they operate their tram 11–8. This tram runs along a 1.6-mile cable from the bottom of the resort to the top. Many people ride the tram to the top (801-933-2147) for $12, and then hike down after satisfying their sightseeing needs. Here's a good hint: You can hike to the top, check out the views, and head down on the tram for no charge. This is great for those seeking exercise, but wanting to save their knees the grief of a more than 3,000-foot descent.

ROCK CLIMBING ↝ **The Front Climbing Club** (801-466-7625; www.front slc.com), 1450 South 400 West. This is Salt Lake's downtown climbing gym. Utah's premier bouldering gym, the Front requires no harnesses or ropes, just shoes, chalk, and a spotter. The most friendly staff and best indoor boulder problems in the city, this gym stays very up-to-date and regularly hosts local and pro competitions, so problems are regularly changed and holds stay fresh and clean.

**IME** (801-484-8073; www.imeutah.com), 3265 East 3300 South. Open since 1987, this is a locally owned, climbing-specific shop. Gear and additional information on the area crags can be obtained here. Despite its location immediately next to REI, they have survived for more than two decades.

**Momentum** (801-990-6890; www.momentumclimbing.com), 220 West 10600 South, Sandy. Visible from I-15 (next to REI). This new gym is located in the far southern end of the valley and has the state's best indoor roped climbing. Opened in 2006, this gym is quite pleasant with plenty of natural light, excellent angles, new holds, and great route setting.

**Rockreation** (801-278-7473; www.rockreation.com), 2074 East 3900 South. This South Salt Lake gym has been around for quite a while and offers roped climbing as well as a bouldering cave. Though not as new and flashy as other gyms, it has been a Salt Lake institution for a few decades and is located in the same building as Black Diamond headquarters.

SKIING, ALPINE **Big Cottonwood Canyon** and **Little Cottonwood Canyon,** just south of Salt Lake City, are the location of some of Utah's best ski areas. At Big Cottonwood are **Solitude** and **Brighton;** in Little Cottonwood are the more famous **Alta** and **Snowbird.** Despite the names of these canyons, the two ski areas in Little Cottonwood are actually quite a bit *larger* than those in Big Cottonwood, in terms of acreage and vertical drop. However, all four of the areas are good to excellent, and your selection will depend on your priorities. Each area has its benefits, and each its downfalls. Brighton is a resort known especially for its terrain parks. Solitude, despite its great snow and moderate-to-expert terrain, enjoys very little crowding—probably due to its smaller size and older lifts. Snowbird is by far the biggest and most aggressive mountain of all of these. This is where the diehard skiers come to pack in as many 3,240-foot tram runs as quickly as possible. On a powder day, the Snowbird experience can be pretty intense, from conditions to the skiers themselves. Alta has somewhat similar terrain to Snowbird but lacks a

Amiee Maxwell

RED PINE LAKE IN LITTLE COTTONWOOD CANYON

bottom-to-top tram and does not have as many high-speed lifts. Alta is also one of the last ski areas that still doesn't allow snowboarders, and it seems likely this will never change. Many of the best runs at Alta require significant hiking and/or traversing—a turnoff to some, and a huge draw for others. Snowbird has a huge village of hotels; the other mountains have much less mass lodging, and guests primarily stay in vacation rentals.

Law requires that all vehicles entering Big Cottonwood and Little Cottonwood have snow chains or four-wheel drive during the winter. Little Cottonwood, because of its steep, U-shaped, thinly vegetated walls, is quite prone to avalanches and is often blocked by road maintenance crews after a storm. These crews work with blasting caps and snow plows to safely trigger potential avalanches and keep the roads clear. During these events, "interlodge" goes into effect; the roads close entirely, and everyone already at the top of the canyon must remain at the ski areas and inside designated buildings until the road opens—sometimes as much as a day later. To check the road conditions, call the **Utah Department of Transportation Hotline** (801-933-2100). Big Cottonwood and Little Cottonwood canyons are both serviced by **Utah Transit Authority** (801-743-3882 or 888-743-3882; www .rideuta.com) Bus Shuttles, which originate in park-and-ride lots at the mouth of each canyon (and from other locations in the city; call for rates). By law, no pets are allowed in Big or Little Cottonwood canyons; these are protected watersheds, and violation of these laws can result in very severe fines and even imprisonment.

For après-ski drinks at the mouth of the canyons, go to **Porcupine Pub & Grille** (801-942-5555), 3698 East Fort Union Blvd. This pub is near I-216 exit 6 and just west of the mouth of Big Cottonwood (just down the hill and toward Salt Lake City from the mouth of Little Cottonwood), and has 50 percent appetizers until 5 PM Monday through Friday, and discounted beers on Tuesday.

## NO, I DON'T WANT TO CLIMB MOUNT EVEREST ONE DAY

Many people innocently hear "rock climbing" and think of blizzardy Himalayan Peaks and, naturally, of Mount Everest. In fact, rock climbing diverged long ago from its mountaineering roots. Today, technical rock climbing is an entirely distinct sport with its own subcategories, professional athletes, and training gyms.

Athletes in this sport strive simply to climb the most challenging route possible, made difficult by size, shape, and orientation of hand- and footholds, distance between the holds, incline of the rock, and friction. Length of a route certainly adds to difficulty, but many of the world's most difficult lines are found on boulders no more 10 or 15 feet tall.

Salt Lake City has long been an epicenter of technical rock climbing in the United States. American Fork Canyon was, to a large extent, where difficult limestone climbing began in North America. A community of very strong climbers, drawn here by the region's climate and rock, has brought with it many of the industry's key businesses and events.

Salt Lake City has three major climbing canyons in its immediate vicinity: Big Cottonwood, Little Cottonwood, and American Fork. Within two or three hours of the city, a huge variety is available; within five or six hours are some of the world's best and unique climbing. Because of its proximity to hot southern deserts and cool northern mountains, Utah climbers can easily climb year-round on weekend road trips.

Climbers, read on. **Little Cottonwood Canyon** is within 20 minutes of downtown and has impeccable white granite. This canyon is home to traditional climbing and world-class bouldering. There is a smattering of sport climbing, but not much. People liken the climbing in this canyon to Yosemite for its old-school grades and style of climbing. **Big Cottonwood Canyon** has mostly sport climbing on quartzite with some traditional climbing in the mix. The climbing here is somewhat blocky, and the walls have a very three-dimensional macrofeaturing.

**American Fork Canyon** is the best sport climbing nearest to Salt Lake City and was one of the most important limestone crags in the country during the

## Big Cottonwood Canyon

**Brighton Resort** (801-532-4731 or 800-873-5512; www.brightonresort.com), 12601 East Big Cottonwood Canyon Rd. Brighton receives an average annual snowfall of 500 inches and has a lift-served elevation between 8,750–10,500 feet. This yields a vertical drop of 1,750 feet over 1,050 acres. The terrain has been roughly determined to be 20 percent beginner, 40 percent intermediate, 40 percent advanced. Special features at Brighton include lighted night skiing, extensive terrain parks, and a combination lift pass with Solitude. $62 for a Brighton and

1990s. Slightly farther south, **Provo and Rock canyons** also offer limestone sport climbing, though not as much. **Maple Canyon,** conglomerate rock near Fountain Green and about 100 miles southeast of Salt Lake City, is yet another best sport area nearby. **Uinta Range,** about one and a half hours east of Salt Lake City, is a moderate climber's high-elevation summer climbing paradise. **City of Rocks,** two and a half hours to the north, stays a bit cooler than Salt Lake City and has some of the most scenic, non-big-wall granite climbing around. **Joe's Valley and Triassic** have some of continent's best sandstone bouldering and are just more than three hours southeast of Salt Lake.

Expand your radius to a half-day's drive, and you get another heap of areas. **Ibex,** very distinctive quartzite bouldering and multipitch route climbing (mixed sport and traditional), is located in the exceptionally unique west-central desert. Surrounded by lunar-type landscape on flat hardpan lake bed, this has some of the nation's more famous bouldering, but its off-the-deck climbing should not be overlooked. **Notch Peak,** just north of Ibex, is North America's largest limestone face, with 3,000 feet of sheer cliffs. Because of loose rock, it is not nearly as popular as El Cap, though some love the added adventure caused by the insecurity. Near Moab are **Indian Creek** and **Castle Valley,** with **Fischer Towers, Castleton,** and other towers. Indian Creek offers the highest concentration of pure-form crack climbing in the world, with splitter Wingate sandstone and virtually no features outside of the crack. Also in Moab are **Wall Street** (Wingate crack routes) and **Millcreek Canyon,** which has some of Utah's best, though difficult and run-out, sport climbing. St. George has a huge variety of climbing options, including **Moe's Valley** sandstone bouldering, various sandstone and limestone sport climbing areas, and sandstone traditional climbing. **Red Rocks,** just west of Las Vegas, has a huge selection of sandstone climbing from single-pitch sport to huge, multipitch traditional. **Northern Nevada** also has a huge amount of limestone, including Mount Clark. **Sinks Canyon** and **Wild Iris** are to the north of Salt Lake, near Lander, Wyoming—both offer a huge amount of sport climbing, and Sinks offers some bouldering.

Solitude combination pass, $47 for adults, $42 children 11–15, $10 children 7–10, $10 for seniors (ages 70 and older), free for ages 6 and under.

As with many ski resorts across the country, Brighton began as a small homestead-turned-mining town. The mining industry faded and was astutely replaced with a luxury vacation business. Brighton's first lift went into operation during 1935, and the rest is history. Today Brighton is most known for its terrain park—which makes it quite popular for aspiring trick skiers—though its affordable lift prices and modest size, by Utah standards, make it very attractive for families. Though the resort lacks the same bounty of aggressive terrain and vertical drop as its sisters Snowbird and Alta, it does enjoy significantly less crowding and less urgency in lift lines. For telemark, Alpine ski, or snowboard lessons, call **Brighton Ski and Snowboard School** (801-532-4731). **Brighton Mountain Rentals** (801-532-5731 or 800-873-5512; www .brightonresort.com) is located in the resort center and offers telemark and Alpine ski rentals, snowboard rentals, repairs, retail, and tuning.

ALBION BASIN AND CECRET LAKE FROM DEVILS CASTLE, ALTA

## On-site Accommodations at Brighton

**Brighton Chalets** (801-942-8824 or 800-748-4824; www.brigtonchalets.com) rental properties are around the resort.

**Brighton Lodge** (801-873-5512; www.brightonresort.com) is a lodge at the resort center.

**Brighton & Solitude Lodging Company** (801-943-5050 or 877-545-6344; www.solitudelodging.com) offers varied lodging at Brighton and Solitude resorts and in Salt Lake Valley near the Cottonwoods.

**Home Away from Home** (801-205-9778; www.skiutahhomes.com) rents guest houses between Solitude and Brighton.

**Mount Majestic Properties** (888-236-0667; www.mountmajestic.com) are single-family slopeside rentals.

THE GRASSY MEADOW AT THE BASE OF SOLITUDE RESORT, WHICH OFFERS HIKING IN SUMMER AND NORDIC SKIING IN WINTER

**Silver Fork Lodge and Restaurant** (888-649-9551; www.silverforklodge .com) is a bed-and-breakfast–style lodge between Brighton and Solitude.

**Solitude Mountain Resort** (801-532-4731 or 800-748-4754; www.skisoli tude.com), 12000 Big Cottonwood Canyon Rd. Solitude receives an average of 500 inches of snow annually (snow phone: 801-536-5777), with lift-served elevation from 7,988 to 10,035 feet. This yields a vertical drop of 2,047 feet over 1,200 acres, which is deemed to be 20 percent beginner, 50 percent intermediate, and 30 percent advanced. Special features at Solitude are a terrain park, Nordic skiing, and a combination pass with Brighton. $62 Brighton & Solitude combination pass, $53 for adults, $32 children 7–13, $25

SOLITUDE VILLAGE

for seniors (ages 70 and older), free for ages 6 and under. Half-day rates start at 12:30 PM and cost $45. There are also multi-day adult lift ticket discounts and beginner discounts.

As early as the 1860s, the Solitude area saw its first heavy traffic when metal ores were discovered in its hillsides—enough to beget hundreds of mines. In fact, today's parking lots were in part constructed from the old tailings piles from these mines. During the 19th century, timber was also harvested from the area to feed a growing Salt Lake City below. Solitude was born as a ski resort in 1957, seven years after the last mine closed. Today Solitude is beloved by those who want to experience light and deep Wasatch powder without vicious competition found at other areas. The name "Solitude" truly does describe the low-key experience at this mountain. Few other ski areas of such quality enjoy such uncrowded skiing, especially so near a metropolis. The drawback for expert skiers is the relative lack of long, steep runs and stiffly challenging terrain. However, for moderate skiers, this mountain might prove superior to its bigger Little Cottonwood siblings—and it certainly has enough terrain to entertain virtually any skier (even an expert skier) for at least a weekend. Relatively low lift ticket prices are also a plus. For lessons, call Solitude's **Snow Sports Academy** (Moonbeam Base Area; 801-536-5730). Child care is available for children four and under at the Snow Sports Academy; reservations at least 24 hours in advance are recommended. Two rental shops, **Moonbeam Lodge Rentals** (801-

BRIGHTON RESORT

THE HELLGATE CLIFFS BETWEEN ALTA AND SNOWBIRD IN LITTLE COTTONWOOD CANYON

536-5630; www.skisolitude.com) in the Moonbeam Base Area and **Villager Rentals** (801-536-5734; www.skisolitude.com) in the Village at Solitude, both offer Alpine ski and snowboard rental, repairs, and tuning.

### On-site Accommodations at Solitude

**Creekside at Solitude** (801-536-5765 or 800-748-4754; www.skisolitude.com). Slope-side condominiums.

**The Crossings** (801-536-5765 or 800-748-4754; www.skisolitude.com). Town homes in the central village.

**Eagle Springs Lodges** (801-536-5765 or 800-748-4754; www.skisolitude.com). Hotel-style lodging in the central village.

**Home Away from Home** (801-205-9778; www.skiutahhomes.com). Guest houses between Brighton and Solitude resorts.

**The Inn at Solitude** (801-536-5765 or 800-748-4754; www.skisolitude.com). Hotel-style lodging in the central village.

**Powderhorn Lodge** (801-536-5765 or 800-748-4754; www.skisolitude.com). Resort center condominiums.

**Silver Fork Lodge and Restaurant** (888-649-9551; www.silverforklodge.com). Bed-and-breakfast–style lodging between Brighton and Solitude.

### Little Cottonwood Canyon

**Alta Ski Lifts Company** (801-359-1078; www.alta.com), eastern terminus of UT 210, Little Cottonwood Canyon, Alta. Alta receives an average of 500 inches of snow each winter (snow phone: 801-572-3939) and has an elevation of 8,530–

10,550 feet. This yields a vertical drop of 2,020 feet spread over 2,200 acres. The terrain is deemed to be 25 percent beginner, 40 percent intermediate, and 35 percent advanced. Special features include: skis only (no snowboards), access to backcountry skiing (conditions permitting), Nordic skiing, snowcat skiing, free skiing after 3 PM, and a combination pass with Snowbird. $71 Alta and Snowbird combination pass, $52 for adults, $23 for kids 12 and under, free for seniors (ages 80 and older); half-day passes $45 (9:15–1 and 1–4). There are also multiple-day pass discounts and beginner lift discounts.

Alta has a special place in the ski world; it is one of Utah's most well-endowed areas. It is consistently among the top snowfall ski areas in the nation and has some of the driest, lightest, and most plentiful snow on earth. It also has some of the best and most varied terrain. Yet it is one of the nation's quirkiest areas, and true Alta skiers *love* Alta for its uniqueness. It doesn't allow snowboarders. It deliberately calls itself "Alta Lifts Company," because it takes pride in being a ski area, *not* a resort. Its lift layout requires a good deal of traversing along cat tracks, even some hiking, to reach the best runs. Alta skiers love all of these quirks. Many find snowboarders bothersome and don't desire the clutter of resort luxuries. They also enjoy the exercise required to reach good runs, and the way it preserves their precious powder stashes.

**Alta Peruvian Bar** (801-742-3000), in the Alta Peruvian Lodge at the Wildcat Base Area, and **Goldminer's Saloon** (801-742-2300) and the Goldminer's Daughter Lodge in the Wildcat Base Area, are two Little Cottonwood après-ski favorites, even attracting skiers from Snowbird. For lessons, call **Alf Engen Ski School** (P.O. Box 8064, Alta, UT 84092; 801-359-1078; www.alta.com). Child care is available though **Alta Children's Center** (801-742-3042), who will care for children as young as six months. Rentals can be obtained at **Deep Powder House** (801-742-2400; www.deeppowderhouse.com) above the Alta Lodge; **Mother Lode Ski House** (801-742-9753; www.deeppowderhouse.com) in the Goldminer's Daughter Lodge; and **Rustler Powder House** (801-742-2705; www.deeppowderhouse

TAKEN FROM THE SOUTH SIDE OF BIG COTTONWOOD CANYON JUST BENEATH THE FAMOUS "S-CURVE" IN THE ROAD, FEATURING THE VERY ANGULAR GEOMETRY OF THE CANYON'S QUARTZITE GEOLOGY

RIDING THE SUPREME LIFT AT ALTA SKI AREA IN LITTLE COTTONWOOD CANYON

Amiee Maxwell

.com), in the Rustler Lodge, all of which do Alpine ski demos, rentals, repairs, retail, and tuning.

### On-site Accommodations at Alta

**Alta Chalets** (801-424-2426 or 866-754-2426; www.altachalets.com). Vacation rentals.

**Alta Lodge** (801-742-3500 or 800-707-2582; www.altalodge.com). Base-area hotel.

**Alta Peruvian Lodge** (801-742-3000 or 800-453-8488; www.altaperuvian .com), a base-area hotel with breakfasts and family-style dinners. **Alta's Rustler Lodge** (801-742-2200 or 888-532-2582; www.rustlerlodge.com). Base-area hotel with breakfast and dinner.

**Alta Vacation Homes** (www.altavacationhomes.com).

**The Blackjack Condos** (800-742-8959).

**Canyon Services** (888-546-5679; www.canyonservices.com). Vacation rentals.

**Cliff Club Condominiums** (877-918-3332; www.snowbirdcondo.net).

**Goldminer's Daughter Lodge** (801-742-2300 or 800-453-4573; www.skigmd .com). Base-area hotel with day spa, restaurant, popular après-ski bar, and ski shop.

**Hellgate Condominiums** (801-742-2020).

**Ironblossom Condominiums** (877-918-3332; www.snowbirdcondo.net).

**The Miles Alta Vacation Home** (801-582-1371).

**Snowpine Lodge** (801-742-2000; www.thesnowpine.com). Base-area hotel with breakfast, dinner, a spa, and guest rooms as well as dormitory-style rooming for those on a budget (or out of other options).

CONDOS BETWEEN ALTA AND SNOWBIRD

**Tobin Powder Ridge Condos** (877-918-3332; www.altacondo.net). Vacation rentals.

**Travis Home** (801-942-5219; www .thetravishome.com). Vacation rentals.

**Snowbird Ski and Summer Resort** (800-232-9542; www.snowbird.com), UT 210/Little Cottonwood Canyon. Snowbird receives an average of 500 inches of snow each year (snow phone: 801-933-2100) and occupies the elevation from 7,760 to 11,000 feet. This yields a 3,240-foot vertical over 2,500 acres. Terrain is deemed to be 27 percent beginner, 38 percent intermediate, and 35 percent advanced. Special features of Snowbird are its tram, with one bottom-to-top ride gaining 3,240 feet of vertical relief, access to backcountry skiing (when conditions permit), small terrain park, and a combination pass with Alta. Rates for a full day are $71 for an Alta/Snowbird combination pass, $64 for adult chair and tram, $54 for adult chair only, $53 for senior chair and tram (ages 65 and up), $46 for senior chair only, $10 for children 7–12, free for ages 6 and under. Half-day passes are $55 for chair and tram or $48 for chair only (9–1 or 12:30–4:30). There are also multiple-day pass discounts and beginner lift discounts.

Snowbird is certainly one of Utah's most famous resorts: huge amounts of snow, huge amounts of terrain, and hugely accomplished skiers. Snowbird is kissed each year by more than 500 inches of Utah's incredibly light powder and has one of Utah's largest acreages. It is served by Utah's only bottom-to-top tram and has some of Utah's best and most extreme in-bounds terrain. Snowbird has two major regions: the main area (facing Little Cottonwood Canyon) and Mineral Basin (the backside). This division allows skiers to somewhat escape strong winds, should they arise.

Snowbird definitely has a much bigger "resort"-style feel than its neighbor, Alta. Similar in some ways to European resorts, it lacks the snobbery of ritzy Aspen-like resorts, yet has enormous hotels and major resort infrastructure. Snowbird (particularly the tram) becomes very crowded on big powder days (even during the week), so be prepared to strategize, if you want to gun for the stashes. Backcountry-ski access to **Whitepine Basin** is permitted at the top of the Mid Gad Lift, conditions permitting. (An avalanche beacon, shovel, probe, and partner are required.) Snowbird's base area, situated in the bottom of narrow and steep Little Cottonwood Canyon, is quite elongated and has multiple entries (with limited parking), so if you are seeking a specific hotel or rental shop, call ahead to be sure you take the proper exit.

THE HIGH TRAVERSE OF SNOWBIRD'S MINERAL BASIN, LOOKING OUT ACROSS THE EASTERN EDGE OF THE RESORT

OFF-PISTE, LOOKING UP TOWARD THE CRAGGY TOP OF SNOWBIRD'S MINERAL BASIN

For lessons, call **Snowbird's Mountain School** (801-933-2170; www.snowbird .com/mtnschool). **Camp Snowbird** (Cliff Lodge; 801-933-2256) is Snowbird's child-care service; call for reservations. Rentals at snowbird can be had at **Christy Sports** (801-742-2871; www.christysports.com), Level 3, Snowbird Resort Plaza; **Cliff Sports Demo & Rental** (801-933-2265; rents telemark equipment in addition to alpine and snowboard gear), Level 1, Cliff Lodge; **Creekside Rentals** (801-933-2414), Gad Valley Building, Creekside Base Area; **Legend Demo Center** (800-232-9542), Resort Plaza Deck and inside Cliff Sports, Level 1, Cliff Lodge; and **Superior Ski and Board** (801-742-2871; www.superiorski.com),

RIDING THE GAD 2 LIFT WITH TWIN PEAKS IN THE BACKGROUND

Level 3, Resort Plaza, all of which offer Alpine ski and snowboard rentals, repairs, tuning, and the like.

Snowbird is home to **The Aerie** (see the *Where to Eat* section later in this chapter). This is a premium contemporary American eatery with a selection of more than 400 wines and fantastic views from the 10th floor of the Cliff Lodge.

### On-site Accommodations at Snowbird

Obtained through **Snowbird's Central Lodging** service (800-232-9542; www.snowbird.com). These include:

**The Cliff Lodge & Spa,** a very large-scale hotel in base area with spa, restaurants (including fine dining, Mexican, and sushi), and lounges.

**The Inn at Snowbird,** which has hotel rooms and apartments.

**The Iron Blosam Lodge,** a base area time-share lodge.

**The Lodge at Snowbird,** a base area hotel with on-site French restaurant.

**Snowbird/Alta vacation rental** listings can be seen in the *On-Site Accommodations at Alta* section earlier in this chapter.

For Salt Lake Valley downtown area lodging, see the *Lodging* section later in this chapter.

SKIING, BACKCOUNTRY, HELICOPTER & SNOWCAT Utah's backcountry is incredibly vast, yet remarkably accessible. The Wasatch Range is the real meat of this out-of-bounds terrain and has many times more acreage than all the resorts put together. Backcountry skiing exists just about anywhere snow falls—including, but not exclusively, at **Big Cottonwood, Little Cottonwood,** and **Millcreek canyons** (and more) in the Salt Lake area alone. The only restrictions are access (to and from the ski run) and avalanche danger. Elevation-supplemented access to backcountry skiing is possible from the tops of **Alta** and **Snowbird,** as well as **Brighton.** In Park City, **The Canyons Resort** has excellent backcountry ski access from the tops of its lifts.

It is a good idea to consult with a number of sources before your trip to be sure your plan is optimized for safety and good snow pack. Volumes of guides to ski touring in the Wasatch exist; many publishers have produced encyclopedic volumes on the matter. The **Salt Lake Public Library Main Branch** (see *To See and Do.*) has a great selection.

**Exum Mountain Guides** (801-550-3986; www.exum.ofutah.com) is one of the area's most respected guide services in case you need or would appreciate assistance.

**Ski Utah Interconnect Tour** (801-534-1907; www.skiutah.com/interconnect) is one of the area's most respected guide services. The Interconnect Tour is a specific

FROM THE SHOULDER OF GRANDEUR PEAK, ACCESSED BY MILLCREEK CANYON, JUST EAST OF SALT LAKE CITY

tour that many consider to be the best around; it visits many different Cottonwood Canyon resorts and Park City resorts in a single day. (Though you wouldn't guess it without looking at a map, the tops of the Cottonwoods are very near Park City as the crow flies.)

**The Utah Avalanche Center** (801-364-1591; www.avalanche.org) is one of the world's foremost avalanche science centers and keeps their hotline and Web site up-to-date throughout the season.

**Wasatch Powderbird Guides** (801-742-2800 or 800-974-4354; www.powderbird .com) is the Wasatch Range's primary independent helicopter skiing service.

↬ **Wastatch Touring** (801-359-9361; www.wasatchtouring.com), 702 East 100 South, downtown Salt Lake City. This is the most backcountry-friendly ski shop in

### GREATEST SNOW ON EARTH

Skiing is arguably Utah's most famous and best attraction. Salt Lake City itself is a prime location for skiers, as the downtown area and airport are each within 30 minutes of four major ski areas, and within 70 minutes of seven more. Each of the four areas in the Wasatch Front's canyons—Snowbird, Alta, Brighton, and Solitude—average more than 500 inches of fluffy champagne powder each winter. What's more, these tens of thousands of inbound acres are dwarfed by endless Wasatch backcountry skiing. Nordic skiing, oft overlooked, is alive and well in the area. In the immediate area, groomed facilities exist at Alta, Solitude, and Mountain Dell—with two more such courses in Park City, and another three more within 80 minutes' drive. As with downhill skiing, these groomed areas are supplemented with many miles of ungroomed nature trails.

Given all this, it is no surprise that Utah has quite a multifaceted winter sports scene. Skiers come here for all different reasons: for recreational resort skiing, helicopter skiing, and ski touring—but also for World Cup ski races, big-mountain competitions, high-school ski racing academies, and Nordic ski jumping. This area's rugged mountains are outfitted with numerous world-class ski competition facilities found in only a handful of places around the world—in large part because of the 2002 Winter Olympics.

Many of the nation's best ski academies are based in Salt Lake City and Park City, including Rowmark Ski Academy, and the Park City Ski Team. The U.S. Ski and Snowboard Team, which includes the U.S. Disabled Ski Team, has its offices in Park City. Many industry giants have relocated their U.S. headquarters to the area, including Rossignol in Park City, and Solomon, Suunto, and Atomic in Ogden. Backcountry.com has its headquarters in Park City, and Black Diamond, longtime maker of backcountry skiing gear (among other things), has been based in Salt Lake City since its birth as a company.

town, renting randonnée and telemark setups. The staff here is a good resource for recommendations.

**Snowcat** skiing is offered at **Alta** (listed in *Skiing, Alpine,* earlier), **Deer Valley Resort** (800-424-3337; www.deervalley.com), **Park City Mountain Resort** (435-649-8111; www.parkcitymountain.com), and **Powder Mountain** (801-745-3772; www.powdermountain.net) in the Ogden Valley.

SKIING, NORDIC Listed below are the areas in the immediate Salt Lake vicinity; many other groomed areas and trails exist near Park City and in the Ogden area, so be sure to see those regions' *Skiing, Nordic* sections as well.

**Alta** (801-359-1078; www.alta.com), UT 210, Little Cottonwood Canyon. Alta offers 5 kilometers of groomed trails for a day fee of $10 (tickets available at the Wildcat base-area ticket office). This trail is groomed for classic and skate skiing alike, and roughly parallels the transfer tow that traverses the grounds between the two base areas. During the heart of the season, when snow cover is sufficient, more trails open up at the midmountain level. This is accessible by the Sunnyside Lift (access to which the Nordic day ticket grants access).

**Millcreek Canyon,** 15 minutes southeast of Salt Lake City, exit 4/3900 South on the eastern side of the I-215 beltway, north one block, then east on 3800 South directly into the mouth of the canyon. This is a popular place for skiers and snowshoers during the middle of winter. The canyon road closes halfway (about 5 miles) up the canyon in November, and the upper portion can be skied as snow conditions allow. The road is sometimes groomed and gives itself to relatively quick skiing, as the upper portion of the canyon has a mild grade—an average of only 7 percent. If the main trailhead is too crowded, many other trails originate down canyon, though are less ideal for Nordic skiing. There is a $2.25 fee for using the canyon, which is paid upon leaving.

**Mountain Dell** (801-582-3812), I-80 exit 134, 10 minutes east of Salt Lake City. This is a golf course by summer, groomed Nordic ski track by winter. Located just a bit up Parley's Canyon (I-80) from Salt Lake City, this system offers multiple loops of varying difficulties around the 18-hole facility. Because of its canyon location, this track does have a distinct slope, though it is much more mellow than many other options in the area. A $5 voluntary fee is asked of all users, and people take this seriously.

**REI** (801-486-2100; www.rei.com), 3285 East 3300 South. Nordic ski and snowshoe rentals (as well as Alpine gear) south of downtown.

**Solitude Mountain Resort** (801-532-4731 or 1-800-748-4754; www.skisolitude .com), 12000 Big Cottonwood Canyon Rd. Solitude has some of the area's most challenging and favorite groomed trails. The proximity to Alpine skiing both at Solitude and Brighton resorts makes it an easy trip for families whose interests split between the two different genres of skiing. Classic and skate rentals, lessons, and clinics available on-site. $15 for adults ($10 after 12:30), free for ages 10 and under and ages 70 and up.

↩ **Wastatch Touring** (801-359-9361; www.wasatchtouring.com), 702 East 100 South, downtown Salt Lake City. For classic and skate rentals (in addition to telemark and randonnée) near downtown. This shop is a Salt Lake institution, locally owned since 1972.

## ✳ Lodging

### BED-AND-BREAKFAST INNS

**Anton Boxrud Bed & Breakfast**
(800-524-5511; www.antonboxrud
.com), 57 South 600 East. This home
was built in 1901 and is outfitted with
antique décor appropriate for the early
20th century. The rooms are clean and
cozy. Each guest room is unique in size
and color schemes, but all have a similar style. There is one suite. Cinnamon
rolls are baked fresh each morning,
and there is a central fireplace. $75–
$170.

**Armstrong Mansion Historic Bed
& Breakfast** (801-531-1333 or 800-
708-1333; www.armstrongmanor.com),
667 East 100 South. This is a higher-
end bed-and-breakfast and is considered one of the most romantic in the
area. This 1893 Queen Anne has a
great, near-downtown location and is
characterized by details like linen nap-
kins, handmade furniture, and marble
fireplaces. Rooms vary quite a bit in
size and opulence; some are rather
simple, and others are quite lavish.
$100–$230.

**Ellerbeck Mansion Bed & Break-
fast** (801-355-2500 or 800-966-8364;
www.ellerbeckbedandbreakfast.com),
140 North B St. The Ellerbeck is
located in the Avenues, a historic
neighborhood on the hills just north of
downtown. This is a quiet bed-and-
breakfast offering a variety of rooms,
each with its own theme. A recent
restoration has modernized the facility
and preserved its historic wooden
floors, stained glass, and original mold-
ing. Special ski packages and extended
stay discounts are possible. $120–$160.

**Inn on the Hill** (801-328-1466; www
.inn-on-the-hill.com), 225 North State
St. The Inn on the Hill is one of Salt
Lake's most deluxe and stately bed-
and-breakfasts. This Renaissance-
Revival home was finished in 1906,
and then completely renovated in
2003. Located just downhill from
Utah's Capitol Building, this has a good
location and ambience especially

THE SHILOH INN IS IN DOWNTOWN SALT LAKE CITY, IMMEDIATELY SOUTH OF THE SALT
PALACE CONVENTION CENTER, A MAJOR CONFERENCE CENTER WHERE THE OUTDOOR
RETAILER SHOW IS HELD TWICE A YEAR.

Craig Bowden

intended for business travelers, and is in one of Salt Lake's finer, historic neighborhoods. $130–$250.

**Wildflowers Bed & Breakfast** (801-466-0600 or 800-569-0009; www.wild flowersbb.com), 936 East 1700 South. This bed-and-breakfast is located on the western edge of Sugarhouse, a neighborhood popular for its historic homes, locally owned shops, cafés, galleries, and restaurants. This 1891 Victorian mansion has adopted a wild-flowers theme. There are extensive flowerbeds and paintings created by co-owner and artist Jeri Parker. $75–$145.

HOTELS **Grand America Hotel** (801-258-6000 or 800-533-3525; www .grandamerica.com), 555 South Main St. The Grand America is Salt Lake City's finest boutique-style hotel, in the style of historic European luxury hotels. Every detail of the Grand is immaculately well appointed, from Italian marble to Richelieu furniture and private balconies, and plasma screen televisions and chandeliers to in-room safes and crystal. The 775-room hotel offers babysitting services, as well as in-house fine dining. $200–$450.

**Hilton Hotel Salt Lake City Center** (801-328-2000; www.hilton.com), 255 South West Temple. The Hilton is located very near downtown's restaurants, clubs, museums, and venues. Upper rooms enjoy a spectacular view of the surrounding area. This familiar international hotel requires little guesswork and has an assured level of quality. $130–$240.

🐾 ⇢ **Hotel Monaco** (801-595-0000 or 877-294-9710; www.monaco-saltlake city.com), 15 West 200 South. As its name might suggest, this is one of Salt Lake's finer hotels with a little bit of flair and decadence. Tasteful bright colors, bold patterns, and eccentric touches make this hotel anything but staid. The Monaco has excellent guest services, including special rooms for taller persons, and has the stylish contemporary American restaurant, ⇢ **Bambara** (801-363-5454; www .bambara-slc.com), on its main floor. $200–$320.

**Little America Hotel and Towers** (801-363-6781 or 800-453-9450; www .littleamerica.com/slc), 500 South Main St. This hotel is Grand America's little sister. Though not as extravagantly deluxe as the Grand, it is still one of Salt Lake's nicer hotels. The building's rather plain exterior does not do its guest rooms and amenities justice. There is also an on-site spa and steak-house. $110–$190.

**Marriott–Salt Lake City Downtown** (801-531-0800; www.marriott.com), 75 South West Temple. This is one of two central Salt Lake Marriott hotels; the other is **Marriott City Center** (801-961-8700 or 866-961-8700), 220 South State St. Both have the reliable quality standards of a Marriott and a great, central location. Each has more than 350 rooms, and the Web site lists current events in the Salt Lake area. $180–$240.

**Peery Hotel** (801-521-4300 or 800-331-0073; www.peeryhotel.com), 110 West Broadway/300 South. The Peery is a small, historic downtown hotel. Dating to 1910, the Perry has 57 guest rooms and six suites with European-style décor, linens, and furniture of great detail. In its early days, it was a rest stop for traveling frontiersmen and miners in town to do business. $150–$290. **Romano's Macaroni Grill** (801-521-3133; www.macaronigrill .com) and **Christopher's Seafood and Steak House** (801-519-8515; www.christophersutah.com) are its two on-site restaurants.

## ✳ Where to Eat

Though you might not guess it, gastronomy is one of Salt Lake City's best assets. The city has a huge variety of excellent cuisine with numerous restaurants in each genre, traditional and contemporary, spanning the range of price and formality. Irish, Thai, Japanese, Austrian, Tibetan, Italian, and much more are available throughout the city. Though the dining quality here is quite high, the cost is surprisingly low, especially when compared with restaurants of similar quality. In many cases, it is not a stretch to compare the excellence and inventiveness of Salt Lake City's restaurants to those of San Francisco.

Savvy locals and visitors mark **Dine O' Round** (801-359-5118; www.down townslc.org/events) on their calendars. This three-week event takes place twice a year, in May and September. At this time, roughly 20 of the city's best restaurants set fixed menus especially for the event, which showcases some of their finest work. For $15 or $30 per plate, depending on the restaurant's tier, you can try a two- or three-course meal. This usually is quite a steal, sometimes costing less than half the price of what they should.

**DINING OUT The Aerie** (801-933-2160), Level 10, Cliff Lodge, Snowbird Resort. For a night out of the city, head up Little Cottonwood Canyon to Snowbird. The Aerie is much more than a slope-side grill; it is Snowbird's premium restaurant, and one of the better in the Salt Lake area. Situated near the very top of the massive base-area Cliff Lodge, The Aerie is encased almost completely with floor-to-ceiling glass windows that offer virtually uninterrupted views of the mountain, Little Cottonwood Canyon, and Salt Lake City far below. Cuisine is contemporary American and draws its ingredients from local producers whenever possible. The 400-item wine list at The Aerie is one of the most extensive around. Just outside The Aerie is the more casual **Aerie Lounge** (same phone number). This is different from the main restaurant in many ways, as it is a sushi bar, private club for members (where guests must be at least 21), and several notches more casual.

↪ **Bambara** (801-363-5454; www .bambara-slc.com), 202 South Main St., on the first ground floor at Hotel Monaco. Open for breakfast, lunch, and dinner daily. Bambara is a very chic, stylish space with contemporary American cuisine. It is beloved by Salt Lake City residents for its high-end fare and bright, bold décor. Many people choose to take cocktails and appetizers here before seeing a show downtown. The menu is created to be interesting and fresh. Entrées $20–$35.

**Café Trio** (Sugarhouse location: 801-533-8746; www.triodining.com), 680 South 900 East; and (Cottonwoods location: 801-944-8746), 6305 South 3000 East. Open for lunch and dinner daily, as well as a famous Sunday brunch. (Cottonwood does not serve Sunday brunch or lunch.) Trio is Salt Lake City's freshest contemporary Italian spot, with upscale cuisine catering to many levels of formality. Its menu has many offerings but seems quite simplified. Divided into "first course" and "second course" listings, it does not follow the typical appetizer-and-entrée template. Rather, the first course is like a mini entrée, and so a huge spectrum of portion sizes is available. You can order any combination of first and second courses in whatever order you want. Trio's flatbread is famous around town and is served with a variety of tapenade and pesto. Entrées $12–$18.

**Cucina Toscana** (801-328-3463; www.cucina-toscana.com), 307 West Pierpont Ave. Open for dinner Monday–Saturday. This family-style old Italian restaurant has long been one of Salt Lake City's best. Voted many times by *Salt Lake Magazine* as Salt Lake's best Italian, this restaurant offers a diverse menu that stays true to its Tuscan roots and fresh ingredients. The menu offers a range of seafood, choice meats, and vegetarian dishes. Entrées $18–$31.

**Market Street Grill** (801-322-4668; www.gastronomyinc.com), 48 West Market St. 350 South St. This restaurant is part of a family of high-end seafood shops and restaurants with seven actual restaurants (three of which are downtown and include the Oyster Bar (801-531-6044), 54 West Market St.; the New Yorker (see below); and three fish markets. These restaurants have elite quality status and, because of their popularity, have the most buying power of fresh seafood in town. This grill does surf and turf with the best of them and has an outstanding menu with exceptional value during the Dine O' Round festival. Though the plates come topped with stately dishes, the old-style black-and-white tile and wooden-booth dining room permits a casual ambience.

**Martine** (801-363-9328), 22 East 100 South. This Mediterranean tapas bar is fairly unique in Salt Lake City for its sampling and plate-sharing dining style. A great wine list and flavorful symbiotic dishes make this a fun gathering place for friends to share conversation and dishes in this cozy, downtown restaurant. The menu is overhauled every two weeks, so it remains zippy.

🍴 ↝ **Mazza** (801-484-9259; www.mazzacafe.com), 1515 South 1500 East. Open for lunch and dinner Monday–Saturday. Mazza Middle Eastern restaurant is located north of Sugarhouse and southeast of downtown. It is considered the best of its kind in Salt Lake City, offering upscale dolaa, kabseh, shawarma, and kabobs with lamb, beef, seafood, and fresh vegetables. The wine list is extensive. The interior of this café adds to the experience, with romantically embellished Middle Eastern style. The service at Mazza is outstanding. Mazza opened another restaurant in the 9th and 9th neighborhood at 912 East 900 South (801-521-4572).

**New Yorker** (801-363-0166; www.gastronomyinc.com), 60 West Market St. 350 South. Open for lunch and dinner, Monday–Saturday. The New Yorker is considered by some to be Salt Lake's finest restaurant, with classic formality, reliable excellence, and first-class service. Open since 1978, this restaurant earns many "best" awards each year honoring the chef, lifetime achievement of the restaurant, cuisine, and wine list. Gourmet seafood and premium meats are the name of the game here.

**Takashi** (801-519-9595), 18 West Market St. 350 South. Takashi serves one of the most inventive, yet incredibly gourmet sushi menus imaginable. While many sushi bars create complex rolls that only achieve novelty, the specialty rolls here are a profound result of masterful culinary skill and creative vision. Standard rolls are over the top as well. Considering all the variety of cuisine represented by Salt Lake's restaurants, it's impossible to objectively declare which the best would be. But if I were required to choose one, Takashi might well be it. This restaurant does not take reservations, but it is located adjacent to **Christoph's Martini Bar,** where you can wait for your table over a specialty martini.

EATING OUT ✧ **The Bayou** (801-961-8400; www.utahbayou.com), 645 South State St. Open for lunch Monday–Friday, dinner nightly. The Bayou has a special place in Salt Lake City, as the city's most famous Cajun-style restaurant and purveyor of nearly 250 beers. This restaurant serves fairly simple, delicious dinners and great appetizers. There is live music most nights and free pool during lunch. This restaurant fills many niches—a place to get dinner, to enjoy appetizers and cocktails with friends, have a lunch meeting, or enjoy an evening at an upscale pub. On the menu are 212 bottled beers (almost all of which are full-strength) and 31 draft beers. Two words of warning: It is rare that every beer on the menu is in stock at all times, and you should expect a full house nearly every night of the week. Still, a distinctive experience and definitely worth it. Reservations accepted. Lunch and dinner $9–$15.

**Blue Plate Diner** (801-463-1151), 2041 South 2100 East. The Blue Plate is located just east of Sugarhouse and is one of the most popular breakfast eateries in town. The restaurant attracts a hip, young crowd. The restaurant is done up à la 1950s but is not kitsch. Even though it has outdoor and indoor seating, it becomes very crowded on the weekends. To enjoy breakfast here but avoid the crowds, come on a weekday or go early, ahead of the party crowd. $8–$13.

**Chanon Thai** (801-532-1177), 278 East 900 South. Open for lunch and dinner Sunday–Friday. Chanon Thai is a small restaurant with an unassuming façade and ambience. Tucked a healthy distance west of Sugarhouse and south of downtown, it has easy parking and a low-key atmosphere. Though prices are very reasonable and the décor is not luxurious, this serves arguably the best Thai food in a city full of such restaurants. The sensory experience commences immediately as you enter the restaurant, as the smell of fresh herbs and individual spices greet your nostrils—this is quite unlike the blanket "Asian-food smell" that many lesser restaurants produce. Entrées $7–$13.

**Himalayan Kitchen** (801-596-8727), 73 East 400 South. Open for lunch and dinner, lunch only on Sunday. This small downtown restaurant is an extremely casual, but renowned Northern Indian establishment serving cuisine marinated in tradition and experience. Locals recognize and love this restaurant for its multigeneration family recipes stewed to perfection, as well as its affordable prices. The lunch buffet attracts downtown businesspeople and is one of the best deals in town for those with a healthy appetite.

**MacCool's Public House** (801-582-3111), 1400 South Foothill Dr., in the Foothill Village. MacCool's is Salt Lake's take on an Irish public house. Though it is located in a shopping village, it still has mustered a pleasant atmosphere and a great comfort food menu.

**Red Iguana** (801-322-1489; www.red iguana.com), 736 North West Temple. Open for lunch and dinner Monday–Saturday. Red Iguana is hands-down the best Mexican eatery in Salt Lake. Opened in 1985 by a family who has been part of the area's restaurateur crowd for more than 40 years, this restaurant is reliably packed. A stacked margarita list and seven Oaxacan-style moles are largely responsible for this. All of the items on the menu are done to perfection. Mexican cuisine at its finest. Entrées $8–$15.

**Red Rock Brewing Company** (801-521-7446; www.redrockbrewing.com), 254 South 200 West. Open for lunch and dinner daily, brunch Saturday and

Sunday at 11 AM. This brewery earned three medals at the 2008 North American Beer Awards and was the 2007 Great American Beer Festival's Best Large Brewpub and Best Large Brewpub brewer of the year in the United States. The menu is a beefed-up pub menu with contemporary American, Italian, and other European accents. Sandwiches, as well as prime cuts of meat, daily specials, salads, pizzas, and seafood can be found on the menu, which really does span a range, from casual to gourmet. Though Squatters, the other big brewpub in Salt Lake, and Red Rock are located very near each other, neither has any problem getting enough business.

**Ruth's Diner** (801-582-5807; www .ruthsdiner.com), 2100 Emigration Canyon. Open daily for breakfast, lunch, and dinner. Ruth's is a Salt Lake City tradition, serving Southwest-influenced cuisine since 1949. Its trolley car location partway up Emigration Canyon is not just for novelty. Ruth, a cabaret singer in Salt Lake City in the 1910s, opened a hamburger shop in 1930 in the valley. She was a caretaker of the townspeople, including girls from a brothel across the street. This earned her no favors from the religious majority of the town, and she was chased out. The restaurant serves three meals a day, but breakfast, with its mile-high biscuits, is its most famous. Most plates $8–$12.

**Squatters** (801-363-2739; www .squatters.com), 147 West Broadway. Open daily for lunch and dinner; brunch on Saturday and Sunday starts at 10:30. Squatters a is a brewpub in a well-dressed building that serves its own beer and a diverse menu that includes appetizers, modest dinners, and entrées. Cuisine ranges from curry to burgers, stir-fry, salad, fish, and Mexican. All beers on tap are Utah 3.2

percent beers, but Squatters does serve its own full-strength beer in bottles.

## ✳ Entertainment

Salt Lake City's performing arts troupes are some of its finest assets. As with its restaurants, the arts tend to be a well-kept secret; people not directly involved with the arts often underestimate the international reputation and skill level of these artists.

**Ballet West** (801-323-6900; www .balletwest.org). Based out of the Capitol Theater, 50 West 200 South. This is a nationally respected institution, created in 1963 by William F. Christensen, founder of the San Francisco Ballet and the nation's first university ballet troupe at the University of Utah. Because of its prestigious beginnings and its continued excellence, this has remained an active and highly esteemed company.

**Repertory Dance Theatre** (801-534-1000; www.rdtutah.org). Located in the Rose Wagner Performing Arts Center, 138 West 300 South Broadway. Reperatory Dance Theater was founded in 1966 as a professional modern dance company under the leadership of Virginia Tanner, and now Linda Smith. The company takes pride in being an integral proponent of modern American dance, yet resurrects classic pieces in addition to performing newly commissioned works.

**Ririe-Woodbury Dance Company** (801-297-4241; www.ririewoodbury .com). Based out of the Rose Wagner Performing Arts Center, 138 West 300 South Broadway. This modern dance company is the antithesis of what is traditional or stagnant. Its performances stretch the senses with powerful coloration of costumes, stages, multimedia effects, and inventive lighting. This company is comfortable in the international spotlight and is sponsored by the National Endowment for the Arts.

**Salt Lake Choral Artists** (801-587-9377; www.saltlakechoralartists.org). Based in the Libby Gardner Concert Hall, 1375 East Presidents Circle, University of Utah. This large ensemble has been under the directorship of Brady Allred since 2004 and is an impressive organization of vocal talent. Individual choirs include a 57-voice women's choir, 38-piece chamber choir, and 155-piece concert choir. Six concerts usually come from this group throughout the year.

**Salt Lake Symphony** (801-463-2440; www.saltlakesymphony.org). The symphony plays many different venues and is a fully amateur, yet highly dedicated and accomplished symphonic orchestra. It is estimated that each year since 1976 more than 10,000 volunteer hours have gone into the annual allotment of 15 concerts.

**Utah Chamber Artists** (801-572-2010; www.utahchamberartists.org), Libby Gardner Concert Hall, 1375 East Presidents Circle. Directed and founded by Barlow Bradford, this chamber group was established in 1991. Each calendar season this string and vocal ensemble prepares a new concert in addition to upholding a fairly rigorous recording schedule. Their repertoire is varied, ranging from jazz to baroque, classical to contemporary.

**Utah Opera Company** (801-533-6683 or 888-451-2787; www.utahopera.org), Capitol Theater, 50 West 200 South. The Opera is one of Utah's most active musical companies with a heavy community outreach component. It draws from a variety of material and performs each year in front of an aggregate audience of 150,000 people. The home stage is the Capitol Theater, but they also put on shows outdoors and in conjunction with other local groups.

**Utah Symphony** (801-533-5626; www.utahsymphony.org), Abravanel Hall, 123 West South Temple. This symphonic orchestra is directed, among others, by Keith Lockhart, who splits his time between this group and the Boston Pops. This professional ensemble adheres to a rigorous schedule, producing more than 200 concerts annually in addition to logging time in the recording studio. Though their home stage is Abravanel Hall, they give concerts outdoors, play at other regional venues, and tour around the world. Their season runs from September through May.

**VENUES Capitol Theater** (801-355-2787; www.finearts.slco.org), 50 West 200 South. This building has had a colorful history since its 1913 opening and is as one of the city's oldest functioning venues. Over the years, it has hosted vaudeville, opera, and dance performances. Restored in 1978 with an $8.6 million budget, it is now home to world-renowned **Ballet West, Ririe-Woodbury Dance Company,** and the **Utah Opera.**

**The Depot** (801-456-2800; www.depotslc.com), 400 West South Temple. The Depot is one of Salt Lake City's major venues for headlining rock, blues, and other big-name bands. With an excellent sound system and two internal levels, this is set up perfectly for large audiences. Both stories have seating and dancing room, as well as their own full bar. Because there is a bar, a minimum age of 21 is required at most shows here.

**In The Venue** (801-359-3219; www.inthevenue.com), 279 South 500 West. Also called **Club Sound,** this is Salt Lake's largest "edgy" venue, with an industrial effect perfect for hip-hop, techno, punk, and hard rock artists. This large club has two main floors, outdoor patio space, large windows (used in the summer), and plenty of standing room—sometimes even dancing cages. Beware: This club often books two consecutive shows in the same evening; if you are arriving for an early (say 7 o'clock) show, you should arrive as punctually as possible, as early shows can be short since time is limited due to the beginning of next performance. A bar section exists in the club for ages 21 and up, so not everyone need be of legal drinking age for all shows.

**Jon M. Huntsman Events Center** (801-581-5445; www.utah.edu), 1825 East South Campus Dr. This indoor arena is the University of Utah's 15,000-seat gymnasium where basketball and gymnastics competitions are held.

**Maurice Abravanel Concert Hall** (801-355-2787; www.maurice-abrava nel.com), 123 West South Temple. This downtown hall is Salt Lake City's go-to performance center for fine, large-scale musical performances. It is home to the Utah Symphony but also hosts a variety of other performances. Known for its immaculate acoustics and clean, modern aesthetics, this hall has not lost any of its prestige or upkeep since its 1979 debut.

**Rose Wagner Performing Arts Center** (801-323-6977), 138 West 300 South. The center is a multifaceted facility with a fine arts gallery and three theaters, the **The Leona Wagner Black Box Theatre, The Jeanné Wagner Theatre,** and **The Studio Theatre.** Here a variety of shows take place, ranging from Sundance film screenings to chamber recitals, piano concerts, dance performances, and more. The individual theaters are fully modern, as each was completed between 1997 and 2002.

NIGHTLIFE The scene in Salt Lake City is somewhat fragmented. Residents find themselves with plenty to do, but it is more of a function of pinning down good events. There is no central bar crawl, so unless you happen upon a party or concert, the scene is likely to be pretty quiet. With that in mind, I've listed a few events and establishments with temporal stipulations.

✦ **The Bayou** (see *Eating Out*) is Salt Lake's most consistent spot for nights out. The clientele here ranges from upper 20s through middle age. This upscale bar and restaurant enjoys live jazz many nights of the week, and an extensive global beer menu. The Bayou fills up but does not become rowdy like many bars do. This is a smoke-free establishment.

**Circle Lounge** is one of Salt Lake City's swankier hangouts for the younger crowd. This lounge has plenty of space for, well, lounging, with couches and tables arranged for intimate conversations. A full-liquor license and sushi bar, as well as outdoor patio open during the summer, add special touches to this establishment. However, as with many places in Salt Lake, this place will be absolutely packed one night, and empty the next. This tends to be popular on summer nights when the Gallivan shows end.

**Fiddler's Elbow** (801-463-9393; www .fiddlerselbowslc.com), 1063½ East 2100 South, tucked off the street. This is a popular sports bar that fills up during big games. Unlike many sports bars, this is located inside a very pleasant, modern, clean building and has a clean atmosphere. An extended pub menu is available here as well.

**Gallivan Center Twilight Concert Series** (801-596-5000; www.slcgov .com/arts/twilight) is a summer event that is probably the most popular social

A SALT LAKE BEES BASEBALL GAME IN FRANKLIN COVEY STADIUM

institution in the city. This smashingly successful series brings to town eight shows each summer, beginning in July. These take place Thursday nights 7–10 PM and are free. Enjoy beers while you watch Grammy-winning groups like The Roots and other nationally known bands like Clap Your Hands Say Yeah and Yonder Mountain String Band. This takes place at the Gallivan Center, an outdoor square in downtown at 239 South Main Street. Parking is difficult. The popularity of this event was so much that the center created **Wednesday Night Rocks,** a 6 PM free concert series each Wednesday during the summer.

**Smith's Tix** (www.smithstix.com) is Salt Lake's biggest tickets seller. This is a great resource to check out shows and events that may be coming through town.

**SPORTS** **Salt Lake Bees** (801-325-2273; www.slbees.com). The Bees are Salt Lake City's minor league baseball team and a part of the Pacific Coast League. They are quite an accomplished team and have the good fortune of playing home games at **Franklin Covey Field**; (801-485-

3800); 77 West 1300 South. This stadium is immaculately well kept and modern. Quite a pleasure to behold, its lush grass and bright signs are backed by a picture-perfect Wasatch ridgeline backdrop.

**Salt Lake Real** (801-924-8585; www.realsaltlake.com) became the state's second major league sports team (behind the Utah Jazz) when it joined the Major League Soccer roster as the 12th team in the U.S. league in 2005. The Real share the **Rice-Eccles Stadium** (400 South Street, southwest University of Utah Campus) with the University of Utah Utes' Division One football team.

**University of Utah Utes** (http://utahutes.cstv.com). These sports teams draw from a nearly 25,000-student pool and include all the big-name sports, such as baseball, golf, football, gymnastics, track and field, skiing, cross country, swimming and diving, softball, and volleyball. **The Rice-Eccles Stadium** (400 South Street, Southwest Campus) is where football and Salt Lake Real soccer games take place, as well as track-and-field meets. Basketball games and gymnastics meets are found at the **Jon M. Hunts-**

man Center (Wasatch Dr., East Campus). **The Ute Fields** (Wasatch Dr., Northeast Campus) is where most Ute soccer takes place.

**Utah Grizzlies** (801-988-8000; www.utahgrizzlies.com) are Salt Lake's representative EHCL hockey team. (Though you would never guess it, the teams of the East Coast Hockey League are now scattered throughout Utah.) The Grizzlies have been a Salt Lake institution since 1969 and have been part of many different hockey leagues. Originally called the Salt Lake Eagles, they have had their current name since 1995. They are based in West Valley in the **E Center** (801-908-0311; www.theecenter.com), 3200 South Decker Lake Dr., West Valley City.

**Utah Jazz** (801-325-2500; www.nba.com/jazz or www.energysolutions arena.com), EnergySolutions Arena, 301 West South Temple. The Utah Jazz has been in Salt Lake City since their 1979 move from New Orleans, and they have enjoyed many successful seasons in this town. The Jazz is a wild success in Utah, both for attracting spectators and excellent players. (Their home, the EnergySolutions Arena, was formerly called the Delta Center.)

## ✳ Selective Shopping

**The Gateway** (801-456-0000; www.shopthegateway.com), 400 West 200 South. The Gateway is a very attractive, two-level, outdoor mall on the western side of Salt Lake's downtown district. A huge number of shops, restaurants, movie theaters, and the like line the meandering pedestrian streets here, including Gap, Hollister, Famous Footwear, Apple Store, Urban Outfitters, and Zumiez. Two underground parking garages are available and free with store-procured voucher.

**Ken Sanders Rare Books & More** (801-521-3819; www.kensanders books.com), 268 South 200 East. This book shop is owned and operated by a longtime friend of Edward Abbey and specializes in Western Americana, the exploration of the Rocky Mountain West, Mormon history, and natural history, particularly that of the Utah and desert Southwest area. Rare editions, as well as more common publications, amount to more than 100,000 volumes in 5,000 square feet of shop space. For

ECCLES STADIUM IN SALT LAKE CITY AT THE UNIVERSITY OF UTAH

history and conservation buffs, or those wanting to learn more about this great region, this shop is a perfect stop.

**Sugarhouse** is the neighborhood and shopping district centered around 2100 South between 900 East and 1000 East. This area has historically been characterized by small, often locally owned cafés, music shops, and clothing boutiques. Recently, more national stores have moved into the area, and more intend to in the future. This area is currently undergoing a massive renovation, which will change its character to an extent. However, it is doubtful that the area will ever completely go the way of the box stores, as it is geographically unfeasible.

**Trolley Square** (801-521-9877; www.trolleysquare.com), 500 South 700 East. This is downtown Salt Lake City's best and least imposing mall. (When the large ZCMI Center was closed and demolished in the name of the Downtown Rising project in 2007, Trolley Square became the only downtown indoor mall by default.) A variety of shops and restaurants are located in these old trolley barns, including Desert Edge Brew Pub, Sharper Image, Banana Republic, and Pottery Barn.

# PARK CITY

Park City is to Utah what Vail is to Colorado. Once a mining town, this town is located in a small valley and is surrounded by thousands and thousands of acres of skiing. It was first a boomtown, then a ghost town (in 1963), and now is Utah's most happening night spot, the home of the U.S. Ski and Snowboard Team, and the host of the star-studded Sundance Film Festival. Park City is located in Summit County, which has 39 of Utah's tallest peaks. It is near enough Salt Lake City to enjoy the company of its airport and metropolitan population, yet is far enough away to have always enjoyed its own politics. As a mining town, it was as rowdy as any. When the mining industry left Park City, the future didn't look so bright, but then the ski industry brought Park City back to life. Now it is a recreation hub—skiing by winter and mountain biking by summer.

Park City residents and visitors enjoy a rare life, with excellent outdoor opportunities and high-end amenities to match. With a mostly affluent population, Park City is endowed with the finer points of culture, but also the allure of a small town. And Park City is a small town—but a small town that can get quite busy. During the summer, the town clears out and there is plenty of breathing room. During the winter, Park City pulsates. The Sundance Film Festival is an absolute madhouse.

Though still a small town by relative standards, Park City has certainly expanded beyond its original size. Main Street is the oldest part of town and where many of the galleries, restaurants, and clubs are located. In all directions from Main Street are residential neighborhoods. The north side of town stretches to Kimball Junction and I-80. This is where the area's big stores and large shopping centers are located, including Park City's famous Tanger Outlet Malls. Quite a few restaurants and some clubs are to the north as well. Nearer to town are three ski resorts. Deer Valley is the southernmost; then Park City Mountain Resort, whose base area is virtually on Main Street; and The Canyons, which is a bit north of downtown.

Park City, like the rest of Utah, was permanent home to no one for the vast majority of its history. Kamas Valley, where Park City is located, was fertile summertime fishing ground for Ute and Northern Shoshone tribes. Winter in Park City was hostile and could support no life. Mountain men like Jim Bridger and Jedediah Smith traversed the lands as well, but not even the U.S. government was able, or had the desire, to establish civilization in the harshly variable and arid Utah climate. This would change forever with the arrival of the Mormons. This industrious bunch found Utah's isolation and desolation to be its greatest asset.

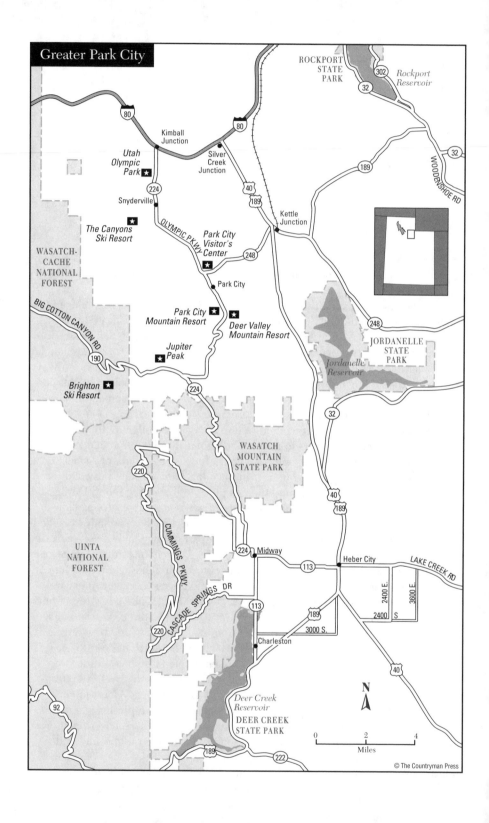

Greater Park City

ROCKPORT STATE PARK
Rockport Reservoir
302
32

80
Kimball Junction
Silver Creek Junction
Utah Olympic Park ★
224
Snyderville
189
40
189
Kettle Junction
WOODENSHOE RD
32

The Canyons Ski Resort ★

WASATCH-CACHE NATIONAL FOREST

OLYMPIC PKWY

Park City Visitor's Center ★
248

Park City

BIG COTTON CANYON RD

Park City Mountain Resort ★
Deer Valley Mountain Resort ★

190

Jupiter Peak ★

Brighton Ski Resort ★

JORDANELLE STATE PARK
248
Jordanelle Reservoir
32

224

WASATCH MOUNTAIN STATE PARK

220

UINTA NATIONAL FOREST

CUMMINGS PKWY

40
189

224  Midway
113
Heber City
LAKE CREEK RD
2400 E.
3600 E.
2400 S.

CASCADE SPRINGS DR

113
189
3000 S.
Charleston
220

92

Deer Creek Reservoir
DEER CREEK STATE PARK

40

N

0    2    4
Miles

189
222

© The Countryman Press

The Mormons had been plagued by persecution since the inception of their religion, and they desired a home isolated from society. In 1848 the first wave of pioneers arrived in the Salt Lake Valley to establish a nation all their own.

Park City went relatively untouched for about two decades. But 1869 changed everything for Park City and for Utah at large. The Young American Lode was discovered in Kamas Valley. Miners who had gorged on the gold rush of '49, but whose appetites were far from quenched, flooded the town. Fed on the gold rush of California and the general mining craze of that time, their enthusiasm was still in full force, but the mining opportunities in other parts of the country had been all but exhausted. Thousands of these prospectors poured into town, and the area was immediately distinguished as a mining district.

On May 10, 1869, the First Transcontinental Railroad was completed, and the commemorative Golden Spike was driven into the ground in Tremonton, Utah. This transportation jugular spanned the width of North America and ran almost directly through Park City by way of Echo Canyon (where present-day I-80 and I-84 merge). Suddenly there was a means to export these precious metals, as well as a way for new workers to come to Utah, and Park City grew rapidly during this time.

Appropriately, Park City was founded on the Fourth of July, 1872. It was called "Parley's Park City" by the miners, after mountain man and Mormon prophet Parley Pratt. The name was quickly shortened to its current version, symbolically leaving behind the Mormon influence. Mining operations grew exponentially, and within a few decades, more than $50 million of silver ore would be extracted from sometimes more than 300 mines in simultaneous operation.

The very small Kamas Valley continued to fill with quickly built wooden structures packed very near to each other. This lack of planning and care would lead to a series of epidemic fires, the first of which happened in the very, very cold month of December in 1882. But the vitality of this mining city saw it reconstructed very quickly afterward, and by 1884 Park City was incorporated. More homes, saloons, theaters, and boardinghouses were packed in, and 1885 brought another massive fire. Still people came from all over the continent and the world—workers came from Scandinavia, Ireland, Scotland, and China; wealthy mine owners relocated from Nevada and California. By June of 1898 yet another fire would effectively destroy the town. Nearly 200 structures, three-quarters of the town, were destroyed.

Mining continued to support the city for several decades—into and through the Great Depression. Park City had its first taste of skiing during this time and held early collegiate and professional ski jumping competitions. A special rail line was even built from Salt Lake City and Provo to Park City in 1936 to transport skiers. Alf Engen, the namesake of Park City's ski museum, was an early record holder in Nordic jumping, flying more than 200 feet by 1940.

The Great Depression took a toll on the city, and despite its status as a ski destination, the town could not be supported in lieu of its waning livelihood of mining. The town suffered a dramatic decline, and by 1950 it was virtually extinct. Despite this, Snow Park (now Deer Valley) built the town's first chairlift in 1946. But in 1963, Park City went onto the national register of ghost towns.

Stubbornly, United Park City Mines struggled to remain in business. It finally closed all mining operations in 1982. However, United and other dead or dying mines were given federal funding. The U.S. government hoped to revitalize old mining towns by creating ski areas and boosting tourism. It worked. Skiers would

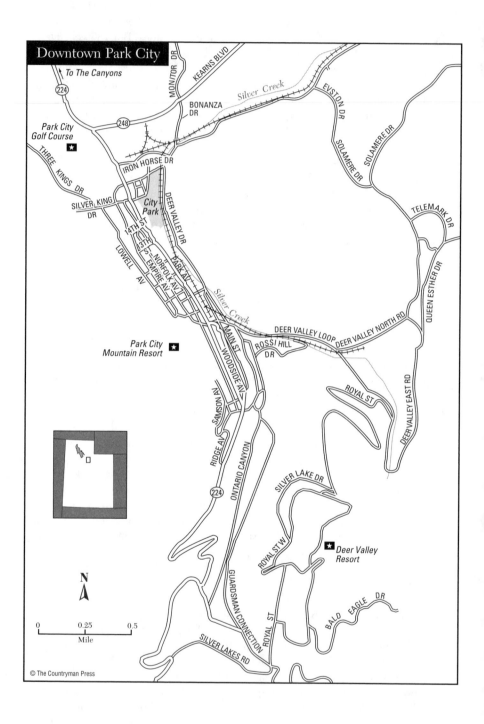

Downtown Park City

To The Canyons

224

Park City
Golf Course ★

248

MONITOR DR

KEARNS BLVD

Silver Creek

BONANZA
DR

EVSTON DR

SOLAMERE DR

SOLAMERE DR

THREE KINGS DR

IRON HORSE DR

SILVER KING
DR

City
Park

14TH ST

13TH ST

DEER VALLEY DR

TELEMARK DR

NORFOLK AV

PARK AV

EMPIRE AV

LOWELL AV

Silver Creek

QUEEN ESTHER DR

Park City
Mountain Resort ★

MAIN ST

ROSSI HILL
DR

DEER VALLEY LOOP DEER VALLEY NORTH RD

WOODSIDE AV

ROYAL ST

DEER VALLEY EAST RD

SAMSON AV

RIDGE AV

SILVER LAKE DR

224

ONTARIO CANYON

ROYAL ST W

★ Deer Valley
Resort

N
↑

0       0.25      0.5
Mile

GUARDSMAN CONNECTION

ROYAL ST

BALD EAGLE DR

SILVER LAKES RD

ride up mining lifts in the old Spiro mineshaft, 1,750 dead-vertical feet, to reach their ski elevation, now the top of Park City Mountain Resort's Thaynes chairlift.

Enter the 1980s, a prosperous national economy, and the era of modern transportation and the interstate system. Utah grew. Park City, isolated from what many consider to be the drawbacks of Utah (i.e., Mormonism), enjoyed its own culture and was one of the few places able to attract newcomers. Its reputation as a ski town made it increasingly popular. In 1985 a series of events would render Park City the lucky host of a World Cup ski race. The town seized this opportunity and went big. It threw a memorable party with concerts, constant festivities, and even skydivers. Park City has been on the map ever since. This reputation was solidified when it became the home of the Sundance Film Festival in 1984, and later by being cohost of the 2002 Winter Olympic Games. Now more than 20,000 people attend the glitzy film festival each year, and Park City is home to the U.S. Ski and Snowboard Team.

GUIDANCE **Park City Chamber of Commerce** (435-658-9616; www.parkcity info.com), 1826 Olympic Pkwy. This visitors center has a great location, immediately just southwest of the Park City/Kimball Junction exit on I-80. Inside are volunteers and hundreds of informational brochures on the area.

GETTING THERE *By car:* Park City is located very near I-80, just 25 miles east of Salt Lake City (where I-80 and I-15 intersect). I-15 runs north through Ogden, Idaho, and Montana, and south through Provo, St. George, and Las Vegas. I-80 runs west into Nevada and east into Wyoming. To get to downtown Park City from the I-80 Park City exit, head south on UT 224. After just more than 5 miles, you'll be near downtown.

*By air:* Just five minutes west of downtown is the **Salt Lake International Airport** (801-575-2400 or 800-595-2442; www.slcairport.com). This major airport is located on I-80, and so is only about 40 minutes away from Park City, most of which is easy, interstate driving.

*By bus:* **Greyhound Bus Lines** (801-355-9579 or 800-231-2222; www.greyhound .com). This bus line has a station in Salt Lake City (300 South 600 West), as well as other Utah cities such as Moab, Provo, Ogden, St. George, and Green River.

*By shuttle:* Even though Park City offers a free bus system within the town, public transportation to get from Salt Lake City to Park City does not exist, so it is useful to know about **ski shuttles,** particularly if traveling by air.

**All Resort Express** (801-575-6420; www.allresort.com). Offers shared ride or limousine service.

**Park City Transportation** (435-649-5466; www.parkcitytransportation.com). Drives private and shared shuttles to any Utah ski resort.

**Resort Transportation** (801-998-8443; www.utahskiguide.com). Gives private shuttle rides only.

**Xpress Shuttle** (800-397-0773; www.expressshuttle.com). Offers private and shared shuttles to the greater Salt Lake area.

**Yellow Express** (801-521-5027; www.yellowcabutah.com). Gives private shuttles only.

**GETTING AROUND** *By rental car:* If arriving by air, you'll most likely rent a car at the airport (see the *Getting Around* section in the "Salt Lake City" chapter). However, if you find yourself needing to rent a car in Park City, you have a few options:

**Budget Rent A Car** (435-645-7555; www.budget.com), 50 Shadow Ridge Rd. This has a central location located just outside of the downtown commotion.

**Enterprise Rent A Car** (435-655-7277; www.enterprise.com), 6560 North Landmark Dr. #300. This national brand usually keeps a pretty good fleet and is located just north of the I-80 Kimball Junction exit.

**Hertz Rent A Car** (435-655-0868; www.hertz.com), 1895 Sidewinder Dr., Marriott Hotel. Hertz is located just off Kearns Boulevard, a major road just north of downtown.

*By bus:* The **Park City Free Bus System** (435-615-5301) offers free transport within Park City, as well as between the ski areas and downtown. These buses and bus stops are very visible around town.

*By taxi:* **Ace Cab Company** (435-649-8294) offers cab service within Park City.

**Advanced Transportation** (435-647-3999 or 866-647-3999) gives rides from the airport to Park City, taxi service within Park City, and to Park City ski areas.

**Daytrips Transportation** (800-649-8294) gives rides from the airport to Park City, as well as rides within Park City.

**Park City Taxi** (435-658-2227 or 800-724-7767) offers taxi service to and from the airport.

**Powder for the People** (888-482-7547) is a company with service to the airport, ski areas, and around town.

**HANDICAPPED SERVICES** **National Ability Center** (435-649-3991; www .nac1985.org) is dedicated to providing the disabled with as many athletic and recreational opportunities as possible. Their scope is quite broad and includes more common sports like cycling and skiing, but also more alternative sports like bobsledding to white-water rafting, rock climbing, and rugby. This excellent center is perhaps influenced by its very near proximity to the National Disabled Ski Team, a division of the U.S. Ski and Snowboard Team (www.usskiteam.com), both of which are based in Park City, and are the training centers for World Cup athletes.

**MEDICAL EMERGENCY** **Park City Mountain Resort Urgent Care** (435-649-8111), 1310 Lowell Ave. This urgent care facility has a great location, just northwest of Main Street downtown. Located at the base of Park City Mountain Resort, it is convenient for summer and winter accidents.

**Snow Creek Emergency and Medical Center** (435-655-0055), 1600 Snow Creek Dr. This is located outside of the hubbub of downtown, slightly northeast of where Park Avenue and Kearns Boulevard intersect.

**NEWSPAPERS** *The Park Record* (www.parkrecord.com) is Park City's daily paper. *Salt Lake City Weekly* (www.slweekly.com) is a free paper distributed profusely, and it covers events in Park City as well as in Salt Lake City. *In Utah This Week* (www.inthisweek.com) is a similar publication with a broader scope.

*Salt Lake Magazine* (www.saltlakemagazine.com) publishes six issues yearly and covers high-end events in Park City as well as in Salt Lake City.

## ✳ To See and Do

**Alf Engen Ski Museum** (435-658-4240; www.engenmuseum.org), 2990 Bear Hollow Dr., inside the Joe Qinney Winter Sports Center and Utah Olympic Park; 4 miles north of Park City, southeast of the Kimball Junction/Park City exit on I-80. Open 9–6 daily, closed holidays. Park City has been part of ski history since the early 20th century, in the realms of recreational skiing, Nordic ski jumping, and World Cup and Olympic competitions. This museum has one of the most extensive collections of ski artifacts in the country, as well an interactive installation that simulates the experience of skiing 90 miles per hour in a World Cup downhill event. Free general admission; bus tours of the park are $7 for adults and seniors, $5 for ages 3–17, free for ages 2 and under.

**Park City Old Town Museum and Territorial Jail** (435-615-9559; www.park cityhistory.org), 528 Main St. Open 11–5 Monday–Saturday, noon–6 Sunday. This is a small museum located inside the 1885 Territorial Jail. Its convenient location on Main Street offers visitors a very easy chance to take a quick look at Park City's history. The museum has exhibits dedicated to the building itself as well as the Silver King Mine, skiing history, and stagecoaches that were all part of Park City's early chapters. Free admission.

## ✳ Outdoor Activities

**Alpine Slide** (800-222-7275; www.parkcitymountain.com), Park City Mountain Resort base area. This is a 0.5-mile track that descends more than 500 vertical feet on which you can drive your own sled, brakes included. The ride is reached by taking the Payday Lift to its midstation.

**Utah Olympic Park** (435-658-4200; www.olyparks.com), 3419 Olympic Pkwy. In addition to the **Alf Engen Ski Museum** (see the *To See and Do* section earlier), the Olympic Park has plenty of thrill-seekers' activities. There are two zip lines

THE ALPINE SLIDE AT PARK CITY MOUNTAIN RESORT IN SUMMER

Liz Gannes

with speeds up to 50 miles per hour. One travels over the K120 Ski Jump Hill (the 120-meter Nordic ski jump), and the other sails down the freestyle bumps course. Perhaps even more exciting are the bobsled rides, available for persons 14 and older. Speeds reach up to 70 miles per hour, with forces exceeding four Gs. For safety, an experienced driver escorts you on these rides. The **Flying Ace All Stars Freestyle Show** takes place each Saturday at 1 PM between the middle of June and end of August, during which the Freestyle portion of the U.S. Ski and Snowboard Team perform their tricks for 25 minutes, using the Nordic jumps to loft them incredibly high above a landing pool.

### BIKING

## Mountain Biking

**Deer Valley** (435-649-1000 or 800-424-3337) has a huge supply of lift-served downhill mountain biking trails—considered to be some of the best in the country. This trail system has a wide range of offerings, some of which are for very advanced riders only. Trails are open from the middle of June through the middle of September each year, conditions permitting. Both the Sterling Express and the Silver Lake run 10–5:30. $28 all day, $19 single ride.

**Glenwild Area/Swaner Nature Preserve Trailhead,** 0.5 mile northeast of the Kimball Junction I-80 exit 145; on Glenwild Rd. via the Frontage Rd. This single trailhead offers access to many different riding options, including the Flying Dog Loop, Bob's Basin Downhill tracks, Cobblestone, and Jeremy Ranch 24-7 trails. These offer a great variety of single-track scenery, length, and technical difficulty. This well-maintained trail system is one of the reasons that Park City is considered one of the best mountain biking towns in the country.

**8,000 Foot Trail** (now "officially" called the **Park City Mid-Mountain Trail**) approximately traverses the 8,000-foot contour for 11.3 miles between The Canyons and Park City Mountain resorts. However, though this trail stays roughly at 8,000 feet, it does feature significant uphill and downhill portions that add up over the length of the ride. Many people do this as a loop (roughly 25 miles, depending on the exact route): Begin at Park City Mountain Resort, and ascend

MOUNTAIN BIKING NORTH OF PARK CITY AT KIMBALL JUNCTION/SWANER NATURE PRESERVE

via the Spiro Trail. About 3 miles later, you reach the junction with the Mid-Mountain Trail; go north 11.3 miles. Descend on The Canyons' access road about 4 miles, and follow pavement back to PCMR.

**Rail Trail,** accessed just south of the intersection of Bonanza Drive and Kearns Boulevard, follows old railroad tracks for 30 miles as it heads northeast toward Echo Canyon. Because it follows old railway, it has an extremely flat grade and is one of the most mellow rides in the area.

## Road Biking

In the immediate Park City area, road biking is limited due to the small size of the Kamas Valley and loopy, dead-end, cul-de-sac–style neighborhood layouts. However, there is great riding just a short drive away, near the town of Kamas, and to the south in Heber Valley (as described in the *Road Biking* section of the "Heber Valley" chapter).

**UT 35** departs from Francis (or Kamas, if you want to extend it by a bit) and heads south and then southeast out of town. This ride passes fields and enters evergreen forests as it winds up rolling hills and small passes. It goes through the small town of Woodland and intersects with a small network of country roads. Bring a map along and create your own variations as you go.

**Mirror Lake Scenic Byway** (UT 150) is yet another ride that departs from Kamas and heads east, though bending north, toward Wyoming, along the western slope of the Uinta Mountains. This ride has significant climbs and is a major ride, starting in Kamas at 6,437 feet and climbing to 10,620 feet at Bald Mountain Pass 29.2 miles later. Bald Mountain Pass is a good turnaround point, or you can continue down the northern slope. The road descends another 49 miles before reaching Evanston, Wyoming. This would be a monster one-day ride out and back or could be split into a multiday tour.

**UT 133** departs from **Coalville**, a bit farther to the east of UT 35 and Mirror Lake. This ride also heads toward Wyoming and is significantly more mellow in distance and elevation gain than the Mirror Lake Highway. This ride climbs very subtly over slightly rolling hills to reach the border. A round-trip ride is just less than 40 miles.

**GOLF** **Mountain Dell Golf Course** (see the *Golf* section in the "Salt Lake City" chapter) is a canyon facility with two 18-hole courses located just down Parley's Canyon, between Park City and Salt Lake City.

**Park City Golf Club** (435-615-5800; www.parkcity.org), 12 Thaynes Canyon Dr. This 18-hole, 6,400-yard, par-72 course is surrounded with trees and crossed by streams and lakes, which present water hazards at every hole. Because of its elevation of 6,700 feet, it remains significantly cooler than many other Utah courses. $32 for residents, $43 for nonresidents.

**HIKING** **Beaver Creek Trail** (see the *Biking* section in the "Uinta Mountains" chapter) is most popular for biking and ATV use. However, this trail also makes for a gentle and open hiking trail along the foothills of the Uintas.

**The Canyons Resort** (435-649-5400) offers several trails. You can either hike from the base, or take a summer gondola ride to bypass some of the elevation gain. This service operates Wednesday through Sunday, starting in the middle of June. Guided tours are available through **All Seasons Adventures** (435-615-8086). Lift rides are $15 for adults, $10 for kids 7–12 and seniors 65 and older, free for ages 6 and under.

**Deer Valley Resort** (435-649-1000 or 800-424-3337) has two trails that run roughly parallel to the Sterling Lift. Or, you can bypass the lift entirely and hike the trails as a loop. This ski area has some of the downhill biking trails in Utah, so keep your eye out for some pretty fancy mountain bikes. $15 for adults, $12 for children 6–12 and seniors 65 and up, and free for ages 5 and under. (Different rates apply for mountain bikers.)

**Nobletts Creek Log Hollow,** 8 miles southeast of Francis on UT 35. This is a trail system that traverses grassy meadows and aspen groves as it passes through two dry canyons on the Park City slopes of the Uinta National Forest. The main route is 5.5 miles out and back. There is a small network of trails here, so you have choices as you encounter various junctions.

**Park City Mountain Resort** (435-649-8111) also has a significant number of hiking trails, accessed either from the base area on foot, or via summer lift rides on the Payday Lift. The 8,000 Foot Trail, named as such because it roughly stays at that elevation as it rolls to the north, is most commonly a mountain bike trail (because of its length) but is a great option for a longer hike. $11 single lift ride.

**HORSEBACK RIDING** **Park City and Deer Valley Stables** (800-303-7256; www.rockymtnrec.com/PCStab.htm) has two Uinta Mountain locations. They offer rides lasting just few hours, as well as longer group rides with meals. Riders must be at least six years old. They have guest ranch lodging as well.

**Red Pine Adventures** (435-649-9445 or 800-417-7669; www.redpinetours.com) offers rides in a convenient location within 10 minutes of downtown. Trips last one and a half hours, two hours, or half a day, and are on private lands.

**Wind in Your Hair Riding** (435-336-4795; www.windinyourhair.com) takes experienced riders only. Rides are customized, and lessons are available.

**ROCK CLIMBING** **Echo Canyon,** just a few miles east of where I-80 and I-84 merge in Echo Canyon along the frontage road (crag locations vary), is the nearest crag to Park City. This is a small, low- to moderate-quality conglomerate sport climbing area. Despite its quality, it's still very fun. Visit www.mountainproject.com or www.rockclimbing.com for more information; no guidebook to this area exists.

The **Uinta Mountains,** as described in the *Rock Climbing* section of the "Uinta Mountains" chapter, are the nearest crags of any real quality and size. For more options, read the *Rock Climbing* section of the "Salt Lake City" chapter.

**SKIING, ALPINE** **The Canyons** (435-649-5400; www.thecanyons.com), 4000 The Canyons Resort Dr., Park City. The Canyons receives an average of 355 inches of snow (snow phone: 435-615-3456) a year and has a lift-served elevation of 6,190–9,990 feet. This yields a vertical drop of 3,190 feet over 3,700 acres. The terrain has been determined to be 14 percent beginner, 44 percent intermediate, and 42 percent advanced. Special features include eight major peaks, two terrain parks, six half-pipes, and access to very good backcountry skiing. $75 for adults, $43 for ages 7–12 and 65 and over, free for ages 6 and under; half-day passes are $45 from 9:15–1 and 1–4.

The Canyons is most famous for its enormous size, excellent backcountry access, and lingering powder stashes. Though the area has 17 major lifts, there is but one primary base area (and one central parking area connected to the base area by the Cabriolet Gondola; guests of The Sundial Lodge and Grand Summit Resort Hotel enjoy underground parking). The terrain here favors the intermediate and expert skier, with five major bowls as well as many tree runs. However, beginners can enjoy the many groomed slopes as well.

**Doc's at the Gondola** (435-615-8068) and **Smokey's Bar and Grill** (435-615-2891), both in the Resort Village, are spots for post-skiing drinks and finger food. Lessons can be arranged at the **Ski School** (435-615-3449 or 877-472-6306; www .thecanyons.com/ski_school.html). Meeting places vary per group. Reservations are required. **Child care** at The Canyons is at **The Little Adventures Children's Center** (435-615-8036; www.thecanyons.com/daycare.html), which will accept children as young as six weeks old.

Rentals can be obtained at the following:

**Aloha Ski and Snowboard Rentals** (877-222-7600; www.alohaskirentals.com), between Sundial and Grand Summit lodges.

**Black Tie Ski Rentals** (435-649-4070 or 888-333-4754; www.blacktieskis.com), delivery service.

**Canyon Mountain Sports** (435-615-3440; www.thecanyons.com), 4000 The Canyons Resort Dr.

**The Canyons Rental and Solid Edge Repair** (435-615-3441; www.thecanyons .com), Canyons Resort Village.

**KinderSport Junior Ski & Snowboard Rentals** (435-615-3385; www.kinder sport.com), The Canyons Resort Sundial Lodge.

**Ski Butlers** (877-754-7754; www.skibutlers.com), delivery service.

**Skis on the Run** (888-488-0744; www.skisontherun.com), delivery service.

## *On-site Accommodations at The Canyons*

**The Canyons Central Reservations** (866-604-4169; www.thecanyons.com) handles all Canyons-owned resort accommodations, including the following:

**Grand Summit Hotel** (866-604-4171; www.thecanyons.com).

**Sundial Lodge** (888-226-9667; www.thecanyons.com).

**Westgate Resort** (435-940-9444). Because The Canyons is such a large guest-service establishment, the larger hotels at the resort are discussed in the *Lodging* section of this chapter.

**Deer Valley Resort** (800-424-3337; www.deervalley.com), 2250 Deer Valley Dr. South, Park City. Deer Valley receives an average of 300 inches of snow annually and has a lift-served elevation of 6,570–9,570 feet. This yields a vertical drop of 3,000 feet over 1,875 acres. Terrain is deemed to be 27 percent beginner, 38 percent intermediate, and 35 percent advanced. Lift rates are $77 for adults, $54 for seniors ages 65 and over, $45 for children ages 4–12, and $20 for ages 3 and under; between 12:30–4:15, half-day passes are $53 for adults, $37 for seniors, $36 for children, and $13 for toddlers.

Deer Valley is Park City's ultra-luxury resort, known for its over-the-top guest service and accommodations. For those who appreciate their attention, this is the place. Everything, from ski rentals to hill grooming, is deluxe. Lined by extremely high-end resort homes, lodges, spas, and fine-dining restaurants, Deer Valley is as much devoted to the other aspects of a resort as it is to skiing. Deer Valley has three major villages: **Empire Pass, Silver Lake,** and **Snow Park.** This is where the vacation rentals, restaurants, lodges, and private homes are located. Snow Park is at the lower base area where skiers first arrive, whether when beginning a resort stay or just for the day.

**Snow Park Lounge,** in the Snow Park Lodge of the Snow Park Base Area, and **The Royal Street Café,** in the Silver Lake Lodge at Silver Lake Village, are Deer Valley's après-ski locations on mountain. Lessons can be arranged with **Deer Valley's Ski School** (435-645-6648 or 888-754-8477). Children between the ages of two months and 12 years may be taken to daycare at the **Children's Center** (435-645-6648), main level, Snow Park Lodge. Reservations are recommended.

**Rentals** are scattered across this huge mountain, and the selection of your rental service will likely depend on your lodging location. For equipment, call or visit the following:

**Black Tie Ski Rentals** (435-649-4070 or 888-333-4754; www.blacktieskis.com), delivery service.

**Cole Sport** (435-649-4601; www.colesport.com), in the Silver Lake Village.

**Deer Valley Rentals** (Snow Park Lodge; 888-754-8477; www.deervalley.com), in the Silver Lake Village.

**KinderSport Junior Ski & Snowboard Rentals** (435-649-8338 and Deer Valley Snow Park Lodge; 435-649-6229; www.kindersport.com), children's ski and snowboard rentals in the Deer Valley Silver Lake Village.

**Ski Butlers** (877-754-7754; www.skibutlers.com), delivery service.

**Ski-N-See Ski and Snowboard** (435-615-1106; www.skinsee.com), Silver Lake Village.

**Skis on the Run** (888-488-0744; www.skisontherun.com), delivery service.

**Stein Eriksen Rental** (435-658-0680; www.steineriksen.com), in The Chateaux at Silver Lake, Stag Lodge, Stein Eriksen Lodge.

## On-site Accommodations at Deer Valley

All accommodations at Deer Valley are arranged through **Deer Valley Central Reservations** (435-645-6528 or 800-558-3337; www.deervalleycentralreservations.com). Because Deer Valley is such a large part of Park City, the larger hotels at the resort are discussed in this chapter's *Lodging* section.

**Park City Mountain Resort** (435-649-8111; www.parkcitymountain.com), 1310 Lowell Ave., Park City. Park City Mountain Resort receives an average of 355 inches of snow annually (snow phone: 435-647-5449) and has a lift-served elevation from 6,900 to 10,000 feet. This yields a vertical drop of 3,100 feet over 3,300 acres. The terrain is deemed 17 percent beginner, 50 percent intermediate, and 33 percent advanced. Special features of Park City Mountain Resort are its terrain park and half-pipes, as well as World Cup racing facilities and snowcat skiing. $77 for adults, $47 for seniors ages 65 and older and for children ages 7–12, and free for ages 6 and under; half-day rates are $60 12:30–4 PM.

Park City Mountain is a resort of many hats. It is at once the training grounds for the U.S. Ski and Snowboard Team, a trick-skiing and terrain-park mountain, and an excellent family-friendly destination. The bulk of the terrain here is moderate, and so it is very popular among intermediate and beginner ski vacationers. However, Park City also has stashes of expert terrain. Because not nearly as many extreme-style skiers come to Park City as go to Snowbird or Alta, steep powder stashes remain fresher much longer. Park City features a fairly uncomplicated layout, with one central (though very busy) base area. Just beneath this resort village is a large parking lot, as well as a parking garage ($5 per day) underneath the base area.

**Legends Bar and Grill** (435-649-8111), on the first level of the Resort Center and adjacent to the base of Payday Lift, and **Pig Pen Saloon** (435-655-0070), on the second level of the Resort Center and next to the National Ability Center, are the mountain's on-hill après-ski spots. **Lessons** can be obtained at the **Mountain School** (group lessons: 800-227-2754; private lessons: 800-222-7275). Disabled persons can obtain lessons and assistance at the **National Ability Center** (435-649-3991; www.nac1985.org); the office is located about 100 feet beneath the base of the Payday Lift. Park City has no on-site child-care facilities, but **Guardian Angels** (435-783-2662; www.guardianangelbaby.com) is a local business that dispatches sitters certified in first aid and CPR.

On-site **rentals** are in high demand at Park City, as it is an extremely popular vacation mountain. Many of these are general rental services, while others specialize in children's rentals and freestyle rentals. (Where there is no description, the name of the company suggests the services available.)

**Aloha Ski and Snowboard Rentals** (877-222-7600; www.alohaskirentals.com), second level of the Resort Center: general ski and snowboard rentals.

**Bahnhof Sport** (435-645-9700; www.bahnhof.com), base of Town Lift, just off Main Street: general ski, snowboard, snowshoe, and children's rentals.

**Bazooka's Freeride Shop** (435-649-0520; www.colesport.com), Resort Center: freeride-specific rentals.

**Black Tie Ski Rentals** (435-649-4070 or 888-333-4754; www.blacktieskis.com) delivery service.

**Breeze Ski Rentals** (435-649-1902; www.skirentals.com), Resort Center: 20 percent discount on ski and snowboard rentals with reservations.

**KinderSport Junior Ski & Snowboard Rentals** (435-649-5463 or 877-350-5463; www.kindersport.com), Resort Center: children's ski and snowboard rentals.

**Ski Butlers** (delivery: 877-754-7754; www.skibutlers.com), delivery service.

**Skis on the Run** (888-488-0744; www.skisontherun.com), delivery service.

**Surefoot** (435-649-6016; www.surefoot.com), Resort Center: boot-fitting specialists.

## On-site Accommodations at Park City Mountain Resort

Lodging options at Park City can be arranged by calling **Park City Mountain Reservations** (435-647-5440 or 800-331-3178; www.parkcitymountain.com). Because Park City Mountain Resort's base area abuts to downtown Park City, the larger hotels at the resort are discussed in this chapter's *Lodging* section.

Craig Bowden

THE NORDIC JUMPS LOCATED AT UTAH OLYMPIC PARKS, NORTH OF PARK CITY

**SKIING, BACKCOUNTRY, HELICOPTER & SNOWCAT** Though you would never guess it, Park City and Salt Lake City are very near each other as the crow flies. Salt Lake City (on the Wasatch Front) is separated from Park City (on the Wasatch Back) only by the ridge of the Wasatch Range. Though the mountains pose quite a geographical barrier, there is not nearly as much distance between the two cities as you would think. Because the barrier between them is the very mountain range on which the skiing takes place, they share the same selection of backcountry skiing and information sources. These opportunities are discussed in the *Skiing, Backcountry, Helicopter & Snowcat* section of the "Salt Lake City" chapter.

**SKIING, NORDIC White Pine Touring Center** (435-649-6249; www.white pinetouring.com), intersection of Park Ave. and Thaynes Canyon Dr., Park City. This full-service facility offers more than 20 kilometers of groomed trails (in 3-, 5-, and 10-kilometer loops), rentals, lessons, and tours.

**Mountain Dell** (as described in the *Skiing, Nordic* section of the "Salt Lake City" chapter) is located in Parley's Canyon between Park City and Salt Lake City.

## ✳ Lodging

**HOTELS Chateau Après** (435-649-9372 or 800-357-3556; www.chateau apres.com), 1299 Norfolk Ave. This hotel has fairly basic accommodations, with two types of guest rooms: one with a twin and a double bed, the other with a queen bed. An Austrian-style façade, 150-yard proximity to Park City Mountain Resort, Continental breakfast, and a no-frills, hard-to-damage interior make this perfect accommodations for low-key winter skiers and summer mountain bikers. Lodging here is extremely affordable, especially compared with most other Park City rates. $100 per room. (For an even more affordable option, dorm-style rooming is available for less than $40 a person.)

**Grand Summit Hotel** (Resort Lodging: 866-604-4171; www.thecanyons .com), 4000 The Canyons Resort Dr. This is The Canyon's large-scale, all-inclusive luxury lodge. This AAA four-diamond rated, 368-room mountain lodge has options ranging from hotel-style rooms to multi-bedroom suites and deluxe penthouses. Guests here enjoy concierge ski service, deluxe furniture, and a long list of amenities, including on-site daycare and spa, and superb customer service. Rates vary depend on season but run from $200 into four digits.

**Marriott's MountainSide** (435-940-2000; www.marriott.com), 1305 Lowell Ave. This Marriott is as slope-side as it gets at Park City Mountain Resort. This hotel has more than 360 rooms and overlooks the base of the Payday Lift. Its outdoor, heated pool is just feet from groomed ski trails. Complimentary parking is available for one vehicle per reservation, a big plus in this crowded town. Rooms vary in size and are reliably nice, though not over the top. Rates start in the mid-$200s, can climb steeply, and are very dependent on the season.

**Park City Peaks Hotel** (435-649-5000 or 800-649-5012; www.parkcitypeaks.com), 2121 Lowell Ave. The Peaks Hotel is located just a few minutes from town. Guests enjoy the accessibility of in-town amenities, as well as the extra breathing room afforded by the short drive to this 2-acre property. An indoor and heated outdoor pool, on-site restaurant (Rustic Creek Grille), and sports bar make it so you don't need to leave if you don't want to. Fresh-baked evening cookies and hot chocolate, complimentary breakfast, and excellent beds add to the experience. Park City's free shuttle bus has a stop here. $170 and up.

**Silver Queen Boutique Hotel** (435-649-5986 or 800-447-6423; www.silverqueenhotel.com), 632 Main St. The Silver Queen, a centrally located small hotel with just 12 suites, is located immediately on Park City's Main Street. Guests staying here are within walking distance of every possible amenity and within a free bus shuttle of all ski areas. Guests also enjoy free parking, which is a considerable perk at this location. Each room is decorated in a unique way and is adorned with fresh flowers, a fully stocked kitchen, dining area, and living room. $250 and up.

**Stein Eriksen Lodge** (435-649-3700 or 800-453-1302; www.steinlodge.com), 7700 Stein Way, Deer Valley Resort. The Stein Eriksen Lodge is, among Deer Valley's omnipresent luxury, the most deluxe of all the lodging. The 175-room mountain lodge is graced by European influences and is located right in the center of Silver Lake Village. A spacious campus leaves room for uncrowded amenities including a spa, the Glitretind Restaurant, lounge, conference center, lobbies, and decks with views of the surrounding mountains. Handsome stonework and woodwork are complemented by choice furniture. $500–$2,500.

**The Yarrow** (435-649-7000; www.yarrowresort.com), 1800 Park Ave. This hotel is, relatively speaking, a budget hotel in a great location. The rooms, despite being located on prime real estate, are reasonably spacious. Though the rooms are not deluxe, they are carefully cleaned and outfitted with solid-quality furniture. $150 and up.

BED-AND-BREAKFASTS **Old Town Guest House** (435-649-2642 or 800-290-6423; www.oldtownguesthouse.com), 1011 Empire Ave. This is a favorite of many, with its low-key tone, comfortable bedding, cozy atmosphere, filling breakfasts, central location, and knowledgeable service. Rooms are outfitted with pine furniture, homey blankets, and a general rustic ambience. With plenty of sunlight, they are cozy and not claustrophobic. $80 (low season) to $230 (peak season).

**Washington School Inn** (435-649-3800; www.washingtonschoolinn.com), 543 Park Ave. This inn has less of the quirkiness and more of the charm than many bed-and-breakfasts seem to have. The rooms are each decorated uniquely, but with more modern furniture, newer bedding, and more reserve than is usual. This building, opened for students in November of 1889, is one of very few to have survived an epidemic town fire of 1898. It was fully refurbished in 1984.

**Woodside Inn** (435-649-3494 or 888-241-5890; www.woodsideinn.com), 1469 Woodside Ave. Unlike many bed-and-breakfasts, this is located inside a modern (circa 2000) structure. Rooms are comfortable and clean, but have no superfluities. This is the closest bed-and-breakfast to Park City Mountain Resort. Prices start at $110 in summer, $250 and up in winter.

VACATION RENTALS Though Park City does have hotels, it is also the land of **vacation rentals.** Many services exist to help you track down your ideal accommodations and include: **Affordable Luxury Lodging** (435-714-1414 or 888-754-9442; www.affordableluxurylodging.com); **David Holland's Resort Lodging and Conference Services** (888-727-5248; www.davidhollands.com); **Deer Valley Lodging** (888-976-2732; www.deervalleylodging.com); **Park City Mountain Reservations** (435-649-8111 or 800-331-3178; www.parkcitymountain.com); **Park City Travel and Lodging** (801-487-1300 or 800-421-9741; www.parkcitytravel.com); **Resort Quest's Central Reservations of** **Park City** (800-401-9913; www.parkcityski.com/cci/html); **Resorts West** (800-541-9378; www.resortswest.com); **Snow Valley Connection** (435-645-7700 or 800-458-8612; www.snowvalleyconnection.com); **Utah Travel Connection** (801-453-1128; www.utahtravelconnection.com); and **Western Leisure** (435-649-2223; www.westernleisure.com).

**Blue Church Lodge and Townhouses** (435-649-8009 or 800-626-5467; www.bluechurchlodge.com), 424 Park Ave. The Blue Church is located in the 1898 building that was the first Mormon church in Park City. There is a choice between seven different suites and four town homes. Each has its own décor, multiple bedrooms, a fully outfitted kitchen, and access to two spas and a common sitting room. There is a Continental breakfast every morning. For such high-occupancy apartment-style lodging in the heart of Park City, this is a good deal. $180–$680 (more during the Sundance Film Festival).

## ✳ Where to Eat

Park City is full of award-winning, nationally and internationally acclaimed restaurants. The hot spots for restaurants are Deer Valley (very high-end), The Canyons, Main Street, and north in Kimball Junction (at the Red Stone Plaza). Unlike in Salt Lake City, the restaurants in Park City consistently charge a pretty penny for their fare. Because of the wealthy resident population and geographical challenges of acquiring ingredients, food here is rarely a bargain, but it is generally of very high quality.

DINING OUT **Bistro Toujours** (435-940-2200; www.bistrotoujours.com), 7815 Royal St. East, inside the Chateaux at Silver Lake Mid Mountain, Deer Valley. Serving breakfast, lunch, and dinner daily; closed mid-April to mid-June, and mid-October through early December. Bistro Toujours is a shoe-in—it was voted by *Condé Nast* as one of the top 50 restaurants worldwide in 2002. This French and American hybrid has a menu that changes with the season to include the freshest, most seasonally appropriate ingredients. Enjoy the elegant, yet casual atmosphere with white linens and an open dinning room. Have a cocktail at Buvez! Private Club (i.e., bar) next door before dinner. Dinner $30 and up.

**Chez Betty** (435-649-8181; www.chez betty.com), 1637 Short Line Dr., inside the Copperbottom Inn. Serving dinner nightly December through March; closed Tuesday and Wednesday during other months. This is a French and American restaurant, open since 1991. The menu utilizes the freshest ingredients possible and stays on the lighter side of French cuisine. Lamb, beef, escargots, salmon, and chicken are each accompanied by complementary and creative sauces, as well as veggies and legumes. A petite portion is an option on every entrée. Dinners $23–$40, petite $12–$21.

**Eating Establishment** (435-649-8284; www.theeatingestablishment .net), 317 Main St. Open for lunch and dinner daily; also open for breakfast in the winter. This low-key restaurant is for many a welcome break from the high-end fare typical of Park City. This restaurant certainly serves a good spread, ranging from Rocky Mountain trout to burgers, ribs, and vegetarian dishes. Completely kid-friendly, it is much more relaxed than most other sit-down eateries. Open since 1972.

**Grappa Italian Restaurant** (435-645-0636; www.grapparestaurant.com), 151 Main St., has the most loyal following of any Italian restaurant in Park City. Located just at the top of Main Street in a three-story historic building whose balconies are trimmed with flower boxes and vines, this restaurant uses only fresh vegetables and herbs to create its slow-cooked sauces and traditional dishes. The menu changes regularly to maintain its loyalty to the highest quality ingredients available. Reservations are required. Open nightly for dinner.

**Mariposa** (435-645-6715; www.deer valley.com), 7600 Royal St., Silver Park Lodge at Deer Valley. Mariposa has been open for decades and is often awarded "best restaurant" in Park City. It menu is varied with contemporary and traditional dishes, as well as sampling options and vegetarian options. And excellent wine list accompanies a menu heavy in seafood and choice meats. Mariposa serves dinner only, Tuesday through Sunday during the ski season, and is closed during the summer. As it is located at Deer Valley, its pricy menu is the name of the game.

**Purple Sage** (435-655-9505; www .purplesagecafe.com), 434 Main St. Open for dinner nightly. This is an "American Western" restaurant that has devoted as much attention to its vegetarian menu as to its meat selections. Smoked trout, elk chili, veal, and duck are served alongside butternut squash ravioli and grilled shrimp polenta. Located in an 1895 Telephone Building on Main Street, this restaurant serves summer diners on its outdoor patio. The atmosphere, with extensive murals, is fun yet refined.

**350 Main New American Brasserie** (435-649-3140; www.350main.com), 350 Main St. Open for dinner nightly. This healthy gourmet establishment, which is in good culinary company in Park City, was chosen as Park City's best restaurant in 2007 by *Salt Lake Magazine* and has a long-standing reputation for excellence. Part of its menu is a gourmet selection of foods especially vitamin-rich and low in saturated fats. Seafood, trout, and fine meats are accompanied by the season's best and freshest vegetables, as well as sauces and mousses created in the kitchen. A distinct Asian influence can be detected on many of the items. Main courses $20–$36.

**EATING OUT** **El Chubasco** (435-645-9114), 1890 Bonanza Dr. Open for lunch and dinner daily. This is considered by many to be Park City's best Mexican restaurant and has a reputation for excellent value. Because of its popularity, it can get very busy. However, service is usually quick; orders are done at the counter, with meals delivered to your table. This is no Tex-Mex place; expect the real thing with chili sauces, old-style recipes, and an extensive salsa bar. This is a fast fix for good food and can be perfect if you're in a rush.

**Main Street Deli** (435-649-1110), 525 Main St. Open daily for breakfast, lunch, and early dinner. This casual eatery serves a great casual meal, generally categorized as sandwiches and soups. However, there is much more available than just turkey and cheese; gyros, liverwurst, and bratwurst are on the list, as well as salads, chilis, milk shakes, pies, and cakes.

**No Name Saloon** (435-649-6667; www.nonamesaloon.net), 447 Main St. The No Name has been "helping people forget their name" since 1903. It has old-time Western ambience with a brass bar, brass glass racks, and mahogany aplenty. The menu is pub food taken up a notch. Though beef is available, the majority of the burgers are buffalo (much more lean and exotic than beef, and delicious). In addition to the carnivorous offerings, there are

a handful of alternatives, from garden burgers to fish (including fish-and-chips, seafood sandwichs, and fish tacos).

**Wasatch Brew Pub** (435-649-0900; www.wasatchbeers.com), 205 South Main St. Open for lunch and dinner daily. This pub is home of the Utah's famous Polygamy Porter: "Why Have Just One?" It has traditional pub fare such as pizzas, beef and buffalo burgers, fish-and-chips, nachos, and calamari, but also extends its menu to include entrées such as filet mignon, baby back ribs, pine nut salmon, and Utah trout.

## ✳ Entertainment

**LIQUOR STORES** Park City has two state-owned liquor stores, the largest of which is in **Prospector Square** (435-649-7254), 1901 Sidewinder Dr. Open 10–8. Another smaller, closer store is **downtown** at 524 Main St. (435-649-3293) and keeps longer hours, 11–10. Another is just north of town at 1612 Ute Boulevard in **Kimball Junction** (435-658-0860), open 11–7. All are state owned and closed on holidays and Sundays.

**VENUES** **Outdoor concerts** of all genres are a big hit in Park City. **The Canyons** (www.thecanyons.com) and **Deer Valley** (www.deervalley.com) each have stages that are used for summer concerts. Deer Valley also hosts World Cup Aerials and Moguls competitions that are usually accompanied by free nightly concerts of some sort. For specific event listings, check the *Special Events* calendar listed in the "Northern Wasatch in Brief" chapter.

**Cisero's** (435-649-5044; www.ciseros .com), 306 Main St. Cisero's attracts big-name DJs, hip-hop groups, rock bands, and the like, particularly in

January around the Sundance Film Festival.

**Eccles Center for the Performing Arts** (435-655-3114; www.ecclescenter .org), 1750 Kearns Blvd. The Eccles Center is just north of downtown and has a main stage that hosts many fine musicians and musical groups with a seated audience.

**Egyptian Theater** (435-649-9371; www.egyptiantheatercompany.org), 328 Main St. Open since 1889, the Egyptian is Park City's oldest stage and is the town's place for drama and comedy.

**Harry O's** (435-655-7579; www .harryos-pc.com), 427 Main St. This club is probably the most popular in Park City, with two floors, go-go dancers, and the like. Its sound system and floor plan are perfect for hosting big parties and concerts.

**Kimball Art Center** (435-649-8882; www.kimball-art.org), 638 Park Ave. Kimball is primarily an art gallery space and community art center but is the starting place of many art strolls, as well as galas and other townwide events such as auctions and dances.

**Park City Performing Arts Foundation** (435-655-3114; www.eccles center.org) is the heart of music in Park City. This organization brings in groups and artists from around the nation and coordinates local performances. They host many shows at Deer Valley, including performances by the Utah Symphony and Utah Opera Company.

NIGHTLIFE **Hungry Moose Sports Pub** (435-649-8600; www.hungry moosepub.com), 438 Main St. This pub is a great place for adults with their families. Unlike a true bar (or "private club"), children are allowed inside this establishment. An extensive pub menu with appetizers, pizzas, and fish-and-chips is available, as well as sports on the television and a full bar with draft beers.

**J. B. Mulligan's Club & Pub** (435-658-0717; www.jbmulligans.com), 804 Main St. This is a cozy Main Street bar with regular live music and occasional comedy acts. Monday nights have 50¢ draft beers.

**The No Name Saloon** (435-649-6667; www.nonamesaloon.net), 447 Main St. The No Name has been open since 1903. In addition to a large pub menu, this bar also has a foosball table and billiards.

**The Spur** (435-615-1618; www.350 main.com/thespur), 350 Main St., behind 350 Main Restaurant. This is one of Park City's most popular venues for local acts. Its hardwood dance floor is often full with people from ages 21 to 70.

## ✳ Selective Shopping

FARMERS' MARKETS **Heber Valley Farmers' Market** (801-654-4555), Heber City Municipal Park, Heber City. Just a short drive to the south, this market takes place Thursday 4–7 PM. Weather permitting, the market begins in the middle of June and lasts through the middle of August.

**Park City Farmers' Market** (435-649-5400; www.parkcityfarmers market.com), Cabriolet Parking Lot, The Canyons Resort. Park City's market takes place Wednesday 3–7 PM. This market begins early—as soon as late May, if the weather allows, and runs toward the end of October.

MALLS AND SQUARES **The Tanger Outlets** (435-645-7078; www .tangeroutlet.com), 6699 North Landmark Dr., Kimball Junction. This nationally famous outlet-mall chain has a huge collection of shops ranging from Coach to Fossil, Guess, Adidas, Banana Republic, and dozens more.

**Redstone Center,** Redstone Dr. northeast Kimball Junction. This spacious center has shops and restaurants galore, from Red Rock Brewpub to World Market, Backcountry.com, and more.

**GALLERIES Artworks Gallery** (435-649-4462; www.artworksparkcity .com), 461 Main St. This gallery showcases variable contemporary media ranging from ceramics to jewelry, glass, steel, and wood.

**Coda Gallery** (435-655-3803; www .codagallery.com), 804 Main St. The Coda Gallery has a wide collection of media, including many paintings, glass, and bronze, and is generally modern, warm, and colorful.

**Crosby Collection** (435-658-1813 or 435-649-6522; www.crosbycollection .com), 419 and 513 Main St. This is perhaps Park City's most Southwestern-influenced gallery, with work by Navajo, Hopi, and Pueblo artists and artisans, new and old.

**David Whitten Gallery** (435-649-3860; www.davidwhittenphoto.com), 523 Main St. A stop at the fine photography gallery is a quick tour of Utah's most beautiful landscapes, captured in their finest light. Other locations from around North America are included in the collection.

**Iron Horse Gallery** (435-615-6900; www.ironhorseartgallery.com), 1205 Iron Horse Dr. This gallery features the work of a few dozen artists, with sculptors and painters being the biggest faction. Enjoy sculpture gardens, fountains, and photography.

**Julie Nester Gallery** (435-649-7855; www.julienestergallery.com), 1775 B

Bonanza Dr. Nearly 30 living artists have their work on display here, with painting, sculpture, and mixed media. This modern warehouse-style gallery is a chic space with fine art written all over it.

**Kimball Art Center** (435-649-8882; www.kimball-art.org), 638 Park Ave. Kimball Art Center is Park City's arts jugular. It is the center for festivals, gallery strolls, musical performances, lectures, auctions, classes, and the like. Within this center are three individual galleries.

**Meyer Gallery** (800-649-8160; www .meyergallery.com), 305 Main St. This Main Street space features the works of more than a dozen artists at a time. The fine paintings and drawings cover a range of themes and styles, from Utah landscape to ultramodern abstraction.

**Phoenix Gallery** (435-649-1006; www.phoenixgalleryparkcity.com), 508 Main St. This is a large gallery for Main Street, with three-levels of display space with several dozen painters, sculptors, and mixed-media artists in a pleasant, Western-influenced interior.

**Stanfield Fine Art** (877-657-1800; www.stanfieldfineart.com), 751 Main St. This fine-art dealer has shops in Aspen, Colorado, and Park City. A wide variety of media and tastes are represented here, from paintings of nature to cityscapes and Picasso-esque abstract works.

**Terzian Galleries** (435-649-4927 or 866-949-4927; www.terziangalleries .com), 309 Main St. This is another excellent Park City collection of many contemporary media and styles, with oil painting, glass, sculpture, and photography.

**The Thomas Kearns McCarthey Gallery** (435-658-1691; www

.mccartheygallery.net), 449 Main St. Offers a distinct break in the pattern from Park City's contemporary and Western-style art galleries, as one of the nation's leading Russian impressionist dealers.

**Wild Spirits Nature Photography** (435-200-0071 or 800-570-8962; www.wildspiritsparkcity.com), 614 Main St. This gallery offers a look into the wild side of the Rocky Mountains. The photography of Utah residents Gary Crandall and Tom Till is on display in prints as well as more portable mementos like books and postcards.

# HEBER VALLEY

Heber Valley is located between the Wasatch and Uinta mountains—20 miles south of Park City, and 30 miles northeast of Provo. It is near both towns as the crow flies, but, it is geographically and socially isolated from the hubbub. It is close enough to the Salt Lake area to be within reasonable distance from the airport, yet is insulated by nature.

Because of its striking topography, this region is nicknamed Switzerland of America. From the valleys rise huge mountains whose slopes begin as lush green hills and top out as snow-covered peaks far above the tree line. Because of the area's beauty and proximity to Park City's money, it has been increasingly on the radar as a vacation destination, and even a place to relocate.

Heber Valley, more than just a spillover from Park City, has its own attractions and niches. Deer Creek Reservoir is in the southern part of the valley, and Jordanelle Reservoir is to the north. Both are beautiful recreation-rich lakes. Midway has a pure line of Swiss ancestry, and it is tastefully reflected in the architecture as much as the surrounding landscape. Soldier Hollow, the former 2002 Winter Olympic Nordic skiing venue, is located in Midway. This is one of Utah's best cross-country skiing facilities and is the host of the International Sheepdog Competitions each year. Many of the area's finest resort and bed-and-breakfast lodging are scattered throughout the valley. All of this, and no urban congestion.

GUIDANCE The Web site **www.gohebervalley.org** is a great, comprehensive site that details each aspect of visiting the valley, and it includes all recreation areas, visitor information, agencies such as the Forest Service, chambers of commerce, and state park offices.

**Heber Valley Chamber of Conference** (435-654-3666; www.hebervalleycc.org), 475 North Main St., Heber City. Open Monday–Friday 8–5. This Swiss-style building is at the northern entrance to the town of Heber as US 40 enters from the north. This chamber maintains a collection of local maps, books, brochures, and events calendars.

GETTING THERE *By car:* Heber Valley is located along **US 40,** which links it to Park City to the north, and eventually to I-80. To the southwest you find I-15, Provo, and Orem, connected to Heber Valley by US 189.

*By air:* **Salt Lake City International Airport** (801-575-2400 or 800-595-2442; www.slcairport.com), about 45 miles northwest of Heber City via US 40 and I-80. This is a major western hub and offers reasonable airfare and many direct flights.

**MEDICAL EMERGENCY** **Heber Valley Medical Center** (435-654-2500; www .intermountainhealthcare.org), 1485 South US 40. This is the area's community hospital connected with the **Heber Valley Clinic** (435-657-4400).

## ✳ To See and Do

**Heber Valley Railroad** (435-654-5601; www.hebervalleyrr.com), departing from the Train Depot at 450 South 600 West. This historic train travels 16 miles of track from Heber Valley to Vivian Park in Provo Canyon. A 1907 steam engine pulls cars dating to the 1920s. Rides last almost three and a half hours round-trip. Special events include hayrides, haunted rides, Christmas rides, barbecue dinners, and raft-and-train combination trips, during which you raft down the Provo River and return by train.

**Wasatch Mountain State Park** (435-654-1791; www.stateparks.utah.gov), just north of Midway on UT 224. This huge state park occupies more than 22,000 acres and is a venerable campus of recreation, including golf, horseback riding, hiking, mountain biking, Nordic skiing, snowshoeing (at Soldier Hollow; see *Skiing*), camping, picnicking, and more. $5 entrance, $20 camping.

HEBER VALLEY, MIDWAY CITY

BIKING

## Mountain Biking

**The Homestead Resort** (888-327-7220; www.homesteadresort.com), 700 Homestead Dr., Midway. This resort rents road bikes, mountain bikes, children's bikes, and helmets by the hour or per day for very reasonable rates.

**Strawberry Reservoir** (435-548-2321), 23 miles southeast of Heber City on US 40. This recreation area has a large number of trails that offer various lengths and difficulties of rides, as well as loops and out-and-backs. The **Shoreline Trail** (as listed in the *Hiking* section) is a great, very easy trail that rolls along the western edge of the lake and can make for a ride as long as 20 miles, if taken the full distance out and back. The **Narrows Trail** is a 12-mile, flat, single-track trail that follows the southern shoreline of the reservoir, accessing the "Narrows," only accessible by boat otherwise. **Willow Creek** is a 9-mile loop that is beginner-friendly and crosses its namesake creek many times (making it best done later in the season when the water is low). Many other rides, particularly loops, are made up in large part by dirt roads, which is as exciting as singletrack to many. These include **Coop Creek, Heber Mountain, Strawberry Ridge,** and **Strawberry River.** For more information on each trail, call the visitors center.

**Wasatch Mountain State Park** (435-654-1791; www.stateparks.utah.gov), just north of Midway on UT 224. This 22,000-acre state park (see *To See and Do*) is considered one of Utah's nicest and most inconspicuous. It has many mountain-biking trails of varying difficulty. **Pine Creek Canyon** is a difficult ride, physically, though it is a very easy ride technically. It ascends this canyon via dirt road, departing just to the north of the visitors center, and summiting about 7 miles later. **Snake Creek Canyon** is another such dirt road with several unmarked, though popular and nicely worn-in, trails that climbs steeply toward the Wasatch ridge. **Sage Creek Loop** is an easy, 3-mile loop that takes a single-track trail from North River Road in Midway and makes a series of right-hand turns to climb a ridge, descend through a meadow to a canyon, and then follow an old jeep road back. More ride suggestions can be obtained by calling the visitors center. $5 entrance.

## Road Biking

**Heber Valley Loop** is a very popular, flat loop that tours the area. It starts in Heber City and hits the towns of Charleston and Midway along the way, as well as Deer Creek Reservoir. Take US 189 southeast out of Heber City southwest toward Charleston. Turn right where the road Ts into Charleston Road/UT 113 at Deer Creek Reservoir. Follow this road north to Midway, and then UT 113 east to Heber City. As you head southeast, there are great views of Mount Timpanogos over the Deer Creek Reservoir. This ride can be extended by continuing along US 189 around the southern point of Deer Creek Reservoir, and into Provo Canyon. To go toward the Sundance Resort, make a right on UT 92 and head just beneath Mount Timpanogos, the most famous peak in the Wasatch Range.

**The Homestead Resort** (888-327-7220; www.homesteadresort.com), 700 Homestead Dr., Midway. This resort rents road bikes, mountain bikes, children's bikes, and helmets by the hour or per day for very reasonable rates.

**FISHING AND BOATING** These two activities in Wasatch County are among the best in Utah, as there is a high number of reservoirs, lakes, and streams in this high county.

**All Seasons Adventures of Park City** (435-649-9619; www.allseasonsadventures .com), 4000 Canyons Resort Dr., Park City. This company operates with tandem, inflatable, and sea kayaks.

**Currant Creek** and **Currant Creek Reservoir** are both southeast of Heber City and are accessed by Currant Creek Road, which departs from US 40, just west of Fruitland. The reservoir has almost 300 surface acres, a boat ramp and a pier and offers brown, rainbow, and other varieties of trout; the creek itself parallels the access road and can itself be fished.

**Daniels Creek** is stocked with many species of trout. This creek is paralleled by US 40, which takes Daniel Canyon southeast out of Heber City. Access points are numerous.

**Deer Creek Reservoir** (in Deer Creek State Park: 435-654-0171), just south of Heber and Midway, has nearly 3,000 surface acres and is one of the Wasatch region's more popular fishing spots, with bass, trout, perch, and walleye. There are four boat ramps.

**Invert Sports** (801-830-8864; www.utahboatrental.com) rents all the necessary motorized gear, including Jet Skis and motorboats with appropriate trailers and vehicles for towing, if necessary, and accessory toys for waterskiing and wakeboarding. This company takes care of everything, including boat delivery and cleanup.

**Jordanelle Reservoir** is just north of Heber City (west of Kamas and Francis) and has 3,000 surface acres. It is a rich trout fishery. Two boat ramps and a marina (with rentals) are at the Hailstone Marina (435-649-9540), along US 40 on the western shore of the lake.

**Provo River** (as described in the *Fishing* section of the "Provo" chapter) is the Wasatch region's best fishing river and has many species of trout. The river begins in the Uintas and travels through Heber Valley and into Provo Canyon, pooling in Jordanelle and Deer Creek reservoirs en route.

**Strawberry Reservoir** is the largest reservoir in the region and is located off US 40, about 30 miles southeast of Heber City. It is considered one of Utah's best bodies of water for fishing purposes and has a surface acreage of 17,000. There are four boat ramps and a marina, Strawberry Bay Marina (on Strawberry/White River Rd.; 435-548-2261), and trout as well as salmon. This reservoir has a reputation for producing very large fish.

**GOLF** **The Homestead Resort Golf Course** (888-327-7220; www.homestead resort.com), 700 Homestead Dr., Midway. Given the "Utah Best of State" award by the State of Utah, this 18-hole, 7,017-yard, par-72 course is one of the most beautiful in the state, with open fairways and the Heber Valley and surrounding mountains as a backdrop. $45 for weekends and holidays, $35 for weekdays.

**Soldier Hollow Golf Course** (435-654-7442; www.soldierhollow.com/golf _course), 1370 West Soldier Hollow Ln., Midway. These public facilities have two 18-hole courses designed by Gene Bates and opened in 2004. Challenging and hilly with open views. $40 for weekends, $37 for weekdays.

**Wasatch Mountain State Park** (435-654-0532; www.golfwasatch.com), 975 West Golf Course Dr., Midway. This is yet another beautiful public course in Heber Valley with two 18-hole courses, one a mountain course and one a lake course.

**HIKING** **Foreman Hollow,** on US 40, 16 miles southwest of Heber City (at Lodgepole Campground). This 4-mile loop is an educational opportunity for visitors unfamiliar with the local plant and animal life. Along the length of this trail, placards point out various bits of information regarding the local wildlife. After crossing through aspen groves and evergreen stands, the trail ascends the hillside to reach an overlook that affords views of Strawberry Reservoir and Daniels Canyon (see below).

**Strawberry Reservoir Shoreline Trail,** accessed by the Strawberry Bay Turnoff, 23 miles southeast of Heber City on US 40. This gently rolling trail, 10 miles in length, follows the western shoreline of the reservoir. The trail is great for walking and trail running, as it covers a lot of ground without too much elevation change. Access points are at Mud Creek Bay, Strawberry Bay, and Chaplain Point. The trail terminates at East Portal Bay. The **Strawberry Visitors Center** (435-548-2321) can alert you to trail conditions and give you general information.

**Thornton Hollow,** on US 40, 12 miles southeast of Heber City. Thornton Hollow is a 3-mile out-and-back hike of moderate difficulty that travels through the varying flora of Daniels Canyon, including aspen groves and grassy parks. This trail follows a stream for part of the way, making it a good hike to do with thirsty dogs. Partway up, the trail departs from the canyon and gains a ridge that offers spacious views.

**ROCK CLIMBING** **Uinta Mountains** (as described in the *Rock Climbing* section of the "Uinta Mountains" chapter) offer the nearest, best climbing in the area. The quartzite climbing is at high altitude and is perfect in the summer heat. There is a wide span of difficulty, but the bulk of the climbs are moderate. Protection is traditional, sport, and mixed.

**SKIING** **Soldier Hollow** (435-654-2002; www.soldierhollow.com), off UT 133, 2 miles southwest of Midway. Soldier Hollow, at the southern end of **Wasatch Mountain State Park** (see *To See and Do*), is first and foremost a Nordic skiing facility. This area was home to the 2002 Winter Olympic Nordic skiing competitions and is regularly a host of national ski and biathlon competitions. Thirty-one kilometers of trails are regularly groomed for skate and classic skiing. These plentiful, meandering loops offer a wide range of difficulty. Soldier Hollow offers classic and skate rentals, as well as lessons at the Rossignol Demo Center. $17 for adults, $15 for ages 65 and older, $9 for children ages 7–17, free for ages 6 and under.

In addition to its top-notch skiing facilities, Soldier Hollow also offers snowshoeing and a tubing hill, and is the host of sheepdog competitions and powwows. The **International Sheepdog Championships** (www.soldierhollowclassic.com) has been at Soldier Hollow for four years. This event takes place over Labor Day weekend, is filled with auxiliary events, and attracts more than 20,000 people. The **Heber Valley Powwow** (www.soldierhollow.com/powwow) has been coming to Soldier Hollow for three years, takes place at the end of June, and features arts and crafts, food, and dancing.

# ✳ Lodging

Because of the natural beauty of the area and its proximity to Park City, lodging in the Heber Valley is largely characterized by high-end resorts and bed-and-breakfasts. However, a fair number of budget lodging is lined up along Main Street in Heber, if you don't mind basic accommodations.

**Blue Boar Inn & Restaurant** (435-654-1400 or 888-650-1400; www.the blueboarinn.com), 1235 Warm Springs Rd., Midway. This inn is a Bavarian-style chateau in Midway that has an award-winning restaurant (Utah's Best-in-State for European-style restaurants) and many best-of awards to its own credit. Inspired by its Alp-like surroundings, this inn is quite fine and truly resembles a historic chateau. To give you an idea of the level of service, the inn gives helicopter picnics. $180 and up.

**Holiday Inn Express** (435-654-9990 or 877-863-4780; www.ihchotelsgroup .com), 1268 South Main St., Heber City. This is a basic, yet reliable hotel in the Heber Valley for those seeking cleanliness and basic quality without spending an arm and a leg. $55 and up.

**The Homestead Resort** (888-327-7220; www.homesteadresort.com), 700 Homestead Dr., Midway. This resort is a huge campus, tucked away from the crowds of Park City and isolated on its own Heber Valley property. Because of its spacious grounds and numerous activities, this is a self-sufficient retreat that really allows guests to escape. At this resort alone is horseback riding, an 18-hole golf course, cross-country skiing, mountain biking, hiking, a spa, and the Homestead Crater (a natural 55-foot-deep beehive-shaped cavern filled with warm water). Lodging options vary from the historic early-20th-century Utah Hotel to private guest condominiums and houses. $160–$700.

**Lodge at Stillwater** (435-940-3800; www.lodgeatstillwater.com), 1364 West Stillwater Dr., Heber City. This is the area's most deluxe lodging outside of the immediate Park City area. Rooms range from studio to three-bedroom suites. On-site outdoor gear shop, as well as a lounge. Beautiful campus; building reminiscent of grand Austrian hunting lodges.

**Johnson Mill Bed & Breakfast** (435-654-4466 or 888-272-0030; www .johnsonmill.com), 100 Johnson Mill Rd., Midway. This bed-and-breakfast is located inside an 1893 mill on the banks of the Provo River. Guests enjoy jogging and walking on the property trails in the summer, and Nordic skiing by winter, as well as a 5-acre lake. Despite the age of the building, the interior is spacious, bright, and renovated to complement its history, yet be uncluttered. $200 and up.

**Rodeway Inn Bear Mountain Lodge** (435-654-2150; www.rodeway inn.com), 425 South Main St., Heber City. This smaller hotel is located right in the center of Heber City and offers basic amenities as well as friendly service for much lower cost than some of the other options. $60 and up.

# ✳ Where to Eat

**Blue Boar Inn & Restaurant** (435-654-1400 or 888-650-1400; www.the blueboarinn.com), 1235 Warm Springs Rd., Midway. Open daily for breakfast, lunch, and dinner. This inn and restaurant, as described in the *Lodging* section above, has won several awards for its chef and menu, and is one of the better fine-dining options in the Heber Valley—and in the state, for that matter. This restaurant features contemporary and traditional dishes alike, drawing from American and European styles, and utilizes the freshest ingredients, many of which are vegetables and herbs from the gardens on the Blue Boar's grounds. Serves a five-course brunch on Sunday. Entrées $30 and up.

**Snake Creek Grill** (435-654-2133; www.snakecreekgrill.com), 650 West 100 South, Heber City. Open for dinner Wednesday–Sunday. This restaurant focuses on contemporary American cuisine—sometimes with a Southwest or even Asian influence, but always showcasing whole foods and homemade sauces. The ingredients are fresh, and the plates creative. Though the quality is high, there is no snobbery. The atmosphere is cozy and comfortable, and service is competent but relaxed. Entrées $15–$25.

**The Spicy Lady** (435-654-4288; www.spicylady.net), 129 North Main St., Heber City. Open Tuesday–Sunday for lunch and dinner, also for brunch on Saturday and Sunday. Located in an old-time Western-style building (Heber's oldest remaining building), the Spicy Lady serves a menu with a focus on peasant dishes. These use simple combinations and old recipes to allow the ingredients to speak for themselves. Beef tenderloin, boiled sausages, lamb shank, pork medallions, and chicken Florentine are some of the classic dishes, though kangaroo meat is on the menu also.

**Spin Café** (435-654-0251; www.spin cafe.net), 220 North Main St., Heber City. Open daily for lunch and dinner. Spin has a range of offerings, from seafood to spare ribs, steak, and chicken, to Alfredo, specialty salads, pulled pork sandwiches, and burgers. Guests enjoy meals in a clean, colorful, and modern space. Homemade gelato and a full bar add to the list of perks. A rotating list of lunch specials applies every day of the week. Sunday brunch is big here.

# Far Northern Utah

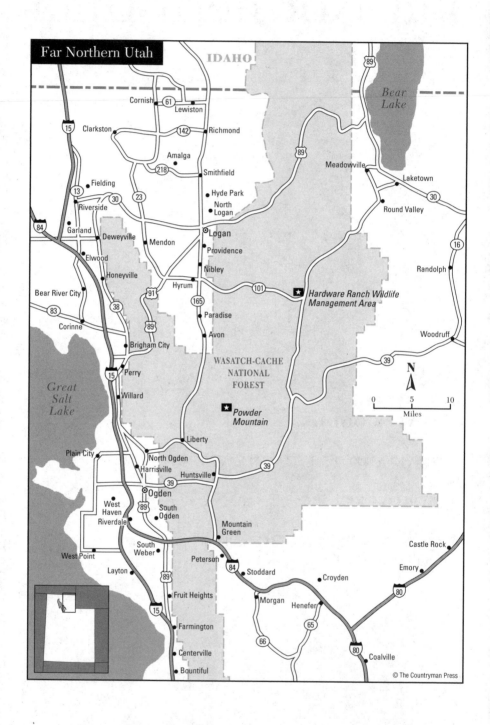

Far Northern Utah

IDAHO

Bear Lake

Cornish  61
Lewiston
15  Clarkston  142  Richmond
Amalga
89
218  Smithfield  Meadowville
13  Fielding  Hyde Park  Laketown
30  23  North  30
Riverside  Logan  Round Valley
84  Garland  Logan
Deweyville  Mendon  16
Elwood  Providence
Honeyville  Nibley  Randolph
Bear River City  Hyrum  101
83  91  165  Hardware Ranch Wildlife
Corinne  38  Management Area
Paradise
Brigham City  Avon  Woodruff
89
Great  Perry  WASATCH-CACHE  39
Salt  15  NATIONAL
Lake  Willard  FOREST  N
0  5  10
Powder  Miles
Mountain
Liberty
Plain City  North Ogden  39
Harrisville  Huntsville
39
West  Ogden  Castle Rock
Haven  89  South
Riverdale  Ogden  Emory
West Point  Mountain
Green  80
South
Weber  Peterson  84  Stoddard
Layton  89  Croyden
Fruit Heights  Morgan  Henefer
15  65
Farmington  66  80
Centerville  Coalville
Bountiful
© The Countryman Press

# NORTHERN UTAH IN BRIEF

Most people think of Utah and imagine only red rock arches, huge ski areas, and Salt Lake City. Utah's oft-overlooked northern region, with its forested mountains, high plains, ranches, and cool canyons, is actually more reminiscent of its neighbor states, Idaho and Wyoming, than its license-plate Utah sister regions like the Salt Lake region, Moab, or St. George. Traveling north into Utah's squat panhandle, the red rocks of the south completely disappear, and the population of the Wasatch Front dwindles, leaving these valleys and mountains covered in grasses and trees, and just barely dotted by small, historic townships.

The townships in the north represent a large physical and cultural variety. Tremonton and Ogden have risen from a different background than the historically Mormon settlements to the south; Logan and the Cache Valley were some of the original Latter-day Saint settlements after Salt Lake City. Ogden and Tremonton, which sprang up along the lines of the First Transcontinental Railroad in the late 19th century, have their roots in rail and related industries. Brigham City and Logan have a history very much rooted in the Mormon church. Today these towns have a very different feel, having originated out of vastly different origins.

Similar to the Salt Lake City region, the landscape in northern Utah is marked by immense vertical relief and dramatic mountains. The Bear River Mountains rise severely from the Great Basin plains and dominate the area's eastern skyline. These mountains are cleft by deep limestone canyons and forested with evergreen trees and aspen groves. Though similar in geology to the mountains and canyons around the Salt Lake City area, they have a distinctly more remote feel, yet have equally abundant recreational resources. Tucked within these mountains is the town of Logan. It is an independent community marked by Utah State University and its excellent ecology programs, a famous local marathon, and the beautiful wilderness of the Cache Valley.

Bear Lake, in the far northeastern corner of the state, is a natural, freshwater lake second in size only to Utah Lake. Set safely to the north of, and away from, the Wasatch Front millions, it offers biking, boating, fishing, and camping opportunities of great beauty in relative seclusion.

## ✳ Weather

As with the rest of Utah, the weather in this region cannot be described without geographical qualifications. However, a safe generalization would describe Ogden as very similar to Salt Lake City, and the valleys of northern Utah as roughly

5 degrees cooler than Salt Lake throughout the year. During the hottest month of the year, July, northernmost Utah stays relatively temperate, seeing average highs around 87°F. This, compared with Salt Lake and Utah valleys, whose average highs extend into the mid-90s, while southern Utah sweats it out in three-digit temperatures. Winter sets in solidly in northern Utah, with the coldest month, January, bringing daytime highs to just over 32°F. Unlike Salt Lake City, the valleys here are generally covered with a blanket of snow throughout the winter. As with anywhere else, valleys will be warmer and drier than canyons and mountains.

This region, as with the rest of Utah, receives very little precipitation, particularly during the summer months. Annually, northern Utah sees only around 17 to 20 inches of precipitation, with less than an inch falling during each of the summer months.

## ✳ Special Events

*Year-round:* Each month the **First Friday Art Stroll** begins at the Eccles Community Art Center (801-392-6935; www.ogden4arts.org), 2580 Jefferson Ave., Ogden. This stroll tours Ogden's galleries, many of which are located in renovated historic downtown buildings, an up-and-coming district.

Many rodeos take place throughout the warmer months with high frequency in northern Utah, often in conjunction with state fairs and other summer celebrations.

*Mid-January:* Ogden celebrates its sister city, Hof, with the **Hof Winterfest German Festival** (www.goldenspike

---

### OUTFITTER SERVICES

**Beaver Creek Lodge** (800-946-4485; www.beavercreeklodge.com), Logan Canyon. This is an all-in-one lodging and adventure establishment (as listed in the *Lodging* section of the "Logan and the Cache Valley" chapter). Located among some of the area's best outdoor opportunities, this lodge gives guided snowmobile tours by winter and horseback outings by summer.

**Red Rock Ranch and Outfitters** (801-745-6393 or 866-826-7625; www.redrock ranch-and-outfitters.com), 13555 East Hwy. 39, Huntsville. This ranch and outfitter service is one of northern Utah's largest all-purpose outfitters. Located about 20 miles east of Ogden and 8 miles east of Huntsville, this 1850 ranch is a center for music, ranch culture, hayrides, sleigh rides, chuckwagon dinners, and cowboy poetry. The outfitter side of Red Rock offers horseback riding and pack trips, snowmobile rentals, and guided fishing trips.

**Rocky Mountain Outfitters** (435-654-1655; www.rockymtnoutfitters.com), as listed in the *Northern Wasatch in Brief* chapter, provide statewide outfitter services in a huge number of outdoor activities.

**Wild Country Outfitters** (801-751-6551; www.wildcountryoutfitters.com), 6531 South Bybee Dr., Ogden. Wild Country offers guided hiking, mountain biking, fly-fishing, and hunting trips.

eventscenter.com), marked by German cuisine, Hof musicians, dancing, and more.

**Sundance Film Festival** is centered in Park City, but quite a few films are screened at the **Peery's Egyptian Theater** (www.peerysegyptiantheater .com), 2415 Washington Blvd., Ogden.

*February:* **Banff Film Festival** (www .banffcentre.ca) visits Ogden each year with its traveling film festival.

*Easter:* ♦ **Easter Weekend Rendezvous** (www1.co.weber.ut.us) comes to Fort Buenaventura (801-399-8099), 2450 A Ave., Ogden. This mountain-man, fur-trapping festival fills the park with canvas tents, historical reenactments, and contests involving canoes, Dutch ovens, black powder guns, children's games, and more.

*Early April:* **Snowbasin Meltdown Race** (www.snowbasin.com), a triathlon of skiing/snowboarding, cycling, and kayaking.

**Snowmobile Hill Climbs** (435-946-3503; www.bearlake.com). These are held at Bear Mountain around the first weekend of this month. During this event, snowmobile drivers try to achieve the "high line" on an incredibly steep hill. Virtually every run ends with a wreck of some sort. Perhaps the greatest spectacle to be seen here are the oversized men who actually *catch* these snowmobiles as they tumble down the slope.

*Early May:* **Annual Bear Lake Classic** (800-756-0795). This 104- and 52- mile bike race circumnavigates the lake. The longer leg is designated for professionals; the shorter is for amateurs.

*Fifth of May:* **Cinco de Mayo** (Ogden City: www.ocae.org) does not go unnoticed in Ogden, a city rich with Mexican American residents. To participate, go to the **Municipal Gardens** (25th

St. and Washington Blvd.) on this date for traditional festivities, or visit Ogden City's Web site for details particular to each year.

*10th of May:* **Last Spike Ceremony** takes place on the 10th day of this month, commemorating the 1869 completion of North America's First Transcontinental Railroad at the Golden Spike National Historic Site (www .nps.gov/gosp) near Tremonton.

*Mid-May:* **Bear River Bird Refuge Festival** (www.brighamcity.utah.gov), Bear River Migratory Bird Refuge, Brigham City. Located aside the northeast apex of the Great Salt Lake, and adjacent to one of the state's most interesting and vital bird habitats, this is one of the nation's most important inland bird refuges. During the festival, exhibits and demonstrations span from the interests of naturalists, to kids, to bird hunters.

**Cache Valley Farmers' Market,** held in Logan at 150 South 100 East, usually begins during the middle of this month and lasts through October, weather permitting.

**Zion's Bank Ogden Marathon** (801-399-1773; www.ogdenmarathon.com). May's moderate temperatures make it a hospitable month for this event, which is notorious for its spectacular canyon scenery enjoyed by way of closed roads.

*June:* **Logan Art and Music Festivals** (www.tourcachevalley.com or www.loganutah.org). Logan's summer months are filled with music, thanks to local chamber music, opera, and ballet groups, as well as the presence of Utah State University. Summer attractions include **Summerfest Art and Jazz Festival** (800-882-4433); the **Summer Art Faire** (435-755-5598), 50 North Main St., on the greens at the LDS Tabernacle, which showcases the works of local artists and features traditional

Dutch oven cooking; **Music in the Parks;** and the **Utah Festival Opera** (beginning in early July).

*End of June:* **Ogden Arts Festival** (www.ogdenartsfestival.com), Ogden's Union Station and 25th St. This festival features the works of local artists. The streets and squares fill with stages, food vendors, and artist booths.

*End of June and through August:* **Snowbasin Free Summer Concert Series** (801-620-1000 or 888-437-5488; www.snowbasin.com) begins toward the end of this month and takes place on Sunday. Music is accompanied by a barbecue.

*End of June:* **Wasatch Back Relay** (operated by Ragnar Relays, 801-295-5536 or 877-837-3529; www.ragnar relay.com). This is a 24-hour, 170-mile, 12-person relay race that takes place in the middle of the month in the vast Wasatch Mountains. The race begins in Logan and finishes in Park City after traversing grueling mountain terrain.

**Multiple Sclerosis 150 Bike Tour** (801-493-0113 or 800-527-8116; www .fightsmsutah.org). The MS 150 is a major fund-raiser and the largest cycling event in Utah. This event is based out of Logan.

*July:* **Utah Festival Opera Company** (435-750-0300; www.ufoc.org). This is held in Logan each summer in the restored neo-classical **Ellen Eccles Theater** (43 South Main St.). The season lasts only a month but includes roughly five separate productions and is enriched by backstage talks, seminars, and the like.

*Fourth of July:* **Logan Cache Valley Cruise-In Car Show** (Logan/Cache County Fairgrounds; 435-563-3406; www.cachevalleycruisein.com). This show is a three-day event with more than 1,000 automobiles and 30,000 spectators.

*July 24th:* ✑ **Pioneer Days** is a festival that commemorates the first Utah arrival of Brigham Young and the Mormon pioneers on July 24, 1847. The festivities, unique to Mormon settlements, are celebrated with fervor and include parades, concerts, fireworks, rodeos, fairs, and the like. In case you were wondering what happened to the typical Independence Day hoopla, this holiday all but replaces the Fourth of July in Utah, especially in smaller, mostly LDS towns.

*Early August:* ✑ **Garden City Raspberry Days** (435-946-2901; www .gardencityut.us) takes place in its namesake town around the first weekend of August, on the western shore of Bear Lake. These red berries are integrated into a creative array of foods. This festival is married to a fair, running race, rodeo, and other small-town festivities.

**Cache County Fair & Great American West PRCA Rodeo** (435-755-1460; www.cachecounty.org/fair). Held in Logan, this features some of the best rodeo in the country.

*Mid-August:* **Railroader's Festival** (435-471-2209) is held in Brigham City every August, illustrating one of Utah's lesser-known historic chapters through reenactments, community historic handcart races, and more.

**Annual Ogden Valley Balloon Festival** (800-413-8312; www.ogdenvalley balloonfestival.com). This fills the Ogden Valley sky with a spectacular amount of color as scores of hot-air balloons take flight and engage in aeronautical competitions and displays. The event takes place between Eden and Huntsville, and also features dozens of bands and an classic automobile show.

**Xterra Mountain Championships** (www.xterraplanet.com). Ogden was named the proud home to this national event in 2006. This brings to Utah some of the world's best off-road triathletes, as well as clinics, parties, film screenings, and concerts.

*Early September:* **Brigham City Annual Peach Days** (435-723-3931; www.bcareachamber.com). This harvest festival attracts 75,000 spectators and includes a parade, street fair, and running race.

**LOTOJA** (801-546-0090; www.lotoja classic.com). Short for "Logan-to-Jackson," this takes riders, either solo or as a team, across three states and over 203 miles. This is North America's longest single-day cycling event.

*Mid-September:* **Ogden Valley Triathlon and Taste of Ogden** (801-791-8801; www.ovba.org/triathlon). The triathlon is one of Utah's largest such events and takes place during the middle of the month. After the triathlon, head to the **Taste of Ogden,** usually held on the same day as, and in conjunction with, the triathlon. Be sure to make reservations.

*Third Saturday of September:* **Top of Utah Marathon** (435-797-2638; www .topofutahmarathon.com). This follows a certified course that gently descends through the Blacksmith Fork Canyon into the Cache Valley and is notoriously scenic. Because it is a fast course, many people use this race to qualify

for the Boston Marathon.

*End of September:* **Fall Harvest Festival & Bear River Heritage Fair** (435-245-6050 or 800-225- 3378; www .awhc.org). This Logan fair is another harvest festival with local wares for sale, as well as artisan bread and cheese-making demonstrations, and performances by local musicians.

**Mountains to Metro** (801-399-1773; www.goalfoundation.com). This is yet another Ogden area athletic bonanza in which contestants can mountain bike, trail run, kayak, or road bike. A cycling criterium is also held during this time. This is followed by extreme-ski film screenings and photography contests. It is during this month that officials release a high volume of water into the Weber River from the Pineview Reservoir upstream, creating a springlike deluge that rushes through the **Ogden Kayak Rodeo Park** (www.ogdencvb.org) in town, creating the prefect setting for a late-season kayak competition venue.

*Last Week of December:* **Railroad Film Festival & Winter Steam Demonstration** (www.nps.gov/gosp). This takes place at the Golden Spike National Historic Site and is one of the largest such festivals in the country.

# GREATER OGDEN

Ⅰf you think Utah is tender and mild, Ogden will come as surprise historically and culturally. Railways, not religion, brought the people to this town, and it shows. Historically Ogden has been the roughest city in Utah. While this is still true of much of the city, it has made great efforts to improve its track record. In recent times, it has advertised itself as one of the greatest outdoor cities in the country, and this is rapidly becoming a reality today.

Seated in Weber County, this town has a distinct flavor whose origin is quite set apart from the Mormon church and its family values. Despite its proximity to Salt Lake City, Ogden's story was dominated by the rail industry surrounding the First Transcontinental Railroad from its onset. During its early days, it was overrun by Old West outlaws, bordellos, and sidearms. Even as recently as 50 years ago, Ogden was considered one of the roughest cowboy towns in the West. Ogden has also always been one of Utah's most ethnically diverse towns. The railroad brought the town its population and industry during the 19th century and was manned largely by a diverse immigrant population, particularly with those of Chinese and Irish heritage.

In the early 19th century, the Ogden Valley was Mexican land coveted by the Hudson Bay trapping company. The region was a rich trapping grounds and was highly trafficked. Utah's first permanent settlement was Fort Buenaventura, in present-day Ogden at the confluence of the Weber and Ogden rivers., founded by mountain man and trapper Miles Goodyear. He reached the area by way of the Oregon Trail in 1845, four years before the Mormons would arrive in Salt Lake City. This fort, which would grow into a city, was a center for trappers, traders, and mountain men.

In 1848, Goodyear sold the rights to the fort and land to the Mormon church for $1,950. For almost 20 years—the only time during its history—Ogden would be strongly influenced by the church. The town served as an agricultural bread-basket for Utah's new LDS settlements until 1869. At this time, the Transcontinental Railroad, which had sprinted to a meeting point from California and Iowa in just seven years, came through Utah through Echo Canyon and the Ogden Valley. This new development would permanently take the town out of the church's hands.

Ogden diverged quickly and drastically from the path of its nearby sister cities. With intimate connections to the railway, it inherited power, industry, and ties to the outside world. The completion of the railroad had several implications. Work-

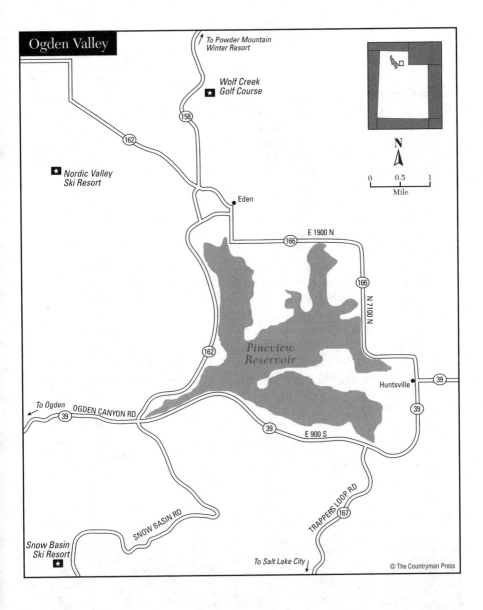

ers who had been employed by this gigantic construction project were suddenly at the end of their tenure; most were immigrants, and few could possibly return home. Secondly, this railroad was, at that time, the ultimate state-of-the-art transportation. This allowed many to move out to the Utah countryside. Many hands came to stake claims here, taking advantage of the infrastructure already created by Mormon occupation. Many more came to pick ore from the hills, with California's gold of '49 virtually cashed out. Still more came for the very reason that the Mormons came: The expansive and harsh Rocky Mountain West afforded outlaws and hermits seclusion unmatched by any other region in the United States.

The sum total was an eclectic new "heathen" town in Utah, forsaken by the LDS church after years of political battles. In 1889 Ogden elected Utah's first non-Mormon mayor. Despite the church's cold shoulder, Ogden flourished economically. At the intersection of the Transcontinental Railroad, and newer north–south line, its depot serviced nine rail companies. It was during this time that Ogden began to earn its reputation as a dangerous and tough town. Al Capone was quoted as saying that the town was too dangerous for his liking.

This industry boom continued until the 1930s when, as in the rest of the country, the bubble burst under the weight of the Great Depression. However, World War II returned prosperity and importance to the region with a need for its metal exports and the founding of the Hill Air Base in 1938. It was also during this time that Ogden, like Salt Lake City, was used as the site of a prisoner of war camp. During the Cold War, many other national and regional organizations relocated headquarters to this area, considering it at once an accessible and safe town, under the radar.

Though Ogden was served well by the railroad, the iron horse could not remain paramount forever. During the middle of the 20th century Ogden would suffer a downturn in prosperity as automobile, and later air, transport eclipsed the railways. Passenger trains had once run through the town at a rate of almost 120 per day, and by the 1960s came through only a few times each week. During this time, the town's economy sank into recession, and crime levels rose.

However, Ogden has adjusted to the modern economy, and today, like Salt Lake City, is on a major upswing. Affordable real estate, prime mountain access, and accessibility are Ogden's sources of new life. Strategic endorsements have made Ogden an attractive place for people, business headquarters, and national athletic competitions to relocate. The ski industry, Weber State University, and the McKay Dee Hospital Center are among the largest employer groups, as well as attractions to the region. Companies like Solomon and Atomic Skis, and international sporting competitions like the Xterra Mountain Games, have already relocated their U.S.

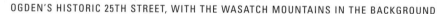

OGDEN'S HISTORIC 25TH STREET, WITH THE WASATCH MOUNTAINS IN THE BACKGROUND

headquarters and national championship competitions to the area. Ushering them in are huge mountains, low crowding, the Weber River running directly through town, low costs, and remarkable accessibility paired with seclusion.

Ogden continues to tame its streets and accelerate its modern appeal. It has taken great measures to up its outdoors scene, artistic vibe, and fine-dining options. It is quickly becoming a less crowded, less discovered, and much more affordable substitute for Salt Lake City or Park City. The city still has a long way to go, but these changes, particularly around the Historic 25th Street district, have laid the foundations for a great future.

GUIDANCE **Ogden City** (www.ogdencity.com). The City of Ogden is its own biggest advocate and best friend. All of the positive changes taking place across the town have been very deliberately orchestrated by the city's leaders. Check the Web site for current events and social projects.

**Ogden/Weber Chamber of Commerce** (801-621-8300 or 866-990-1299; www .echamber.cc2484). This is another online resource that lists local businesses and events.

**Ogden Utah Convention and Visitors Bureau** (866-867-8824; www.ogdencvb .org), 2501 Wall Ave., Suite 201, Ogden. Stop by the office to speak with staff or obtain area brochures, maps, and literature.

**Brigham City Area Chamber of Commerce** (435-723-3931; www.bcarea chamber.com). This organization focuses on the southern end of the area and highlights events and businesses that might be overlooked by the larger city of Ogden.

GETTING THERE *By car:* If driving to Ogden, you will find that it is in a very interstate-rich area. It is immediately adjacent to I-15, which runs north–south through Montana, Idaho, Utah, Nevada, and California. I-80 runs east–west through Utah just 35 miles south of Ogden and intersects with I-15 in Salt Lake City. I-84 originates at I-15 in the southern Ogden area and heads southeast through the Wasatch, eventually joining I-80 before heading into Wyoming.

*By air:* **Salt Lake International Airport (SLC)** (801-575-2400 or 800-595-2442; www.slcairport.com), just 40 miles southwest of downtown Ogden by way of I-15 and I-80. Most arriving by plane will fly into Salt Lake City, as it is a major hub in the western United States.

**Ogden-Hinckley Airport (OGD)** (801-622-5600), 3909 Airport Rd., just west of I-15 exit 340. Ogden does have a small municipal airport, though arriving and departing from here is significantly more expensive and tedious.

*By bus:* **Greyhound Bus Lines** (800-231-2222; www.greyhound.com), 2393 Wall Ave., Ogden. Greyhound has a station in Ogden, as well as other Utah cities such as Salt Lake City, Moab, Provo, St. George, and Green River.

*By train:* **Amtrak** (800-872-7245; www.amtrak.com). This company crosses Utah daily with stops in St. George, Provo, Salt Lake City, and Green River, with direct lines to Los Angeles, San Diego, San Francisco, Denver, Portland, Seattle, and Vancouver. The nearest station to Ogden is in Salt Lake City (340 South 600 West), where Greyhound also has a station.

**Utah Transit Authority (UTA)** (888-743-3882; www.rideuta.com) operates a new commuter train. Called the **Frontrunner,** this shuttles between Salt Lake City and Ogden.

OGDEN'S CITY MUNICIPAL BUILDING LOCATED AT THE INTERSECTION OF WASHINGTON BOULEVARD AND HISTORIC 25TH STREET, DIRECTLY WEST OF HOTEL BEN LOMOND

**GETTING AROUND** *By mass transit:* **Utah Transit Authority (UTA)** (888-743-3882; www.rideuta.com). This is an ever-growing public transportation company that runs bus routes primarily focused in and around the downtown area. Call for specific information, or look online in the Weber County section for route maps and scheduling information.

*By car:* For information navigating the Utah's famous and feared **grid system,** see *Driving and the Grid System* in the "What's Where in Utah" chapter at the beginning of this guidebook.

*By shuttle:* **USS Ogden Express** (801-393-5438 or 866-746-5438; www.ogden express.com). This bus company's primary offerings are airport and ski-resort shuttles. They also offer chartered tours; online reservations are available.

**Ogden Tourist Ski Shuttle** (operated by USS Ogden Express) caters to the area's booming ski industry. Shuttles orginate at several hotels around the city and terminate at Wolf Mountain, Powder Mountain, and Snowbasin Resort. Reservations should be made the night before the desired service, either by contacting the hotel front desk or USS Ogden Express. Participating hotels are the Best Western High Country Inn (801-394-9474), Comfort Inn & Suites (801-544-5577), Holiday Inn Express (801-392-5000), Marriott Ogden Hotel (801-627-1190), Hampton Inn & Suites (801-394-9400), and the Ben Lomond Historic Suites Hotel (877-627-1900).

**MEDICAL EMERGENCY Intermountain North Ogden Clinic** (801-786-7500; www.intermountainhealthcare.org), 2400 North Washington Blvd., North Ogden. This is the region's northernmost medical facility and is prepared to handle most minor medical concerns.

**McKay-Dee Medical Center** (801-387-2800; www.intermountainhealthcare.org), 4401 Harrison Blvd., Ogden. This hospital is located on the eastern end of South Ogden, very near the Wasatch slopes.

**Ogden Regional Medical Center** (801-479-2111; www.ogdenregional.com), 5475 South 500 East, Ogden. This hospital is located just southeast of the junction of I-15 and I-84, and just north of I-84 exit 85.

**Brigham City Community Hospital** (435-734-9471; www.brighamcityhospital .com), 950 South Medical Dr., Brigham City. This hospital, located at the southern end of this conglomerate, is located east of I-15 exit 362 and just north of US 91.

**Intermountain South Ogden Clinic** (801-387-6200; www.intermountainhealth care.org), 975 East Chambers St., South Ogden. This clinic is ideal for people in the southern end of the city needing attention without an appointment, but not requiring an emergency room.

# ✳ To See and Do

🦶 **Red Rock Ranch and Outfitters** (801-745-6393 or 866-826-7625; www.red rockranch-and-outfitters.com), 13555 East Hwy. 39, Huntsville. This ranch is an active, farm-life center just 20 minutes east of Ogden in the Upper Ogden Canyon. Activities include sleigh rides, a petting farm, concerts, Dutch-oven dinners, and much more.

**The Salomon Center** (801-399-4653; www.salomoncenter.com), 2261 Kiesel Ave., Ogden. Built in 2007, this is a new addition to Ogden that at once symbolizes and promotes Ogden's emergence as one of America's best outdoors towns. Within this megalocolypse is indoor skydiving; a rock climbing wall; wave pool for surfing, wakeboarding, and boogie boarding; a Gold's Gym; a fun center with bowling, pool, bumper cars, mini golf, and an arcade; as well as a pizza joint and Mexican restaurant.

**MUSEUMS Eccles Community Art Center** (801-392-6935; www.ogden4arts .org), 2580 Jefferson Ave., Ogden. This is Ogden's major fine-arts hub and is starting point for the art strolls, which take place on the first Friday of each month. In addition to art exhibits, this center holds classes, local competitions, and sculpture gardens. Free admission.

🦶 **George S. Eccles Dinosaur Park** (801-393-3466; www.dinosaurpark.org), 1544 East Park Blvd, Ogden. Open 10–8 Monday–Saturday, noon–6 Sunday during summer; slightly restricted hours during the winter season. Drawing from Utah's wealth of fossil beds and paleontology, this museum is a child's paradise, with more than 100 assembled, true-to-size sculptures, including a tyrannosaurus rex. Some replicas are even animated by robotics. Also at the museum are hands-on exhibits and a working paleontology lab, whose fossils come from nearby digs. $6 for adults, $5 for students and for seniors ages 62 and older, $4 for children ages 2–12, free for infants 1 and under.

OGDEN ARTS COUNCIL IS LOCATED AT THE DOWNTOWN INTERSECTION OF WASHINGTON BOULEVARD AND HISTORIC 25TH STREET.

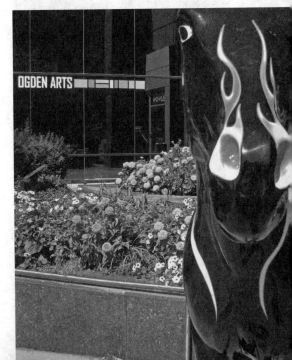

**Hill Aerospace Museum** (801-777-6868; www.hill.af.mil), 7961 Wardleigh Rd., Building 1955, Hill Air Force Base. Open daily 9–5; closed holidays. This museum covers 5 acres of the Hill Air Force Base and has more than 80 aircraft, aerospace vehicles, and missiles, as well as other illustrative military equipment and memorabilia on display. Free admission; donations encouraged.

**Ogden Union Station** (801-393-9886; www.theunionstation.org), 2501 Wall Ave., Ogden. Open Monday–Saturday 10–5, closed Sunday and holidays. The Ogden Union Station is a museum, gallery, and historic center whose exhibits appeal to the full range of ages. The Station has five museums and two art galleries. The **Utah State Railroad Museum** depicts the history and scenery of the First Transcontinental Railroad of the 19th century and includes several model trains. The **Eccles Rail Center** showcases historic full-sized locomotives and rail cars, dating from steam engines to the 2002 Salt Lake City Olympic Cauldron Car. The **John M. Browning Firearms Museum** features original designs and actual guns crafted by Ogden local John Browning—the internationally famous creator of many military and sporting guns. A collection of antique cars illustrating automobile history can be found at the **Browning-Kimball Classic Car Museum.** The **Natural History Museum** surveys Utah's paleontological, geological, and geographical past with fossil, mineral, and floral displays. Two art galleries are the **Gallery at the Station** and **Myra Powell Gallery** (neither of which charge admission). $5 for adults, $3 for children ages 2–12 and seniors 65 and up, $12 family (two adults and up to four children).

OGDEN'S UNION STATION, ON THE WESTERN END OF HISTORIC 25TH STREET, NOW HOUSES THE JOHN M. BROWNING FIREARMS MUSEUM, UTAH STATE RAILROAD MUSEUM/ECCLES RAIL CENTER, THE NATURAL HISTORY MUSEUM, BROWNING-KIMBALL CAR MUSEUM, GALLERIES, SHOPS, AND THE UNION GRILL RESTAURANT.

✂ **Treehouse Children's Museum** (801-394-9663; www.treehousemuseum .org), 347 22nd St., Ogden. Open 10–4 Monday, 10–6 Tuesday–Thursday, 10–8:30 Friday; closed Sunday and holidays. Children must be accompanied by a chaperone at least 16 years old, and (oddly) adults must be accompanied by a child. This youth-focused museum covers a wide range of interests, from geography to dinosaurs, music, politics, and domestic activity. All exhibits have an easy-to-digest, colorful presentation that gives kids some insight into the world's goings-on. $3 for adults, $5 for children ages 5–15, free for ages 4 and under.

**GARDENS AND PARKS Brigham City** (801-734-6600; www.brigham city.utah.gov) has fewer parks than Ogden, but the parks do cover a variety of interests. **Constitution Park** (450 East 700 South) is one of the city's main parks, with horseshoe pits, a bowery, soccer fields, volleyball courts, a football field, and a skate park. Other major parks are **John Adams Park** (600 East 100 North), with disc golf course and tennis courts, and **Rees Pioneer Park** (800 West Forest St.).

**Ogden City** (801-629-8284; www.ogdencity.com/parks.main.html) alone has nearly 40 parks, and Brigham City (435-734-6600; www.brighamcity.utah.gov) has another nine. Ogden is home to the area's biggest city parks with the most offerings.

**Municipal Gardens** (25th St. and Grant Ave.) is one of Ogden's main events venues, hosting concerts, plays, farmers' markets, and film screenings. The **MTC Learning Park** (1750 Monroe Blvd.), with botanical gardens and visitors center, abuts to the **Big D Sports Park** (1396 Park Blvd.), a spacious park with grounds for baseball, volleyball, soccer, basketball, fishing, and picnics, as well as a regionally famous man-made ice climbing tower. Another, **Lorin Farr Park,** has a public, Olympic-sized swimming pool (complete with toboggan-style water slide) and skateboard park.

**Ogden Nature Center** (801-621-7595; www.ogdennaturecenter.org), 966 West 12th St., Ogden. Open Monday–Friday 9–5, Saturday 9–4, closed Sunday. Guests can explore different ecosystems and wildlife species by way of pond walkways, forest trails, treehouses, picnic grounds, and observation towers among diverse fauna, as well as indoor exhibits at the visitors and education centers. On the campus is also a wild-bird rehabilitation center and bird habitat. $3 for adults, $1.25 for children ages 2–12, free for infants.

**Ogden River Parkway** (www.weberpathways.org), access points at the intersection of 18th St. and Washington Blvd.; 1700 Monroe Blvd.; at the eastern ends of Park Blvd. and Valley Dr. This 3.4-mile-long paved trail follows the Ogden River through town, past gardens, picnic areas, soccer fields, Ogden's Dinosaur Park, a swimming pool, and skateboard park.

**LANDMARKS Ben Lomond Hotel** (801-627-1900), 2510 Washington Blvd., Ogden. The Ben Lomond Hotel was completed in 1927, in the era when hotels were constructed on a grand scale with boutique style. This hotel is still one of Ogden's finest.

**Brigham City Historic Depot** (435-723-2989), 833 West Forest St., Brigham City. Brigham City's Depot was built in 1906 and is still located immediately near tracks still in use by Amtrak today. Inside and out the building is preserved. When this depot was in operation, it had a "ladies waiting room" in which no spitting, vulgarity, or smoking was allowed. Today there is a gift shop and a very small selection of historical items on display. Hours are irregular, as the depot is operated by a volunteer staff; call ahead.

OGDEN 25TH STREET FOUNTAINS, WEST OF THE 25TH STREET AND WASHINGTON BOULEVARD JUNCTION

**Eccles Building** (801-394-9400), 2401 Washington Blvd., Ogden. Located in the same district as the Ben Lomond, and built 14 years earlier, this eight-story art deco structure is now likely one of the world's most historic and stately **Hampton Inn & Suites.**

**Fort Buenaventura** (801-399-8099), 2450 A Ave., Ogden. This fort was built in the prerailroad, pre-Mormon days when trappers, traders, mountain men, and Native Americans were first becoming acquainted in the Rocky Mountain West. Though the original structures no longer remain, exact replicas stand in their place.

**Huntsville Trappist Monastery** (801-745-3784; www.holytrinityabbey.org), at the Abbey of Our Lady of the Holy Trinity, 1250 South 9500 East, Huntsville. This is one of the Intermountain West's earliest Catholic establishments of its kind. It was founded by monks who came to the valley in 1947. Admission is free and open to anyone over 20.

**Miles Goodyear Cabin** (801-393-4460), 2148 Grant Ave., in Tabernacle Square, Ogden. The actual cabin built by Goodyear in 1845, this was the first permanent structure in Utah's first permanent settlement. The cabin was relocated from its original location at Fort Buenaventura. Open during summer only.

**Ogden Tabernacle** (21st St. and Washington Blvd.) was built in 1956 and is open to all; the **Ogden Temple** (350 22nd St.), designed by the same architect as the Provo Temple and opened to select Latter-day Saints in 1972, is closed to the general public. **The Brigham City Tabernacle** (251 South Main St.) is one of Utah's more historical LDS buildings, whose construction dates back to 1890.

**Ogden Union Station** (801-393-9886; www.theunionstation.org), 2501 Wall Ave., Ogden. Discussed earlier in the *Museums* section of this chapter, this is one of Ogden's most alive historic landmarks on the western end of Historic 25th Street. Originally a switching station, this is presently occupied by five museums and two art galleries.

**Relief Society Building** (801-393-4460), 2150 Grant Ave., Tabernacle Square, Ogden. Now the home for the **Daughters of Utah Museum,** the Relief Society is a historically important charitable Mormon institution in which women promote education and philanthropy. Originally created in 1842 in Illinois, the society has played a major role in the successful establishment of Utah and the livelihood of needy Mormons. Built in 1902.

**Washington Boulevard and 25th Street Historic District.** Ogden put down its strongest roots in the railroading days of the late 19th century, during which the town's epicenter was at this intersection. Near the switching stations and rail infrastructure, this was the location of the banks, brothels, and bars of Ogden's roaring boom days. As the railways became less important to life of the city, this district faded into decay and despotism. Recently, as with many other urban regrowth situations, artists seized upon this low-rent historic space; the artists were then followed by restaurants, shops, and more. Today this is one of the most lively sections of town.

# ✳ Outdoor Activities

Ogden, an undiscovered town with a premium geographical location, has taken it upon itself in recent years to become one of the country's biggest outdoor recreation hubs—and the plan is working. Major players in the outdoor industry have relocated their headquarters here, and new sporting infrastructure is being built all the time, from the Ogden installment of The Front Climbing Club (out of Salt Lake City) to the new Ice Tower, the Salomon Center, and the Ogden Whitewater Park.

**Ogden Ice Sheet** (801-399-8750; www1.co.weber.ut.us/icesheet), 4390 Harrison Blvd., Ogden. This is an indoor, 20,000-square-foot slab of ice used as the curling venue in the 2002 Olympic Games. This is a community recreation center as well as a venue for hockey, figure skating, and other events, and has a seating capacity of 2,000.

**Ogden Whitewater Park** has been constructed on the Weber River in town and is where kayakers engage in trick boating. There are four man-made holes in which boaters practice maneuvering through eddies and the like. See the *Boating* section of this chapter.

**The Salomon Center** (801-399-4653; www.salomoncenter.com), 2261 Kiesel Ave., Ogden. As listed in at the beginning of the *To See and Do* section of this chapter, this 2007 center has a multitude of outdoors activities inside.

## BIKING

### Bike Rentals & Shops

**Diamond Peak Mountain Sports** (801-745-0101; www.peakstuff.com), 2429 North UT 158, Eden. This sporting-goods store rents hard tail, full suspension, and downhill-specific mountain bikes in the Ogden Valley for half-day and full-day rates.

**Snowbasin's Grizzly Center Rental Shop** (801-620-1120; www.snowbasin.com), Snowbasin Resort. This base area shop rents mountain bikes, which can be used anywhere but that are typically ridden immediately at the mountain (see Snowbasin in *Mountain Biking*, below). Adult and children's bikes are available for half- and full-day rates, and can be rented in conjunction with a lift pass.

A BIKER ON ANTELOPE ISLAND, GREAT SALT LAKE

Craig Bowden

www.utahmountainbiking.com is a comprehensive Web site that maintains information on trails across the state. It has trail descriptions, access information, photographs, and even the occasional video. Most of the information is accurate, but once in a while access directions can be a bit off.

**Bonneville Shoreline Trail** (as described in the *Hiking* section) is an extensive network of trails in the Ogden area that traverse the foothills of the Wasatch along the former shoreline of the ancient Lake Bonneville. Salt Lake City, Ogden, and Provo all have their own installments of this trail system. Because of the relatively low elevation and high sun exposure on this trail, it is best done in the spring and fall; summer is too hot (unless done early in the morning).

**Mueller Park** is one of the Utah's classic rides, in season from late May through October. The ride is at the southern end of the greater Ogden area, departing from the eastern edge of Bountiful. This forested, relatively low-elevation ride can be done as an out-and-back ride, or a loop when connected to North Canyon. The first half (7 miles) leading to Big Rock is generally more well traveled and less steep. A good beginner or intermediate ride, the trail is smooth and wide, particularly on the bottom portion. The trailhead is on 1800 South in Bountiful, just 2 miles east of the intersection with Orchard Drive. Parking is on the south side of the road.

**Northern Skyline Trail,** popular for skiers and hikers, is also considered one of the area's best mountain bike rides. The technical difficulty of this ride is only moderate, but the fitness requisite is high; the trail climbs about 2,600 vertical feet over 6.7 miles to reach the flanks of Ben Lomond Peak. The large amount of climbing yields plentiful views of Ogden and the Great Salt Lake. The trailhead nearest Ogden is the Northern Divide Trailhead, as described in the *Hiking* section.

**Snowbasin** (801-620-1000; www.snowbasin.com). This ski area has nearly 3,000 vertical feet of terrain and 25 miles of bike-friendly trails. From mid-June through mid-September (weather and snow cover permitting), the resort operates a gondola to its Needles Lodge. Those not wanting to pedal up may pay a fee to ride the lift. Maps that detail the trails from the top of the resort all the way down to Pineview Reservoir are available online and at the Grizzly Center in the base area. The **Wasatch-Cache National Forest** (801-236-3400) maintains a number of trails that connect directly to these Snowbasin trails. Lift rates: $16 for adults onetime, $20 all day, $14 for children 12 and under all day.

## Road Biking

**Ogden River Parkway** is Ogden's in-town, go-to nature path. Paved, this 3.5-mile strip is very popular among joggers, Rollerbladers, and casual bikers. Speeds should be kept low for the safety of all user groups. This is located along the Ogden River from the mouth of Ogden Canyon to Washington Boulevard.

**Ogden River Scenic Byway** (also UT 39/Ogden Canyon Rd.) departs from Ogden as 12th Street and enters the cool and winding Ogden Canyon alongside the Ogden River. Almost immediately upon entering the canyon, the Ogden Waterfall appears on the left side of the road. This steep and tall waterfall cascades from high atop a craggy ridge. The parkway passes Pineview Reservoir 5 miles up canyon from these falls as it enters the scenic Ogden Valley, before ascending into the Monte Cristo Range, which adorns the valley's skyline. This road ends at UT 16 in Woodruff after 63 miles, but the ride is not necessarily over, as many state highway loop options exist with UT 16. This landscape is rural and open.

**Snowbasin Road** begins in the broad, scenic Ogden Valley and ascends steeply about 1,500 feet to the base area of the resort at 6,400 feet above sea level. To extend this ride, begin by doing a loop around the Pineview Reservoir. From Pineview Reservoir, take UT 226 toward Snowbasin Resort.

**Trapper's Loop Road** is a mountainous, 9-mile stretch of paved road connecting Huntsville to Mountain Green, also popular as a scenic drive. Though it is called a "loop," it really is an out-and-back trip for cyclists, as the road eventually ends in Mountain Green, which is bordered on the south by I-84. This meandering road stays atop small ridgelines and is especially scenic during fall foliage season.

**BOATING Club Rec** (801-614-0500; www.clubrecnorth.com), 2479 North UT 162, Eden. This Ogden Valley operation rents many kinds of toys, including watercraft such as Jet Skis, motorboats, and kayaks. Call for reservations.

**The Great Salt Lake** is a unique body of water, with almost 10 times the salinity of the ocean and an average depth of only around 15 feet (depending on seasonal precipitation). Surprisingly, it is possible to operate powerboats in this water; the engines must simply be flushed after use. Still, most watercraft on this lake have sails because of the ideal wind conditions and expansive surface. Even though the unique experience would seem inviting, many people avoid the lake because of its oft-briny smell and periodic insect populations.

**Invert Sports** (801-830-8864; www.utahboatrental.com). This full-service rental company stocks all kinds of motorized gear, including Jet Skis and motorboats with appropriate trailers and vehicles for towing. This company delivers boats and cleans them when you're done.

**Ogden River,** east of Ogden along UT 39 in Ogden Canyon. This river, narrow and steep as it is, is popular for river running during the springtime. Both the South Fork of the Ogden (which follows UT 39 in Ogden Canyon), and the portion of the river beneath Pineview Reservoir, are considered passable. The former section has rapids rated class I–III according to the International Whitewater Rating System; the latter is rated class II–V.

**Ogden Whitewater Park** has been built into the Weber River in the middle of Ogden. Here kayakers practice maneuvering in and around man-made holes. Check out Utah Whitewater Club's Web site, www.utahwhitewaterclub.org, for more information. To get there, take B Street north from its intersection with 24th Street, and make a right where it ends at a T-intersection. Continue for less than a mile, and the river will appear to the side of the road.

**Pineview Reservoir,** in the Ogden Valley between Eden and Hunstville. This is a 2,900-acre reservoir popular for boating and fishing. Located in a valley surrounded by mountains, this lake is particularly scenic and popular for its close proximity to Ogden.

**Weber River,** roughly parallel to I-84. This river has many discrete, boatable sections, most of which are mellow. Devil's Gate (or Scrambled Egg Bend), just outside of Ogden, is the most technical section of river, with difficulty up to 4+.

**Willard Bay Reservoir** (as described in the *Fishing* section). This is the best flat water boating nearest to Ogden. This freshwater partition of the Great Salt Lake, just northwest of Ogden, is a state park is popular for waterskiing and other motorized boating sports, as well as fishing and camping. Two marinas, north and south, service the area for a combined total surface acreage of nearly 10,000. This reservoir is often severely drained for irrigation purposes, so call ahead just in case.

FISHING Most of the fishing in the Ogden area is on man-made reservoirs, or along the two rivers that run directly into Ogden: the Ogden and Weber rivers. The Bear River, a bit more distant, is also an option. For more information on northern Utah's fishing, visit www.utah.com/fish. Utah State publishes its own guidebooks, complete with area recommendations and fishing-related laws. These books are available as free downloads at www.wildlife.utah.gov/guidebooks or can be obtained at any Utah Division of Wildlife Resources Office or licensing agent— where you'll need to stop anyway.

**Bear River** runs from Bear Lake (in the far northeast corner of Utah) into the Great Salt Lake just north of Willard Bay. The 5 miles between Corrine and the Great Salt Lake are known for its catfish. Access can be tricky because of property issues and thick brush.

**Causey Reservoir,** 15 miles northeast of Ogden on UT 39, on Causey Road. At an elevation of 5,700 feet is a small reservoir with approximately 140 surface acres. Located on the South Fork of the Ogden River, the reservoir is generally in season from June through October. Fish here include rainbow, cutthroat, and brown trout. This reservoir is perched among mountain peaks, has steep shores, and no official boat ramps.

**Hyrum Reservoir** is a state park on the southwestern edge of Hyrum and about 10 miles northeast of Brigham City. Contains perch, bluegill, rainbow trout, and bass. This is a beautiful valley reservoir of modest size that, despite its proximity to Hyrum, feels geographically isolated.

**Pineview Reservoir,** 6 miles east of Ogden via UT 39. This Ogden Valley lake is known for its tiger muskie and bass. With 2,900 surface acres, the reservoir has two boat ramps, a beach, and is popular for many kinds of water recreation. Fishing here is most popular near its inlets. The reservoir is in the scenic valley between Eden and Huntsville with 360-degree views of surrounding mountains.

**Ogden River,** which runs into Ogden from the east, through Ogden Canyon, alongside UT 39, contains several varieties of trout and is stocked with rainbow. Much of the land along the river is public, and there are many fishing facilities and campgrounds in the area.

**Red Rock Ranch and Outfitters** (as described in *Outfitter Services* sidebar in the "Northern Utah in Brief" chapter), offers trips on Pineview and Causey reservoirs.

**Weber River** flows into the Ogden area from the southeast, along I-84. Another trout-filled, fisherman-friendly body of water, this river has access that is a bit trickier than that of the Ogden River, as less of the shoreline is public property. This river originates in the Uinta Mountains and flows through Wanship and Echo reservoirs before converging with the Ogden River just east of the Great Salt Lake.

**Wild Country Outfitters** (801-751-6551; www.wildcountryoutfitters.com), 6531 South Bybee Dr., Ogden. This is a local tackle shop that has an online fishing report, guided trips, and gear rentals.

**Willard Bay Reservoir** (Willard Bay State Park: 435-734-9494), Willard Bay Rd., exit 357 on I-15. Strangely enough, this is a freshwater portion of the Great Salt Lake, fed by the Ogden River and artificially barricaded from the rest of Salt Lake. This is the only place in Utah where the wiper species can be caught. This portion of the lake is often drained for irrigation purposes. Two marinas are located in this state park. $10 day use fee.

**GOLF** **Eagle Lake Golf Course** (801-825-3467; www.eaglelake-golf.com), 2885 West 5200 South, Roy. This public facility has a nine-hole, 2,161-yard, par-33 course, as well as a driving range and a mini golf course. The surrounding scenery and its namesake lake at the course add to the sensory experience.

**❧ Eagle Mountain Golf Course** (435-723-3212; www.eaglemountaingc.com), 960 East 700 South, Brigham City. This public course has 18 holes, 6,780 playing yards, and some of the most open and spacious greens in the state. It is located near the mouth of Sardine Canyon, and has a tilted and rolling topography and open feel with small trees dotting the course. This very scenic course, about 20 minutes south of downtown Ogden, offers great views of the surrounding foothills. $23 weekdays and weekends.

**El Monte Golf Course** (801-629-0694), 1300 Valley Dr., Ogden. This public facility has a nine-hole, 3,009-yard, par-35 course and driving range at the scenic mouth of Ogden Canyon. This course has a parkland layout and was built in 1931 as part of the New Deal programs of the Great Depression. The clubhouse is constructed of stone quarried from the Ogden River during that time. $10 on weekdays, $12 on weekends.

**Mount Ogden Golf Course** (801-629-0699), 1787 Constitution Way, Ogden. This public course has 18 holes, 6,294 yards, and a rating of par 71. This hilly, challenging, and incredibly scenic course is perched on the eastern bench. The course is craftily integrated into the rolling and steep natural grounds, with great views overlooking the city below and mountains dwarfing it immediately to the east. $18.

**Remuda Golf Course** (801-731-7200; www.remudagolf.com), 2600 West 3500 North, Farr West. This public course is Utah's newest, with 18 holes, 6,300 yards, a par-72 rating, and driving range. This flat course is located in the valley and has a pleasant suburban setting, with great mountain views. Because the course is new, all of the facilities are modern and inviting. $24; $29 after 3 PM.

**Wolf Creek Resort** (801-745-3365; www.wolfcreekresort.com), 3900 North Wolf Creek, Eden. The Ogden Valley, just 25 minutes east of Ogden City, is an incredibly beautiful location, free from the major population of the cities along the Wasatch Front. Surrounded by the mountains where Snowbasin and Powder Mountain sit, this public course has 18 holes, 6,845 yards, and a par-72 rating. Wildflowers, water hazards, and occasional cottonwood trees visually integrate this course into the wilds beyond. Check the Web site or call for dress code information and reservations. $150.

**HIKING** **Ben Lomond Peak,** elevation 9,712 feet, is one of Ogden's more popular, nearby "big" hikes. During the summer, its grassy shoulders and ridges bloom with wildflowers. During winter this is also well liked for backcountry ski touring. Very few trees interrupt the views, especially toward the top. There are many different trailheads that begin at different elevations and offer a selection of lengths and different vistas. The **North Skyline Trail** (also called North Ogden Pass) is accessed at the northeastern tip of 3700 North Street in North Ogden, at the Ogden Divide Trailhead. It is the longest and least steep of the bunch, beginning at 6,180 feet above sea level and 11.4 miles each way. This trail trends due north from the trailhead. (**Lewis Peak,** 8,031 feet, can be reached by heading south from this parking area instead of north.) Another option for accessing Ben Lomond Peak is by the trailhead at **North Fork Park,** as described in the *Skiing* section of this chapter. Two shorter and steeper trails lead to the top from here.

**Bonneville Shoreline Trail: North of Ogden Canyon.** This is a rolling trail that traverses the former shoreline of the ancient Lake Bonneville. This huge lake, created by earthen dams and a moist ice-age climate, covered a region almost half as large as present-day Utah. This lake filled and drained multiple times, the last of which was approximately 12,000 years ago. The ancient shores of this bygone lake are still visible today in most places along the Wasatch Range, several hundred feet above the current surface level of the Great Salt Lake. The shoreline trail is a massive network of pathways that exists in the Ogden area as well as Salt Lake City and Provo. There is no map for this system, but the sparse nature of the vegetation allows for intuiting one's way around this web. Because of its nearness to town and variety of options, this system is popular for mountain bikers as well. This stretch of trail offers roughly 3.5 miles of trail from end to end, though parallel trails offer more variety of experience than this would suggest. Elevation is between 4,400 and 4,840 feet. This trail system, like its sister in Salt Lake City, has multiple access points from south to north: at the mouth of Ogden Canyon, at 1725 East 1175 South, at the eastern end of Douglas Street/350 South Street, at 420 North Harrison Boulevard, and at 1180 North Mountain Road.

**Bonneville Shoreline Trail: South of Ogden Canyon.** This portion of the Bonneville system offers roughly 6.4 miles of trail from end to end. Like the Bonneville Shoreline Trail north of Ogden Canyon, this is also generally traversing and rolling trail. Elevation is between 4,400 and 5,680 feet. Multiple access points from north to south include the intersection of Valley Drive and UT 39/Rainbow Gardens, and the eastern ends of the following Ogden streets: 22nd, 29th, 36th, and 46th.

**Mount Ogden Trail** is located at the Snowbasin Resort. It tops out at a classic peak and respectable elevation but requires only moderate distance. This trail, open for hiking during the summer only, follows the dirt service roads of Snowbasin to the top of Mount Ogden. Elevation starts at 6,560 feet and reaches 9,572 feet after 4.5 miles of hiking. Snowbasin operates the Needles Gondola each Friday, Saturday, Sunday, and holidays between the middle of June and the middle of September, conditions permitting. $14 for adults, $10 for ages 7–12, and free for children ages 6 and under. For more information call 801-620-1014. (Separate rates apply to mountain bikers using the gondola.) The trailhead is at the Snowbasin Resort parking lot.

**Indian Trail** is of moderate difficulty and has an elevation between 4,840 and 6,100 feet. It is 4.3 miles one-way and heads east into Ogden Canyon along the southern walls of the canyon. This trail historically was used by the Shoshoni to navigate up and around the steep rocks of this narrow canyon during times of high water. The end of this trail connects to the Cold Water Canyon Trail. From this trailhead, the **Hidden Valley Trail** (1.4 miles each way) can be accessed as well. This steep trail is followed by maintaining a southerly direction of travel (as indicated by HIDDEN VALLEY painted on a rock near the correct fork in the trail) and gains views of Mount Ogden above and Taylor Canyon below. Both trails are generally only used by hikers. To reach Indian Trail, go to the eastern end of 22nd Street in Ogden, or go to the Cold Water Canyon trailhead about 1.5 miles east of the canyon mouth along UT 39.

ROCK CLIMBING Rock climbing in the immediate Ogden area exists but is not nearly as plentiful as in the Salt Lake City or Logan areas. The most comprehensive information for the area is found in the guidebook *Wasatch Climbing North*, by Stuart and Brett Ruckman, or in *Ogden Area Climbing Guide*, by David G. Robb. For an overview on climbing in Utah as a whole, see the *Rock Climbing* section in the "Northern Wasatch" chapter of this book. The statewide Web site, www.utah climbers.org, represents one of the nation's most active climbing communities and is a very active online forum for discussion and a dispatch center for news.

**Ben Lomond Climbing Gym** (801-737-7274; www.geocities.com/blclimbing center), 2370 North US 89, Ogden. This has historically been Ogden's local gym. This gym has 4,000 square feet of climbing, including face climbing as well as crack climbing.

**Canyon Sports** (801-621-4662; www.canyonsports.com), 4598 South 700 West (just south of Riverdale Rd.), Ogden. This shop is preferred among Ogden climbers because of its knowledgeable staff, who can give you more personalized information on surrounding areas and perhaps sell you a guidebook or equipment.

**9th Street Crag,** eastern terminus of Ninth St. This is Ogden's local, user-friendly sport-climbing and top-rope crag, and has a reputation for being the best wall in the area. Quartzite walls approximately 40 feet tall are protected with bolts and affixed with permanent anchors. Parking for this crag is limited.

**Ogden Canyon,** east of Ogden on UT 39. This canyon has a smattering of short sport climbs on strange quartzite with granitelike qualities. The highest concentration of climbs is on the north side of the canyon. Park as for the Ogden Canyon Falls, cross a railroad bridge, and walk up canyon about 500 yards. The cliffs are located about 100 yards up a very steep talus field.

**Salomon Center/I Rock Utah** (801-399-4653; www.salomoncenter.com), 2261 Kiesel Ave., Ogden. This 2007, very modern sports complex has a 50-foot indoor climbing wall.

**Schoolroom Wall,** top of 21st and 27th St., as for 26th Street Bouldering. This is the most densely concentrated wall in the area, with nearly 100 routes spanning the difficulty range. This west-facing quartzite wall is the very obvious cliff band above the bouldering field. It is completely sun soaked in the afternoons; climb here in the early morning during summer, or afternoons during early spring and late fall. Protection is a mix of sport and traditional.

**26th Street Bouldering,** at the topographical crest of 21st and 27th St., on the eastern edge of town. This boulder field is one of Ogden's best outdoor climbing assets, with notoriously unforgiving ratings. More boulders can be accessed by hiking above the first boulder field (which is visible from the road), or by driving to the eastern end of either 25th or 27th St. More information on this area can be found in the book *A Bouldering Guide to Utah,* by Beck, Baldwin, and Russo. A short PDF guidebook is available online at www.drtopo.com.

**Willard Street Spires,** Brigham City's nearest crag, is the several-pitch, alpine-style, quartzite climbing accessed by notoriously rugged hiking. Climbs here protect with traditional gear and are moderate, with difficulty ratings between 5.7 and 5.9, and commitment ratings between Grade III and IV. The main formation here is the London Spire, though there are other cliffs including the Ogre, Birdie's Wall, and the Prow.

## SKIING

### Alpine

Ogden has the good fortune of being less than 20 miles from two major ski resorts, Snowbasin and Powder Mountain—as well as one small area, Wolf Mountain (formerly Nordic Valley). These areas receive more than 400 inches of annual snowfall and contain excellent terrain. Yet because they are removed from the immediate vicinity of Salt Lake City or Park City, they endure much less crowding than those resorts.

**Powder Mountain** (main office: 801-745-3772, snow phone: 801-745-3771; www.powdermountain.net), northern terminus of UT 158, Eden. Powder Mountain's elevation is 6,895–8,900 feet, and it has 5,500 acres of broad bowls, scattered trees, and chutes. *There is more lift-served terrain here than any other resort in the United States.* Relatively inexpensive snowcat tickets are available for purchase for those wanting even more terrain. An intelligent layout requires only five major lifts to service this vast mountain. All base area services and parking are at the Timberline Area. By law, no pets are allowed at Powder Mountain, as the area is located within a protected watershed. The two biggest après-ski hits at the mountain are the **Sundown Lodge** (adjacent to Sundown Lift, Resort Center) and the **Powder Keg** (lower level, Powder Mountain Lodge). Also serving beer, but closing by 4:30, is the **Powder Mountain Restaurant** (Resort Center). A variety of on-site accommodations are available, from ski-in, ski-out condos to lodge style.

**Snowbasin Resort** (801-620-1000 or 888-437-5488; www.snowbasin.com), 3125 East Snowbasin Rd., Huntsville. Snowbasin is Ogden Valley's other

POWDER MOUNTAIN IN OGDEN VALLEY IS KNOWN FOR ITS HUGELY SPACIOUS SLOPES AND LONG-LASTING POWDER STASHES.

THIS OGDEN VALLEY SKI RESORT IS JUST MORE THAN AN HOUR NORTH OF SALT LAKE CITY AND IS A VIABLE ALTERNATIVE TO THE OFT-CROWDED COTTONWOOD CANYONS' SKI AREAS.

major ski area. The terrain is generally more rugged than at Powder Mountain, though all abilities will find plenty of skiing. The mountain itself is striking; its ridges are crowned with dramatic, craggy spires. A Sun Valley resort, this Snowbasin is adorned with the opulent lodges designed to aesthetically complement the environment. Resplendent furniture, gourmet cuisine, varied and plentiful terrain, and small crowds are enhanced by surprisingly reasonable ticket rates. The elevation at this resort ranges from 6,400 to 9,469 feet, with 3,200 acres of skiable terrain, nearly two-thirds of which is considered advanced terrain. **Earl's Lodge Lounge** (Earl's Lodge, Main Plaza) is where Snowbasin skiers head for a quick beer.

✦ **Wolf Mountain** (801-745-3511; www.wolfmountaineden.com), 3567 Nordic Valley Way, Eden. This is the third alpine area in the Ogden area and is the smallest by a long shot. With a 1,000-foot vertical drop and 110 acres, Wolf Mountain is perfect for those wishing to learn to ski and not waste money on advanced terrain they'll never see. For beginner skiers and families with young children, Wolf Mountain is ideal. A kid-friendly learning environment with very affordable lift tickets.

## Nordic

**Art Nord Trailhead** area is a sometimes-groomed trail system with many variations. Most trails trend north and west, through Wheeler Canyon. Ski far enough to the west, and you'll end up at the Snowbasin parking lot. Be advised that avalanche danger can be a factor in this canyon. Take UT 39 east out of Ogden, and turn south onto UT 167 (also called Trapper's Loop Road) about 0.5 mile after the Snowbasin turnoff. Turn right (west) onto UT 226, the old Snowbasin Road.

**North Fork Park Campground** is another starting point for groomed skiing. This is an unusually snowy area for its elevation, which gives it reliable snowpack for cross-country skiing and ski touring alike. The terrain here is varied and satisfies different skill levels. Directions are a bit complicated: North Fork Park

Campground is reached by following UT 39 east through Ogden Canyon, as if going to Powder Mountain or Wolf Mountain. At the westernmost point of the Pineview Reservoir (its spillway), turn left onto UT 158. Take another left onto UT 162 at the T-intersection where UT 158 ends. Follow this highway; to do so, you will have to take a left onto 4100 North in about 3 miles, followed by an immediate right onto 3300 East. At this point you should be able to follow signs to North Park. You will be led to a left-hand turn on North Fork Road in about 2 miles, followed by another left-hand turn onto 5950 North. This is the last turn you will make, and at this point, the parking lot should be visible. This trailhead is used by backcountry skiers accessing Ben Lomond Peak, as well as Nordies.

**North Ogden Divide** generally sees consistent snowpack because of its higher elevation. Trails branch off in every direction, so you can select the slope aspect that best suits your needs. Most trails here are fairly steep, so skiing is considered difficult. This is the same trailhead from which you can reach Ben Lomond Peak to the north and Lewis Peak to the south in summer (as described in the *Hiking* section in this chapter).

**Pineview Reservoir** is a popular starting point for off-piste cross-country skiing with convenient access. Most skiers begin at the **Anderson Cove Campground** (along the south shoreline, shortly after the turnoff to Snowbasin), where trails are intermittently maintained by a grooming machine. This area is largely without much vertical relief and is thus beginner-friendly. Dogs are allowed anywhere at the reservoir except near developed beaches, one of which is at this campground.

**Snowbasin Resort** (as in the *Alpine* section, above) offers slick and speedy, resort-style Nordic skiing with 26 kilometers of trails that are regularly groomed—much of which is beginner-friendly. Information and gear can be obtained at the base area of the resort. Nordic skiers will ideally park in Lot 2, though it is immediately adjacent to Lot 1. Use of Snowbasin's trails is free of charge.

**South Fork of the Ogden River Campgrounds** is a collection of campgrounds in a small pocket of national forest with roads and trails that roughly follow the Ogden River's South Fork. The skiing here is very popular and generally considered easy. Moose, which can be dangerous, have a healthy population here. Go 8 miles east of Huntsville on UT 39. Parking is on the highway. You may wish to consider another location if it is actively snowing, as people's cars have been buried by snowplows clearing the road.

## Backcountry

If Utah lift-served skiing is awesome and enormous, its backcountry is better and more vast. Naturally, backcountry skiing requires expertise and ambition much beyond that of resort skiing, especially with regard to avalanche safety, emergency preparedness, familiarity with the terrain, and willingness to hike. Nonetheless, Utah has an extremely large population of backcountry skiers and an excellent avalanche-safety organization. The **Utah Avalanche Center** is one of the world's premier avalanche-safety organizations and is staffed by many of snow science's leading authorities. Their Web site, **www.avalanche.org,** gives daily updates per region, covering the state in seven sections. Discussed are trends of increasing or decreasing danger, likelihood of avalanche with respect to slope aspect, recent avalanches (with photographs), and more. Another local resource is the

THE BASE AREA AT SNOWBASIN

**Ogden Ranger District Office** (801-625-5112), whose staff can also discuss conditions with you.

**Ben Lomond Peak** (access described in the *Hiking* section, above) is a popular place for ski touring in the Ogden area, with miles of trails and pleasant skiing approaches. The generally higher elevation of this area ensures more consistent snow cover than many other places in the vicinity.

**Powder Mountain** (as discussed in the *Alpine* section) has a ski patrol that is very kind to Alpine ski touring. When the backcountry is deemed safe, access gates open, and ski patrol even blasts some of the main out-of-bounds slopes—unheard of at most resorts. If you forgot skins, you can use plastic to buy a ride on any of their available machinery, from snowmobiles to shuttle buses, snowcats, and helicopters. For those unfamiliar with the area, using their guide service might prove very helpful, if not crucial.

**Snowbasin Resort** (as discussed in the *Alpine* section) backcountry skiers enjoy very easy access from the top of the lifts. However, where grunt effort is lacking, technical skills and safety know-how requirements are greatly elevated. In addition to generally elevated avalanche danger, skiers face difficult route finding on the return trip. Generally speaking, terrain on the south side of the mountain is considered less technical, while the west and north sides are generally much more serious.

## ✳ Lodging

**HOTELS Hampton Inn & Suites Ogden** (801-394-9400; www.ogden suites.hamptoninn.com), 2401 Washington Blvd., Ogden. Formerly known as the Ogden Plaza Hotel, this does not have the structure typical of most Hampton Inns. This downtown boutique-style hotel was built in the early 20th century. The updated rooms have been furnished with a clean, simple, modern style.

**Hotel Ben Lomond** (801-627-1900 or 877-627-1900; www.benlomond suites.com), 2510 Washington Blvd., Ogden. This is perhaps one of Ogden's finest boutique-style grand hotels.

THE AWNING OF THE HOTEL BEN LOMOND, A 1927 ITALIAN RENAISSANCE REVIVAL BUILDING ON THE NATIONAL REGISTER OF HISTORIC PLACES

Opened in 1927, the building is graced by aesthetic detail that was important in the era of its construction. Centrally located in downtown Ogden and outfitted with upscale amenities, this is suitable for tourists and business travelers alike. Rooms are handsomely decorated, ranging in style from modern to Victorian. The overall effect is tasteful, without extravagance. Special packages are available, from ski and spa bundles to deals that include drinks at the on-site lounge. $70–$200.

**The Red Moose Lodge & Hotel** (801-745-6667; www.theredmoose lodge.com), 2547 North Valley Junction Dr., Eden. The thick-timbered Red Moose Lodge is reminiscent of a ski lodge, whose rooms are furnished with rustic, woodsy-feeling décor. However, this modern lodge is quite spacious and offers guests contemporary comforts. The lodge has a pool table, and picnic areas and gazebos for relaxing during warm months. $99–$200.

**BED-AND-BREAKFASTS** **Alaskan Inn & Suites** (801-621-8600 or 888-707-8600; www.alaskaninn.com), 435 Ogden Canyon Rd., Ogden. This woodsy establishment incorporates its mountain surroundings into an Alaskan-lodge theme, with its lodge and cabins constructed of large logs and filled with hand-made pine furniture. The ambience here is that of a rustic retreat, and packages are available, from ski deals to massages and picnics. $150 and up, more for private cabins and packages.

**The Atomic Chalet** (801-745-0538; www.atomicchalet.com), 6900 East 100 South, Huntsville. Designed by skiers for skiers, this is a European-style bed-and-breakfast with morning meals intended to fuel a full day of exercise. The chalet caters to serious skiers and outdoors enthusiasts, and asks that guests respect each other's early wake-up times. Young children and pets are not allowed.

**VACATION RENTALS** **Lakeside Resort Properties** (866-745-3194; www.lakesideresortproperties.com), 6486 East UT 39, Huntsville. This lodging company owns a complex of modern, lodge-style condominium units that sit on the scenic shores of the Pineview Reservoir, surrounded by the beautiful Ogden Valley mountains just beyond. These units, located in Huntsville, have convenient access to ski resorts and outdoor activities. There are also on-site tennis courts, pool, and private hot tubs. Roughly $200–$500.

**The Snowberry Inn** (801-745-2534; www.snowberryinn.com), 1315 North UT 158, Eden. This is one of the area's more quaint, family-oriented bed-and-breakfasts. Rooms have homey, country-style decorations, and much of the building is dedicated to a community game room with darts, board games, pool, a piano, and ski-memorabilia decorations. Home-style cooking is another draw for guests, and the breakfasts are quite well liked. $90–$150.

## ✳ Where to Eat

As in many western cities, chain restaurants abound in the Ogden area. (These are most concentrated around I-15 and on Riverdale Road.) Despite the seeming saturation of national restaurants, Ogden surprises new residents and visitors with its local dining and low costs. Located on and near Historic 25th Street, the restaurants tend to have a bit more flair and variety.

**DINING OUT** **The Artisan Grille** (801-395-0166; www.artisangrille.com), 172 25th St., Ogden. Open for lunch and dinner Tuesday–Saturday. The Artisan Grille has one of Ogden's more attractive menus and a great atmosphere. The food is mainly contemporary American, with French, Italian, Asian, and other influences. This restaurant has a raw-brick dining room that is outfitted with sleek furniture, clean lines, and smaller, bistro-style tables. The overall impression is elegance that is not stuffy. Large parties are possible, but this is best experienced in a group of four or less. During the warm months, a patio is available for seating out back. Entrées $11–$26.

**Bistro 258** (801-394-1595), 258 25th St., Ogden. Open Monday–Saturday for lunch and dinner. This is one of Ogden's finer dining establishments for those seeking a svelte, yet casual evening experience. The mixed American and Continental menu centers around fine preparations and cuts of meat, much of which is from local sources. The dining room is long and

narrow, enriched by deeply hued wood. Entrées $9–$25.

**EATING OUT** **Grounds for Coffee** (801-621-3014), 3005 Harrison Blvd., Ogden and (801-392-7370), 111 Historic 25th St., Ogden. This hip local chain is one Ogden's favorite coffee shops, now at several locations and two major locations in Ogden. Each location runs a different weekly special, sometimes partnering with neighboring restaurants. Occasional evening music.

**La Ferrovia Ristorante** (801-394-8628), 232 25th St., Ogden. Open Tuesday–Saturday for lunch and dinner. This Italian joint earns enthusiastic raves from locals and visitors alike. This restaurant stews in the deliciousness of generations-deep family sauces, dressings, and pasta recipes. Family owned, La Ferrovia serves what many consider to be the best Italian food perhaps in all of Utah, and is yet fairly inexpensive. $7–$18.

✿ **Prairie Schooner** (801-621-5511; www.prairieschoonerrestaurant.com), 445 Park Blvd., Ogden. Open for lunch Monday–Friday, daily for dinner. This is a family pleaser, making a shameless bid for fun with full-blown prairie décor that begins with an Old West façade as the restaurant front and covered-wagon booths as tables. The Schooner is a good venue for a large, carnivorous meal. Battered and fried appetizers give way to even larger dinners. House-aged steaks of all cuts and preparations and seafood are the house specialties.

**Rooster's 25th Street Brewing Company** (801-627-6171; www.roostersbrewingco.com), 253 25th St., Ogden Don't knock Utah beer until you've tried it. In spite of the lowered alcohol content, the flavor is generally delicious—and if you're accustomed to the oxygen levels at sea level, "3.2" beer might well suffice. Additionally, you probably didn't know that Utah brewers are actually permitted to brew full-strength beer; it must simply be served in bottles, as state law prohibits the sale of full-strength beer from kegs. Naturally, the food is another important aspect of Rooster's. The menu here is of the high-end brewpub variety and offers contemporary entrées as well as gourmet-style pizza, burgers, sandwiches, pasta, seafood, and Mexican cuisine. The atmosphere is a blend of modern brick, ample natural light, artistic twists, open space, and brushed-steel vats.

**Tona Sushi** (801-622-8662), 210 25th St., Ogden. This little sushi bar on Historic 25th Street is one of the favorites in Ogden and fits right into the gentrification trend of this street. Though it is no San Francisco joint, this has reliable sushi and fair pricing. Tona has a

very solid menu, with traditional and creative sushi offerings, as well as tempura dishes, noodles, grilled items, salads, and even stews. Rolls are generally familiar but span the complexity range and include an expansive variety of ingredients. The atmosphere is a modern take on traditional Japanese décor.

**Union Grill** (801-621-2830; www .uniongrillogden.com). 2501 Wall Ave., Ogden. Under the same ownership of Rooster's Brewing Company (listed earlier), this grill is located at Ogden's Historic Union Station. The décor is thus another dose of railroading, as is appropriate tribute to this original lifeblood of the city. The causal atmosphere and low-key menu complement each other well. The food is mainly sandwiches, pastas, and a few entrées. It is fresh and prepared with slight ethnic twists, ranging from Thai to Italian influence.

## ✳ Entertainment

**David Eccles Conference Center** and adjacent **Peery's Egyptian Theater** (801-395-3227; www.peerys egyptiantheater.com), 2415 Washington Blvd., Ogden. Originally built in 1924, this is a downtown film and performance arts theater that now hosts workshops in addition to performances.

**Golden Spike Events Center** (801-399-8798; www.co.weber.ut.us/gsec), 1000 North 1200 West, Ogden. This center is a massive complex of many trades, with indoor and outdoor venues suitable for events ranging from rodeos to concerts and fairs.

**Heritage Community Theater** (435-723-8392; www.heritagetheatreutah .com), 205 South Hwy. 89, Perry. Originally built as a church, now home to Brigham Community Theater. Located in Perry, just a few miles south of Brigham City.

THE ROOSTER'S BREWPUB ON THE ONCE-ROWDY, NOW GENTRIFIED HISTORIC 25TH STREET IN OGDEN

OGDEN'S ECCLES CONFERENCE CENTER, LOCATED AT 24TH STREET AND WASHINGTON BOULEVARD, IS HOME OF BALLROOMS AND PEERY'S EGYPTIAN THEATER.

**Municipal Park,** 25th St. and Grant Ave. Part of this city park is an outdoor amphitheater where outdoor concert series are held during the summer months.

**Terrace Plaza Playhouse** (801-393-0070; www.terraceplayhouse.com), 99 East 4700 South. This is one of Ogden's homes for local theater.

NIGHTLIFE **Brewskis** (801-394-1713; www.brewskisonline.net), 244 25th St., Ogden. This is one of Ogden's more popular watering holes. This is a bar's bar with sports, pool tables, neon signs, and live music.

**Ogden First Friday Art Stroll** takes place on the first Friday of each month and begins at the Eccles Community Art Center (801-392-6935; www.ogden 4 ts.org), 2580 Jefferson Ave.

**Shooting Star Saloon** (801-745-2002), 7350 East 200 South, Huntsville. About 20 minutes to the east of Ogden, the Shooting Star is among the oldest bars in Utah and still retains its hitching post outside to vouch for that fact. The Star has a reputation for making one of Utah's best burgers.

**Time Out Sports Deli** (801-392-5565), 4396 Harrison Blvd., Ogden. This is the bar of choice around Weber State Athletics events and is a good place to watch big games on television.

**Wiseguys** (801-622-5588; www.wise guyscomedy.com), 269 25th St., Ogden. This comedy chain/beer bar has acts performing each Friday and Saturday evening.

SPORTS **Ogden Raptors** (801-393-2400; www.ogden-raptors.com), home games at Lindquist Field, 2330 Lincoln Ave., Ogden. This minor league baseball team is a farm team of the Los Angeles Dodgers. Established in 1994, the team is part of the Pioneer League and has been in Ogden since 1997.

**Ogden Rhino Raiders** (801-499-6262; www.eteamz.active.com/rhino -raiders). This is an oft-successful minor-league football team that holds the all-time national 84-game winning streak record. The Raiders play in many different locations, as they do not have a home stadium.

**Weber State University Wildcats** (www.weberstatesports.com) has a full range of collegiate athletics. Varsity sports include men's football; women's softball, soccer, and volleyball; men's and women's basketball, cross country, track and field, golf, and tennis.

## ✳ Selective Shopping

**MALLS Newgate Mall** (801-621-1161; www.newgatemall.com), 3651 Wall Ave., Ogden. This is Ogden's only major mall, with 95 stores, a 14-screen movie theater, and a variety of mall-style dining options, from cookies to fast-food restaurants.

**GALLERIES Artists and Heirlooms** and **Loft Gallery** (801-399-0606; www.artistsandheirlooms.com), 115 25th St. This is a small gallery located in the historic 25th district. Here pieces from various artists are mixed with antiques.

**Artstop Ogden** (www.artstopogden .org) is a community database, with theater, visual arts, events, and art education listings—including information on Ogden City's 15 established galleries, the highest concentration of which is along Historic 25th Street.

**Cara Koolmees Gallery** (801-540-2299; www.carakoolmees.com), 256 25th St., Ogden. This small gallery showcases the brightly colorful watercolor works of namesake Southern California artist.

**Eccles Community Art Center** (801-392-6935; www.ogden4arts.org), 2580 Jefferson Ave., Ogden. This is Ogden's major fine-arts hub. It is the starting point for the art strolls, which take place on the first Friday of each month. In addition to art exhibits, this center holds classes, local competitions, and sculpture gardens.

**Fine Arts Gallery** (801-393-3771; www.fineartson25th.com), 290 25th St. This establishment is part framing shop, part art gallery with monthly rotating featured local artists.

**Gallery 25** (801-334-9881; www .gallery25ogden.com), 268 25th St. Owned and staffed by nine local artists, this busy little gallery has one of the most diverse collections of Ogden's galleries.

**Ogden Blue** (801-392-7573; www .ogdenblue.com), 175 25th St. An instructional center, and drafting and arts supplies shop, Ogden Blue has a grassroots gallery featuring rapidly rotating shows by local artists, including novice and professionals alike.

# LOGAN AND THE CACHE VALLEY

The Cache Valley is in the northernmost part of Utah and is flanked by the Wellsville Mountains to the west and the Bear River Mountains to the east. It is a broad and green valley, dotted with towns and agriculture. The parallel, north–south running ranges enclosing the valley jut out as great blue walls. Logan, a town of just under 50,000 residents tucked away in the Cache Valley, is just underpopulated enough to feel like a small town, yet large enough to have a few big-town amenities and attractions. It is close enough to the Salt Lake metropolis to have convenient access, yet is far enough away that it is isolated. Its roots are in Mormonism and farming, but it is also home to Utah State University, as well as strong arts and outdoor-enthusiasts communities.

The first peoples to cross through the lands of Cache County were the ancestors of the Plains Indians and Shoshone. These tribes traversed the longitudes and elevations yearly, fleeing during the colds of winter and returning during the pleasant spring and fall months. Just like many other regions in the Rocky Mountain West, the Cache Valley was late in being tamed by would-be settlers because of its extreme topography, climactic harshness, and tremendous isolation. Thus, long after the Atlantic and Pacific coasts of North America had been settled, the valley's only inhabitants were transients: indigenous peoples, outlaws, fur trappers, and missionaries.

The first wave of Mormon pioneers landed in Salt Lake City in 1847. They came to the area with nothing other than what could be carried in small handcarts, having survived a difficult and treacherous journey. The first winter in Utah was extremely harsh, and the Mormons were, by nature of their situation, scarcely prepared to handle it. Narrowly surviving starvation and exposure during this first winter, the Mormons quickly fortified themselves in springtime, establishing permanent residence and agriculture in what they considered to be their holy land.

More waves of Mormons arrived, and Salt Lake City became ever more established. As soon as was possible, the Mormons set about expanding their domain to the north and south, reaching Moab within seven years and arriving in the Cache Valley by 1856. The first successful settlement in the Logan area was Maughan's Fort, which later became Wellsville. In 1859, Logan was expressly selected as a site for a new city.

The Utah Mormons had already overcome tremendous difficulties to arrive and survive in Utah. For them, Utah was not only a home, but it was also their mecca. They established communities with speed and ambition, entrenching themselves

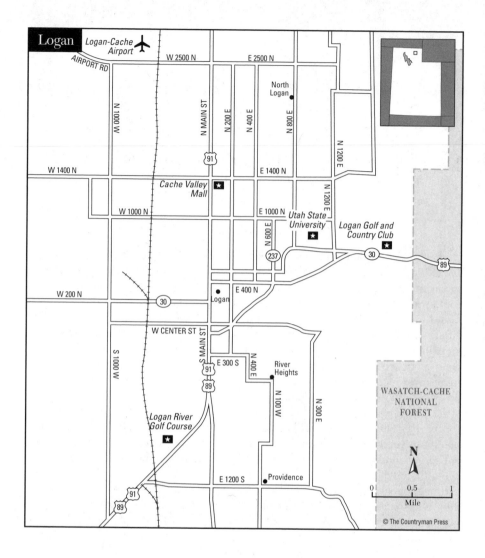

wherever possible in order to lay the foundations for a future nation of their own. Immediately after their arrival in the Cache Valley, the settlers went about felling timber for homes and plowing earth for crops. By June 10, only four days after their arrival, many crops had already been planted. Within a year, 100 houses had been built. In 1866 the City of Wellsville was incorporated.

Industries contemporary to the 19th century began to develop in the valley, including a railroad and businesses dealing in timber and mining. By 1873 the Northern Utah Railroad, a railway connecting the main line near Brigham City to the Cache Valley, was completed. Every local industry responded positively, connected now to a greater economy. Logan continued an uneventful modernization and growth. The LDS church and agriculture have played perhaps the biggest role in the town's development and are a very tangible presence today. Utah State University, founded in 1888, has played a role in the cultural shaping of the town as well, bringing to it a culture of higher education and fine-arts appreciation.

GUIDANCE **Cache Valley Visitors Bureau** (435-755-1890 or 800-882-4433; www.tourcachevalley.com), 199 North Main St., Logan. This visitors bureau has the best, most user-friendly Web site of any in the area. Its physical installment has knowledgeable staff and printed information on the area.

**Logan City** (435-716-9000; www.loganutah.org). Logan City maintains a tidy Web site with current headlines and events, as well as businesses across the valley per field.

**Cache Valley Chamber of Commerce** (435-752-2161; www.cachechamber .com), 160 North Main St., Logan. This Web site contains a countywide list of tourist information and businesses categorized by genre, from restaurants to lodging and general travel. The building itself hosts a small Daughters of Utah Pioneers museum.

GETTING THERE *By car:* If driving, you will approach the vicinity by way of the north–south running I-15. From the south (Salt Lake City), depart from I-15 at Brigham City exit 362, and take US 89/91 as it heads northeast through the Wasatch Range and out of the Salt Lake Valley. If driving from northern Utah or I-84, the best access is via UT 30. If coming from Idaho, take US 91 southeast, exiting I-15 about 36 miles north of the Idaho/Utah border.

*By air:* The most cost-effective way to reach Logan by plane is via the **Salt Lake International Airport (SLC)** (801-575-2400 or 800-595-2442; www.slcairport .com), only five minutes west of downtown Salt Lake City on I-80, and about 90 miles southwest of Logan. Shuttle services to and from the Salt Lake Airport are available with advanced reservation by calling **Cache Valley Cab** (435-752-4555), **Cache Valley Limo Service** (435-563-6400), or **CVC Shuttle** (435-752-4555).

**Logan-Cache Airport (LGU)** (435-752-8111; www.logancache.com), 2850 Airport Rd., Bldg. FL-6A, Logan. This is the local option and is open to the public.

*By bus:* **Logan/Cache Valley Transit District** (435-752-2877 or 435-753-2255; www.cvtdbus.org). This public transportation service offers express bus shuttle services between the Cache Valley and Salt Lake City, as well as local mass transit (as listed below). Call ahead for special needs.

GETTING AROUND *By mass transit:* **Cache Valley Transit District** (435-752-2877 or 435-753-2255; www.cvtdbus.org). This local transit company offers regional bus services, with handicapped services available by telephone arrangement. Various local and commuter schedules exist, and all services are free of charge. Route maps can be found on the Web site. Call for more information.

*By car:* Car rental agencies in Logan include **Enterprise** (435-755-6111 or 800-325-800) and **Hertz** (435-752-9141 or 800-654-3131 ), who have offices in Logan. Otherwise, car rental is best done at Salt Lake International Airport.

*By cab:* **Cache Valley Cab** (435-752-4555) and the **Cache Valley Limo Service** (435-563-6400) are the region's only two taxi services.

MEDICAL EMERGENCY **Intermountain Logan InstaCare** (435-752-1010; www.intermountainhealthcare.org), 235 East 400 North, Logan. This clinic offers speedy attention daily 9–9.

**Cache Valley Specialty Hospital** (435-713-9700; www.cvsh.com), 2380 North 400 East, North Logan. This is one of two hospitals in the valley, in a modern facility with an emergency room.

**Logan Regional Hospital** (435-716-1000; www.intermountainhealthcare.org), 1400 North 500 East, Logan. This hospital is located in the center of town, just northwest of Utah State University.

NEWSPAPERS *Cache Citizen* (www.cachecitizen.com) and *The Logan Herald Journal* (www.hjnews.townnews.com) are the two local newspapers that publish local events listings, happenings, and weather.

## ✳ To See and Do

MUSEUMS **Cache Museum–Daughters of Utah Pioneers** (435-752-5139 or 435-753-1635), 160 North Main St., Chamber of Commerce Building, Logan. Open 10–4 Tuesday–Friday, June through September only; by special arrangement otherwise. This small museum focuses on Mormon pioneer history of the area, illustrating the early days of Mormon life in the valley with artifacts from the 19th century. Some items in this small museum include furniture crafted by Brigham Young and an early Mormon organ. Located in the Cache Valley Chamber of Commerce Building, this stop may already be on your schedule.

**Everton Genealogical Collection** (435-716-9143), 290 North 100 West, Logan Justice Building, Logan. Utah is quite an authority on family history—a fact that arises from the strong family values of the Mormon religion. Though the study is

GREAT SALT LAKE CAUSEWAY AT ANTELOPE ISLAND. THIS STATE PARK FEATURES THE LAKE'S LARGEST ISLAND, HOME TO A HERD OF BISON OF WHICH THERE IS AN ANNUAL NOVEMBER ROUNDUP AND AUCTION.

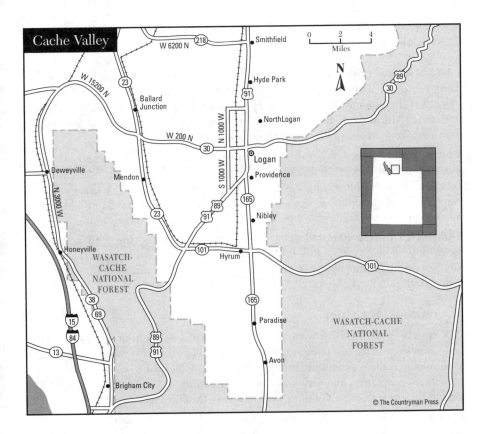

rooted in Mormonism, the product is hardly limited to Utah or this young faith. Rather, the information spans continents and centuries. This Logan installment of genealogic collections has more than 82,000 media items, including periodicals, microfiche, maps, books, and digital media.

**Intermountain Herbarium** (435-797-1584 or 435-797-0061; www.herbarium .usu.edu), Room 252, Old Main Building, University of Utah, Logan. Open 8–5 Monday–Friday. This herbarium reflects the work of Utah State University's nationally famous ecology department, showcasing almost 240,000 plant photographs and specimens, about half of which hail from the region.

**Nora Eccles Harrison Museum of Art** (435-797-0163; www.usu.edu), 650 North 1100 East, Utah State University, Logan. Open 10–4 Tuesday–Friday, noon–4 Saturday. This large museum has ownership of one of the largest collections in the Rocky Mountains, including ceramics and Native American artifacts. A free brochure detailing the outdoor art across campus is available at the museum. Free admission.

**GARDENS AND PARKS** ✒ **Willow Park and Zoo** (435-750-9265), 419 West 700 South, Logan. Open daily 9 AM–dark, closed on holidays; exhibits open only as weather allows. This small zoo is home to a variety of mammals, including bobcats, foxes, lemurs, and elk—but the real attraction of the park is its avian collection.

The more than 100 species make this one of the area's largest such collections. $1 for adults, $.50 for children under 12.

**LANDMARKS** **Logan LDS Temple,** 175 North 300 East. Though the Salt Lake Temple was the first temple to undergo construction, this temple, completed in 1884, was the second Utah temple to open (behind the St. George Temple). As with other Mormon temples, this is only open to particular members of the church and is available to the public for viewing from the outside only.

**Logan Tabernacle,** 100 North Main St. Like Logan's temple, the tabernacle is also one of Utah's oldest, built between 1864 and 1891. Unlike most other Mormon architecture, this was built with dark limestone blocks that give them a look reminiscent of ancient churches and cathedrals abroad. Here non-Mormons are allowed inside the building and welcome to partake of free guided tours.

**Old Rock Church,** 10 South Main St. Now the **Providence Inn Bed & Breakfast** (see *Lodging,* below), this was completed by Mormon settlers in 1871 as the Rock Meeting House, after two years of construction. This stone building is the oldest in the Cache Valley.

## ✳ Outdoor Activities

**Al's Sports** (888-752-5151; www.alssports.com), 1617 North Main St., Logan. This shop is perhaps the most comprehensive in all of Logan. It covers rock climbing, golf, hiking, running, camping, fitness equipment, team sports, water sports, and all winter sports from telemark skiing to snowboarding and snowshoeing. In addition to the breadth of gear, they also have a very friendly staff.

**Campsaver** (435-752-5524; www.campsaver.com), 31 North Main St., Logan. This outdoors shop keeps inventories in all of the backwoods-type sports, particularly backpacking, hiking, trekking, and camping.

**Common Ground** (435-713-0288; www.cgadventures.org), 335 North 100 East, Logan. This organization is dedicated to extending the area's many recreational opportunities to disabled members of the community. Sports and activities include canoeing, cycling, fishing, hiking, rock climbing, skiing, snowshoeing, and even art projects in the surrounding **Wellsville and Bear River Mountains.**

**Logan Aquatic Center** (435-716-9266 or 435-716-9280), 451 South 500 West, Logan. A beautiful outdoor facility, this has an Olympic-sized lap pool and a recreation pool with water slides and other fun features. Unfortunately this is closed during the winter months (for good reason).

✍ **Logan Celebration Centre** (435-752-4215; www.logancelebrationcentre.com), 1903 South 800 West, Logan. The "centre" has a spectrum of family-friendly recreation. Mini golf, three different levels of go-kart racing, many different gigantic human pendulums and freefalls, an arcade, a rock climbing wall, and even snowmobile drag racing. Prices and times vary by activity and season.

**Sports Authority** (435-752-4287; www.sportsauthority.com), 1050 North Main St., Logan. This store covers gear for many recreational activities, from indoors to outdoors.

**Trailhead Sports** (435-753-1541), 117 North Main St., Logan. This shop is has a special emphasis on mountaineering, rock climbing, skis, canoes, kayaks, and camping gear.

## Bike Shops & More

**Al's Sports** (435-752-5151 or 888-752-5151; www.alssports.com), 1617 North Main St., Logan. No stores in Logan rent bicycles, but Al's has a large selection of cycling accessories and clothing.

**Cache Valley Veloist Bicycle Touring Club** (www.cvveloists.org). This is a welcoming, community-based club that wants to share the joy of the sport among friends and newcomers.

**Joyride Bikes** (435-753-7175; www.joyridebikes.com), 65 South Main, Logan. This retail and demo shop specializes in bikes and can offer good ride suggestions, if you're looking for advice.

**Sunrise Cyclery** (435-753-3294; www.sunrisecyclery.net), 138 North 100 East, Logan. This is purely a retail shop, but it has a full selection of bike parts and a tuning shop. They also put on the famous Logan-to-Jackson bike tour, and their Web site hosts a community forum.

## Mountain Biking

**Jardine Juniper** (access is described in the *Hiking* section). This is one of the area's technically intermediate, yet highly strenuous classic single-track rides that takes riders up nearly 1,900 vertical feet to Utah's oldest living tree, estimated to be 3,200 years old. This trail is just about 6 miles long and is in season mid-May through September.

**Logan River Trail** (as described in the *Hiking* section) demands very little technically and physically, and takes a wide dirt path that parallels the Logan River. The trail is 3.7 miles long and has virtually no incline or decline as mountain biking is concerned. There is just 1 mile of mildly technical single-track riding in the middle of its length.

**Richards Hollow Trail** is a loop trail that gives riders the chance to bomb down a single track after ascending on a dirt road. The climb is 9 miles (11 if you want to access a higher drop-in point) and is mellow compared with ascending on single track. The descent is 5.6 miles (or 7.3) with 2,000 feet elevation loss. From Hyrum, head east on Main Street (UT 101) 6.8 miles up Blacksmith Fork Canyon. Turn left onto Left Hand Fork Road and travel 3.6 miles; parking is just above the Friendship Campground.

**Sherwood Hills Resort** (435-245-6055; www.sherwoodhills.com), 12 miles southwest of Logan in Sardine Canyon, along US 81/91, Wellsville. This resort has its own trail that is used for serious regional races but is open to customers otherwise.

**BOATING** **Bear Lake** (as described in the "Bear Lake" chapter), is by far the largest freshwater lake in the vicinity of the Cache Valley. It offers the area's most accessible still-water boating. The town of Garden City has boat rentals and launch sites, as well as creature comforts including lodging and restaurants.

**Logan River** (as described in *Fishing*) represents the area's best white-water boating. Paddling this river is tricky, as it is a steep and narrow river interrupted by three dams. This river requires great skill to run, and ratings along this section are Grades II–V. The Web site www.riverfacts.com describes this river in detail and lists hotel recommendations along the way.

**FISHING** **Bear Lake** (as described in the "Bear Lake" chapter) is Utah's second-largest freshwater lake and just 30 miles northeast of Logan. This sizable body of water has two state parks and ample infrastructure for lake fishing, including boat ramps and boat rentals. Fish in this lake include cisco, and cutthroat.

**Logan River,** which runs directly through town, is a popular trout fishery with ample access along US 89 in Logan Canyon and several species of trout. There are 30 miles of easily accessible roadside fishing, divided into sections by dams called the First, Second, and Third dams. Above these dams there is a very clear river dominated by cutthroat and brown trout; beneath these it is common to sometimes catch large brown and rainbow trout.

**The State of Utah** publishes its own guidebooks, complete with area recommendations and fishing-related and wildlife conservation laws. These books are available for free download at www.wildlife.utah.gov/guidebooks or can be picked up at any Utah Division of Wildlife Resources Office or licensing agent (locations listed on the Web site)—somewhere you'll need to stop anyway in order to pick up the necessary conservation licenses.

**GOLF** **Birch Creek Golf Course** (435-563-6825; www.birchcreekgolf.com), 600 East Center St., Smithfield. This is a public course with 18 holes, 6,877 yards, and a par 72 rating. This course is much more flat and open than many in the area and is well liked for its value and playing speed. $24 on weekdays, $25 on weekends.

**Logan River Golf Course** (435-750-0123), 550 West 1000 South, Logan. This public, par-71, 18-hole course has 6,502 yards. This very lush and scenic course is thickly lined with trees, frequent water hazards, and high grasses. The Logan River runs through the property. $35.

**Sherwood Hills Golf Course** (435-245-6055; www.sherwoodhills.com/golf), 12 miles southwest of Logan in Sardine Canyon, along US 81/91, Wellsville. This public course is located at the Sherwood Hills resort. It is a nine-hole, 3,315-yard, par-36 course that is one of the area's most immaculately manicured and maintained. The course is generally hilly and tree lined, set immediately beneath mountain slopes. $28.

**HIKING** **Bonneville Shoreline Trail,** in the foothills east of town, has many access points; to get to the Logan Canyon access, park at the intersection of Canyon Road and UT 89 (at mouth of Logan Canyon). This system, like that of Salt Lake City, Provo, and Ogden, is Logan's installment of this popular Utah trailway. This 2-mile trail more or less traverses the terrain around the former shoreline of ancient Lake Bonneville. This lake, caused by a moist ice-age climate and earthen dams, occupied an area approximately half the size of modern Utah in the Great Basin. Having emptied and filled many times, its last appearance was about 12,000 years ago. Today the former shorelines are still visible.

**Crimson Trail** is a moderate trail in Logan Canyon, 2 miles long with 800 feet of climbing. It is generally forested, though has nice views of the surrounding canyon walls and its limestone cliff bands. This out-and-back trip can be partially converted into a loop hike by taking the **Riverside Nature Trail.** This trail stays fairly near the Logan River, connecting Spring Hollow to Guinavah Campgrounds (the trailhead for Crimson Trail). The Crimson Trail is particularly colorful during the fall foliage season. The trailhead is at Guinavah Campground, about 6.5 miles into the canyon on US 89 on the south side of the road.

**Jardine Juniper Trail** is another area classic, whose featured attraction is "Old Jardine," a 1,500-year-old Rocky Mountain juniper. Jardine, which is still alive, is almost 9 feet wide and 45 feet tall. To reach the tree, you must climb almost 2,000 vertical feet over the course of 5.7 miles. The trailhead is at Wood Camp Campground, 10 miles into Logan Canyon on US 89.

**Logan Cave** is another natural spectacle in Logan Canyon. This limestone cavern extends almost 1 mile (4,000 feet) into its parent mountain. It used to be a popular cave to explore. However, vandalism forced a closure, and so the cave is now only viewable from the mouth. Still worth the stop, if you're in the canyon; the hike is very short, and the cave is visible from the road. The trailhead is 12.2 miles into the canyon on US 89.

**Logan River Trail** is a quick 'n' easy option with almost no elevation gain or loss and many points of access. This 3.7-mile trail presents as a perfect option for jogging or light hiking near town in a riverside setting. Access is at multiple points east of Logan along US 89, starting just 2.5 miles into the canyon at Second Dam, but also at the Bridger Campground, Gus Lind Flat, Third Dam, and Spring Hollow.

**Wind Cave Trail** offers a 1-mile journey that steeply ascends just more than 1,000 vertical feet to fairly peculiar limestone arch and cave formations. This short hike also offers pleasant views of steep and forested Logan Canyon and its limestone cliff bands. The trailhead is roughly 5.2 miles east of Logan on US 89.

**HORSEBACK RIDING Beaver Creek Lodge** (as described in the *Lodging* section) offers guided horseback rides during the summer months. Horses provide a great way to see more of the national forests, public lands, wilderness, and trails surrounding the Cache Valley.

**ROCK CLIMBING Logan Canyon Bouldering** has two main fields: the Beaver Boulders and the Scree Boulders. These boulders are limestone and have seen very little development, yet offer a few dozen established problems each. The Beaver Boulders are generally fairly committing at 10–20 feet high, and the Scree Boulders' established problems are relatively moderate, usually V0–V5. These two fields are located along the Beaver Mountain Ski Road.

SCENIC LOGAN CANYON IS HOME TO THE LOGAN MARATHON AND MANY LIMESTONE CLIFFS POPULAR FOR SPORT AND TRADITIONAL ROCK CLIMBING.

Page Kyle

**Logan Canyon Sport Climbing,** east of Logan on UT 89. The climbing in this canyon is, for the most part, bolted sport climbing on limestone. However, there is some quartzite in the canyon, and occasional traditional protection is required on some routes. The canyon's easier routes are found at the First and Second Practice walls, with the Second consisting of mostly top-rope routes. On the other end of the difficulty spectrum is The China Wall Cave. This is the location of Boone Speed's route Super Tweak, the country's first 5.14b. There are two guidebooks on the area: Tim Monsell's *Logan Canyon Climbs* and *Northern Utah Limestone* by Casey Hyer.

**Rock Haus** (435-713-0068; www.rockhausgym.com), 1780 North 200 East, North Logan. This is a well-designed climbing gym with lead climbing, varied angles, crack climbing, and a bouldering wall. Novices and families are also welcome here, as gear rentals, top roping, and instruction are available. More than 12,000 square feet of climbing space is represented by a realistic variety of angles and features.

## SKIING

### Alpine

**Beaver Mountain** (office: 435-753-0921 or 866-703-1483, snow phone: 435-753-4822; www.skithebeav.com), 27 miles east of Logan on US 89. Beaver Mountain is Utah's northernmost resort. It receives around 400 inches of snow each year, has an elevation of 7,200–8,800 feet, and has 664 acres. Though the amount of snow is slightly less than that of the Wasatch Resorts, the northern location keeps the temperatures low enough that snow sticks. This is a low-key, hometown resort—small and inexpensive, but still with 25 percent of its terrain considered advanced and 40 percent intermediate. $38 for adults, $30 for children ages 12 and under, $22 for seniors ages 65 and up.

### Nordic

Logan's ski clubs **Nordic United** (www.nordicunited.org), the **Logan Ranger District** (435-755-3620), the **Utah Conservation Core,** and the **Utah State Outdoor Recreational Center** (435-797-3264) all pool together to make Nordic skiing in the Logan area possible and pleasant. Much of the skiing is along forest roads. If there is enough snow to ski, then there is enough snow to snowmobile, and many people prefer to avoid encounters with these motorized vehicles, so an effort is made to keep both enthusiasts happy. There are no Nordic ski supply or rental shops in the vicinity, so plan ahead if you wish to partake.

**Green Canyon.** Start at 1900 North 1600 East, and head east 1 mile along 1900 North to the obvious parking area. A groomed trail heads up this fairly open, yet narrow, canyon for about 4 miles.

**Franklin Basin,** 22.8 miles east of the mouth of Logan Canyon/Ranger Station on UT 89. This is a popular scenic trail by summer, where many people fish and ride horses. A groomed trail by winter, this is shared by skiers and a large population of snowmobilers. (If you wish to avoid encounters, ski early in the mornings or on weekdays.)

**Sink Hollow,** base of Beaver Mountain Ski Resort, 27 miles east of Logan on US 89. In winter this is a skier-only area, allowing you to enjoy snowmobile-free solitude. This trail crosses the Idaho/Utah border, is very popular, and is the site of many community races.

Tony Grove and Tony Grove Lake, 19.6 miles east of the mouth of Logan Canyon/Ranger Station on UT 89. This area is characterized by flat, open meadows dotted with the occasional evergreen tree, and rimmed by hills and small mountains. In summer, a 7-mile paved road reaches the lake from the turnoff; in winter, this is a popular area for skiers and snowmobilers.

## ✳ Lodging

HOTELS The Cache Valley has more than its share of familiar chain and basic hotels, most of which are located directly on Main Street in Logan and are easy to spot and easy on the wallet. These include the **Best Western Baugh Motel** (435-752-5220 or 800-462-5220), 153 South Main St., Logan; **Best Western Weston Inn** (435-752-5700 or 800-532-5055), 250 North Main St., Logan; the **Comfort Inn** (435-752-9141 or 800-228-5150), 447 North Main St., Logan; **Crystal Inn** (435-752-0707 or 800-280-0707), 853 South Main St., Logan; **Hampton Inn** (435-713-4567 or 800-426-7866), 1665 North Main St., Logan; the **Logan Inn** (435-753-5623), 364 South Main St., Logan; the **Old Trapper Inn** (435-753-5602), 43 East 100 South, Logan; **Ramada** (435-787-2060 or 800-272-6232), 2002 South US 89/91, Logan; and the **Super 8 Motel** (435-753-8883 or 800-800-8000), 865 South US 89/91, Logan.

**Beaver Creek Lodge** (Logan Canyon, Utah; 800-946-4485; www.beaver creeklodge.com), located 27 miles east of Logan in Logan Canyon. This lodge is remote enough to feel secluded, yet, it's also within reasonable commuting distance to in-town amenities. The mountain-style hotel, surrounded by an expansive property, has continuous balconies on each level, raw timber furniture, cozy decorations, and common sitting areas. Package deals at the lodge include home-cooked meals, snowmobile rentals, and guided horseback trips. $100–$140 for lodging only.

**University Inn** (435-797-0017 or 800-231-5634; www.usu.edu/univinn), 4300 Old Main Hill, Logan. Located right on the edge of the Utah State campus, this hotel is extremely affordable, for its central location. Sizes of rooms vary from standard hotel style to expansive suites. The hotel is outfitted with conference rooms for academic and business guests. $70–$110.

BED-AND-BREAKFASTS
**Providence Inn Bed & Breakfast** (435-752-3432 or 800-480-4943; www.providenceinn.com), 10 South Main, Providence. Just five minutes south of Logan, this bed-and-breakfast has 33 rooms, each decorated in slightly individual style, but each with tasteful reserve. Each well-kept room has the aura of a historic New England home. Options range from queen guest rooms to deluxe king suites. This building, one of the oldest in the valley, dates back to 1871, when it was completed and began service as the Old Rock Meeting House. $100–$200.

**Seasons at the Riter Mansion** (435-752-7727 or 800-478-7459; www.the ritermansion.com), 168 North 100 East, Logan. The Riter Mansion in downtown Logan is among the area's most elegant accommodations. Historic, yet polished, modernized, and full of natural light, the mansion's entrance is inviting. Size and cheer of the rooms do vary significantly, so be sure to call well in advance for the room of your preference. Delicious breakfasts, fireplaces, and a whirlpool add to the experience. $100–$170.

**RESORTS Sherwood Hills Resort** (435-245-5054 or 800-532-5066; www .sherwoodhills.com), 7877 South US 89/91, Wellsville. The Sherwood Hills Resort, located in the Wellsville Canyon, is a true retreat with its own golf course, spa, pool, tennis, volleyball, and trails for hiking, mountain biking, birding, and cross-country skiing. Such a large property gives guests a feeling of escape. Rooms range in their elaborateness, from standard hotel-style rooms to deluxe suites. Special packages are available to help integrate guests into the surroundings and include dinners at nearby restaurants as well as recreation opportunities.

## ✳ Where to Eat

**DINING OUT Le Nonne** (435-752-9577), 129 North 100 East, Logan. Le Nonne is a refreshing, upscale Italian restaurant whose focus is on quality of service, cuisine, and atmosphere. The chefs here manage to bring fresh vegetables and herbs to northern Utah throughout the year, dare to prepare fresh seafood, and are not afraid to serve a rare steak. The restaurant is housed in a historic Victorian mansion just north of the tabernacle. Among the best dining in northern Utah. $12–$30.

**EATING OUT ✐ The Bluebird** (435-752-3155), 19 North Main St., Logan. Open for lunch and dinner Monday–Saturday. This 1914 restaurant has the styling of an old soda fountain, with hometown-type American cuisine and very affordable prices. In addition to soups, salads, sandwiches, and other comfort foods, ice cream, milk shakes, and ice cream floats are available. $7–$13.

**Caffe Ibis** (435-753-9515 www.caffe ibis.com), 52 Federal Ave., Logan. Open daily. Logan's most hip and tuned-in café—rich with local happenings and information on international issues—is a distinct detour from today's brushed-steel, corporate café. Instead of expensive pastries, this café serves salads, sandwiches, and even tacos.

**Café Sabor** (435-752-8088), 600 West Center St., Logan. Open for lunch and dinner Monday–Saturday. Café Sabor treats the Cache Valley to upscale, fresh Mexican cuisine in a fresh, upscale setting. Fresh fruits, herbs, and vegetables go into the homemade salsas and entrées. Outdoor seating, occasional live music, and the old switching station location add to the ambience. Because this is a popular restaurant, prepare to wait on peak nights. $10–$22.

**Formosa Restaurant** (435-753-7889; www.formosalogan.com), 890 North Main St., Logan. Open daily for lunch and dinner. This is where Logan eats Chinese cuisine. Prices are reasonable, food is fresh, and the service is prompt. As a perk, this restaurant is open on Sunday. $8–$15.

**Indian Oven** (435-787-1757; www .indianovenutah.com), 130 North Main St., Logan. Open for lunch and dinner Monday–Saturday; closed 2:30–4:30. Spicy, rich traditional Indian fare is the name of the game here. This restaurant hits the spot for those craving curry, vindaloo, kurma, paneer, and more. A generous selection of vegetarian entrées is available in addition to lamb, chicken, and seafood dishes. $8–$14.

**Kamin Thai** (435-755-6543), 51 West 200 South, Logan. Open for lunch and dinner Monday–Saturday. This restaurant has a very polished air with outdoor dining and excellent presentation. This is Logan's option for the light and intricate dishes of Thailand. $9–$14.

**Tanpopo** (435-750-7099), 55 West 1000 North, Logan. Open for lunch and dinner Monday–Saturday. Tanpopo brings sushi and traditional Japanese fare to the Cache Valley. The atmosphere is extremely simple and subdued, but the food is fresh. Though the main draw is sushi, a variety of cuisine is available, including an abundance of noodle dishes in substantial portions. If in town on Tuesday or Thursday, happy hour occurs 3–5 PM, at which time every item on the menu costs only $2. $8–$18.

## ✳ Entertainment

**Cache Valley Center for the Arts** (435-752-0026; www.centerforthe arts.us), 43 South Main, Logan. This is a community art umbrella that facilitates and coordinates performing arts, community involvement, and more. Check their Web site for upcoming cultural events and an extremely comprehensive alphabetical arts listing that names the community's musicians, performance groups, artists, and more.

**Caine Lyric Theatre** (435-797-1500; www.usu.edu/lyric), 28 West Center, Logan. This theater was constructed in 1913 and has hosted opera and theater ever since. Each summer the **Old Lyric Repertory Theater** puts on comedies, dramas, and musicals here. This theater was restored in 2000 and seats 364 people.

**The Chase Fine Arts Center** (435-797-3040; www.usu.edu), 4030 Old Main Hill, Utah State University, Logan. This major facility has several performance venues, including the **Kent Concert Hall, Morgan Theatre,** and **Caine Lyric Theatre.**

**Dansante Building** (435-750-0300 or 800-262-0074), 59 South 100 West, Logan. The offices of the **Utah Festival Opera** and its permanent home are located here. This building is one of the oldest remaining in Utah. Built in 1900, it was fully restored in 1997.

Today it contains a 124-seat performance hall, as well as many rooms for the various production elements of the opera, from costumes to props.

**Ellen Eccles Theater at Cache Valley Center for the Arts** (435-752-0026; www.centerforthearts.us), 43 South Main St., Logan. Built in 1923 and restored in 1993, this is the home of the **Utah Festival Opera** each summer.

The **Manon Caine Russell Kathryn Caine Wanlass Performance Hall** (2970 Old Main Hill, Utah State University, Logan; 435-797-0305). Opened in January of 2006, this state-of-the-art performance hall on the Utah State campus was designed specifically for chamber music performances. Though the stage has capacity for a maximum of 22 musicians, there is enough room for 424 audience members.

SPORTS **Utah State University Aggies** (www.utahstateaggies.cstv .com). This NCAA school was admitted to the Western Athletic Conference in 2005 and includes the following teams: basketball, cross country, football, golf, gymnastics, soccer, softball, tennis, track, and volleyball. Gymnastics is one of the school's best sports on the women's side. On the men's side, the basketball team is one of the teams in the league with a history of most wins.

## ✳ Selective Shopping

**North Main Street** has the highest concentration of shops outside of a mall in Logan and is where most locally owned shops are located.

FARMERS' MARKETS **Gardeners' Market** (www.gardenersmarket.com), Pioneer Park, 100 South 200 East, Logan. 9–1, mid-May through mid-October. The Gardeners' Market is where Cache Valley farmers, artists, artisans, and restaurants bring their wares to sell in the company of live music and fresh air.

**Wednesday Produce Market,** 199 North Main, Logan. 4:30–8 PM July through August. Though there are fewer accessory goods for sale, you can get farm-fresh produce here during the summer.

MALLS **Cache Valley Mall** (435-753-5400; www.cachevalleymall.com), 1300 North Main St., Logan. This mall offers the most concentrated shopping in the area. In case you've forgotten an important dress, or simply need to pass away a rainy day, this mall has shops that will cover your needs. Here you will find a full variety of mall stores, national and local, from jewelers to electronics and department stores.

GALLERIES **Alliance for the Varied Arts** (435-753-2970; www.varied arts.org), 35 West 100 South, Logan. Utah's oldest nonprofit arts group, this gallery organizes a gallery stroll and Art on the Lawn, as well as other events. The strolls take place Friday 6–9 PM but are not necessarily a regularly scheduled event. (See the Web site for the date of the next stroll.)

**Jerry Fuhriman Studio-Gallery** (435-753-9446), 28 Federal Ave., Logan. This gallery features the works of local watercolor and oil painter Jerry Fuhriman. These are landscapes inspired by the many regions of Utah, from the plains to red-rock deserts.

**Paint Utah—Michael Bingham** (435-750-5066), 90 North 100 East (downstairs), Logan. This is one of many galleries featuring the work of Bingham's prolific career. Now a Logan resident, he has filled this gallery with his impressions of local scenery.

**Ten Thousand Villages/Global Village Gifts** (435-713-4347; www.ten thousandvillages.com), 146 North 100 East, Logan. This is an international fair-trade imports store designed to bring income to artists and artisans in developing countries.

**Winborg Masterpieces Gallery** (435-792-4278; www.winborg.com), 55 North Main St., Logan. This space is filled with religiously saturated depictions of local life and history.

# BEAR LAKE

Bear Lake is a huge freshwater body of water, about 20 miles long and more than 5 miles wide. This lake occupies the bottom of a canyon formed as recently as 150,000 years ago by geological faults. At the time of the ice ages, when the climate was much cooler and wetter, Lake Bonneville occupied a region in the Great Basin half the size of Utah. Bear Lake filled almost the entirety of its basin and was more than double its present size.

For the last 10,000 years or so, Bear Lake Environs were traversed by Shoshone, Ute, and Bannock tribes. These tribes considered the lake home but were never permanent residents, as the winter temperatures were much too harsh to allow for permanent inhabitance without significant infrastructure. In fact, this corner of the state remained untouched by civilization much longer than the rest of Utah.

The first recorded sightings of the lake by European settlers were in 1818 by French-Canadian Hudson Bay trappers. In the 1820s and 1830s, western legends and mountain men Jedediah Smith and Jim Bridger frequently visited the shores of Bear Lake and maintained good relations with the local tribes. The Oregon Trail, in heavy use from 1836 to 1850, ran very near Bear Lake to the north. Though the trail might have impacted the lake's history—and the lake might have impacted the trail's—it seems likely that no one using the trail ever dipped south to see the lake.

Mormon settlers arrived in Salt Lake City in 1847. After quickly establishing that city, they began to settle towns in what they hoped would have become a sovereign nation called the State of Deseret. Bear Lake was first visited by the Mormons in 1863 at the site of modern-day St. Charles. Led by Charles C. Rich, these Mormons created an agreement with the "locals," which would leave nearly the entire southern portion of Bear Lake Valley untouched by whites. Of course this was never meant to last, and soon Mormons encroached on the entire inhabitable shoreline, establishing Fish Haven, Garden City, Pickleville, and Lake Town. Even though these towns never grew substantially, such a large and beautiful lake would inevitably develop into a recreation destination. Today the lake is shared almost equally by Idaho and Utah, and its striking blue waters are enjoyed by boaters and water-sports enthusiasts. Two state parks and seven boat ramps provide recreation access to the lake. Garden City, whose year-round population is fewer than 500 people, and Lake Town, whose population is only 188, are Utah's two Bear Lake villages; Fish Haven and St. Charles are in Idaho. Despite the lake's

## WHAT'S IN THE WATER?

Bear Lake has its share of mysteries and tall tales. Dating to prehistory, long before the Mormons came to the area, tribal lore told of a large, serpentine monster that lived in the waters of the lake. This monster had, in years long past, eaten a group of warriors and was called the "water devil." Accordingly, the local peoples would not swim in the lake, sleep near it, or bathe in it. Fast forward several centuries and swap residents. According to reports in the *Deseret News* from 1868, many, many Mormon settlers reported sightings. These men and women, alone and in groups, reported observing an extremely large, slender animal as long as 200 feet (some said much smaller) moving at incredible speeds across the lake's surface and sometimes even crawling awkwardly on land by way of short legs.

small population, it hosts a number of popular summer festivals and winter events that cater to the area's visitors, including snowmobile hill-climb competitions and Raspberry Days, which in addition to raspberry-based culinary treats, brings a rodeo, parades, dances, fireworks, a fair, talent shows, running races, and concerts to the area.

GUIDANCE The Web site www.bearlake.com is dedicated to providing visitor information on the entire Bear Lake Valley, for both Idaho and Utah.

**Bear Lake Convention & Visitors Bureau** (208-945-3333 or 800-448-2327; www.bearlake.org). This is another such Web site organized into categories such as lodging, events, dining, and activities per season.

**Bear Lake Rendezvous Chamber** (800-448-2327; www.bearlakechamber.com). The chamber's Web site has a list of area businesses as well as visitor-specific information.

GETTING THERE *By car:* Utah's half of Bear Lake is in the northeasternmost corner of the state's blunt panhandle; Idaho's portion of this oblong lake is in the far southeastern corner of Idaho. All of the townships along the lake are on the western shore. Utah's on-location settlement is **Garden City;** Idaho's nearest Bear Lake towns are **Fish Haven** and **St. Charles.** Utah's only major highway accessing the lake is US 89, which trends northeast out of Ogden, passes through Logan, grazes the western shore of the lake, and finally bends north to follow the Idaho/Wyoming Border. If coming from Idaho, follow US 30 east from I-15. This intersects with US 89 just north of the Lake; take US 89 south. All of the Bear Lake–area towns are located along this highway.

*By air:* **Pocatello Regional Airport** (208-234-6154; www.pocatello.us), 117 miles north of Garden City. Pocatello Regional is a midsized airport about 85 miles to the northwest of Bear Lake.

**Salt Lake International Airport** (801-575-2400 or 800-595-2442; www.slcairport.com), about 5 miles west of Salt Lake City on I-80. This is about 120 miles away from Bear Lake via US 89, I-15, and I-80.

**MEDICAL EMERGENCY Bear Lake Community Health Center** (435-946-3660), 325 West Hogan Hwy., Garden City. This facility was opened in 2003 and performs the full spectrum of health services, from urgent to primary care, on an ability-to-pay basis.

**Bear Lake Hospital** (208-847-1630; www.blmhospital.com), 164 South Fifth St., Montpelier, Idaho. Montpelier is at the junction of US 89 and US 30, about 15 miles northeast of St. Charles, Idaho, the northernmost town in the immediate vicinity of Bear Lake—and about another 12 more from Garden City, to the south.

## ✳ To See and Do

**Bear Lake Raspberry Days** (www.gardencity.us or www.bearlake.org). This is a three-day festival that takes place usually toward the end of July or beginning of August. Originating out of a raspberry harvest, this massive celebration now includes rodeo, craft fairs, pancake breakfasts, live music, a running race, fireworks, cook-offs, a beauty pageant, and, of course, delicious raspberry confections. This is a townwide celebration, and shuttle buses operate from many locations to transport participants around town.

**Pickleville Playhouse** (435-946-2918; www.picklevilleplayhouse.com), 2049 South Bear Lake Blvd., Garden City. This company puts on shows June, July, and August of each year. They usually do two different musicals, both of which are performed throughout the season. All shows are family friendly and begin with an (optional) preshow Western-style dinner (as listed in the *Where to Eat* section of this chapter). Themes are often Western, but not always.

BEAR LAKE STRADDLES IDAHO AND UTAH, AND, SECOND TO UTAH LAKE, IS THE STATE'S LARGEST FRESHWATER LAKE.

Craig Bowden

**Bear Lake Fun** (435-946-3200; www.bearlakefun.com). This group of stores has six rental locations with snowmobiles, motor boats and Jet Skis, ATVs, and even cabins for rent. They rent in both Idaho and Utah, and have boating advice on their Web site.

**Bear Lake Sails** (435-946-8600 or 866-867-5912), 2129 South Bear Lake Blvd., Garden City. This company rents motor boats and Jet Skis, an integral part of the experience of many.

**Rendezvous Beach/Bear Lake State Park** (435-946-3343). Bear Lake straddles Idaho and Utah in the far northeastern part of the state. Stretching north–south, it is about 20 miles long and 5 miles wide, and is the second-largest freshwater lake in (or partly in) Utah. This state park is an especially attractive home base for boaters wishing to explore these waters, though biking, jogging, and camping are popular here as well. Boat ramps, marinas, beaches, picnic grounds, and a paved 4-mile trail make nature a bit more accessible to users here. Entrance $7 per vehicle. Camping $10–$25.

BIKING **Bear Lake Loop** is a 52-mile loop around the entirety of the lake. The western portion of the ride is flat, while the eastern side has enjoyable rolling topography. Each year at the beginning of August, this is the location for a road race put on by the Logan Cycling Club. Clockwise from Garden City, you will head north on US 89, then east onto North Beach Road just north of St. Charles. This road curves to the south, and you'll want to take a slight right onto Eastshore Road, which will bring you very near the lake, through Bear Lake State Park–East Beach, before turning into Cisco Road as it enters Utah. Follow this road to the southern tip of the lake as it curves to the south and turns into Main Street just north of Laketown. Take a right onto UT 30/Bear Lake Boulevard, and take this road all the way back and north into Garden City.

BOATING **Bear Lake** has an average depth of 85 feet and a surface area of about 150 miles. Its northern location and reasonable depth shorten the swimming season of the lake just a bit, but nonetheless boating is very popular here. Boaters and rental agencies are serious about it, too.

**Bear Lake Sails** (435-946-8600 or 866-867-5912), 2141 South Bear Lake Blvd., Garden City. This company rents motorboats, Waverunners, paddleboats, canoes, and kayaks, as well as water toys like tubes, water skis, and wakeboards.

**Cisco's Landing** (435-946-2717; www.ciscoslanding.com), 1865 North Bear Lake Blvd., Bear Lake State Marina, Garden City. This is your complete boating facility, with boat ramp, marina, and rentals including jet boats, kayaks, canoes, and motorboats.

FISHING Bear Lake, the second-largest freshwater lake in Utah, is one of the state's main boating and fishing destinations. The two main species fished at Bear Lake are the cutthroat and lake trout, and to a lesser extent yellow perch and other types. Trout in this lake can grow to be quite large. In winter, Bear Lake freezes over completely, and ice fishing is a popular activity here.

Interestingly, Bear Lake has four unique species that have evolved since the formation of this lake as little as 150,000 years ago. These are the Bear Lake Whitefish, Bear Lake Sculpin (a homely, bug-eyed creature), the Bonneville Cisco, and Bonneville Whitefish.

For more information on northern Utah fishing, visit www.utah.com/fish. Utah State publishes its own guidebooks, complete with area recommendations and fishing-related laws. These books are available as a free download at www.wildlife .utah.gov/guidebooks or can be picked up at any Utah Division of Wildlife Resources Office or licensing agent—somewhere you'll need to stop anyway.

**GOLF** **Bear Lake Golf Course** (435-946-8742), 2176 South Bear Lake Blvd., Garden City. This course is somewhat mountainous and challenging, with nine holes and a par-36 rating.

**Bear Lake West Golf Course** (208-945-2744), 155 US 89, Fish Haven, Idaho. This broad, generally flat and open course is open to the public and marked by occasional water hazards. Golfers catch great views of Bear Lake along the nine holes located on 2,715 yards. $28.

**HIKING** **Bear Lake Summit/Limber Pine Nature Trail,** parking at Sunrise Campground, about 4 miles west of Bear Lake at milepost 491.9 in Logan Canyon on US 89. This is a short and easy 1-mile loop with just 100 vertical feet of elevation gain. The trail gains what was once thought to be the oldest tree in the world. Recently it has been learned that, in fact, this tree is actually five trees that appear to be just one. Still, this "tree" is more than 550 years old, which is more than 2,500 years younger than the world's oldest. The tree is almost 8 feet wide and is 44 feet tall. Perks include views of the azure-colored Bear Lake to the east.

**Minnetonka Cave** (435-245-4422 or 208-942-2407), 9 miles up St. Charles Creek Rd. in St. Charles Canyon, west of St. Charles, Idaho. This cave has nine rooms, more than 480 steps, and is almost 0.5 mile long. The cave maintains a constant temperature of around 40°F, so be sure to dress accordingly. Bats, stalactites, stalagmites, and the like are the main attraction. The mouth of the cave is one of the area's highest cave entrances, at around 7,700 feet above sea level. The largest room on the tour is about 300 feet wide and 90 feet tall. Guided tours are available from the second week in June through Labor Day every year.

**SKIING**
*Alpine*
See **Beaver Mountain** in the *Skiing* section of the "Logan and the Cache Valley" chapter.

**Barrie's Ski And Sports** (208-945-2770 or 800-421-2896; www.barriessports .com), 45 South First West St., Bloomington, Idaho. This is the nearest ski shop to Bear Lake, about 5 miles north of St. Charles and 17 miles north of Garden City. This store offers a selection of downhill skiing equipment.

*Nordic*
**Bear Lake Golf Course** (435-946-8742), 2176 South Bear Lake Blvd., Garden City. In winter the golf course offers plenty of groomed Nordic ski trails at a convenient location.

Craig Bowden

THE SHORES OF BEAR LAKE

**SNOWMOBILING** The Bear Lake region is one of the Rocky Mountain's hot spots for snowmobiling. Because of its elevation and climactic trends, it enjoys consistently good winter snow cover. Lack of population and abundance of land also add to the advantages for sledders. In fact, the area has more than 350 miles of groomed trails. For avalanche danger, visit the Web site www.avalanche.org. For general information, grooming reports, and restrictions, call Bear Lake State Parks–Utah (435-946-3343 or 800-322-3770) or Bear Lake State Parks–Idaho (208-847-1045). The season usually lasts from the end of November into April.

## ✳ Lodging

**Bear Lake Lodging** (435-946-3300 or 888-642-2327; www.bearlake lodging.com). This central lodging agency rents a handful of cabins, homes, and condominiums to those wishing to stay in a vacation home instead of a hotel room. Their properties are generally located within **"Harbor Village"** in Garden City, which offers access to outdoor and indoor pools, a bike path, and tennis courts.

**Ideal Beach Resort** (435-946-3361; www.idealbeach.net), 2176 South Bear Lake Blvd., Garden City. Ideal Beach offers lakeside suites and rooms of various sizes, sleeping four to 20 people. Guests have access to campus amenities such as tennis, outdoor swimming

pool, children's playground, mini golf, sauna, laundry facilities, arcade, and bike and snowmobile rentals. Spacious lawns offer the chance to spread out and enjoy the outdoors. There is an on-site gift shop, and a small selection of groceries is available.

## ✳ Where to Eat

**Bear Lake Pizza** (435-946-3600), 240 South Bear Lake Blvd. This pizzeria offers a quick, simple meal perfect for families or large appetites earned recreating in the outdoors.

**Bear Trapper Steakhouse** (435-946-8484), 216 South Bear Lake Blvd., Garden City. This is the local carnivore-friendly eatery with rustic atmosphere, friendly service, and filling portions.

Also one of the only sit-down dinner restaurants in town.

**Hometown Drive-In** (435-946-2727), 105 North Bear Lake Blvd. This style of restaurant perfectly complements the summertime lakeside atmosphere of Bear Lake. The drive-in serves a variety of oversized, multipattied burgers, fried baskets, grilled sandwiches, and other cold specialty sandwiches. There are many shakes from which to choose—however, the raspberry shake is the most classic. Made with the area's famous local raspberries, these thick, monster shakes are enough to feed a family.

**Pickleville Playhouse Western Cookout** (435-946-2918; www.pickle villeplayhouse.com), 2049 South Bear Lake Blvd., Garden City. The playhouse offers Western cookout-style dinners on the evening of each show, starting at 6:30 PM in the Pickleville Pavilion (adjacent to the playhouse, as listed in the *To See and Do* section of this chapter). Huge slabs of meat are grilled over an open flame and served with cowboy beans, baked potatoes, salad, dinner rolls, punch, and dessert. Choices of meat include lemon-herb chicken, rib-eye steak, and pork ribs.

# GOLDEN SPIKE NATIONAL HISTORIC SITE

T he **Golden Spike National Historic Site** (www.nps.gov/gosp) commemorates the May 10, 1869, meeting place of the Central Pacific Railroad and Union Railroad. On this day, two golden spikes were driven into the ground to celebrate the landmark accomplishment that was the completion of the First Transcontinental Railroad—and one of the most important accomplishments in the history of modern Utah.

Since the successful inception of the locomotive as transportation in the 1830s, it had a goal to connect the East and West coasts of North America with rails. Existing track and the extreme topography of the Intermountain West dictated that the line would have to run through Echo Canyon in northern Utah, the most passable canyon in the vicinity. The Central Pacific and Union Railroad began designing and constructing their own lines that would aim to include this passageway.

On April 9, 1869, it was agreed that "Promontory Summit," in what would later become Box Elder County, was to be the meeting place for the Central Pacific Railroad to join with the western-bound Union Railroad. This sparked great rigor in the two rail companies, their goal clearly in sight; Central Pacific set a one-day construction record of 10 rail miles, which will likely never be broken. A mere month after deciding where to meet, the two companies ran together at Promontory Summit, just 25 miles west of modern-day Tremonton, on May 10, 1869. This would forever change Utah's history and catalyze Utah's industrial and multicultural development.

Over the next few months, this region saw an extreme boom. Corrine would become the first primarily "gentile" town in Utah. At the time of this initial railroad boom, it flooded with economy, culture, and population from around the world. People projected that it would overtake Salt Lake City as Utah's major city and political capital. The streets were filled with rowdy Old West types, prostitutes, saloons, and the like.

As a matter of course, politics flared. Utah was still decades from becoming a state. In the 1870s, the Latter-day Saints were still earnestly attempting to persuade the United States of America to grant them their own sovereign nation. Making every effort to establish such a nation, Mormon leaders established outpost cities around the Rocky Mountains and desert Southwest, and most importantly worked hard to maintain a stronghold on the existing Utah government and towns.

So it goes without saying that significant pressure was applied to reduce Corrine and other rail towns—havens for gamblers, prostitutes, drifters, and other "heathens"—to nothing more than stops along the line, ghost towns. These towns, with the exception of those in the Tremonton and Ogden areas, succumbed to the pressure and indeed slowly died.

At the Golden Spike National Historic Site, 2 miles of track remember the original location where railways from the East Coast and the West Coast connected the entire breadth of North America for the first time. Though the area now is quiet and isolated, it was, for a moment, the most important place in the United States. Today this historic location is celebrated by historians and train buffs with multiple demonstrations and festivities year-round. Every Saturday and each holiday between May 10 and Labor Day you can watch reenactments from 11 AM to 1 PM. Working replicas of the key locomotives of the time, *119* and *Jupiter,* animate the ceremonies. The Last Spike Ceremony kicks off the season and is held every year on May 10, the date of this historic anniversary. Winter sees very little activity, with the exception of the Steam Festival, held during the last weekend of December every year. Tourists can experience the park via a 1.5-mile hiking trail and several driving loops that pass different remnants of these early days. $5 per vehicle.

GUIDANCE **Golden Spike National Historic Site Visitors Center** (435-471-2209; www.nps.gov/gosp). This is the official center to the historic site, listing events schedules, activities, and fees.

**Box Elder County Tourism** (www.boxelder.org). This Web site maintains a short outline of tourist attractions and amenities in the county.

**Tremonton City** (435-257-2625; www.tremontoncity.com). This Web site has accommodations, dining, recreation, and store listings.

GETTING THERE *By car:* This region falls in the immediate vicinity of the junction of I-84 and I-15. Promontory, the location of Golden Spike National Historic Site, is about 20 miles west of this junction and Tremonton, near the northern tip of the Great Salt Lake. UT 83 and 102 are the two state highways connecting the interstate to this site.

*By air:* The **Salt Lake International Airport (SLC)** (801-575-2400 or 800-595-2442; www.slcairport.com), just 90 miles south by way of I-15 and I-80, is a major hub with inexpensive flights and many direct flights around the nation.

MEDICAL EMERGENCY **Bear River Valley Hospital** (435-257-7441), 440 West 600 North, Tremonton. This hospital is the biggest, nearest hospital to the region.

**Intermountain North Ogden Clinic** (801-786-7500; www.intermountain healthcare.org), 2400 North Washington Blvd., North Ogden. About 30–40 minutes from the Tremonton/Promontory area, this is the nearest nonappointment, nonemergency-room facility.

NEWSPAPERS *Tremonton Leader* (www.tremontonleader.com). Tremonton's local daily, this is a small-town affair with local news and events listings.

## ✳ To See and Do

**Big Fill Loop** is a 1.5-mile walking trail that follows a short portion of the Central Pacific's original path. Because of railway standards, this line could never be steeper than 2 percent. In order to achieve this standard, massive landfills and digs were implemented. On this walk is the "Big Fill," a large ravine backfilled as such. This is especially impressive when considering the lack of modern implements used to complete such jobs. The Central Pacific used more than 500 workers and almost as many animals over the course of a few months to span this ravine about 175 feet deep and 500 feet across. Cuts into the earth and evidence of blasting are also visible from the trail; these, too, were created using only basic means of that time. Because of the relative isolation of this National Historic Site, the vistas along this walk are very similar to those the workers would have seen at the time of the project.

**East Auto Tour** is a 2-mile road that follows the old Union Pacific line. Features of this drive are Union's final cut, trestles, fills, and abutments. The Chinese Arch, named after the Chinese immigrants who played an enormous role in the railroad's completion, is a small limestone arch that can be reached by a short walk. This remains open during the winter season, though hours are restricted.

**West Auto Tour,** a 5-mile drive (10 miles out and back), tours another portion of the original Central Pacific line, with vistas of fills, cuts, and old-fashioned culverts crafted of wood and stone. Scenic views of the Great Salt Lake to the south. Also along this drive is the record-breaking 10-mile section of track that was laid in one single day. This road closes during winter, as regulated by snow cover.

## ✳ Lodging

The nearest lodging to Golden Spike National Historic Site in Tremonton are fairly basic accommodations as follows: **Hampton Inn** (435-257-6000; www.tremonton.hamptoninn.com), 2145 West Main St., Tremonton; **Marble Motel** (435-257-3524), 116 North Tremont St., Tremonton; and **Sandman Motel** (435-257-5675), 585 West Main St., Tremonton. For more options or more deluxe lodging, see the Lodging sections in the "Greater Ogden" and "Logan and the Cache Valley" chapters.

## ✳ Where to Eat

Tremonton is also the nearest area for dining in the Golden Spike National Historic Site region. Most eateries are also basic (either fast food, chain, or country-diner style) and can be found right in the center of town. Almost every establishment closes on Sunday.

# Southern Wasatch

PROVO

SUNDANCE RESORT

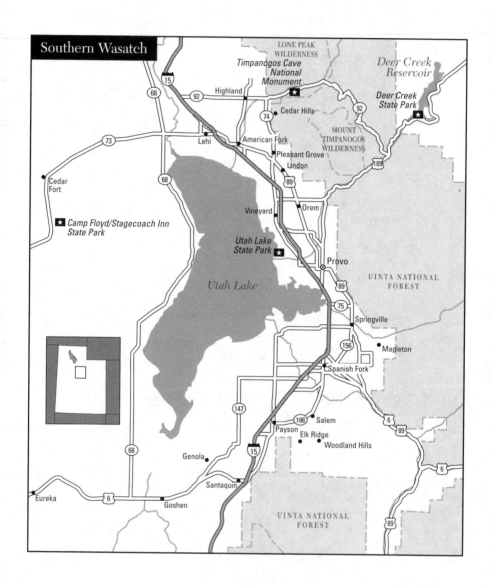

# SOUTHERN WASATCH IN BRIEF

Central Utah is home to the southern Wasatch Range, Provo, Brigham Young University, Utah Lake, and the Sundance Resort. Utah Lake is the largest freshwater lake in the state, with a surface area of almost 100,000 acres and an elevation of 4,500 feet. The southern Wasatch is the highest portion of the range, and Mount Nebo is 11,928 feet above sea level. The valley is broad and open, and is quickly being filled with the homes of Provo's many growing families.

Utah Valley is a unique place. While most urban areas have increased crime, rubbish, graffiti, high-rise buildings, and liberal thinkers, Utah Valley is markedly low-profile in its structures and is full of conservative politics and dress. It is a community held together by faith and morals to which the people strictly adhere. Though Salt Lake City was the early capital of Mormonism, and today still has many of its key buildings and offices, Provo has in many ways become the heart of the Church of Jesus Christ of Latter-day Saints.

Because Provo—with Brigham Young University, the Missionary Training Center, and so forth—is in many ways the functional center of the Mormon religion, this attracts many such devotees from around the world. These people have brought with them many things, the most noticeable of which are their arts and cuisine. If you stroll up University Avenue, you will see tiny restaurant after tiny restaurant filled with exotic aromas and décor. More so than common foreign fare found elsewhere in the United States, these offer even more exotic cuisine.

The Sundance Resort, tucked up in Provo Canyon along the Alpine Scenic Loop, is quite unlike Utah Valley. In some ways the differences between Provo and Sundance are parallel to those between Salt Lake City and Park City—and in other ways, they are completely dissimilar. Sundance has grown, just as Park City, to become an entity all its own. By choice, it is tucked up in the folds of tall mountains, isolated from the majority Mormon population below. However, unlike Park City, Sundance Resort has maintained its small, rustic charm and has not become overrun by beefed-up resorts.

## ✳ Weather

The weather in Utah Valley and nearby mountains is nearly identical to the weather in the Salt Lake Valley and its canyons. During the hottest month of the year, July, Provo sees average highs around 94°F; January, the coldest month of the year, brings highs just above 40°F. The most pleasant months, temperature-wise, are generally April, May, and October, during which high temperatures are somewhere in the 60s and 70s. As with any similarly mountainous region, the canyons remain significantly cooler than the valleys because of river-induced refrigeration effect, and elevation differences. The highest peaks in the Provo-Wasatch area are about 7,000 feet above the valley floor, so temperature differences are generally quite dramatic. Mountains are also much more susceptible to high winds and sudden precipitation.

Generally this region is extremely dry. Utah, after all, is a desert state. For most of the summer, and much of the winter, the valleys remain dry. Provo's annual precipitation totals only around 20 inches. Yet the Wasatch mountains have among the highest annual snowfall in the lower 48—with an average snow accumulation of 500 inches (or about 54 inches, if you measure it as liquid precipitation). This is because the enormous peaks squeeze the bellies of the clouds, forcing them to release most of the moisture that they've carried with them across the Great Basin.

## ✳ Special Events

*Early February:* **Winter Choir Fest** (800-978-8457) takes place at various locations across Utah Valley and features the area's best collegiate choirs.

*April:* **Semiannual LDS World Conference** (www.lds.org) takes place directly in Provo, but it does bring many thousands of Latter-day Saints to the area. BYU and the Missionary Training Center are particularly active during this time. The second yearly occurrence of this event is in October.

### OUTFITTER SERVICES

**Rocky Mountain Outfitters** (435-654-1655; www.rockymtnoutfitters.com). Guides for just about any kind of mountain-style outing in Utah you could imagine, from snowmobiling to horseback riding, fly-fishing, horse-pack trips, and chuckwagon dinners. Their office is in Heber City (30 miles northeast of Provo), and they operate trips around the state.

**High Country Rafting** (801-224-2500 in Provo or 435-649-7678 in Park City; www.highcountryrafting.com). A company based in Provo, this specializes in rafting, kayaking, and fly-fishing. In addition to these activities, the company also offers tubing and a ride on the Historic Heber Railroad as a means to reach the put-in for rafting trips.

**Red Elk Outfitters** (in American Fork; 801-763-9036) has a niche in customized scenic tours of Utah, as well as hunting, fishing, and fly-fishing trips.

**Rental Toys** (888-785-8697; www.rentaltoys.com), 1451 West 40 South, Lindon. This company stocks snowmobiles, ATVs, boats, and Jet Skis for rent. They serve the entire state of Utah and purchase a new fleet every year. Located in Lindon, just south of Salt Lake City (and north of Orem/Provo), this is a good stop for those coming in at the Salt Lake International Airport.

*Early June:* **Scottish Festival and Highland Games** (www.utahscots .org), at Thanksgiving Point in Lehi. This is a festival of Scottish culture and athletics, including many hefting activities: stone throws, weight tosses, and hammer throws.

*Last Week of June:* **Lehi Roundup Rodeo** (801-766-3951; www.lehicity .com/roundup). This is a community-wide event celebrating the town's Western culture and history.

*June and July:* **Blue Skies Concert Series,** which takes place at Pioneer Park, 500 West Center Street, on Monday nights at 7 PM.

*First Two Weeks of July:* **Springville World Folkfest** (801-489-4811; www .worldfolkfest.com) takes place at various locations across Springville, with folk dancers hailing from around the world.

*July:* **Summer Theater** (801-225-4107; www.sundance.org), Sundance Resort. This brings people up into the cool canyons to enjoy drama in the idyllic Sundance environment.

*July 24:* **Pioneer Day** (www.freedom festival.org) is perhaps one of the Latter-day Saints' most fervent and unmatched celebrations. This holiday commemorates the July 24, 1847, arrival of Brigham Young and the early Mormon pioneers in Utah. In Utah this almost completely replaces the Fourth of July holiday—and Provo is no exception. The parades and festivities resemble those of Independence Day but are celebrated zealously.

*Labor Day Weekend:* ✍ **Timpanogos Storytelling Festival** (801-229-7050; www.timpfest.org), Timpanogos Cave Park, American Fork Canyon State Park. This is a huge, family-friendly event that utilizes the beautiful American Fork Canyon as its backdrop.

*October:* **Semiannual LDS World Conference** (see *April*) comes to Utah for its second yearly installment during this month.

*November and December:* **Holiday Concerts** (around the valley). Jesus is the reason for the season, and this fact is not overlooked in Utah Valley. Many, many churches around the area put on quite a show during the last part of this month, with Christmas concerts and ornate lighting. Other performance sources during this time are **Brigham Young University** (www.byu.edu) and **Utah Valley State College** (www .uvsc.edu).

*New Year's Eve:* **First Night** (www .provo.org) is a celebration that takes place on the last day of the year, during which Provo's businesses invite you to become acquainted with them outside of normal business hours.

# PROVO

T he Utah Valley community is nestled against the base of the Wasatch, whose sweeping incline spans from the fresh waters of Utah Lake to the imposing range that explodes 7,000 vertical feet above the cities below. The Utah Valley contains a collection of suburban towns whose total population is just under 450,000 people. Roughly half of these people reside in Orem and Provo, two adjacent cities whose streets and communities run together.

This community is the most pure spiritual stronghold of the Latter-day Saints. Though Salt Lake City was the original landing site of early Mormon pioneers (and is still the home of the original temple and World Headquarters), Provo remains much less diluted by outside faith and customs. It has essentially replaced Salt Lake City as the capital of Mormonism. This is the place where Mormons are educated to go forth into the world and spread the word as missionaries and to go forth into the world as college graduates. Provo is the home of the World Missionary Training Center, as well as the well-respected Brigham Young University. Orem is home to Utah Valley University (formerly Utah Valley State College). Both academic institutions have around 30,000 students each. Despite these huge educational institutions and significant population, the area is incredibly quiet.

Mount Timpanogos, whose pinnacle sits at 11,750 feet above sea level, is the most striking peak of the Provo-area Wasatch fortress. Within the jagged and geometric peaks of the Wasatch Mountains are several canyons popular for recreation. American Fork Canyon is the most popular limestone rock climbing in the Wasatch and has several picnic areas and campgrounds, as well as the enormous and fascinating Timpanogos Cave. This canyon is also part of a scenic loop that connects Lehi to the Sundance Resort and Provo area. Farther south is Provo Canyon and Rock Canyon. Though not accessible to vehicles, these canyons have offerings of their own, including more rock climbing and miles of trails for jogging and mountain biking. Utah Lake, unlike the Great Salt Lake, is composed of entirely fresh water and is thus popular for water recreation, including boating, fishing, and swimming.

The Utah Valley has historically been one of the most hospitable environments in Utah. For centuries, before Europeans knew about the valley, the Timpanogotzis (or "Fish Eaters") lived a settled, bountiful life in the valley. Unlike most tribes of the Rocky Mountain West, they were able to remain in one location, nourished by the fresh waters of Utah Lake.

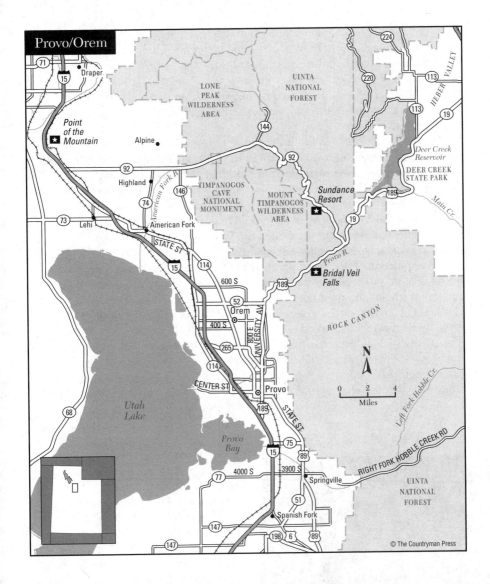

The first Europeans to come to the area, as with the rest of Utah, were nomadic. The Franciscan priests Dominguez and Escalante entered the valley on September 23, 1776, and recorded their first European contact with the Timpanogotzis tribe. Utah Valley was the turnaround point of an attempted inland mission from Mexico. Despite their favorable impressions of the people and environment, the area would remain protected for nearly a century from impending civilization by geography, distance, and harsh climate. In the meantime, trappers and traders would traverse the area only occasionally, as none of the rivers in the vicinity were large enough to see much substantial traffic.

The Mormons arrived in Salt Lake Valley in July of 1847 and were the first organized group of European Americans to take interest in the area and successfully settle here. They possessed unique qualities that matched them perfectly with the region. The strangeness of their new religion had rendered them perpetually persecuted among other populations; Utah was extremely isolated from society. The sacred values of work and efficiency inherent in the religion facilitated their survival in these harsh lands. It allowed them to design and realize infrastructure that would allow them to capture and allot water proportionately, as was essential in this desert environment.

Once Salt Lake City was firmly established, rhizomes of the Church of the Latter-day Saints began to spread outward as the Mormons prepared the foundations for an empire. Provo was established in March of 1849, and it began to send out shoots of its own. These other communities originated as small, isolated agricultural communities thick with orchards. A Mormon nation would have occupied about two-thirds of the American West and would have been called the State of Deseret, had the federal government not denied the Saints this request a dozen times. Salt Lake City would have been the capital.

The population of the area grew as quickly as the region could support, and as the loins could produce. The residents relished in the community of the religion, and the Mormon faith would become forever entrenched here. Even as Salt Lake City and Ogden became increasingly infiltrated by the outside world by way of rail work, mining, ranching, and other commerce, Utah Valley remained a Mormon mecca. Any such industry was fully integrated into the church. Mormon infrastructure was not diluted; rather the residents focused on strengthening its economy, environment, and education entirely on its own. Brigham Young Academy (later University) was founded in 1875 to provide young people with the highest degree of faith-based education possible. Since that time, Utah Valley has modernized and grown enormously. It still is home to mostly Mormon residents. Still, it is a friendly, respectful, and safe community with all the G-rated offerings of a city in a beautiful natural setting.

CENTER STREET IN PROVO

This area is indeed a cultural center for the Church of Jesus Christ of Latter-day Saints. As with anything of strong flavor, some will love this area, and some will not. For members of the church, it is a wonderful place to be among friends of the faith, learn more about their spirituality, and be inspired. For others, this is a beautiful area with a new culture to be explored.

GUIDANCE The Web site www.hello provo.com offers information on all of what is going on in the area, including events, area artists, real estate, attractions, movies, and the like.

**Provo-Orem Chamber of Commerce** (801-859-2555; www.the

chamber.org) has a good Web site linking the two interconnected community resources.

**Utah Valley Convention and Visitors Bureau** (801-851-2100; www.utahvalley .org), 111 South University Ave. This visitors center is located very near the quiet heart of Provo. Staff and brochures are present to assist you with your visit.

GETTING THERE *By car:* I-15 runs the length of Utah Valley and services it from exit 230 to exit 285. US 189 runs north–south through the Provo-Orem area and bends east into Provo Canyon, and eventually into the Heber Valley. UT 52 runs east–west along the northern edge of this compact and merges with US 189 at the mouth of the Provo Canyon.

*By air:* Most everyone flying to Provo will arrive at the **Salt Lake International Airport** (SLC) (801-575-2400 or 800-595-2442; www.slcairport.com), about 5 miles west of Salt Lake City on I-80 at exit 115B. This major airport offers the most affordable and direct flights in the region and is within about 50 interstate miles of the Utah Valley.

*By bus:* **Greyhound Bus Lines** (801-373-4211 or 800-231-2222; www.greyhound .com) 124 North 300 West. There is a station in Provo, as well as other Utah cities such as Moab, Salt Lake City, Ogden, St. George, and Green River.

*By train:* **Amtrak** (800-872-7245; www.amtrak.com), 300 West 600 South. Amtrak operates stops in St. George, Provo, Salt Lake City, and Green River. Provo's station is a dozen blocks southwest of Brigham Young University. Salt Lake City's station (340 South 600 West) shares a location with the Greyhound bus station.

GETTING AROUND *By car:* You may want to take a look at the *Driving and the Grid System* section in the "What's Where in Utah" chapter at the beginning of this book. Car rental agencies in Provo include:

**Avis Rent A Car** (Sears; 801-494-1529; www.avis.com), 1200 Towne Centre Blvd., Provo.

**Budget Rent A Car** (801-377-9300; www.budget.com), 1475 North State St., Provo.

**Enterprise Rent A Car** (800-377-7100; www.enterprise.com), 875 South 100 East, Provo.

**Hertz Rent A Car** (801-434-4520; www.hertz.com), 656 South State St., Orem.

*By cab:* Provo's two cab companies are **Affordable Cab & Limousine Service** (801-375-0000) and **Taxi Van** (801-375-8833).

*By mass transit:* **Utah Transit Authority** (UTA) (801-377-7433; www.rideuta .com) has an ever growing bus and rail line that services the length of Provo and Orem, especially the downtown and university districts.

MEDICAL EMERGENCY In a region so large and thoroughly developed, it is a good idea to know of a number of hospitals and clinics across the valley. These services are listed clockwise, starting toward the northwestern edge of Utah Lake.

**Intermountain Saratoga Springs InstaCare** (801-766-4567; www.inter mountainhealthcare.org), 250 East UT 73, Saratoga Springs. This clinic is one of the only medical facilities near the western edge of Utah Lake.

**Intermountain Highland InstaCare** (801-763-2900; www.intermountain healthcare.org), 10968 North Alpine Hwy., Highland. If you're in northern Utah Valley and don't need an emergency room, but would like medical attention without an appointment, this is the place for you.

**American Fork Hospital** (801-855-3300; www.intermountainhealthcare.org), 170 North 1100 East, American Fork. This is one of the northernmost hospitals in Utah Valley with the full spectrum of hospital services, including an emergency room.

**Intermountain North Orem InstaCare** (801-714-5000; www.intermountain healthcare.org), 1975 North State St., Orem. This is located toward the northern end of Orem on the uncrowded State Street.

**Orem Community Hospital** (801-224-4080; www.intermountainhealthcare.org), 331 North 400 West, Orem. This hospital is in the center of Orem, about 1 mile east of I-15 as the crow flies.

**Utah Valley Regional Medical Center** (801-357-7850; www.intermountain healthcare.org), 1034 North 500 West, Provo. In the heart of Provo, this is just slightly west of Brigham Young University.

**Intermountain Springville InstaCare** (801-429-1200; www.intermountain healthcare.org), 762 West 400 South, Springville. This Springville clinic is just about 1 mile east of I-15 exit 260 on UT 77.

**Mountain View Hospital** (801-465-7000; www.mvhpayson.com), 1000 East 100 North, Payson. Mountain View is toward the southern tip of Utah Lake, about 1 mile off I-15 on UT 198.

NEWSPAPERS *Deseret News* (www.deseretnews.com) is the main Utah Valley daily newspaper that speaks to Mormon Utah and reports general statewide, national, and global news.

THE UTAH COUNTY COURTHOUSE IN PROVO

# ✳ To See and Do

**MUSEUMS Alpine Art Center** (801-763-7173; www.alpineartcenter.com), 450 South Alpine Hwy., Alpine. Open Monday–Friday 9–5, Sunday 3–6, closed Monday. The Alpine Art Center is a modern facility on a 10-acre campus of lawn, wildflowers, natural streams, trails, and sculpture gardens. Within the building itself is 33,000 square feet of galleries, meeting spaces, and the **Adonis Bronze Fine Art Casting Facility.** In addition to traditional daytime art displays, the center hosts evening functions as well, including dances, dinners, and chamber concerts. Call or look on the Web site for upcoming events. Free admission.

**Conservation Mountain Museum at Cabela's** (801-766-2500; www.cabelas .com), 2502 West Grand Terrace, Lehi. Open Tuesday–Saturday 10–5, Sunday 3–6, closed Monday. This is one of the most out-of-the-ordinary museums of the area. Included in this outdoors store/museum is a 30-foot-tall wildlife habitat exhibit, taxidermy of wild game from the corners of the earth, fish ponds and streams, and even waterfalls. This gives visitors an all-in-one look into hunting, firearms, and fishing history as well as modern practice, with a gun library, shooting and archery ranges, a 55,000-gallon aquarium filled Utah's native fish and mock habitat, and a restaurant featuring wild game, among other dishes. Free admission.

**Earth Science Museum** (801-422-3680; http://cpms.byu.edu/ESM), 1683 North Canyon Road, Provo. Open Monday–Friday 9–5, closed Saturday and Sunday. This museum showcases the paleontological labors of Brigham Young University, enriched by the bounty of fossils of local and regional digs located in Utah, Montana, Idaho, and Wyoming—some of the most endowed fossil beds in the world. The museum was founded in 1976 and is home to skeletons dating from 15,000 years old to 380 million years old. Displays are rich in information and low on flashy gimmicks. Admission is free except for special exhibits.

**Harris Fine Arts Center** (801-422-2881), accessed by North Campus Dr., north of the Wikinson Student Center. Open 9–5 Monday–Friday. Located at **Brigham Young University** (www .byu.edu), this center has two main art galleries, the **Gallery 303** and **B.F. Larson Gallery.** Both are on the third floor. Free admission.

THE AMERICAN FAMILY SCULPTURE IN FRONT OF THE UTAH COUNTY COURTHOUSE

**L. Tom Perry Special Collections** (801-422-3514; http://sc.lib.byu.edu), Room 1130, Harold B. Lee Library, west of Wilkinson Student Center, Brigham Young University, Provo. Open Monday–Thursday 8 AM–9 PM, Friday 8–6, Saturday 10–6; closed Sunday. In these collections you will see rare and historic texts, with an emphasis on historic Mormon documents and texts. The Perry Special Collections are a working part of many departments at BYU and are thus one of the

THE THEATER AT THANKSGIVING POINT,
LOCATED IMMEDIATELY WEST OF I-15 IN
LEHI, UTAH

best collections of its kind in the region. Additionally, the collections include historic Americana texts, World War II volumes, and books from many other categories, such as fine prints, the Renaissance and Reformation, science history, Victorian and Edwardian, and an extensive collection of Larson Yellowstone's Yellowstone National Park art. Free admission; fee for special exhibits.

**Monte L. Bean Life Science Museum** (801-422-5051; http://mlbean .byu.edu/home), 645 East 1430 North, Brigham Young University, Provo. Open Monday–Friday 10–9; Saturday 10–5; closed Sunday. This museum possesses a collection of student, community, and professional exhibits ranging from permanent to temporary wildlife photography competitions. Some exhibits focus on wildlife from around the world, others on local topics. This museum helps oversee the **Lytle Ranch Preserve** near St. George. This 462-acre Mojave oasis is a sanctuary to hundreds of fragile fauna and flora species, 20 of which are found nowhere else in Utah. Free admission.

**Museum of Art** (801-422-8287; http://moa.byu.edu), 492 East Campus Dr., Brigham Young University, Provo. Open Monday–Friday 10–9, Saturday noon–5, closed Sunday. As with many other museums in the area, this art museum has a heavy preference for items pertaining to the Mormon faith. The museum hosts a variety of exhibits spanning a range of eras and media. More than 350,000 visitors come to this museum each year, allowing it to acquire art from prestigious institutions and attract the works of notable artists. The host building is a very modern space with more than 100,000 square feet of floor space as well as sculpture garden outside. Free general admission; fee for special exhibits.

✒ **North American Museum of Ancient Life** (801-766-5000; www.thanksgiving point.com/museum), 2929 North Thanksgiving Way, Thanksgiving Point, Lehi. Open Monday–Saturday 10–9, closed Sunday. This museum, located on the entertainment campus of Thanksgiving Point, is a classic dinosaur museum that will light up the imagination of children of all ages. Within the 122,000 square feet of floor space is everything from dinosaur eggs and footprints to enormous dinosaur skeletons and small crèchelike scenes. Aside from the 60 skeletons housed within, additional features include a "Night Sky Tunnel" and working paleontology room available for viewing. Life-sized dioramas illustrate the pioneer way of life and are replete with artifacts. Also in the building is the **Mammoth Screen Theater,** whose screen is 70 feet wide and 50 feet tall. $9 for adults, $7 for seniors ages 65 and older and children ages 12 and under.

**Springville Museum of Art** (801-489-2727; www.sma.nebo.edu), 126 East 400 South, Springville. Open Tuesday–Saturday 10–5, Sunday 3–6; closed Monday. This museum, housed in a spacious Spanish Revival building, was founded in 1937 and is Utah's oldest remaining visual arts museum. The subject matter is very often related to Mormonism but addresses unrelated subjects as well. Events include concerts and seminars, as listed on the Web site. Free admission.

**Woodbury Art Museum** (801-426-6199; www.uvu.edu/museum), 575 East University Pkwy., Second Level, University Mall, Orem. Open Tuesday–Saturday noon–8, closed Sunday and Monday. The art in this gallery includes sculpture, painting, and photography with local, national, and international origins. The Woodbury and Utah Valley State College often work in conjunction to bring in guest speakers and put on special exhibits. Because of its affiliation with the 30,000-student Utah Valley University, this small museum has a fairly substantive draw. Free admission.

GARDENS **Thanksgiving Point Gardens** (801-768-2300 or 888-672-6040; www.thanksgivingpoint.com), 3003 North Thanksgiving Way, Thanksgiving Point, Lehi. Open late March through November. Roughly 55 acres of gardens exist here amid vines, promenades, brick walkways, and trees. Each garden has its own theme, including the Monet Garden, Fragrance Garden, Waterfall Gardens, Parterre Garden, and Secret Garden. During the summer months, concerts are put on in the gardens. The gardeners here share their expertise with home gardening tips and workshops for adults and children. $10 for adults, $9 for ages 65 and up, and $6 for children ages 3–12.

LANDMARKS The **Historic Buildings Tour Booklet** and **Utah County Historic Sites Brochure** are free and can be picked up at the **Utah Valley Convention and Visitors Bureau** (801-851-2100; www.utahvalley.org), 111 South University Ave., Provo. Most of the historic buildings in the Historic Buildings Tour Booklet in town are just north of the bureau along Center Street and University Avenue. If you are strolling through here, try lunch at one of the hole-in-the-wall international restaurants. The Utah County Historic Sites Brochure will send you on a broader tour of the valley to sites like the Lehi Roller Mills, the American Fork Presbyterian Church, and Peteetneet Academy.

**Camp Floyd–Stagecoach Inn State Park,** about 20 minutes to the southwest of Lehi in Fairfield on UT 73. Open 9–5 daily (closed Sunday mid-October through early April). In its heyday, Camp Floyd housed 3,500 soldiers whose primary job was to oversee Mormon activities and suppress any rebellion, if necessary. Though

CENTER STREET IN PROVO

there was good reason to expect one, the Mormon Rebellion never broke loose, and the fort's role slipped into more common responsibilities such as Indian relations, surveying, and overseeing Overland Coach and Pony Express routes. $2 per vehicle.

**Historic Academy Square** (801-852-6651; www.provo.lib.ut.us), 550 North University Ave. Now Provo Academy Square Library, this was the original building of the Brigham Young Academy, built by Don Carlos Young, son of the most famous Mormon pioneer, Brigham Young. Founded in 1892, this later became Brigham Young University. In 1968 the building was vacated for what would be 20 years, with demolition seemingly inevitable. However, the community rallied and produced enough funds to rescue it from harm. Today it houses the Provo City Library.

**Historic Lehi Bus Tour** (801-768-0307), 394 West Main St., Lehi. Passengers on this tour are driven out to the remnants of Camp Floyd (today an inn), once the Western military hub of the U.S. government in the 1850s. The driving route follows the old Overland Coach and Pony Express route past historic buildings and massacre sites on this six-hour tour.

**Provo Mormon Temple** (801-375-5775), 2200 Temple Hill Dr. This temple is a much newer building than the tabernacle, constructed between 1969 and 1972. Though a young building by comparison, it is the busiest LDS temple in the world. Just down the hill (to the west) is Brigham Young University and the Missionary Training Center, arguably the religion's most important educational facilities for Mormons.

**Provo Tabernacle** (801-370-6655), 100 South University Ave., Provo. This tabernacle was opened in 1898 after 15 years of construction and has been in near constant service ever since. The original tower, too massive for the roof beneath it, was removed in the 1950s, after partial condemnations and safety closures. However, the four original corner towers remain in place today. Every holiday season this Tabernacle is graced by a performance of Handel's *Messiah*.

**AMUSEMENT PARKS**  **Seven Peaks Resort Water Park** (801-373-8777; www.sevenpeaks.com), 1330 East 300 North, Provo. Open seasonally. Utah Valley

THE TEMPLE IN PROVO

can get truly hot in the summer—and few things can refresh a family better than a trip to a water park. Seven Peaks has done a lot to make water entertaining, with water slides, tubing falls, a wave pool, and a children's pool. For those with pruney fingers and toes, there is a burger stand, multiple picnic areas, volleyball courts, and lawns for towel lounging. Admission is variable.

🦈 **Thanksgiving Point** (801-768-2300 or 888-672-6040; www.thanksgivingpoint .com), 3003 North Thanksgiving Way, Lehi. Open Monday–Saturday 10:30–7:30, also Sunday noon–7:30 during summer. Thanksgiving Point is a campus of family-friendly entertainment with features for diverse ages and interests. **Farm Country** has a collection of barnyard animals to be seen, pet, and fed by children who get to learn how these animals are raised. You might luck out and see chicks hatching or foals being born.

Wagon rides are available on the farm. Kids also love the **North American Museum of Ancient Life** (as described in the *Museums* section of this chapter), which boasts the world's largest collection of dinosaur skeletons. All generations will enjoy the **Thanksgiving Point Gardens** (as discussed in the *Gardens* section). Covering 55 acres with gardens of many varieties, it includes a Secret Garden that tickles the imagination of little girls. For adults, there is the 7,730-yard **Golf Club** at Thanksgiving Point. This Johnny Miller course has an enormous clubhouse and 18 holes. Price variable by ride and access.

🦈 **Trafalga Family Fun Center** (801-224-6000; www.trafalga.com), 168 South 1200 West, Orem. Open seasonally with some winter closures. Recently remodeled, this has both indoor and outdoor opportunities. Go-kart racing, mini golf, and batting cages can be enjoyed during the warm months; arcade games, indoor mini golf, and billiards tables can be enjoyed under a roof. Colorful, giant mini golf obstacles and tidy landscaping make this a colorful, pleasant family-fun area. Price variable, depending on activity.

## ✳ Outdoor Activities

### BIKING

### *Bike Rentals/Shops*
**Bingham Cyclery** (801-374-9890; www.binghamcyclery.com), 187 West Center St., Provo. For in-person recommendations, bike tuning, supplies, or cycling-specific guidebooks, visit Bingham. Though they don't rent, this shop is staffed by experienced, local cyclists who can point you in the direction of classic rides that are suited to your schedule and ability.

**Outdoors Unlimited** (801-422-2708; http://outdoors.byu.edu), 1151 Wilkinson Student Center, on the northeast corner of 1060 North and East Campus Dr. Amazingly, this is the only bike rental facility in the immediate area. In addition to road and mountain bike rentals, they also offer helmets, two-way radios, and child trailers. It is advised that you call well ahead for rentals.

**Racer's Cycle Service** (801-375-5873; www.racerscycle.net), 159 West 500 North, Provo. In addition to their retail supplies, this shop offers weekly group road rides that depart from the shop every Saturday at 10 AM. (Though the ride is no-drop, they expect you to maintain an 18–20 mph pace.) The usual ride is about 55 miles, with a refreshment break along the way in Payson. Some riders engage in mountain sprints along the way but will wait for the group on the flats.

## Mountain Biking

Utah has just about the most perfect biking climate one could imagine. The only season generally considered unsuitable for riding is winter. Spring and fall are perfect. Summers, though hot, can be enjoyed in the reprieve of cooler canyons or early mornings. The hottest days, when the canyons can even be too warm, enjoy perfect temperatures in the morning. The Web site **www.utahmountainbiking .com** is about as comprehensive as possible, with routes listed per region and descriptions illustrated by maps, mileage, elevation profiles, photographs, and sometimes even video.

**Bennie Creek Trail** starts at an elevation of 6,200 feet and gains 1,200 feet of elevation over the course of 4.5 miles. This easy gradient and pleasant single track make for a very popular mountain biking trail with serious cardiovascular benefits. To get there, take the I-15 exit 250 for North Payson/Benjamin (formerly exit 254). Travel south on Main Street to 100 North and turn left (east). Continue east to 600 East and turn right (south) for approximately 3.5 miles to the mouth of Payson Canyon, the beginning of the Mount Nebo National Scenic Byway (Nebo Loop road, #015). The trailhead is marked.

ACCESSED VIA US 6 BY TRAVELING NORTHWARD ON DIAMOND FORK ROAD, WHICH DEPARTS TO THE NORTH FROM US 6 TEN MILES EAST OF SPANISH FORK

Amiee Maxwell

**Bonneville Shoreline Trail** is one of the most easily found and easily ridden trails in the area. The Utah Valley portion of this trail system, like its Salt Lake City counterpart, hugs the modern-day foothills of the Wasatch. Formerly the shores of ancient Lake Bonneville, these were lapped by lake waters 12,000 years ago. One of Provo's most readily accessible trailheads is **Provo Canyon at the Bridal Veil Falls** pullout (see *Hiking*), on the south side of the road. This portion of the trail can be connected with the graded **Provo Canyon Parkway.** Another ride that traces the perimeter between Orem and Pleasant Grove can be reached by taking 800 North Street east, then 800 East Street north. Make a right onto Cascade Drive, which will wind back and forth until it reaches the parking area. This ride is 9 miles one way.

**Squaw Peak Road** is a more out-of-the-way trail with high enjoyment potential, and low risk of being marooned (due to its popularity among other bikers). This road is accessed by entering Provo Canyon via US 189, and traveling about 1.5 miles before making a right-hand (southward) turn onto

Squaw Peak Road. This paved road winds up into the mountains and turns to dirt after about 5 miles of travel. Free parking is available beneath the campground. From here, continue on past the campground. This ride is an out-and-back that summits and descends from two major ridges. Along the way it connects Provo, Rock, and Hobble Creek canyons as it travels south. The two high points along the ride are the Rock Canyon Outlook and Horse Mountain Pass. The riding along this these dirt and jeep roads is technically less difficult than single-track trail, but the aerobic challenge is plentiful. (Be careful along the way to not turn into the Rock Canyon Campground about 5 miles into the ride, and at the bottom of the first major canyon you enter; rather, continue south along Forest Road 27.)

## Road Biking

**Alpine Loop** is one of northern and central Utah's best rides, if you feel like pushing it. This is also a popular scenic drive that departs from the Utah Valley and ascends east into the Wasatch. The ride begins in Orem, ascends the **Provo Canyon** on into the Uinta National Forest on US 189, joining with UT 92 North, and looping west into Lehi through **American Fork Canyon.** Along the way, you pass **Bridal Veil Falls, the Sundance Resort,** and **Mount Timpanogos.** This ride is best done during late spring and early fall, as the mountainous beauty comes with lowered temperatures. If this is too much, but the scenery sounds just right, you can cut the ride short by doing an out-and-back up Provo Canyon. Make sure you've brought plenty of fitness, fluids, and fuel, because this ride brings with it 40 miles of mountain climbs and no amenities.

**Utah Lake Loop** is one of the most popular long-distance rides in the area. This ride covers 100 miles of very low-profile terrain around the perimeter of Utah Lake. Taken counterclockwise, the loop traverses the urban and suburban compact around the Provo/Lehi area, then Saratoga Springs (a small and isolated Western town), and finally stark, wind-swept plains along the western shore. The arid landscape of Utah Valley is juxtaposed strangely against the massive lake, on which the peaks of the Wasatch are reflected. Though the ride is flat, be advised that winds can pick up (especially in the afternoon), and the stretch along the west side of Utah Lake is devoid of services. If you're curious or doubtful about weather conditions, contact the **Utah Lake State Park** (801-375-0731), and bring plenty of supplies for nutrition, hydration, and weather.

**BOATING** As with the best fishing in Utah, most of the big white water is in the eastern side of the state. White-water specialists and flat-water expeditions find the best of their sport on the Green, Colorado, and sometimes Yampa rivers. However, the Provo River comes through again for the Wasatch Region, with some of the only navigable river rafting and kayaking in the vicinity. However, Utah Lake is a freshwater lake, and its marina (as described in *Fishing*) has ample facilities for boaters.

If you want to descend the frothy waters of eastern Utah, you will most likely use a guide service. These rivers are remote and often highly dangerous and technical. Accessibility and regulatory issues make these rivers difficult to attempt independently without large amounts of planning and previous experience. **Adrift Adventures** (in Jensen; 800-758-5161; www.adrift.com), **Dinosaur River Expeditions** (in Park City; 800-345-7238; www.dinoadv.com), and **Sheri Griffith Expeditions** (in Moab; 435-259-8229 or 800-332-2439; www.griffithexp.com) are certified, permit-holding companies in Utah that run these rivers regularly and have the means to access some of the trickier put-ins and take-outs.

**Daytrips Outfitters** (800-649-8294; www.daytrips.com) operates along the same lines as Invert Sports, with motorized boats including Jet Skis and waterskiing boats, and additionally fishing boats, pontoons, kayaks, and canoes.

**High Country Rafting** (801-224-2500 in Provo or 435-649-7678 in Park City; www.highcountryrafting.com). This guide service leads raft and tubing trips down the Lower Provo. This river has an American Whitewater difficulty rating of I–IV. (The ratings on the Provo are generally considered soft.)

**Invert Sports** (801-830-8864; www.utahboatrental.com). You can rent all the necessary motorized gear, including Jet Skis and motorboats with appropriate trailers and vehicles for towing, if necessary, and accessory toys for waterskiing and wakeboarding. This company takes care of everything, including boat delivery and cleanup.

**Utah Lake** has 96,000 acres of freshwater surface area for fishing, canoeing, kayaking, and sailing, and Provo City is practically waterfront property on the eastern shores of Provo Bay.

FISHING  Utah's biggest fishing hot spots are generally considered to be in the northeast portion of the state, by Flaming Gorge and Dinosaur National Monument, along the Green River. That said, the **Provo River** is considered to be some of the best fishing near the greater Salt Lake City and Provo area.

**Eddie Robinson's Fly Fishing** (801-434-3166; www.eddierobinsons.com) is based less than 1 mile from the Provo River and offers half- and full-day trips, with all equipment, including rods, reels, and waders. Trips are generally restricted to one or two people. This company also offers an excellent variety of classes, from tying a fishing fly to rod building and fly-fishing techniques and strategies. The Web site gives current river conditions.

**Four Seasons Fly Fishing** (435-657-2025 or 800-498-5440; www.utahflyfish .com), 44 West 100 South St., Heber City. Based out of Heber City, Four Seasons has a physical and online retail shop. They also offer guide services on the nearby Provo River, as well as the more distant Strawberry and Green rivers. Four Seasons offers lodging with partner accommodations to clients on longer trips.

**Provo River** is one of north and central Utah's most popular fishing spots and is stuffed "to the gills" with brown and rainbow trout that are consistently large by reputation. The Provo begins at Trail Lake high in the beautiful Uinta Mountains and flows through two reservoirs, Jordanelle and Deer Lake, en route to Utah Lake. These three segments are aptly named the Upper, Middle, and Lower.

**Provo River Outfitters** (888-776-8824; www.utahflyfishing.com) offers classes and trips in four-, six-, and eight-hour lengths. Trips are offered on the Provo, Green, and Strawberry rivers, and guests stay at the Sundance Resort or Stein Eriksen Lodge in Park City, among other places.

**Utah Lake** is where the Provo River finds its terminus. This is a 100,000-acre freshwater lake where you can expect to catch white and black bass, channel catfish, panfish, and walleye. Launch ramps, campsites, and restrooms are at **Utah Lake State Marina** (801-375-0731), 4400 West Center St., Provo. $9 day use fee.

**GOLF** Utah's yearly temperatures give visiting and local golfers quite a long season. As with the rest of Utah, many golf courses here are public courses—many of which beautiful and award-winning, yet affordable. Because of golf's popularity in Utah, reservations are recommended.

**Cascade Fairways Golf Course** (801-225-6677; www.cascadegolf center.com), 1313 East 800 North, Orem. This public, 18-hole course was designed by William Neff. The course is generally open and slightly rolling, with trees here and there. In addition to the main course, there is a driving range and mini golf course. $25.

**Cedar Hills Golf Club** (801-796-1705; www.cedarhillsgolfclub.com), 10640 North Clubhouse Dr., Cedar Hills. This Graves & Pascuzzo course is public, hilly, and beautifully incorporated into its natural surroundings. At the mouth of American Fork Canyon, this course has 18 holes, 6,700 yards, par 72, and fairly significant topography. $36 for weekdays, $40 for weekends.

Craig Bowden

MAPLE CANYON, SOUTHWEST OF FOUNTAIN GREEN, UTAH, IS POPULAR WITH CLIMBERS, AS WELL AS WITH CAMPERS AND HIKERS.

**Hobble Creek** (801-489-6297), Hobble Creek Canyon, Springville. This public course, designed by William F. Bell, is surrounded by nature and steep hills. The 18 holes over 6,300 yards are not particularly long but are known for their beauty. *Golf Digest* gave this four and a half stars (out of five) in 2006–2007. There is a driving range as well. $24 for weekdays, $26 for weekends.

**The Links at Sleepy Ridge** (801-434-4653; www.linksatsleepyridge.com), 700 South Sleepy Ridge Dr., Orem. This public Matt Dye course is Orem's newest. It is very flat and utterly unobstructed by trees or geography other than a few water hazards. The 18 holes cover 7,000 yards at par 71. $23 Monday–Thursday, $26 Friday–Sunday.

**Ranches Golf Club** (801-789-8100), 4128 East Clubhouse Dr., Eagle Mountain. This is one of the area's more upscale public courses. The 18 holes and 7,400 yards of this course were designed to facilitate a true links experience. The clubhouse has a rather Western theme, and light beer is available for sale. $42 Monday–Thursday, $48 Friday–Sunday.

**Spanish Oaks** (801-798-9816), 2300 Power House Rd., Spanish Fork. This public course has 18 holes and 6,400 yards. Located west of Spanish Fork Canyon, this course is generally considered to be short, but fun and inexpensive. Located very

MAPLE CANYON IS A DREAM FOR CONGLOMERATE/COBBLESTONE SPORT CLIMBING (AND ICE CLIMBING, BY WINTER).

near the new power-generating windmills—a step forward in Utah environmentalism.

**Thanksgiving Point Golf Course** (801-768-7400; www.thanksgiving point.com), 2095 North West Frontage Rd., Lehi. This Johnny Miller course is extremely convenient for families; one parent can golf, and the other can visit the gardens, museum, or shops. This challenging and picturesque course has 18 holes, 7,730 yards, and is par 72. With more than 200 acres, it is the largest club in the state and was recognized as one of the best new courses in the country by *Golf Digest* in 1997. $65 Monday–Wednesday, $75 Thursday, $85 Friday, Saturday, and holidays; discounts to residents.

HIKING **Mount Timpanogos,** east of Higland in American Fork Canyon along Alpine Scenic Loop/UT 92. This is one of the most famous and massive peaks in the Wasatch Range, and so many access trails exist. The most popular trail nearest Provo departs from **Timpooneke Campground** about 10 miles into the canyons and is 13 miles each way. Another hike on the same mountain (that does not gain the peak) departs from the **Timpanogos Cave National Monument Visitors Center** (801-756-5238; www.nps.gov/tica), about 2.5 miles east of the mouth of American Fork Canyon on UT 92, east of Alpine. Here a steep 1.5-mile hike departs to the entrance to **Hansen Cave.** This cave, discovered in 1887, is the first in a series of three colorful, connected caves. $6 at Timpanogos Cave National Monument.

⚓ **Bridal Veil Falls,** about 8 miles east of Provo on US 189 or along the Provo River Parkway. This two-tiered cataract waterfall drops 600 feet, accessible at the marked scenic pullout. Follow a trail higher, and you'll reach the **Cascade Springs,** clear water pools among limestone steps.

**Rock Canyon,** on the eastern edge of Provo, is accessed by taking North Temple Drive to its eastern terminus, then turning right at a four-way stop sign to enter the parking lot. Rock Canyon, just south of, and parallel to, American Fork Canyon is a craggy Wasatch Canyon that offers more solace than some of the others, as it is accessed by foot and bicycle only. This canyon offers long, flat hikes free from vehicles. A broad trail follows the bottom of the canyon near the stream below. Look for rock climbers on the canyon's many quartzite and limestone walls, some of which are very near the pathway.

**Sundance Resort** (801-223-4121; www.sundanceresort.com), RR3, Box A-1, Sundance. If you are visiting Utah Valley in the summer, it is definitely worth a detour for a cool hike and resort dinner of organic and local ingredients. Many trails of varying difficulty depart from the resort base, and guide hikes are available for a price. Trail maps are available in the base area, and online.

ROCK AND ICE CLIMBING Utah has long been considered one of the best places in the country to live as a rock climber. Not only is the weather ideal, the number of excellent destinations within a short drive is incredibly high. For more information on these, see the sidebar *No, I Don't Want to Climb Mount Everest One Day* in the "Salt Lake City" chapter of this book. If you need to purchase any gear, guidebooks, or would like to talk to someone about route whereabouts and current conditions, visit **Hansen Mountaineering** (801-226-7498; www .hookedonclimbing.com), 1799 North State St., Orem; or **Out-N-Back** (801-224-0454), 1797 South State St., Orem.

MAPLE CANYON

Craig Bowden

☗ **American Fork Canyon** is east of Alpine and northeast of Provo. This is generally considered the best local sport climbing in the Wasatch Range, and is indeed popular. The climbing community in the greater Salt Lake area is one of the strongest and most able in the country, and so American Fork Canyon is one of the more serious training grounds. Fittingly, there is a high concentration of difficult routes (5.11 to 5.13) and a low concentration of easy routes. In fact, anything less than 5.11 is rarely found in any concentration. If you are looking for easy or moderate routes, the south-facing **Escape Buttress** is your best bet, with a gridwall of mostly 5.10. The next most moderate wall is the **Division Wall,** a mostly north, northwest-facing wall of primarily 5.11, but with a range of 5.10 to 5.12+. For 5.12, the **Billboard** is one of the most popular, with as dense a concentration at that grade as the Escape Buttress has at 5.10. The **Hell Cave** is the 5.12+/ 5/13 hot spot where steep, extremely strenuous routes ascend from the depths of a gritty cave. Stuart and Bret Ruckman's

*Climber's Guide to American Fork Canyon, Rock Canyon* is the definitive guide to the area.

✐ **Momentum Climbing** (801-990-6890; www.momentumclimbing.com), 220 West 10600 South, Sandy. Exit 293, about 20 miles north of Provo and Orem. Just over Point-of-the-Mountain, this is Utah's newest and best-roped climbing facility. This beautiful, well-designed gym courses with the enthusiasm of the Wasatch climbing community and is embellished by excellent route setting, excellent wall angles, very realistic (and oft challenging) crack climbing, plenty of lead climbing, and even bouldering and top roping, as well as high-quality fitness equipment.

**Provo Canyon** is, by winter, one of the region's best ice climbing destinations. Slide Canyon, a tributary canyon to Provo Canyon, is located on the north side of the road 0.7 mile past the turn off to Bridal Veil Falls on US 189 (about 5 miles east of Provo).

✐ **The Quarry** (801-418-0266; www.thequarry.net), 2494 North University Pkwy., Provo. This rock gym has been around for years and maintains roughly 100 routes of all difficulties and steepness, spread among top rope, lead climbing, and bouldering walls. Shoe and harness rental available for use on the premises.

**Rock Canyon** is mostly a limestone sport-climbing canyon, though some quartzite, traditional, and mixed routes can be found here. The number of established lines is somewhere around 130, most of which are in the 5.8 to 5.12 range and are bolted with fixed anchors. The Ruckmans' guide mentioned in **American Fork Canyon,** above, is also a guide to this area. Rock Canyon is accessed at the parking lot at the eastern end of 2300 North. See a map for details.

## SKIING

### Alpine

**Park's Sportsman** (801-225-0227 or 800-789-4447; www.parkssportsman.com), 644 North State St., Orem. This shop offers Alpine and Nordic ski and snowboard rentals, and a retail selection.

**Pedersen's Ski & Sports** (801-225-3000), 575 University Pkwy., University Mall, Orem. Pedersen's rents Alpine skis and snowboards, and offers a retail selection.

**Sundance Resort** (801-223-4121 or 800-892-1600; www.sundanceresort.com), RR3, Box A-1, Sundance. Sundance is located just 20 minutes east of Provo along the popular scenic drive (and road biking route), the **Alpine Loop.** See the *Skiing* section of the "Sundance Resort" chapter.

### Nordic

**Park's Sportsman** (801-225-0227 or 800-789-4447; www.parkssportsman.com), 644 North State St., Orem. This shop offers Alpine and Nordic ski and snowboard rentals, and a retail selection.

**Sundance Nordic Center** (801-223-4170 or 800-892-1600; www.sundance resort.com), RR3, Box A-1, Sundance. East of Provo in the Provo Canyon, the Sundance Resort grooms at least 26 kilometers of trails daily, with an on-site Nordic Center in which lessons and rentals can be procured. See the *Skiing* section of "Sundance Resort" chapter.

## ✴ Lodging

If you would prefer to stay in an upscale or nonchain hotel, your best bet in the Provo area is a bed-and-breakfast. Provo has a bevy of tidy midlevel hotels but generally lacks high-end establishments. The upside of Provo's lodging is that it is generally somewhat inexpensive. Another viable option for discerning visitors is a vacation rental at the **Sundance Resort** (801-225-4107 or 800-892-1600; www.sundanceresort.com), as listed in the *Lodging* section in the "Sundance Resort" chapter.

HOTELS **Best Western Cotton Tree Inn** (801-373-7044 or 800-662-6886; www.bestwesterncottontreeinn.com/provo), 2230 North University Pkwy., Provo. This installment of the familiar chain is located on the banks of the Provo River, just five blocks from the BYU campus. It's also just three blocks from the LaVell Edwards stadium, so guests here don't have to concern themselves with parking if attending a game. A complimentary Continental breakfast is available, as well as local, regional, and national papers. Wireless Internet and meeting spaces make this a good option for business travelers. Pets are not allowed. $95–$105.

**Courtyard by Marriott** (801-373-2222; www.marriott.com), 1600 North Freedom Blvd. 200 West St., Provo. This is one of the nicer, more modern hotels in Provo. The location is ideal for many business travelers, just two blocks north of the Utah Valley Regional Medical Center, and two blocks west of the BYU campus. Additional perks are close proximity to the junction of historic Center Street and University Avenue and the Riverside Country Club. Though the hotel is one of many of its kind, it is in fact aesthetically adorned and affords its guests ample space and natural light. Standard guest services include wireless Internet, voice mail, and buffet-style breakfasts. Pets are not allowed. $130–$220.

☃ **Days Inn Provo** (801-375-8600 or 877-308-3356; www.cottontree.net/provo), 1675 North Freedom Blvd. 200 West St., Provo. This hotel should require little explanation with regard to the accommodations—but what requires some touting is the special recreational deals, among which are golf course and amusement park packages and discounts for Missionary Training Center guests. The inn is within walking proximity to restaurants, sporting events, and the like. Personal business accommodations, such as fax, are available upon request. Pets are allowed here conditionally. $75–$90.

☃ **Hampton Inn** (801-377-6396; www.hamptoninn.com), 1511 South 40 East, Provo. This hotel has adapted its Provo, making hot breakfasts available in the morning, as well as to-go snacks. Though a bit farther from the BYU district, this is nearer the University Mall. Other perks are a small indoor pool, hot tub, and modest fitness facility. Romantic and family package deals are available. Business facilities, including meeting rooms, lounge, and 24/7 coffee, are obtainable. Pets are allowed conditionally. $180–$220.

☃ **La Quinta Inn Provo Town Center** (801-374-9750; www.lq.com), 1460 South University Ave., Provo, and **La Quinta Inn & Suites Orem University Parkway** (801-226-0440; www.lq.com), 521 West University Pkwy., Orem. These are two basic, clean, modern hotels in the area operated by the same company. Guests are privy to complimentary hot breakfast buffets and modern facilities. Breakfasts include fresh waffles, fruit, cereal, and bagels. Pets are allowed at both locations. $99–$110.

**Provo Marriott Hotel & Conference Center** (801-377-4700 or 800-777-7144; www.marriott.com), 101 West 100 North, Provo. The Marriott is near the top echelon for Utah Valley hotels. This is a large, business-ready hotel with 330 guest rooms and an aggregate 28,000 square feet of modern meeting facilities. Rooms are generally simple, yet colorfully decorated with contemporary overtones. Two restaurants exist on the premises: **Allie's American Grill** (breakfast, lunch, and dinner; American cuisine) and **Season's Private Club** (dinner only). Pets are not allowed. $170 and up.

**Travelodge** (801-373-1974; www .travelodge.com), 124 South University Ave., Provo. This is perhaps Provo's most centrally located, simplest lodging option. It is inexpensive, yet outfitted with modern resources like a small fitness center and free wireless Internet. Free off-street parking and daily newspapers are available. Pets are not allowed. $65–$105.

**BED-AND-BREAKFASTS Hines Mansion Bed & Breakfast** (801-374-8400 or 800-428-5636; www.hines mansion.com), 383 West 100 South, Provo. This is Provo's only luxury bed-and-breakfast and is located right in the center of town. Built in 1895, this has the gift of historic elegance and a 1995 remodel. Carefully selected furniture and décor integrate stately tastes and the building's age, creating a handsome style. Each room is one of a kind and outfitted with a private, jetted hot tub. Floral arrangements, strawberries and cream, or even a horse-drawn carriage ride are available upon request. Special vacation packages include fly-fishing trips and other

recreational getaways. If you are not accustomed to Utah's customs, you will be surprised to find a bottle of sparkling apple cider in your room in place of champagne. (The consumption of alcohol is not permitted in the Mormon religion.) Pets are not allowed. $130–$240.

**Somewhere Inn Time** (801-785-9777; www.somewhereinntime.com), 175 North State St., Lindon. This bed-and-breakfast is located in a modern mansion with a complete wraparound balcony that oversees the property's 5 greenly landscaped acres. Though the furniture is not extravagant, it creates a cozy ambience. Rooms vary quite a bit in size and feel. Breakfast is served to each room every morning. Beware the many wedding parties that reserve this establishment. Special deals for weekday stays and weddings. Pets are not allowed. $105–$200.

**Victorian Inn Bed & Breakfast** (801-489-0737 or 888-489-0737; www .myvictorianinn.com), 94 West 200 South, Springville. This mansion was originally built in 1892 as a private residence. It was sold and transformed into the Kearns Hotel in 1909. Today this is called the Victorian Inn and has undergone basic and luxury modernizing improvements like electricity, plumbing, and Jacuzzi tubs. Located in Springville, this is set quietly outside the Provo/Orem conglomeration and offers lower rates than other such establishments. $99 and up.

## ✳ Where to Eat

Perhaps one of the more surprising things about Provo, with its small-town, conservative overtones, is the plentiful hole-in-the-wall, high-quality, low-cost ethnic eateries along University Avenue and Center Street. Brigham Young University and the Missionary Training Center bring Mormons to Utah Valley from all around the globe, and with these international citizens come their cuisine. Of course, Provo also has its fair share of chuckwagon, family-friendly, American eateries designed to cater to the large families encouraged in the Mormon religion. On the same note, expect many—well, almost all—of the restaurants in Utah Valley to be closed on Sunday. Many restaurants do not serve alcohol, and even the ones that do will not set the dining table with an alcohol or wine list. These must be requested if desired.

If you would prefer a high-end meal of locally grown foods amid natural surroundings—and perhaps accompanied by alcohol—you might consider the short trek to the mountainous **Sundance Resort** (801-225-4107 or 800-892-1600; www.sundanceresort.com), whose restaurants, **The Tree Room, The Foundry Grill,** and **The Owl Bar** (a bar more than restaurant) are listed in the "Sundance Resort" chapter of this book.

**DINING OUT** **Chef's Table** (801-235-9111; www.chefstable.net), 2005 South State St., Orem. Open Monday–Saturday for dinner and Monday–Friday for lunch. This contemporary American restaurant gives guests a distinctive experience from the first glimpse of its peaked roofs and turrets. Chef's Table outdoes its Utah Valley peers in every sensory measure. Inside is a menu considered to be among the top 10 in all of Utah—a state whose cuisine is well regarded nationally and internationally by experts. Among the headlining dishes are savory preparations of seafood, fish, and fine cuts of beef. The restaurant is saddled with awards for its cuisine and service alike. Call for reservations. Entrées $16–$35.

**Harvest** (801-768-4990; www.thanks

givingpoint.com), 3003 North Thanksgiving Way, Thanksgiving Point, Lehi. Open Monday–Saturday for lunch and dinner. Harvest offers a chance to sample some of the region's homegrown food prepared according to Mediterranean and contemporary American methods. After a day at Thanksgiving Point's gardens, golf course, museum, or shopping center, you can enjoy fresh herbs, flatbread, pastas, poultry, and seafood. $18–$25.

✐ **Magleby's Grill & Oyster Bar** (801-374-6249; www.maglebys.com), 4801 North University Ave., Provo. Serving lunch and dinner Monday–Saturday. Open since 1980, this locally owned restaurant serves surf and turf with casual style, in half and full portions (for most entrées). The seafood ranges from halibut to mahi-mahi, roughy, and crab legs. Other categories include pasta, chicken, steaks, other house specialties, and informal fare like sandwiches. $10–$30.

**Ottavio's Ristorante Italiano** (801-377-9555; www.ottavios.com), 77 East Center St., Provo. Open for lunch and dinner Monday–Saturday. Murals lend the space a Mediterranean feel. The lengthy menus offer abundant choices and cover the range of possible traditional fare. Wholesome, home-cooked food arrives with tasteful plating in substantial portions with robust aromas preceding them. During dinners an accordion player strolls the dining room aisles; if you are interested (or uninterested) in being present for the live music, call for specific days and hours. Patio dining is popular during the summer. $11–$22.

**EATING OUT** **Bombay House** (801-373-6677; www.bombayhouse.com), 473 North University Ave., Provo. Open Monday–Saturday for dinner only. Bombay House is the first example of Provo's tasty international cuisine served in an unassuming restaurant. The house recipes come uninterrupted from Chennai, India, whence the owner hails. Called to Utah by BYU and the Mormon religion, Daniel Shanthakumar still imports ingredients from his hometown. This restaurant has been serving rich tandoori, saag, curry, kurma, and more since 1993. A full spectrum of meat and vegetarian dishes is available. Most entrées $10–$17.

**Brick Oven** (801-374-8800; www .brickovenprovo.net), 111 East 800 North, Provo. Open Monday–Saturday for lunch and dinner. This serves gourmet pizzas with fresh ingredients, yet is casual and very family friendly. Hefty pizzas are complemented with simple pasta dishes, a salad bar, and classic desserts. This is regularly voted the best family restaurant in Utah Valley—which means a lot in such a family-oriented community. In business for more than 50 years, the proprietors have pizza making down to a science, creating their own aged marinara sauce, as well as home-brewed apple and root beers. Reservations are available for large parties only. Most people are fed for $9 or less.

**La Casita** (801-489-9543), 333 North Main St., Springville. Open for lunch and dinner Monday–Saturday. For a Mexican restaurant to last three decades in a small town, something about it must be good. The success of this establishment has originated in time-perfected family recipes, fresh ingredients, friendly service, and large portions. This has a reputation among Utah Lake Loop cyclists as a perfect lunch stop on the home stretch en route to Provo. $10–$15.

**Osaka Japanese Restaurant** (801-373-1060), 46 West Center St., Provo. Open for lunch and dinner Monday–Saturday. Combine the familiarity of traditional

Japanese fare with a cozy restaurant, and you've got Osaka. This is far from some of Salt Lake's trendy Japanese establishments, but it is the go-to establishment for Provo locals. Friendly service, fresh food, and reasonable pricing have earned it this honor. Sushi and miso soup are offered in the same breath as tempura, teriyaki, and katsu dishes. Open since 1985, the restaurant has special signature dishes including salad and dumplings. $15–$20.

**Touch of Seoul/Spicy Corea** (801-377-7330), 43 North University Ave., Provo. Also called Spicy Corea, this is a great lunch stop, convenient because of its location at the University Avenue/ Center Street intersection. The atmosphere is very plain, and the dishes extremely affordable. However, flavors are outstanding and exotic for the American tongue. Fresh vegetables and bold, distinctive flavoring make the diner want to learn more about Korea's cuisine. Tofu, chicken, beef, and even squid dishes are often of the rice or noodle bowl variety, and are accompanied by national sides like seaweed, pickled cabbage, and teriyaki vegetables. $8–$13.

## ✳ Entertainment

**Center Street Musical Theater** (801-764-0535; www.csmtc.com), 177 West Center St., Provo. At this theater you can eat dinner and catch a show all at once. The environment is family friendly, and the cuisine is Western and Italian.

**The Hale Center Theater** (801-226-8600; www.haletheater.com), 225 West 400 North, Orem, performs shows alternating between the classics and homespun tales. Ruth and Nathan Hale, founders of the company and highly active LDS church members, have penned more than 80 plays.

**The Provo Theatre Company** (801-379-0600), 105 East 100 North, Provo. This is the area's only professional drama troupe, whose performance season consists of six different productions and lasts from September to June in its renovated 132-seat theater.

**Utah Valley Symphony** (www.utah valleysymphony.org). This orchestral group is one of the most solid artistic institutions in the valley. This is a non-profit congregation of 75 musicians that performs at the **Provo Tabernacle** (100 South University Ave.). The

**Brigham Young University** has a large number of performing groups. Listed here are some of the groups who may be performing while you are in town. For more information on music at the university, visit www.music.byu.edu, or for performance schedules visit http://pam.byu.edu.

**The BYU Singers** is a score of men and women that perform hits from folk to the classics and Broadway.

BYU's **Chamber Orchestra** gives intimate performances in close quarters.

The **Concert Band** (also known as the **Wind Symphony**) is a 47-piece set of percussion, brass, and wind musicians whose repertoire includes classical and contemporary pieces and marches.

**Folk Music Ensemble** is composed of five individuals creating bluegrass and country renditions with vocals, banjo, mandolin, guitar, and fiddle.

The **Jazz Legacy** is a Dixieland ensemble of piano, banjo, brass, and other instruments that performs in attire that matches their music.

The **Jazz Singers** is composed of 14 vocalists that usually perform a cappella, but occasionally with accompaniment.

**Living Legends** represents the diverse faction of the student body and is composed of Polynesian, Native American, and Latin American musicians who bring their traditional music to the Utah Valley through musical and dance performance.

The **Men's Chorus**, a 230-piece group, has an enormous sound and claims to be the largest collegiate choir of its kind in the United States.

The **Philharmonic Orchestra** is composed of 80 musicians playing stringed and woodwind instruments and fine music from many eras.

**Synthesis** is an all-brass band amalgamation of jazz, blues, Latin, and swing.

A cappella at BYU is represented by **Vocal Point**, the main on-campus glee club.

**Young Ambassadors** is a dance group and musical theater combo that creates its own blend of American drama.

The **Young Company** is a colorful troupe that employs bold and amusing costumes to bring the joy of performance art to children and their families.

symphony prepares and performs five concerts each year.

**NIGHTLIFE** Nobody, local or tourist, would claim that Provo is known for its nightlife. However, though Utah Valley most certainly lacks bars and nightclubs, it does have its own variety of amusement. Utah Valley is proud of its lack of bars and debauchery, and takes pride in its wholesome entertainment. If indeed you would like to sip cocktails among like-minded folk, the short drive to the **Sundance Resort** (801-223-4121; www.sundanceresort.com) might be in your cards. See the *Entertainment* section of the "Sundance Resort" chapter.

**A. Beuford Gifford's Libation Emporium** (801-373-1200; www.abgsbar.com), 190 West Center St., Provo. This Provo bar actually serves liquor, despite rumors that Utah County is dry. Guests frequently enjoy live music and billiards.

**Club Omni** (801-375-0011), 153 West Center St., Provo. Unlike the Libation Emporium, this is an alcohol-free establishment that offers three dance floors and is an all-ages club.

**Comedy Sportz** (801-377-9700), 35 West Center St., Provo. This small establishment offers a very home-grown improvisational comedy scene and is located very near BYU and the Center Street/University Avenue intersection.

**Wise Guys Comedy Club** (801-377-6910; www.wiseguyscomedy.com), 1350 West 1140 South, Orem. This is a small comedy chain in Utah and is considered one of the better ones in the Utah Valley. Local and national performers fill the calendar.

**SPORTS Brigham Young University Cougars** (www.byu.edu). This 35,000-student NCAA school has foot-ball, basketball, soccer, baseball, gymnastics, volleyball, and more. The University of Utah Utes (of Salt Lake City) and BYU are forever entangled in a rivalry, and fans are about as enthusiastic as they come. If you're interested in the history of the teams, check out **Legacy Hall** (801-422-2118; www.byucougars.com), in the Student Athletic Center, south of 1230 North and east of University Avenue. There are 110 years of sporting history commemorated here. The hall is open 7 AM–9 PM daily, and there is no charge for admission.

**VENUES** Around town there are a few major events centers. The **LaVelle Edwards/Cougar Stadium** (between Stadium Ave. and University Pkwy. on North Canyon Rd., Brigham Young University Campus, Provo) is a large football, track, and soccer stadium with the capacity for large crowds and many events of different varieties. The **Marriott Center** (500 East University Pkwy., Provo), also on the BYU campus, has nearly 23,000 seats and hosts many events, from basketball games to gymnastics competitions and notable speakers.

## ✴ Selective Shopping

**SPECIALTY SHOPS Cabela's** (801-766-2500; www.cabelas.com), 2502 West Grand Terr., Lehi. This is the outdoorsman's 150,000-square-foot dream come true. These sportsman's hobbies are represented not just with purchasable goods, but also with museum installations, a 55,000-gallon aquarium with a selection of Utah's native fish, a 30-foot-tall wild game mock habitat, archery and shooting ranges, a gun library, and a restaurant where you can devour or sample a huge variety of wild game from around the world.

**Lehi Roller Mills** (801-768-4401; www.lehirollermill.com), 833 East Main St., Lehi. This is a specialty food shop that represents the local traditions and LDS history. What began in 1906 as a church farm and flour mill has flourished and grown into a greater food dispensary. This has been a community pillar, having served the valley in times of need, dispensing treats during happier times. Products are limited to baking kits and the like.

**FARMERS' MARKETS The Provo Downtown Business Alliance Farmers' Market** takes place 8–1 every Saturday (weather permitting) in the northwest corner of Pioneer Park, 500 West 100 South.

**MALLS AND SQUARES The Provo Towne Centre** (801-852-2401; www.shopprovotownecentre.com), 1200 Towne Centre Blvd., Provo. This is a haven of familiar national brand stores and has over 100, including Victoria's Secret, Gap, and Dillards. This mall also has a 16-screen movie theater and a conventional food court.

**The Shops at Riverwoods** (801-802-8430; www.shopsatriverwoods.com), 4801 North University Ave., Provo. This outdoor mall boasts a bounty of high-end establishments, including theaters, restaurants, and stores—a few of which are even local. This center sometimes hosts live music and festivals.

**University Mall** (801-224-0694; www .shopuniversitymall.com), 575 East University Pkwy., Orem. This is another large Utah Valley mall with many of the country's favorite big stores, including clothing and specialty shops, salons, and on-the-go eateries.

**GALLERIES Coleman Studios** (801-225-5766; www.colemanart.com), 117 North University Ave., Provo. This gallery features the work of around 20 artists with fairly conservative themes.

**Downtown Provo Gallery Stroll** occurs on the first Friday of each month. Each stroll is enhanced by some combination of live music and refreshments. The strolls last from 6 to 9 PM, are free of charge, and visit the galleries listed in this section.

**Freedom Gallery** (801-375-1150) 230 West Center St., Provo. This gallery has art of various themes, including modern sculpture and painting.

**Gallery OneTen** (801-623-0615), 110 South 300 West, Provo. Gallery OneTen features traveling shows relating to Utah's history and people.

**Terra Nova Gallery** (801-374-0016; www.terranovagallery.com), 41 West 300 North, Provo. This fine-arts collection is fairly new, open since just 2003. This is a very active gallery with receptions, lectures, and regular participation in the downtown strolls. Many of the works focus on Utah landscape, and some on LDS heritage.

# SUNDANCE RESORT

Sundance Resort has a special place in Utah and is much more than just a ski resort. In addition to winter activities, it is a year-long cultural center for artists, musicians, and some of the best cuisine and nightlife anywhere near Provo. Concerts, artists' galleries and workspaces, and environmental activism draw people to the area—as well as Alpine and Nordic skiing, snowshoeing, mountain biking, and hiking.

As a ski area, it is markedly different than many modern resorts. Conspicuously absent are the parking garages, large hotels, condominium clusters, or flashy shops that typically clutter the woods and hillsides at other areas. Billboards and sponsor logos are replaced by works of art from resident artists. Guests of Sundance stay in cottages, and architecture is small, intimate, and woodsy. Though humble in size and noninvasive in appearance, the resort is quite refined. It artfully employs simplicity in allowing the natural beauty of the area to speak for itself. In essence, the Sundance Resort is a breath of fresh air in a world of corporate ski resorts and intrusive infrastructure.

Historically, this region of Utah was home to the Ute Indians and their ancestors—as long as 10,000 years ago. Through the fall and spring they lived along the shores of freshwater Utah Lake. Because of this huge body of water, they lived much better than many other tribes in the Intermountain West, eating a hearty diet of fish. Though dubbed "Utes" by European settlers, they had called themselves Timpanogotzis, or "fish eaters." Today Mount Timpanogos retains this more proper name. Summer heat often drove these tribes up into the cooler Wasatch canyons, making them seasonal residents of the modern Sundance Resort.

The first white settlers in the immediate Sundance vicinity were a family of Scottish immigrants by the name of Stewart. They came to the canyon early in the 1900s and made a living by surveying and shepherding. A few decades after the initial homesteading, skiing became popular as a national pastime. Ray Stewart opened the ski area Timp Haven in 1944. It was serviced by a single rope tow and burger stand.

This small resort operated for more than 20 years under the Stewart family, with some chairlifts finally being added at the end of their tenure. In 1969, Robert Redford purchased the ski area and surrounding land to create what is now the Sundance Resort. From the outset, the resort was created with environmentalism in mind, and so today lacks the stacks of condominiums and lodges typical of most resorts. Instead, this area retains an intimate feel, connection to nature, and culture of artists and environmentalists.

The skiing at Sundance is not as expansive as at an area like Snowbird, but the trails offer a full variety of terrain and enjoy significantly less crowding. Trails include open bowls, tree runs, chutes, corduroy groomers, and wide-open beginner slopes. These trails are serviced by three main lifts and one central base area. There are 2,150 vertical feet of lift-served terrain, between 6,100 and 8,250 feet elevation. The 450 acres offer 17 percent beginner terrain, 50 percent intermediate terrain, and 33 percent expert terrain. Lift tickets are affordable, too, with adults paying a mere $45 for a full day of skiing. In summer there are hiking trails, horseback rides, lift rides, mountain biking, children's camps, concerts, fly-fishing, and more. The restaurants and bars at Sundance eclipse most others in the area and are popular retreats for locals as well as visitors.

GUIDANCE **Sundance Resort** (general: 801-225-4107; lodging: 800-892-1600; www.sundanceresort.com) has information on the area as a whole, from summer recreation to lodging, nightlife, dining, and skiing.

GETTING THERE *By car:* If arriving from Salt Lake City or the south, the most direct route is via I-15. Take exit 272 (800 North in Orem) and head east, and connect with UT 189 at the mouth of the Provo Canyon. Take a left onto UT 92 (7 miles up the canyon and the first left turn after passing through a tunnel), and 2 miles later you will arrive at the resort.

If traveling from Park City, take UT 248 (Kearns Blvd. in Park City) south out of town to US 40. In Heber City, make a right and head southwest on UT 189. Just 3 miles after passing Deer Creek Reservoir, head right on UT 92. Sundance offers a $10 discount on ski passes to each person in a vehicle with four or more people.

*By shuttle:* **Utah Transit Authority** or **UTA** (801-377-7433; www.rideuta.com) offers a very comprehensive shuttle schedule between Provo/Orem and Sundance during the winter. There is also service between Salt Lake City and Utah County.

MEDICAL EMERGENCY There are no hospitals immediately in the Sundance Resort. During winter, ski patrol is the emergency health service. By summer, Heber City and Provo are the nearest facilities. (See the *Medical Emergency* sections in the "Heber Valley" and "Provo" chapters.)

## ✳ Outdoor Activities

BIKING Sundance Resort has significantly lower elevation than many of Utah's ski resorts and is thus able to open its trails to bikers about a month earlier. Due to variations in snow pack and length of the season, this changes yearly. However, Sundance can usually open its trails in May. For safety reasons, mountain bikers are not allowed on hiking trails. Helmets are required for on-property riding, and passes (which do not include lift fare) cost $10 per day. All trails have been designed for both directions of travel, so do not assume any right-of-way as a downhill cyclist. Mountain biking instruction is available in clinic form at the resort's **Mountain Bike School** (801-223-4849). Over 25 miles of single- and double-track trails are maintained on the property, and different major routes include **Archies Loop, Ray's Run,** and **Scotts Pond.** Riding at the resort is generally accessible for riders at the beginner and intermediate level, though trails are scenic and challenging enough to entertain more advanced riders. Trail maps are available online or with ticket purchase in the base area.

**FISHING** **Provo River,** with cutthroat, rainbow, and German brown trout, is one of Utah's better fisheries and is also within very close driving distance. See the *Fishing* section of the "Provo" chapter.

**Sundance Resort** (801-226-1937; www.sundanceresort.com). Sundance offers its guests guide services in cooperation with **Rocky Mountain Outfitters** (435-654-1655; www.rockymtnoutfitters.com). Fishing, meals, and accommodations packages are available.

**HIKING** The Sundance Resort has 10 miles of trails on its property, but many more connect to the greater forests beyond, including the Great Western Trail and Ridge Trail. (There are 25 more miles of single-track biking trails on the property as well; see *Biking*) Sundance Resort offers guided hikes at hourly rates that depend on group size and destination. Hiking trail maps are available on the resort Web site (www.sundanceresort.com). The resort trails can be started at the base area, or by taking Ray's Lift to Ray's Summit ($8 per ride).

**Stewart Falls** is one of the area's more popular hikes. Requiring only about two hours, it can either be done as an out-and-back or a loop hike, and it accesses waterfalls named after the Scottish family that originally owned the land and built the predecessor ski area.

**Arrowhead Summit Trail** takes hikers upward and northward to Arrowhead Summit overlooking Heber and Utah valleys, with good views of the greater Wasatch Range. This summit is the highest point in the resort, at 8,250 feet above sea level.

**Black Forest Loop** is the least-strenuous trail in the area and enjoys the cover of the forest canopy, keeping hikers cooler during warm months.

**HORSEBACK RIDING** This is yet another way to enjoy the resort and surrounding area in summer. Rides begin at the **Sundance Stables** (801-223-6000) and are conducted by **Rocky Mountain Outfitters** (435-654-1655; www.rockymtnout fitters.com). All trips are guided and vary in length. Lessons, clinics, and overnight trips are available in addition to day trips.

## SKIING

### Alpine

**Sundance Resort** (801-223-4170 or 800-892-1600; www.sundanceresort.com), RR3, Box A-1, Sundance, just 20 minutes east of Provo via US 189 and Alpine Loop Scenic Byway. Sundance has three major lifts servicing 41 runs, 2,150 vertical feet, and 450 acres of skiing, on a yearly average of 320 inches (that's 26 feet, 8 inches) of snow. The terrain is considered 17 percent beginner, 50 percent intermediate, and 33 percent advanced. $45 for adults, $36 for half day, $22 for children ages 6–12, $12 for seniors ages 65 and up, free for ages 5 and under.

Sundance enjoys being at once a secluded retreat and an elegant destination. The resort, created by Robert Redford, is the namesake of the independent film festival. It has roots squarely in the fine arts, with artists-in-residence drawing from the peaceful surroundings as they create their work. Though modern, all of the lodging and infrastructure have been designed with backwoods charm to complement its fantastic backdrop, the 11,749-foot-tall Mount Timpanogos.

The skiing at Sundance is on a smaller scale than many of the big Utah resorts, and that is no accident. Sundance was created to exist harmoniously with nature. Its terrain of bowls, groomers, trees, chutes, flats, and steeps is of the same variety as Snowbird and Alta, but on a much smaller scale. However, by simply being removed from the large Salt Lake City and Park City ski populations, the slopes of Sundance enjoy much less crowding and greater solitude. Rentals are in the **Creekside Lodge** (801-223-4140), in the base area. Private, semiprivate, and group adult lessons, as well as children's and women-only lessons, are available for skiers and snowboarders, also located in the Creekside Lodge.

## Nordic

There are 26 kilometers of wide, regularly groomed trails available for classic and skate skiing at Sundance. A spectrum of difficulty is available to choose from, with longer trails usually offering more difficult terrain. Rentals can be obtained at the **Nordic Center** (801-223-4170), open daily during the winter 9–5. Classic, skate, and telemark ski packages are available for rent, as well as snowshoes and sleds. $14 for a day pass.

## ✳ Lodging

**Sundance Resort Reservations**
(800-892-1600; www.sundanceresort
.com). Lodging at the resort is all done through its central reservations service. The resort has three genres of private rentals scattered throughout the floor of the resort, each with its own unique flavor:

**Mountain Suites and Lofts** are the largest option, with around 900 square feet per unit. These offer a full master bedroom and kitchen, and special features such as steam showers and large porches.

**Sundance Suites** are a step down in size and are marked by the same high-level comfort and rustic, woodsy aesthetic. Stone, woodwork, and Native American craftsmanship trim the 700-square-foot units. Each has a kitchenette.

**Sundance Studios** offer guests just more than 400 square feet of accommodations, including some basic kitchen fixtures. These cozy units are accented with down comforters, fireplaces, and queen-sized beds; a few have private balconies.

## ✳ Where to Eat

**DINING OUT The Foundry Grill**
(801-223-4220; www.sundanceresort
.com/dine), Resort Main Building, base area. Open Monday–Saturday for breakfast, lunch, and dinner; open Sunday for brunch. The Foundry Grill is the exemplary casual dining experience at Sundance. As with the rest of the resort, the grill has a casual air, yet exceptional quality. The cuisine is American, crafted from the freshest ingredients possible. Entrées and accompaniments are delicately prepared and succulent. An applewood oven makes dishes unique. Each drinking glass is blown from recycled glass at the resort. A kid's menu makes the grill more relaxing for families.

**The Tree Room** (801-223-4250; www
.sundanceresort.com/dine), Resort Main Building, base area. Open Tuesday–Thursday 5–9, Friday and Saturday 5–10. The Tree Room is Sundance's finest dining experience, serving guests exquisite preparations of Rocky Mountain–accented fare. In the style of greater Sundance, the dining room is rustic yet elegant. Attention is given to the quality of the dish, not showiness

or trends of the times. Holistic preparations allow the food to speak for itself. Main dishes include exotic and local game, seafood, and poultry, and are complemented by locally grown greens and vegetables when available.

**EATING OUT** Sundance Resort has two slope-side, high-end grills typical of a ski resort. The **Creekside Restaurant** is located in the base area, and the **Bearclaw Restaurant** is Utah's only mountaintop restaurant. Both afford diners excellent views of Mount Timpanogos, and the Bearclaw has uninterrupted panoramic views of the Wasatch Mountains and Utah and Heber valleys below. These are open during ski season and available for private party booking during the off-season. Information for both can be attained by calling 800-818-1010.

**The Deli** (801-223-4211; www .sundanceresort.com/dine), base area. Open Sunday–Thursday 7 AM–9 PM, Friday and Saturday 7 AM–10 PM. The Deli is Sundance's most casual eatery, offering portable goods from pastries and organic espresso drinks in the morning, to barbecue and sandwiches at lunch, and homemade jams and such that can be taken home. Lunch fare is generally toned down a bit but still high-end; dinner entrées span the complexity and price range. If you are staying at Sundance, The Deli will deliver to your room with a $5 fee.

## ✳ Entertainment

Though Sundance is a ski area, it also hosts a good number of central Utah's concerts and performing arts events, including summer Shakespearean theater and independent film screenings. All venues are located in the base area and include the **Eccles Outdoor Stage** (along the far western edge of the base area), the **Rehearsal Hall**

(just to the east of the Eccles Stage), and the **Screening Room** (farther east still). Information can be obtained by calling Sundance's central line, 801-223-4535.

**The Owl Bar** (801-225-4107; www .sundanceresort.com/dine), Resort Main Building, base area. Open Monday–Friday 5 PM–12 midnight, Saturday and Sunday noon–midnight. This is Sundance's nightlife spot, arguably one of the better hangouts in the entire Provo area. The actual bar is made of antique rosewood and was relocated from Wyoming. This was the very bar frequented by real-life Butch Cassidy and the Sundance Kid in between their frontier adventures. Hungry Owl Bar customers can order off The Foundry Grill menu.

## ✳ Selective Shopping

**The Deli** (801-223-4211), Resort Main Building, base area. As listed in *Eating Out,* The Deli offers fresh pastries, customized sandwiches, gourmet spreads, cheeses, pastes, dips, and the like. All of these are produced in the region—some have even been crafted at Sundance itself.

**Gallery** (801-223-4535), behind the General Store and next to the Art Shack, base area. Open 10–5 daily. Perhaps the best dry goods shop at the resort, this sells the goods of Sundance's and Utah's painters, sculptors, photographers, jewelers, and glass blowers.

**The General Store** (801-223-4250), Resort Main Building, base area. Open 9–9 daily. This is far from a rinky-dink hardware store. What began as a fine clothing store, among other things, became so popular that the Sundance Catalog was born to serve loyalists around the nation and the world. Also featured here is the work of artists and jewelers.

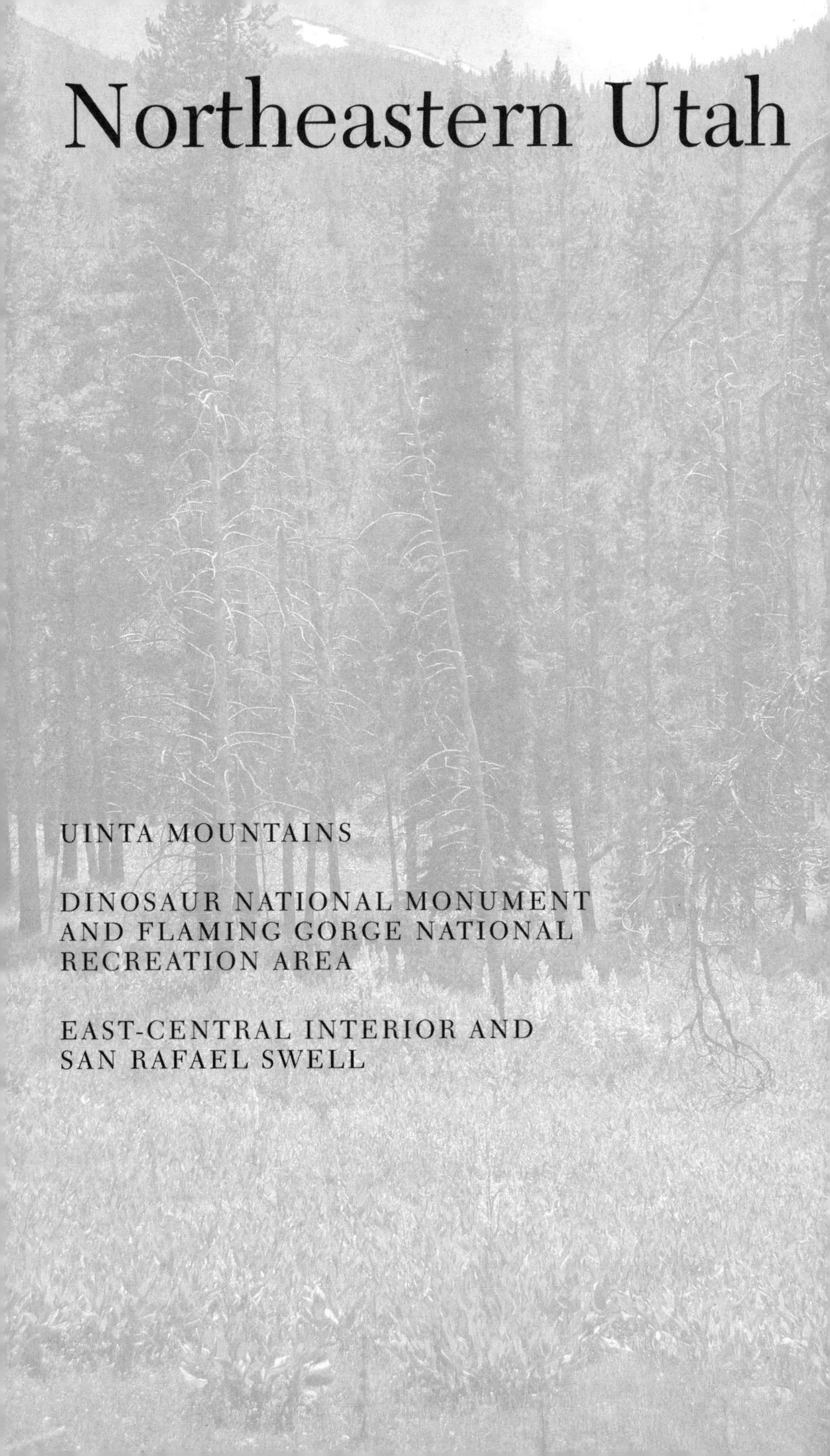

# Northeastern Utah

UINTA MOUNTAINS

DINOSAUR NATIONAL MONUMENT
AND FLAMING GORGE NATIONAL
RECREATION AREA

EAST-CENTRAL INTERIOR AND
SAN RAFAEL SWELL

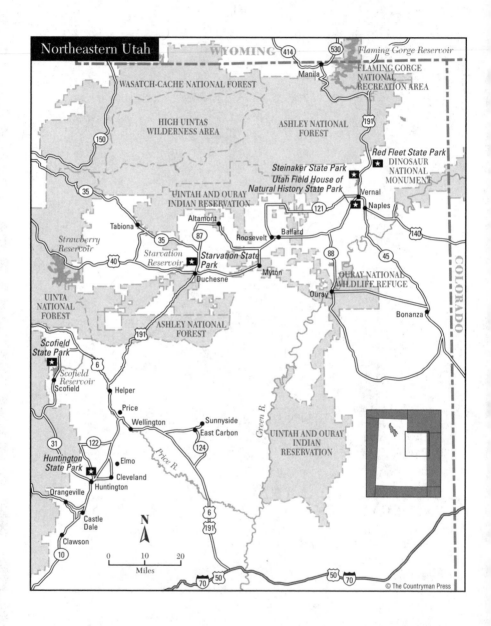

**Northeastern Utah**

WYOMING

*Flaming Gorge Reservoir*

414

530

Manila

FLAMING GORGE
NATIONAL
RECREATION AREA

WASATCH-CACHE NATIONAL FOREST

HIGH UINTAS
WILDERNESS AREA

ASHLEY NATIONAL
FOREST

191

150

*Red Fleet State Park*
DINOSAUR
NATIONAL
MONUMENT

*Steinaker State Park*
*Utah Field House of*
*Natural History State Park*

Vernal

35

UINTAH AND OURAY
INDIAN RESERVATION

Tabiona

Altamont

121

Naples

87

Roosevelt

Ballard

140

35

*Strawberry*
*Reservoir*

*Starvation*
*Reservoir*

*Starvation State*
*Park*

88

45

40

Myton

Duchesne

OURAY NATIONAL
WILDLIFE REFUGE

UINTA
NATIONAL
FOREST

Ouray

Bonanza

COLORADO

ASHLEY NATIONAL
FOREST

191

*Scofield*
*State Park*

6

*Scofield*
*Reservoir*
Scofield

Helper

Price

*Green R.*

Wellington

Sunnyside

East Carbon

UINTAH AND OURAY
INDIAN
RESERVATION

31

122

124

*Huntington*
*State Park*

Elmo

*Price R.*

Cleveland

Huntington

Orangeville

Castle
Dale

N

Clawson

10

0    10    20
Miles

6
191

70    50

50    70

© The Countryman Press

# NORTHEASTERN UTAH IN BRIEF

Northeastern Utah is a special region with its own characteristics. It does not have the same desert environment as the southern red-rock landscapes, or the salt flats of the Great Basin in the western part of the state. It also doesn't have the population of the Wasatch Front, or the interstate system of central Utah. With its high plains, even higher mountain ranges, and major rivers, it is more similar to Wyoming than to other parts of Utah, and it is one of the state's more remote areas.

The geography in this region is intense and rugged, and its natural features are proud and remote. The Uinta Mountains occupy 3,500 square miles of this area and comprise the state's tallest range. Most of the peaks are around 11,000 to 13,000 feet above sea level, and Utah's highest point, King's Peak (at 13,528 feet above sea level), is in the central part of the range. The Uintas are composed primarily of quartzite, shale, and slate, and contain wilderness lands as well as National Forest lands. They are unique in North America as it is the largest east–west running range, an uncommon orientation.

DRIFTWOOD ON THE GREEN RIVER IN NORTHEASTERN UTAH

The Green River is Utah's largest river, entering the state from Colorado through Dinosaur National Monument, and looping along the eastern border of the state all the way down to Lake Powell at the Hite Marina. This river carves a cleft, sometimes more than a mile deep, into the mountainous eastern edge of the San Rafael Swell. The Swell, a region loved for its remoteness and simultaneous accessibility, is a massive horseshoe-shaped uplift. Though it is not distinguished by anything as obvious as a mountain peak, it is easy to sense when you are at or "on" the Swell. Indeed, one gets

ROCKY MOUNTAIN BIGHORN SHEEP ON THE SHORES OF THE GREEN RIVER SOUTH OF DUCHESNE

the distinct feeling of being on a swollen part of the earth. Tucked within the swell are innumerable canyons in which people camp, canyoneer, and rock climb. Certain parts of the Swell have distinct sandstone outcroppings where it is obvious uplift was too much for the bedrock and fractured the sandstone strata into rows of teeth that point upward into the sky.

Most towns in the area are small and unadorned, and many are predominantly occupied by Native Americans or generations of industrial workers. The space between them is open, large, and mostly unsettled. Much of this land is held by the Ute tribe as reservation and should be respected as such. Aside from the far southeast portion of the state, this area has the highest concentration of tribal lands in Utah, the Uintah and Ouray Reservation.

## ✳ Weather

This northern portion of the state shares very similar weather systems and patterns with its neighbors, Wyoming and Idaho. The region's weather cannot be described categorically, but in-town temperatures usually reach daytime heat-of-the-summer highs in the low to upper 80s. Winter daytime highs are a bit cool, usually in the low 30s. The hugely tall Uinta Mountains see much different weather and are considered accessible for recreational use usually no sooner than mid-July at the earliest. As with the rest of Utah, this region is generally very dry, seeing as few as 7 inches of precipitation a year on the plateaus.

# UINTA MOUNTAINS

Uintah County, named for its indigenous Uintah and Ute tribes, is a largely Native American–occupied ranching and reservation region. Where these townships and ranches end, great mountains rise more than 13,000 feet above sea level—8,000 feet above the valleys—into the sky.

The Uinta Range runs roughly parallel to, and just south of, the Utah-Wyoming border. It is approximately 100 miles long and reaches from Heber Valley (near Park City) in the west and into Colorado in the east. In this range there are an estimated 1,000 natural lakes that resulted from heavy glacial sculpting during the ice ages. These lakes have excellent alpine fishing opportunities during the heat of the summer, as their high elevation keeps them cool. Many other forms of recreation, including rock climbing and backpacking, are popular during the summer months, as this is often the coolest place within several hundred miles. There is but one paved road that enters this range, the Mirror Lake Highway, which slices into a small slice of the massif on the far northwestern tip. This beautiful road is rich with convenient recreation and becomes intensely busy during summer weekends. You can find seclusion along this road on weekdays and in the off-seasons, as well as during peak tourist season, provided you venture into the backcountry and off the beaten path.

On the northwestern end of the range is the historic Echo Canyon, through which the First Transcontinental Railroad ran. Today I-80 comes through Echo and runs the northern rim of the Uinta Range. At the northeastern corner of the range is the Flaming Gorge Reservoir, a dammed portion of the Green River, beneath

AFTERNOON THUNDERSTORMS IN UTAH'S TALLEST MOUNTAIN RANGE ARE VIRTUALLY A DAILY OCCURRENCE.

which is some of the state's best fly-fishing. Along the southern aspect of the range is the Uintah and Ouray Reservation, as well as a network of small communities along US 40 and 191. Towns here are small but have enough provisions for restocking. Vernal (population 6,644), Maeser (1,850), Naples (1,334), Ballard (644), Jensen (400), LaPoint (250), Whiterocks (200), and Fort Duchesne (200) are the most sizable towns here.

The Uinta Range is geologically part of the Colorado Plateau, a Montana-sized portion of land straddling Utah, Colorado, New Mexico, and Arizona that is drained by the Colorado River. The primary rock is an estimated 700–800 million years old and is composed of quartzite, slate, and shale; the mountains themselves were created by a tectonic uplift that occurred roughly 60 million years ago. The Uinta Basin, just to the south of the range, has remained relatively unlifted by these geologic events and has an elevation between 5,000 and 5,500 feet above sea level.

Though the Uinta Basin receives very little precipitation—less than 8 inches a year—there is plenty of water flowing into it by way of a multitude of streams and rivers that drain the Uinta and Wasatch mountains. Thus people have occupied the Uinta Basin for as many as 12,000 years. The most documented tribes were the Fremont (who existed at the same timeframe as the Anasazi) and the ancestors of the modern Uintah Tribe, a band of the larger Ute Tribe. The Uintahs enjoyed the basin's wealth of streams and good habitat, which provided them with a healthy supply of animal and plant nourishment. Northern Shoshone also visited the area occasionally but did not have the same presence as the Utes.

Dominguez and Escalante, Spanish explorer-priests who based out of Santa Fe, were the first known Europeans to see the basin. Later, based on their records, trappers and mountain men crossed through the lands, drawn in by the abundance of wildlife. Some of the most notable names of that era were Etienne Provost, William Ashley (after whom the Ashley National Forest is named), Kit Carson, and Antoine Robidoux. Two trading posts were established in the area in the 1830s and 1840s, forts Robidoux and Kit Carson, but no permanent townships were formed. Major John Wesley Powell, arguably the Western Interior's most important and accomplished explorer, made two major investigative voyages down the Green River, first in 1869 and then again in 1871. At the time he took these trips, no one before had even boated in white water, and no information about the continent's interior existed. Essentially, survival seemed highly unlikely. Against all odds, this one-armed man successfully completed the first, and then second, trip, making fixatedly detailed sketches and written observations along the way.

BIRD PRINTS ON THE BANKS OF THE GREEN RIVER IN NORTHEASTERN UTAH

Mormons arrived in Utah in 1848. Despite their overwhelming speed and vigor in establishing new towns, they left the Uinta Basin very much untouched. Brigham Young sent a party to investigate the area for its potential worth, and it was reported to be a wasteland unsuitable for habitation. In keeping with tradition, the federal government assigned these lands

MULE EARS ARE ABUNDANT IN THE HIGH, WET, ALPINE MEADOWS OF THE UINTAS.

to Indian Reservations, beginning in the late 1860s. The reservations were continually reduced and eventually pared down to what remains today. Though the reservations today are much smaller than their original size, they have left more of an impact on the area than any other civilization. By nature of this region never having been occupied by Mormons, this corner of the state retains a distinctly different feel than a lot of the rest of Utah.

GUIDANCE **Bureau of Land Management Salt Lake: Northern Uintas** (801-539-4001; www.blm.gov/ut), 440 West 200 South, Suite 500, Salt Lake City. This portion of the BLM keeps its office in Salt Lake City.

**Bureau of Land Management Vernal: Southern Uintas and Uinta Basin** (435-781-4400; www.blm.gov/ut), 170 South 500 East, Vernal. In this portion of the state, the BLM oversees much of the Uinta Basin, Eastern Uintas, east and west Tavaputs Plateau, Book Cliffs, and more.

**Dinosaurland Travel Board** (435-789-6932 or 800-477-5558; www.dinoland .com), 55 East Main St., Vernal. This is a very typical tourist-friendly Web site representing eastern Utah, with tips on recreation, lodging, dining, and so forth.

**Duchesne County Chamber of Commerce** (435-752-4598; www.duchesne .net), 50 East 200 South, Roosevelt. Though not its express purpose, this chamber keeps a list on its Web site of all the area's recreational opportunities, from hunting to llama tours.

GETTING THERE *By car:* The Uinta Range has very limited roadways and is best accessed from the south. US 40 is a major highway running along the southern flank of these mountains through Heber City, Duchesne, Myton, Roosevelt, Vernal, and eventually Dinosaur National Monument. In Vernal, US 191 departs from US 40, heading due north toward Flaming Gorge National Recreation Area and into I-80/Rock Springs, Wyoming. Mirror Lake Highway/UT 150 is an incredibly scenic drive, the only paved road that penetrates the range. This road goes

## UINTA MOUNTAINS INFORMATION RESOURCES

**Ashley National Forest** (435-789-1181; www.fs.fed.us/r4/ashley), 355 North Vernal Ave., Vernal. This Forest Service agency presides over the southern and eastern swath of the range, part of which is the High Uintas Wilderness, in the center of the range.

**Wasatch National Forest** (801-466-6411; www.fs.fed.us/r4/uwc), inside REI, 3285 East 3300 South, Salt Lake City. This is another major administrational presence in the region.

**Uinta National Forest** (801-342-5100; www.fs.fed.us), 88 West 100 North, Provo. Though the office for this district is in Provo, some of its jurisdiction is in the western and southwestern portion of the Uinta Range.

from Kamas and makes a crescent-shaped loop northeast toward Evanston. This is the most popular road for casual access to recreational opportunities.

*By air:* **Salt Lake International Airport** (801-575-2400 or 800-595-2442; www.slcairport.com), about 50 miles west of Heber City and another 70 miles to Duchesne, or 130 miles to Vernal, is the nearest, biggest airport to the region.

**Uintah County/Vernal Regional Airport** (435-789-3400), located just more than 1 mile south of Vernal, operates small shuttle flights to Denver (formerly Salt Lake City).

GETTING AROUND *By car:* Car rentals can be obtained through **All Save Car Rental** (1245 South US 40, Vernal; 435-789-4777 or 800-440-5776; www.allsave carrental.com), **Enterprise Rent A Car** (835 South 500 East, Vernal; 435-781-3009; www.enterprise.com), or **Lissage Rent A Car** (450 East 100 South, Vernal; 435-781-0312). The area's cab service is **Vernal City Cab** (435-790-1212).

THE FLATLANDS SOUTH OF DUCHESNE

COTTONWOOD TREES IN NORTHEASTERN UTAH NEAR DUCHESNE

**MEDICAL EMERGENCY Ashley Regional Medical Center** (435-789-3342 or 866-725-2862; www.amvc-hospital.com), 151 West 200 North, Vernal. This is a standard hospital with emergency services, among others, toward the eastern end of this region.

**Uinta Basin Medical Center** (435-722-6186; www.ubmc.org), 250 West 300 North, Roosevelt. This medical center is toward the central part of the range's southern slopes, about 30 miles west of Vernal.

## ✴ To See and Do

**Mirror Lake Highway** is one of Utah's most scenic byways, which originates in Kamas and heads north through the northwestern swath of the Uintas. Immediately as the highway begins to ascend into the range, you'll come to the **Kamas Ranger District Office,** a good source of up-to-date information regarding climate, accessibility, permits, and the like. From the ranger's office, 6 miles of driving brings you into the Ashley National Forest, which is filled with campgrounds, picnic areas, and trailheads. Between mile 6 and 19, there are roughly a dozen such major pullouts, and numerous others. Around mile 25, the highway enters distinctly more rugged terrain, passing Bald Mountain Pass at mile marker 29.1, at 11,947 feet elevation. Here the road is above the tree line

A SMALL WATERFALL IN THE UINTAS ALONG THE TRAIL TO HAYDEN PEAK, AS ACCESSED BY THE MIRROR LAKE HIGHWAY

and passes through several sweeping bends that afford excellent views from many perspectives of the alpine landscape below. High-elevation campgrounds, scenic pullouts, and alpine trailheads line the highway. The road descends for another 25 miles or so, passing the Bear River before entering Wyoming and eventually Evanston. A day-use fee of $3 is required to recreate anywhere along UT 150, payable at the ranger booth east of Kamas. For specific recreation recommendations such as hiking or rock climbing, see those sections later in the chapter.

MUSEUMS **Daughters of Utah Pioneers Museum** (www.dupinternational .org), 500 West 200 South, Vernal. Open 10–4 Wednesday–Saturday, June through August. The Daughters of Utah Pioneers is one of the state's oldest and most active historical associations, with many museums across the state. This museum is small, yet has an interesting collection of artifacts dating back to the early history of the area and the 19th century. These frontier items include guns, wool spinners, clothing, furniture, and the like. Free admission.

**Dry Fork/McConkie Petroglyphs,** west of Vernal. Take UT 121 to 3500 West; head north on 3500 West roughly 7 miles to marked parking area. These petroglyphs are located on the private property of the Sadie McConkie Ranch. Respect access privileges by staying on the trails and obeying all signs. This dense collection of illustrations was created by the Fremont Indians and are among the best in the nation, especially for such easy access. Figures carved into the Navajo sandstone are as tall as 9 feet. Free admission; donations accepted. No restrooms or other facilities are available.

**John Jarvie Ranch** (435-885-3307), northeast of Vernal about 75 miles (the final 2 miles are on very steep dirt roads); call for specific directions particular to your direction of travel. Open daily 10–5 May through October. This ranch, established in Browns Park in 1880, was a hub for shady characters of the Wild West, including Butch Cassidy and his gang, Ann Bassett, and more. Jarvie himself was murdered, his body sent down the Green River, and his safe robbed. Four original structures dating back to the 1880s exist, including a dugout and blacksmith shop, as well as a replica of the general store and gravesites of four murdered men.

**Utah Field House of Natural History State Park Museum** (435-789-3799; www.stateparks.utah.gov), 496 East Main St., Vernal. Open daily 8–7 Memorial Day through Labor Day, 9–5 during winter. This 22,000-square-foot facility is located within one of the world's richest fossil regions and houses a large number of assembled skeletons and exhibits illustrating the area's history in terms of paleontology, geology, biology, and archaeology. The geology represented here dates as far back as 3 billion years, and life represented here dates back 600 million years. The Fremont and more recent Ute tribes, indigenous to the area, are represented through replicas of art, tools, and through murals. A dinosaur garden outside includes life-sized replicas of a tyrannosaurus rex, a ceolophysis, and 15 other species. $6 for adults, $3 for children ages 6–12, free for ages 5 and under.

## ✳ Outdoor Activities

BIKING If you plan to bike in the area, come prepared with your own equipment, as there are no retail or rental shops in the area. (The nearest are in Evanston and Park City.) Also come equipped with all of your repair tools, food, and water, as there are no towns or shops in the high Uinta Mountains. Finally, be ready to breathe in thin air, as even the paved Mirror Lake Highway gains an elevation of 10,600 feet at Bald Mountain Pass.

**Beaver Creek Trail,** 6 miles east of Kamas on UT 150/Mirror Lake Highway, Yellow Pine Parking Area. Beaver Creek is a popular mountain biking trail because of its gentle gradient and long season. The trail is approximately 5 miles each way and climbs from 7,100 to 7,600 feet altitude, with much earlier snowmelt than most other Uinta trails. The first portion requires little technical ability as it follows a glaciated valley; the final 1.5 miles of the main route are slightly more technical and rocky. This trail is shared by ATV users and is a high-quality trail slightly wider than most single-track trails, making it very open and easy to

A THUNDERSTORM AS SEEN FROM BALD MOUNTAIN

follow. The trail runs parallel to the Uinta Mountains and a small creek spotted with occasional beaver ponds. About 3 miles into the ride, an information board names a few other possible side loops, some of which are more challenging and include the Cedar Loop, Aspen Pass, and Pine Valley Trail.

**Wolverine Ridge,** trailhead at Bear River Lodge, 49 miles northeast of Kamas on UT 150/Mirror Lake Highway. This fairly extensive trail system offers a 16-mile loop, shorter loops, as well as out-and-back ride options. This network is on the northern flanks of the Uintas and is shared by ATV users. The lowest elevation is 8,400 feet and the highest is 9,500; the entire loop requires just more than 2,000 feet of climbing. The main trail is generally moderate but has occasional technical cruxes, including a 0.5-mile 500-foot climb. Lilly Lake is a good beginner option that follows a dirt road for 2.5 miles. These trails are generally broad and smooth, which allows beginner to intermediate riders to enjoy themselves.

GATES OF LODORE, COLORADO, A CATARACT THROUGH WHICH THE GREEN RIVER FLOWS INTO THE MOUNTAINS JUST NORTH OF DINOSAUR NATIONAL MONUMENT

**BOATING** Most of the area's boating is best done on the Green River (white water) and on Flaming Gorge Reservoir; these areas are discussed later in the "Dinosaur National Monument and Flaming Gorge National Recreation Area" chapter.

**Mirror Lake,** access as described in *Fishing.* Located at one of the most

scenic portions along the Mirror Lake Scenic Byway, and with very convenient access, this high-elevation lake permits motorboats. This lake has an elevation of 10,000 feet, almost 90 campsites, and proximity to trailheads accessing Bald Mountain. This lake becomes very crowded on summer weekends.

**Smith and Moorehouse Lake,** 2 miles east of Oakley on UT 213, then south on Forest Service Road 033 for 2 miles, is a popular lake for boating as it has a nice, gravelly boat ramp on the eastern shore. This scenic lake fills the bottom of a steep, wooded basin. Motorized boats are permitted here. With an elevation of 7,600 feet, this comes into season later than valley reservoirs, but before the high Uinta lakes.

FISHING The Uinta Range, which underwent heavy glaciation through the ice ages, is the location of some 1,000 alpine lakes, roughly 500 of which have great fishing opportunities. Additionally, the range is the headwaters for many of the state's largest rivers and best fisheries. For more information on fishing conditions, permits, and the like, call any of the listings in *Guidance.* For outfitter-style accommodations, see the *Lodging* section of this chapter.

**Green River,** especially beneath (south of) the Flaming Gorge Dam and above the Gates of Lodore/Lodore Canyon, is considered one of Utah's best fly-fishing spots. For more information on this body of water, read the *Fishing* section of the "Dinosaur National Monument and Flaming Gorge National Recreation Area" chapter.

**Jans Mountain Outfitters** (800-745-1020; www.jans.com) run guided-fishing trips across the state, including in the Uintas. Based out of Park City, this company is not too far from the Uintas and has available everything you'll need, from apparel to tackle.

**Mirror Lake,** just east of Bald Mountain Pass, about 31 miles northeast of Kamas. Located in the western Uintas, this is the namesake of the Mirror Lake Scenic Byway and offers views of Bald Mountain and Hayden Peak. This lake is stocked

A POPULAR FISHING SPOT TWO-THIRDS OF THE WAY FROM KAMAS TO THE WYOMING BORDER ALONG THE MIRROR LAKE HIGHWAY, TO THE NORTH OF THE HIGHWAY

Amiee Maxwell

with trout and becomes very busy during summer weekends. Powerboats are now permitted on these waters.

**Provo River** begins in the southwestern portion of the range and is fished from its origin in the Uintas to its terminus in Utah Lake, just west of Provo. There are three sections of this river, divided by bodies of water. The upper section in the Uintas is located between Trail Lake and Jordanelle Reservoir. For more information on the lower and middle sections of this river, see the *Fishing* sections in the "Heber Valley" and "Provo" chapters.

OFF THE MIRROR LAKE HIGHWAY ON THE EASTERN SLOPE OF BALDY PASS

**Uinta River** drains the south slope of the mountains, and its many small tributaries and creeks supply fishermen with plenty of fishing opportunities. Fish include rainbow, wild brown and brook trout, and mountain whitefish. This river is north of Roosevelt in Uinta Canyon and offers good fly-fishing in relative solitude.

**Weber River** begins in the northeastern part of the range and drains west into the Great Salt Lake through the Ogden area. This generally mellow river is a popular spot for trout fly-fishing.

GOLF **Dinaland Golf Course** (435-781-1428), 675 South 2000 East, Vernal. This public, 18-hole course is only lightly dotted with trees, giving the course an open feel and views of the Uintas beyond. The course is nearly flat, with some slightly rolling terrain, many water hazards, 6,773 yards, par 72, and a driving range. $18.

**Roosevelt Golf Course** (435-722-9644), 1155 Clubhouse Dr., Roosevelt. This public, par-72 course has 18 holes, 7,034 yards, a slope rating of 121, and a driving range. It is made challenging by its many hazards. The newer greens on the back are more challenging.

HIKING The Uinta Range is more than 100 miles long and 30 miles wide, and is largely comprised of national forest, with some of its interior designated as wilderness. The interior of the range, with Kidney Lake, Clements Lake, and Mirror Lake, is High Uinta Wilderness. On every side this is surrounded by national forest: Uinta to the west and southwest, Wasatch to the north, and Ashley to the east and southeast. Roughly 100 trails access the interior of this region. The Uintas are Utah's highest range and one of its most northern, and as such the trails here generally do not open until mid- to late summer, depending on the year's snowpack. For more information on trail variety or accessibility, call the ranger districts listed in the *Guidance* section at the beginning of this chapter. A day-use fee of $3 is required to recreate anywhere along UT 150, payable at the ranger booth east of Kamas.

**Bald Mountain**, trailhead at Bald Mountain Pass Picnic Area, 29 miles east of Kamas on UT 150/Mirror Lake Hwy. Bald Mountain is the highest peak in the western Uintas, at 11,943 feet. This hike, just 2 miles each way, gains just 1,250 feet of elevation and has excellent vistas-per-effort economy. The trail begins with gentle switchbacks up the steep mountainside and finishes by traversing the summit ridge. Also from this trailhead is a trail up Notch Mountain. Both peaks are visible from the trailhead.

**King's Peak** is accessed via many different trailheads. It is the tallest point in Utah, at 13,528 feet, and is a very popular hiking destination. The easiest route to the summit is via the **Henry's Fork Trail,** accessed by taking WY 410 and then Forest Service Road 077 south out of Mountain View, Wyoming, for about 24 miles to Henry's Fork Campground. This trail follows the Henry's Fork River for 6 miles and arrives at lakes and good camping sites after the first 8 miles. From these lakes is a selection of trails that reach the summit, anywhere from 5 to 9 miles long. The mountain can also be enjoyed by a **loop trail,** which never gains the top but offers great views at lower elevations. This 8-mile loop, popular for mountain bikers as well as hikers, is just 4 miles east of Browns Park/John Jarvine Ranch. (To get there, take Browns Park Rd. south from UT 191 for 22 miles. Signs will indicate the presence of the ranch.)

**HORSEBACK RIDING** The Uintas are composed entirely of public lands and have more than 100 distinct trails. Horseback riding is excellent here, though riders should be advised that many of these trails (outside of the Uinta Wilderness) are shared by ATV riders. Check the *Lodging* section; many lodging options in the Uinta area are also outfitters of some sort of guided horseback riding trips.

**NORDIC SKIING** **Bear Creek Cross-Country Trail** originates 6 miles east of Kamas along UT 150/Mirror Lake Scenic Highway. This moderately pitched trail travels roughly 5 miles into the woods and gains only 450 feet along the way; it is the main line from which more difficult trails branch.

**ROCK CLIMBING** The Uinta Range is one of Utah's best moderate sport and traditional climbing locations. Salt Lake City residents love the area because it allows them to escape summer heat without driving long distances; summer temperatures here are usually around 20–30 degrees cooler than in the Salt Lake Valley. The rock here, Uinta Quartzite, is extremely compact. Climbs here are generally vertical, though a few are slightly slabby, and others are quite overhanging. In other words, a variety of good routes are available here between 5.7 and 5.12. In addition to excellent climbing, the Uintas offer climbers excellent, sometimes unregulated camping in a scenic alpine setting. The range usually doesn't come into season until the beginning of July at the earliest.

Almost all of the climbing is along or near to the Mirror Lake Highway (UT 150) and is mostly moderately difficult. A 5.10 climber will have a heyday here, but 5.8 climbers and 5.12 climbers will get theirs, too. Sport

ROSES, NEAR RUTH LAKE, ALONG THE MIRROR LAKE HIGHWAY

climbers should look to climb at **Ruth Lake** as well as the **Moosehorn** and **Jax** crags; traditional climbers will prefer the concentration of lines at the **Portal, Recess, Wall of Tiers,** and **Scout Lake** crags. More information on climbing in the Uintas is available in Nathan Smith and Paul Tusting's *Uinta Rock*.

## ☀ Lodging

**HOTELS** Hotels in the area are generally very basic and include: **Best Western Inn** (435-722-4644 or 800-528-1234), 2203 East US 40, Roosevelt; **Frontier Motel** (435-722-2201 or 800-248-1014), 75 South 200 East, Roosevelt; and **Holiday Inn Express** (435-654-9990; www.ihchotelsgroup.com), 1268 South Main St., Heber City. For more moderate and higher-end selections, Park City, Kimball Junction, and Heber Valley are your best bet; see the *Lodging* sections in the chapters of the Northern Wasatch section of this book.

**MOUNTAIN LODGES AND OUT-FITTERS** **Bear River Lodge** (800-559-1121; www.bearriverlodge.com), 49 miles north of Kamas on UT 150/ Mirror Lake Hwy. This property has cabins in a variety of sizes and on-property fishing ponds, convenience store, service station, and a restaurant (which, as of the summer of 2008 was temporarily closed due to construction). This lodge is located in a pleasant and flat scenic valley near Amethyst Lake and rents snowmobiles and ATVs. Cabins $130–$370.

**Falcon's Ledge Lodge** (435-454-3737 or 877-879-3737; www.falconsledge .com), from Duchesne, north 15 miles on UT 87. Falcon's Ledge is an all-around outfitter and lodge that offers hunting, wing-shooting, and falconry, but specializes in fly-fishing. This Orvis-endorsed lodge is one of the most attractive options around for fly-fishermen. Rooms are noticeably more luxurious than many other options in the area. The lodge is located near Altamont on the southern slope of the Uintas. The very modern-looking lodge is located in a private 600-acre canyon, and three meals a day are prepared fresh in the kitchen; call to inquire.

TRAIL JUNCTION LEADING FROM CHRISTMAS MEADOWS WITH OPTIONS TO KERMSUH, AMETHYST, AND RYDER LAKES

PASILLAS MEXICAN RESTAURANT IN THE CENTER OF KAMAS

Breakfast is included for guests; other meals can be purchased. Reservations are recommended. Children must be 12 and older. Legalities require that you bring your own beer, wine, and liquor. $175; includes breakfast.

**LC Ranch** (435-454-3750; www .lcranch.com), about 0.25 mile east of the intersection of Bluebell Road/ UT 87 and 3750 North St., Altamont. A lodge, outfitter, and guide service, LC Ranch offers elk hunting, private trout ponds, and catch-and-release fly-fishing. Located on the southern ramp of the Uintas, this is a campus of private cabins, some of which are huge, and others sufficiently large. $200 and up.

🎣 **Moon Lake Resort** (435-454-3142 or 970-731-9906; www.moonlakeresort .com), about 30 miles north of Duchesne via UT 87 and Moon Lake/ Mountain Home Rd. This is a family-style lakeside lodging option in the Ashley National Forest. The resort campus provides guests with tidy cabins, boat rentals, horseback rides, fishing in lakes and streams, hiking, biking, and a small general store. Though cabins have plumbing, electricity (and a refrigerator, heater, and stove), bed linens and kitchen gear are not provided and either must be rented or brought from home. Open seasonally, usually from the end of March through November. $65–$135.

**Rock Creek Store Bed & Breakfast** (435-454-3853; www.rockcreekstorebb .com), 30 miles north of Duchesne via UT 87 and Mountain Home Rd.

THE GATEWAY GRILL, IN THE CENTER OF KAMAS

This mom-and-pop operation has a general store with basic supplies ranging from food to hunting and camping gear, as well as breakfast. Very basic, yet cozy accommodations. $70–$110.

**Spirit Lake Lodge** (435-880-3089; www.spiritlakeutah.com), at Spirit Lake, on the northeastern slope of the Uintas. Complex directions; see Web site or call for more information. Accommodations here are a series of very charming and rustic cabins that sleep anywhere from two to eight people. Also here are a small restaurant and store. $60–$120 per cabin.

## ✳ Where to Eat

There is not much at all in this vicinity for fine dining, aside from on-site venues at select guest ranches (as described above). However, most small towns especially have small restaurants located along their main streets. Be warned that in many small towns, restaurants and other services are closed on Sunday, and have very limited hours on days when they are open. Typical restaurants include Mexican eateries and chains such as JB's.

# DINOSAUR NATIONAL MONUMENT AND FLAMING GORGE NATIONAL RECREATION AREA

This is a region much more marked by its prehistory (and study thereof) than its recent history. This area is among the world's richest fossil beds and has one of Utah's smallest human populations. The Green River, which runs through Flaming Gorge Dam and Dinosaur Monument, is one of the most fished and boated rivers in the state—and is one of its largest, with almost 600 uninterrupted miles within Utah's borders. The arid lands of this region are home to Utah's second-largest collection of Indian reservation land, belonging to the Uintah and Ouray Reservation.

Dinosaur National Monument (970-374-3000; www.nps.gov) is split between Utah and Colorado, with Colorado having just slightly more than majority holdings and its headquarters, at 4545 East US 40, Dinosaur, Colorado. Though more of the monument is within Colorado, Utah's portion has the best access for motorists and also contains the Cleveland-Lloyd Dinosaur Quarry. In general, this area is highly remote and rugged. Access is possible from the north (via CO 318 and connecting gravel and dirt roads) and from the east (via US 40 and connecting gravel roads).

NAVAJO SANDSTONE AFTER A STORM, TAKEN FROM THE SHORES OF THE GREEN RIVER, LOOKING EAST FROM DINOSAUR NATIONAL MONUMENT

The quarry, opened in 1957, was closed due to bedrock and structural instability. Though this major attraction is not available, there is still plenty of hiking and exploring to do on the premises. Entrance to this national monument is $10 for vehicles and $5 for pedestrians, cyclists, and motorcyclists.

Many boaters enter the monument from the north via the Green River as it flows into the monument from the spillways of Flaming Gorge Dam and into Dinosaur through the scenic and intimidating Gates of Lodore and Lodore Canyon. The Green River is a river of many personalities: at points, it is a flat, lazy river flowing atop high plains; at other times it meanders calmly through beautiful sandstone canyons (Labyrinth and Stillwater, just south of Green River City), and yet at some points it has some of the state's best white-water boating and even features some of North America's biggest drops (as in Cataract Canyon, beneath its confluence with the Colorado).

The Flaming Gorge Reservoir, part of the Green River, is itself a flat-water boater's and fisherman's paradise, with 91 miles of length and roughly 300 miles of shoreline. Trout in excess of 50 pounds have been caught in this lake. The majority of the lake is in Wyoming, but the most scenic and accessible portions are in Utah. Fishing permits, as given by Ashley National Forest, are required. (See *Guidance*.) Day use is $5 per vehicle.

Dutch John and Green Lake are two very small Utah towns near the recreation area, and Manila (www.manillautah.us), though just a slight bit farther away, is slightly larger. Sheep Creek Canyon and Little Hole National Recreation Trail are two highlights for hikers in the vicinity, each with impressive crossectional geology and brilliant rock colors.

**GUIDANCE Dinosaur National Monument Canyon Visitors Center** (435-781-7700; www.nps.gov/dino), 2 miles east of Dinosaur, Colorado, on Harpers Corner Rd. Open 8:30–4:30 Wednesday–Sunday, May 2–October 6; closed Monday and Tuesday. This is the Colorado-side entrance station with much more restricted hours.

**Dinosaur National Monument Temporary Visitors Center** (in place of **Quarry Visitors Center,** 970-374-3000; www.nps.gov/dino), north of Jensen on UT 149. Open 8:30–4:30 daily Labor Day through Memorial Day, open until 5:30 in summer, closed holidays. This temporary center does not have the fossils and exhibits of the Quarry Visitors Center, but it does have informative staff and brochures, and is within a 0.5-mile hike of a fossil bed.

**Flaming Gorge Dam Visitors Center** (Bureau of Reclamation: 435-885-3106, or Flaming Gorge Dam Visitors Center: 435-885-3135), about 43 miles north of Vernal on US 191. Open daily

CLIFFS ALONG THE GREEN RIVER, NEAR DINOSAUR NATIONAL MONUMENT

10–5 April–October, restricted hours in winter. The Bureau of Reclamation owns the dam itself and has erected a visitors center at its location to explain the engineering, geology, and history of the project.

**Flaming Gorge National Recreation Area Headquarters** (435-789-1181; www.fs.fed.us/r4/ashley), junction of UT 44 and UT 43 in Manila. This national recreation center is managed by the Ashley National Forest, and so any questions may be answered by calling or visiting in person.

**Red Canyon Visitors Center** (435-889-3713), just 3.5 miles west of the UT 44/ US 191 junction on UT 44. Open 8–6 daily Memorial Day through Labor Day. This visitors center has been perched atop a canyon wall with cliffs, steep banks, and 1,300-foot exposure. Enormous windows overlook these expanses. From here a trail departs and tours the canyon rim, offering you a chance to stretch your legs for up to 4.2 miles each way.

GETTING THERE *By car:* The most central and substantial town in this far northeastern corner of Utah is Vernal, which is at the junction of US 40 and US 191. US 40 heads west from there, skirting the southern underbelly of the Uinta Mountains before winding up in Heber, and eventually Park City and I-80.

**Dinosaur National Monument's Temporary Visitors Center** (and western entrance point) is just north of, and signed from, Jensen, Utah, 14 miles east of Vernal on US 40. The Canyon Visitors Center and eastern entrance point is just 2 miles east of Dinosaur, Colorado, on US 40 (just east of the Utah/Colorado border) via Harper's Corner Road. Other access points exist but are much less easily accessed due to unimproved roadways and utter lack of signage. One such access point is beneath the Flaming Gorge Dam along the Green River, where boaters and fishermen access the river. A gazetteer, though helpful, actually is not detailed enough to give reliable directions to this access point in this maze of unimproved ranch roads.

**Flaming Gorge National Recreation Area** is a teardrop-shaped area of land encasing Flaming Gorge Reservoir, just more than 90 miles in length. This reservoir, formed by the Flaming Gorge Dam at its southern end, is filled with the waters of the Green River. At its northernmost tip is the town of Green River, Colorado, at the junction of CO 530 and I-80. CO 530 runs the western length of the reservoir, and CO 373/US 191 flanks the east. UT 44 cradles the bulbous southern end of the reservoir. Manila sits at the junction of UT 44 and 373, and Dutch John is just north of the UT 44 and US 191 junction.

*By air:* **Salt Lake International Airport** (801-575-2400 or 800-595-2442; www .slcairport.com), 5 minutes west of Salt Lake City on I-80 and 180 miles west of Vernal via US 40 and I-80. This is the largest airport anywhere in the vicinity of this region.

**Denver Aiport** (303-342-2000; www.flydenver.com), Denver, Colorado. This airport is another major airport about an hour or more farther than Salt Lake's airport.

**Uintah County/Vernal Regional Airport** (435-789-3400), just more than 1 mile south of Vernal, operates small shuttle flights to Denver (formerly Salt Lake City).

MEDICAL EMERGENCY The nearest medical services to this region are in Vernal and Rangely, Colorado. Be advised that, though cellular service is randomly available, it should be expected phones will *not* work in the majority of this region.

**Ashley Regional Medical Center** (435-789-3342 or 866-725-2862; www.am vc-hospital.com), 151 West 200 North, Vernal. This regional hospital is located in Vernal, just a few blocks away from the junction of US 40 and 191.

**Rangely District Hospital** (970-675-5011; www.rangelyhospital.com), 511 South White Ave., Rangely, Colorado. This hospital is about 60 miles due north of Fruita, Colorado, on CO 139.

**Uinta Basin Medical Center** (435-722-6186; www.ubmc.org), 250 West 300 North, Roosevelt. This hospital has surgical facilities and an emergency room.

## ✳ To See and Do

**Dinosaur National Monument Main Quarry,** north of Jensen, at the monument's western entrance. This quarry, opened in 1957, has been indefinitely closed due to major structural problems considered irresolvable. For a substitute, albeit more remote, experience, see the **Cleveland-Lloyd Dinosaur Quarry** in the "East-Central Interior and the San Rafael Swell" chapter.

**Flaming Gorge Scenic Byway,** also **UT 44,** is a 28-mile stretch of highway that tours the southwestern corner of the gorge, with overlooks of the reservoir, Sheep Creek Bay, and pleasant evergreen and aspen forests.

**Sheep Creek Bay Scenic Loop,** 14.5 miles south of Manila by way of US 40. This loop is a designated 12-mile stretch of road that tours through severe canyons rift into the earth's crust at the site of the Uinta Crest Fault. This geologic feature has millions of years of strata uplifted and visible as tilted red and white stratified ridges extending for many miles in most directions. A mostly paved road travels among these twisted stone layers west along Sheep Creek. This loop is closed in winter. $3 per vehicle.

**Utah Field House of Natural History State Park Museum** (435-789-3799), 496 East Main St., Vernal. This is a 2004, 22,000-square-foot facility with paleontological exhibits filing the entire space. Animated life-sized dinosaur mock-ups, educational exhibits, and murals illustrate prehistory for guests here.

## ✳ Outdoor Activities

BIKING & HIKING TRAILS **Bear Canyon Bootleg Trail,** trailhead at Flaming Gorge Resort, 4 miles north of the UT 44/US 191 junction. This is an easy hike along a 1.5-mile double-track dirt road that gains views of the Flaming Gorge at its terminus.

**Canyon Rim Trail,** trailhead about 3 miles west of the UT 44/US 191 junction at the Red Canyon Visitors Center, or at the Greendale Overlook parking very near the junction. This is a popular trailhead for mountain bikers and hikers. From here departs a 4-mile trail that tours the rim of the Red Canyon, with views down into the canyon below and across to the distant Uinta Mountains. The site of a wildfire in 1993, this open landscape is notorious for wildflowers.

**Dry Fork Canyon,** in Vernal; head west on 500 North to parking for Remember the Maine Park/Red Cloud Loop, about 4 miles west of US 191. This ride is about 11 miles each way but requires little commitment. The ride out is uphill, so the return trip is effortless. For such a short ride, there are many attractions, including the **McConkie Ranch** (3 miles into the ride) and its huge collection of Fremont petroglyphs. Two miles after this, make a right at the junction, and in 3 more miles you will pass the ghost town of **Dry Fork Village.** This is a good turnaround spot, though the route continues another 3 miles.

**Flaming Gorge National Recreation Area** is cradled under its southern belly in Utah by UT 44 (Flaming Gorge–Uintas Scenic Byway) and US 191. Along these roads are many gravel and unimproved dirt roads.

**Little Hole National Recreation Trail,** as described in *Fishing,* is generally used the most heavily by anglers for its superb Green River fishing access, but it is a very pleasant, scenic, flat, and very worthwhile hike as well.

**BOATING** **Buckboard Marina** (307-875-6927), 24 miles south of Green River, Wyoming, on WY 530 and 23 miles north of Manila on WY 530. Open 7 AM–8 PM Monday–Wednesday April through November. This marina offers rentals, storage, gasoline sales, boat repair, and guided fishing and sightseeing trips.

**Cedar Springs Marina** (435-889-3795; www.cedarspringsmarina.com), 2 miles south of Flaming Gorge Dam. Open daily 8–6 May through September. This is a full-service marina with pontoon, ski boat, and fishing boat rentals; a boat ramp; and morning and evening guided-fishing trips.

**Lucerne Valley Marina** (435-784-3483 or 888-820-9225; www.flaminggorge .com), 7 miles east of Manila. Open daily 7 AM–9 PM March through November. This company rents houseboats and small boats alike, and has storage facilities and lakeside cabins.

**FISHING** **Green River,** beneath the spillways of Flaming Gorge Reservoir, is Utah's best fly-fishing spot, absolutely thick with trout. As many as 20,000 fish per mile have been reported here and represent the brown, rainbow, and cutthroat species. Fishing is permitted year-round on the river at this location, 24 hours a day. The **Little Hole National Recreation Trail** is a 7-mile pathway along the northern shore of the Green that tours Red Canyon and has several good holes along the way. The trailhead is located at the boat ramp beneath Flaming Gorge Dam. For more information on fishing the Green, including directions on how to navigate the largely unmarked back roads, visit the Web site www.quickbyte.com/greenriver.

**Green River Drifters** (435-885-3344 or 970-879-0370; www.greenriverdrifters .com). This guide service offers trips of varying length and Dutch-oven meals, and specializes in Green River fly-fishing.

**Flaming Gorge Reservoir,** part of the Flaming Gorge National Recreation Area, is 90 miles long and is known for its "trophy fishing." Read: big fish. Fishing on the reservoir is permitted year-round, 24 hours a day. Given the size of this reservoir, the best fishing is done by boat; for information on marinas at the reservoir, see the *Boating* section of this chapter.

**Old Moe Guide Service** (435-885-3342; www.oldmoeguideservice.com). This northeastern Utah fishing company offers wading and drift boat trips *all year long.*

## ✳ Lodging

**Flaming Gorge Resort** (435-784-3483 or 888-820-9225; www.flaming gorge.com), 7 miles northeast of Manila on WY 530. Open daily 7 AM–9 PM March through November. **Lucerne Valley Marina** (as described in *Boating*) is a full-service marina that is part of this resort. This company rents houseboats and small boats alike, and has storage facilities and *floating* cabins. Each of these unique units is equipped with a kitchenette.

**Red Canyon Lodge at Flaming Gorge** (435-889-3759; www.red canyonlodge.com), 4 miles west of the US 191/UT 44 junction on UT 44 (790 Red Canyon Rd.). This lodge is a resort campus with private cabins in a variety of sizes. Each is a hand-made log cabin with similarly crafted furniture and rustic outfitting. It has an on-site restaurant with American cuisine, including salads, pastas, and various meat entrées, including elk, beef, and chicken. Horse packing trips, as well as nonmotorized boats, mountain bikes, and snowshoes, are available through this lodge.

HORSE PACKERS CROSS ONE OF THE MANY SMALL FOOTBRIDGES IN CHRISTMAS MEADOWS.

# EAST-CENTRAL INTERIOR AND THE SAN RAFAEL SWELL

U tah is a state of variety. It contains fully populated metropolitan areas as well as completely desolate, empty desert expanses. It sees summer temperatures well above 100 degrees in the south and winter lows significantly below zero in the mountains. From high-altitude alpine zones to grassy plains, red-rock canyons, and lush riparian zones, Utah has it all. The center of Utah contains something representative of all these categorizations. It offers excellent wildlands and some of Utah's deepest seclusion, yet also supports some townships and is cut by some of Utah's busiest highways. It is arid and contains red rock, but also mountains, plains, rivers, and deep canyons.

This central region is best described as a swollen uplift in the center of the state. This is the region where Utah begins to ascend to the Colorado Plateau. If coming from the north, you will climb into the regions along US 6 from Spanish Fork. The road continuously gains elevation, but it never reaches dramatic mountains; rather it seems that the earth just becomes taller and taller. Price, halfway between I-15 and I-70 along the diagonal US 6, is the last major town before Green River on the trip south. The San Rafael Swell, in Emery County, sits just south of this area, girdled in its middle by I-70.

The San Rafael Swell, or just "Swell," was formed by tectonic uplift and is quite distinctive. It is an area 40 miles wide and 70 miles long. Prior to this region becoming "swollen," horizontal sandstone, limestone, and shale strata composed the crust here. Uplift from below 60 million years ago thrust these layers skyward, which broke and eroded into toothlike formations as part of this massive anticline. Other portions of the Swell feature desert towers, sandstone bluffs, and buttes. These clefts, the dominant rock of which is a variety of sandstone, are now home to canyons that host some of the state's best canyoneering, relatively uncharted rock climbing, and largely unregulated camping. **Goblin Valley State Park** (day admittance $7 per vehicle; 435-564-3633; www.stateparks.utah.gov) is at the southern end of this feature. On the eastern end is the Book Cliffs. Desolation Canyon, thought to be the single most remote area in the lower 48—deeper and more isolated than even the Grand Canyon—is cut into this bedrock to the east of the Swell by the Green River.

Throughout the Swell run wild herd of burros and horses. Be advised that rainstorms easily produce flash floods in this region due to lack of absorptive topsoil

SAND WASH RUINS, TOP OF DESOLATION CANYON. DESOLATION CANYON IS A POPULAR WHITE-WATER RAFTING SPOT AND IS AMONG THE REMOTEST REGIONS IN THE LOWER 48.

layers; it is advised to stay out of any narrow canyons if a rainstorm is anywhere in the region.

**GUIDANCE Emery County** (888-564-3600; www.emerycounty.com). This county has only about a dozen towns, the largest of which is Huntington, with a population of 2,131 at the time of the 2000 census. However, this county is home of the San Rafael Swell and maintains a travel department on their Web site to help answer questions you may have with regard to lodging, recreation, dining, and the like.

**Goblin Valley State Park** (435-564-3633; www.stateparks.utah.gov), 24 miles south of I-70 on UT 24. This state park represents the southern portion of the San Rafael Swell and is a worthwhile destination.

**Green River** (www.greenriverutah.com). This interstate town is located just east of where US 6 and I-70 intersect. A classic town in its genre, Green River has gas stations, diners, and truck stops galore.

**Price** (www.priceutah.com). Price is the largest town in this region on the northern end and is the most likely to have resources you might need.

**GETTING THERE** *By car:* This area of the state has some of Utah's busiest highways, but outside of that very few major roads. No paved roads access the interior of the San Rafael Swell, with the major exception being the east–west running I-70. US 6 is a major highway that runs from I-15 in Spanish Fork, southeast through Price and Helper, and into I-70 near the city of Green River. For travelers heading between Salt Lake and the southeastern part of the state, this is a very popular route, as it cuts off a huge chunk of driving compared with the I-70/I-15 route.

*By bus:* **Greyhound Bus Lines** (801-355-9579 or 800-231-2222; www.greyhound .com), 525 East Main St., Green River. This national bus line keeps a station in Green River as well as other Utah cities such as Salt Lake City, Moab, Provo, Ogden, and St. George.

*By train:* **Amtrak** (800-872-7245; www.amtrak.com), 250 South Broadway, Green River. Amtrak stops in Green River, St. George, Provo, and Salt Lake City, with direct lines to Los Angeles and San Diego, San Francisco, Denver, Portland, Seattle, and Vancouver.

**MEDICAL EMERGENCY Ephraim Intermountain Clinic** (435-283-4076; www.intermountainhealthcare.org), 525 North Main St., Ephraim. Along US 89, and south of Mt. Pleasant, this nonhospital medical facility is a bit far to the west of the region, but still useful, if needed.

**Sanpete Valley Hospital** (435-462-2441; www.intermountainhealthcare.org), 1100 South Medical Dr., Mt. Pleasant. This hospital is also on the far western end of this region, but if you're recreating in a region this desolate and remote, it is worth knowing about.

## ✳ To See and Do

**Cleveland-Lloyd Dinosaur Quarry Visitors Center,** east of Huntington, about 30 miles south of Price. Open 10–5 Monday–Saturday, noon–5 Sunday Memorial Day through Labor Day. This quarry exists in what is known as the "Upper Jurassic Beds" and is one of North America's most prolific quarries of that era. Opened in 1927, this was the Bureau of Land Management's first ever visitors center. This building was renovated in April of 2007.

THE SLOT CANYONS OF THE SAN RAFAEL SWELL ARE ONE OF THE REGION'S MAJOR ATTRACTIONS AND SPAN THE FULL RANGE OF TECHNICAL DIFFICULTY.

Kami Hardcastle

**Goblin Valley State Park** (435-564-3633; www.stateparks.utah.gov), 24 miles south of I-70 on UT 24. This state park is perhaps one of Utah's most famous state parks, often mistaken for a national park. The first-known Westerners to lay eyes on it were cowboys in the late 1920s, when the distinctive sandstone features earned it the name "Mushroom Valley." The area immediately became as much of a tourist destination as such a remote region could be, given the transportation of the time. The land was acquired by the State of Utah and assigned as a state park in 1964.

The cause of these very unlikely, distinctive, and numerous globular formations is uneven erosion of parallel strata of sandstone. This has allowed softer layers to erode more quickly than the more sturdy layers they support, creating tens of thousands of globelike formations. Today the park is roughly 3,700 acres large and has several pay campgrounds and hiking trails. **Caramel Canyon Trail** is a 1.5-mile

SPLIT MOUNTAIN NEAR DINOSAUR NATIONAL MONUMENT, ON THE GREEN RIVER

hiking tour of the park, which begins at the picnic area at the end of the paved state park road. The trail follows blue cairns and can be a bit tricky to follow exactly. The **Little Wild Horse/Bell Canyon Loop,** whose trailhead is about 5 miles south of the park (see p. 231), is the most popular hike in the Swell, and is one of Utah's best slot canyons. Be advised that rainstorms easily produce flash floods in this region due to lack of absorptive topsoil layers; it is advised to stay out of any narrow canyons if a rainstorm is anywhere in the region.

**The Green River.** This flowing body of water is a substantial and long river—the largest fork of the Colorado River that in the western side of the Wind River Range in Wyoming. As it passes through Utah, it has one of the longest stretches (roughly 600 miles) of river uninterrupted by dams in the United States. Except for one low-head dam just north of Green River City, the river runs freely from Flaming Gorge Dam (in Wyoming) all the way until its confluence with the Colorado River, and still farther into Lake Powell, a reservoir created by the Glen Canyon Dam. The Green River also holds a special place in history, as it was the passageway for the historic exploratory journeys of Major John Wesley Powell in 1869 and 1871—the first time the heart of the Rocky Mountain West was ever truly charted.

After leaving the Wind River Range, the river skirts around the eastern flank of the Uinta Range, entering the Flaming River Gorge (now Reservoir) as named by Powell for its brilliant colors. It leaves the spillway of the dam, passes through 6 miles of Utah's most desirable fly-fishing regions, and heads through **Lodore Canyon** (via the very dramatic and intimidating **Gates of Lodore**), **Split Mountain,** and **Dinosaur National Monument.** At **Steamboat Rock,** it is joined by the Yampa River (a distinctly less green shade than the Green River) and traverses some less-exciting vistas in the **Uintah and Ouray Indian Reservation** and **Ouray Wildlife Refuge.** Over the next few dozen miles, it acquires the water of quite a few tributaries before heading into **Gray** and the more famous **Desolation Canyon.** These are taken by river runners as one stretch of river, as access is so tricky. This stretch of river, often more than a vertical mile beneath the surrounding landscape, is considered the most remote region in the lower 48, as it is separated by sheer canyon walls and as many as 50 completely impassible miles from the nearest, very much unimproved and unmapped, dirt roads. Despite (and perhaps because of) its extreme isolation, this is still an attractive stretch of river for boaters, offering roughly 60 class I–III rapids.

After anticlimactically emerging from these deep canyons onto the plains north of Green River, it begins to again weave its way deeper into the earth's sandstone crust just south of I-70 as it creates **Labyrinth and Stillwater Canyons.** These two gentle and extremely loopy canyons flow together calmly and are often done in conjunction as a three-day canoe trip. These canyons are walled in by smooth sandstone walls, often rising several hundred feet immediately off the water. However, these sheer walls sometimes yield to good side canyons and hiking opportunities.

After these canyons, it flows through **Canyonlands National Park,** where it joins with the **Colorado River.** At this confluence, whirlpools of the muddy Colorado and the very *green* Green form along the line between the two bodies of water. The peninsula above this is absolutely filled with fossils of many sizes, undisturbed by man; even though they are located in a national park, they are removed from roads by vast terrain and are almost inaccessible. Very quickly after the two rivers meet, they plunge into **Cataract Canyon,** with its famous **Big Drops One, Two,** and **Three.** One and Three are considered two of North America's biggest river drops.

A hundred years ago, the river would have flowed wildly through **Glen Canyon,** reported by early river travelers as a much longer and nastier stretch of river than any of the rapids left undammed today. Today the river flows rather uneventfully into **Lake Powell,** a body of water almost 190 miles in length. Recently, though, as speedy evaporation has dropped the lake's surface level as much as 120 feet, huge blocks of old lake sediment have been known to break off into large mud boulders and land in the river, causing potentially large rapids to spontaneously develop and then disappear just as quickly as they appeared.

THIS MAJOR UNDIVIDED HIGHWAY IS A POPULAR SHORTCUT FOR THOSE TRAVELING BETWEEN I-70 AND I-15, FROM WHICH ACCESS ROADS TO THE EASTERN EDGE OF THE SAN RAFAEL SWELL DEPART.

THE CAPITOL REEF FORMATION IN SAN RAFAEL SWELL RUNS FOR MORE THAN 100 MILES
NORTH–SOUTH AND IS A UNIQUE SANDSTONE FORMATION FILLED WITH SLOT CANYONS
AND PICTOGRAPHS.

**San Rafael Swell.** This dome-shaped anitcline of central Utah is unique; though
it is spectacular and ecologically fragile, it is owned for the most part by the
Bureau of Land Management and is largely unregulated. This kidney-shaped uplift
has only one paved road crossing it, I-70, which splits it into a northern and southern half. Though the Swell is only accessible by dirt roads, it is often possible to
take two-wheel-drive cars to many of the places within.

Major features of the northern half are: the **Little Grand Canyon** carved by the
**San Rafael River,** the crack climbing of **Buckhorn Wash, Upper and Lower
Black Boxes, Cane Wash, Saddle Horse Canyon, Mexican Bend, North and
South Coal Wash, Salt Wash,** and **Black Dragon Canyon.** The northern part,
particularly the interior, offers open, flat areas, large cliffs, tall towers, and skele-
tons of old homesteads and uranium mines.

The southern half of the Swell is marked by numerous slot canyons, some of which
are **Reds Canyon, Eagle Canyon, Devils Canyon, Copper Globe, Eardley
Canyon,** and the **Temple Mountain** vicinity slot canyons—**Little Wild Horse**
and **Bell**—among others, and **Muddy Creek Drainage.**

**Little Wild Horse/Bell Canyon Hiking Loop** is one of Utah's best and most
casual slot canyon hikes in the southeastern portion of the Swell. It can be done as
an 8-mile loop, or as shorter, out-and-back hikes of the individual canyons. (Little
Wild Horse is considered to be the better hike of the two.) The canyons include
very narrow passages, as well as more open sections reminiscent of Canyonlands.
Sandstone here varies from planar to wavy, and even eroded to look like a sponge.
Be aware that storms anywhere upstream of these canyons easily produce flash
floods due to lack of absorptive topsoil layers; it is advised that you stay out of any
narrow canyons if a rainstorm is anywhere in the region. Approach as for Goblin

Valley State Park on UT 24 and Goblin Valley Road, and turn right (east) just before the park entrance so as to follow signs for Wild Horse Mesa and Muddy Creek; travel 5.3 miles on dirt and sand road to the parking area. The trail is unmarked and without infrastructure, so be prepared to do you own navigating and bring your own hydration and emergency supplies.

**Canyoneering** in the San Rafael Swell is prime, with dozens and dozens of slot canyons and a generally dry climate. Some of the canyons here can be done with little, if any, technical gear, and many require a high level of skill to navigate and good route finding to locate. The Web site www.climb-utah.com/SRS has excellent route descriptions illustrated with photographs and maps. For more specific information on how to navigate the nebulous backcountry roads (and whether your vehicle can handle the task), call the **BLM Price Field Office** (435-636-3600).

## ✳ Outdoor Activities

BIKING **Bike the Swell** (www.biketheswell.org) is a supported, three-day festival of mountain biking that takes place at the end of September at a different place in the Swell each year and is open to all levels and ages of rider. In addition to pasta dinners, Dutch-oven cook-offs, and campfire stories, riders are also educated about the sport and the area.

**Nine Mile Canyon** is an awesome place for long-distance grinds as well as pleasant family rides. Located north of Wellington, this canyon has interesting sandstone geology, as well as many petroglyphs and old ranch ruins. This ride can be as long as 45 miles out and back, or a short as you like. To get there, take US 6 south of Wellington. Just past the town, head left (north) on Soldier Creek Road. Stay left at the first fork, and expect the pavement to end after about 12.5 miles. Stay right at the next fork, and drive straight through the dude ranch, parking at Cottonwood Glen Picnic Area.

HORSEBACK RIDING AND BOATING **Hondoo Rivers & Trails** (435-425-3519; www.hondoo.com), 90 East Main St., Torrey. This guide service offers horse packing and river trips of varying lengths all over the region that highlight local wildlife (including wild horses), petroglyphs, and ruins.

ROCK CLIMBING **Joe's Valley and Triassic** are two sandstone bouldering areas fairly near each other. Joe's Valley has longer seen attention and development, but both are excellent and offer something to do at every ability level. These boulders are famous for being among the best and most concentrated sandstone boulders in the country. To get to Joe's, head south on UT 10 out of Price. About 10 minutes after Huntington, head east on Route 29 and make a right at a T-intersection; this will lead you to the parking area. To get to Triassic, head south from Price on UT 10, turning east on UT 155 at the Dinosaur Quarry sign. Turn right at the first stop sign in Elmo and follow signs for the quarry. After passing two DIP signs, take a right. Don't worry if you don't see any boulders; they only pop into view at the last moment. See Mike Beck and Mark Russo's *Utah Bouldering* or www.drtopo.com for more information.

**Maple Canyon** is in the western end of this region, in the inconspicuous hills just southwest of Fountain Green and the tiny town of Freedom. This spectacular canyon has the best conglomerate climbing in the United States. Though you'd

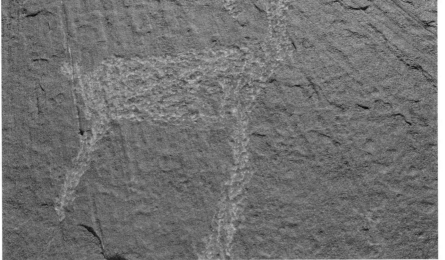

Kami Hardcastle

THE SAN RAFAEL SWELL, POPULAR FOR CAMPING, HIKING, MOUNTAIN BIKING, AND ROCK
CLIMBING, ALSO HAS A HEAVY HELPING OF PICTOGRAPHS, OFTEN VISIBLE FROM THE
ROAD.

never guess it, looking at the scruffy hills that it cuts into and the surrounding
turkey farms, this deep and narrow canyon has miles and miles of climbable walls,
branching dozens of times. The walls of this canyon vary in angle, but most are
vertical to very overhung. The **Minimum Wall** is the land of pumpy, juggy 5.11
and 5.12 routes overhanging 20 degrees. The **Pipe Dream Cave** is one of Maple's
most defining walls, stretching the definition of endurance. This wall is 100 feet
wide and 80 feet deep, and for much of its roof, nearly horizontal. This is home to
knee pads, mutants, and hard 5.13 and 5.14 jug hauls. Maple Canyon is accessed
by arriving in Fountain Green on UT 132. At the southern end of town, head west
on 400 South, and stay with it as it bends south. Continue on this for about 6
miles. In the town of Freedom, take a right and head west on Freedom Road, then
right again at the first road. This will bend left and take you into the canyon.

**San Rafael Swell** has no guidebook and sees few crowds, but it has a limited
amount of very good Wingate sandstone crack climbing. The reason climbing here
is overlooked is the relatively near and very famous Indian Creek, which has miles
of the same style climbing and a very explicit guidebook. Additionally, it is difficult
to get a passenger car into this region of the Swell if the roads have been washed
out. The walls are most concentrated near the intersection of Mexican Mountain
Road and Cottonwood Wash Road. There is a campground here with a pit toilet.
The largest concentration of routes is at the Dylan Wall. All protection is traditional, and a massive rack of cams is advised. This general area is reached by taking
exit 129 off I-70. Take a right onto Buckhorn Wash Road, which heads north and
then east for a short bit before heading north for about 20 miles. Eric Bjornstad's
*Desert Rock: Wall Street to the San Rafael Swell* has information on some of these
routes.

## ✳ Lodging

**Best Western Carriage House Inn**
(435-637-5660; www.bestwesternutah
.com), 590 East Main St., Price. This is
a new and clean Best Western that has
40 rooms of different sizes and free
wireless Internet. $60 and up.

**Holiday Inn Hotel & Suites Price**
(877-863-4780; www.ichotelsgroup
.com), 838 Westwood Blvd., Price.
This Holiday Inn has almost 2,000
square feet of meeting spaces, a small
fitness gym with treadmills and weight
machines, and almost 175 rooms and
suites. $60 and up.

🐾 **Ramada Inn** (435-564-8441; www
.ramada.com), 1117 Main St., Green
River. This is one of the nicer hotels in
Green River's strip of national accommodations typical of an interstate
town. A bonus for people traveling
with their animals: This hotel allows
pets.

## ✳ Where to Eat

In this corner of the state, almost all of
the restaurants are fast-food joints. In
Price, these restaurants line Main
Street (US 6 Business Loop), and in
Green River, these are concentrated
nearest the interstate exits.

**Ray's Tavern** (435-564-3511), 25
Broadway, Green River. This bar and
grill is the best place to eat in Green
River and has a reputation statewide
with climbers and boaters. This is a
beer and burgers place, perfect for a
fairly quick meal with no formality.
This is a welcome change from the
convenience stores and truck stops in
the vicinity.

# Southeastern Utah

MOAB

ARCHES NATIONAL PARK

CANYONLANDS NATIONAL PARK

THE FAR SOUTHEAST CORNER:
HOVENWEEP, NATURAL BRIDGES,
AND LAKE POWELL

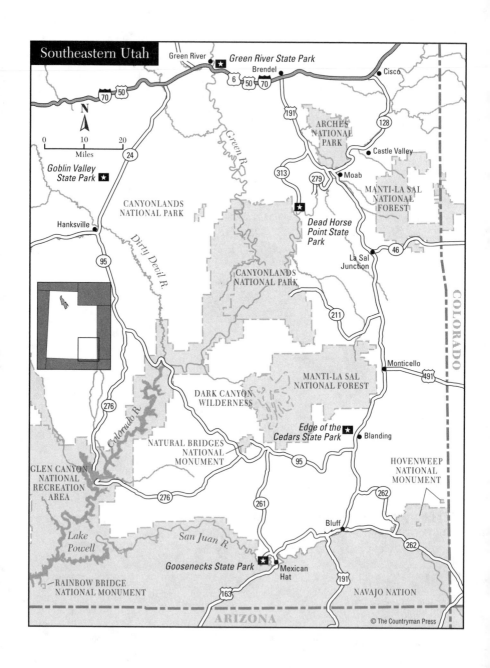

Southeastern Utah

Green River — Green River State Park
Brendel
Cisco

ARCHES NATIONAL PARK
Castle Valley

N

0   10   20
Miles

Goblin Valley State Park

MANTI-LA SAL NATIONAL FOREST

CANYONLANDS NATIONAL PARK

Green R.

Moab

Dead Horse Point State Park

Hanksville

Dirty Devil R.

La Sal Junction

CANYONLANDS NATIONAL PARK

MANTI-LA SAL NATIONAL FOREST

Monticello

DARK CANYON WILDERNESS

Colorado R.

Edge of the Cedars State Park
Blanding

NATURAL BRIDGES NATIONAL MONUMENT

HOVENWEEP NATIONAL MONUMENT

GLEN CANYON NATIONAL RECREATION AREA

Lake Powell

San Juan R.

Bluff

RAINBOW BRIDGE NATIONAL MONUMENT

Goosenecks State Park
Mexican Hat

NAVAJO NATION

ARIZONA

COLORADO

© The Countryman Press

# SOUTHEASTERN UTAH IN BRIEF

Southern Utah is a mixed bag. It is a collection of national parks, small Mormon townships, and tourist destinations. It has alternating stark plains, high mountains, and beautiful red-rock scenery spanning the distance among these areas. Of course the geology here is dominated by the red and orange desert sandstone, but even still there is quite a bit of diversity. The La Sal Mountains, a strikingly lofty and isolated range, thrust into the sky atop the already high Colorado Plateau. This snowy blue range is surrounded by sandstone of all varieties representing ancient seabeds. Through these strata cut the Colorado and Green rivers, which flow into each other just south of Moab in Canyonlands National Park. In addition to the famed deep-orange arches and burnt-red mesas that come immediately to mind, a

NORTH OF GREEN RIVER CITY, THE LANDSCAPE IS OPEN, VIRTUALLY UNPOPULATED, AND CHARACTERIZED BY CRUMBLING SANDSTONE BUTTES AND FRAGILE DESERT FLORA.

full palate of sandstone colors and formations have been sculpted by the desert winds and waters.

Varying rock quality and mineral contents have yielded a huge variety of rock formations: buttes with sheer Wingate sandstone walls that tower hundreds of feet above angular talus slopes, photogenic arches, hoodoos of bulky capstone atop thinner pillars, blobs, smooth cliffs, and deep canyons in colors of white, purple, yellow, orange, and red. These colors are highlighted by the deepness of the desert sun. They are complemented in winter by snow and in spring by the greening of desert sage and other plants.

What exists within the landscape is a variety of settlements, recreational opportunities, and national treasures. The very history of the land and peoples is preserved here by the arid climate and can be seen in the form of petroglyphs and fossils. Canyonlands and Arches national parks are very near Moab and offer visitors the chance to view many different instances of these ancient stone etchings, as well as fossilized dinosaur bones and even footprints. Outside of these parks are many more less-regulated instances of these pieces of history.

Otherwise, Moab is the biggest attraction. Since the popularization of mountain biking, Moab and the surrounding slick rock have been considered the national capital of the sport. In addition to this, the town serves as a hub for white-water rafting and paddling, rock climbing, off-road driving, road biking, hiking, and more. Skydiving is even a major draw. Lake Powell, in the far southern portion of the state, is Utah's largest reservoir and brings boating enthusiasts from across the southwestern United States. The Colorado and Green rivers are the largest rivers in the region and draw many white-water and still-water boaters to the area, offering some of the most scenic and accessible still water, as well as some of the most serious white-water mileage around.

## ✳ Weather

Despite its location in the southern part of Utah, this southeast corner tends to run significantly cooler than its southwestern counterpart. Moab, at just over 4,020 feet above sea level, has temperatures fairly representative of valley floors. Highs in the

MILL CANYON, ABOUT 10 MILES NORTH OF MOAB, IS THE LOCATION OF MANY IN-GROUND FOSSILS AND OPEN PUBLIC LANDS POPULAR FOR HIKING AND OFF-ROAD DRIVING KNOWN AS "JEEPING."

summer typically reach the mid- to high 90s. The coldest months of the year are December and January, with highs in the low 40s. However, many of the natural attractions in the area are in stream-cooled valleys or at higher elevation. Keep in mind that temperatures generally drop just more than 5 degrees for every 1,000 feet of elevation gain. All things considered, it is wise to bring a range of clothes—even for just a daily outing.

It is important to keep in mind that southwestern Utah is a very exposed environment; vegetation is generally low lying and sparse, thus leaving any sun or wind to be felt intensely. Only 9 inches of precipitation touch the dirt annually, and humidity is almost nonexistent. With very little moisture in the earth and atmosphere, temperature is highly localized. Shade is much cooler than sun, and temperatures drop quickly and drastically at night. Though there is virtually no humidity, the intensity of the sun and the absolute lack of protective canopy allow the unprepared to bake. Fortunately, you put the odds in your favor with ample water, electrolytes, sunscreen, and light-colored, lightweight clothing.

Additionally, the lack of vegetation leads to more vulnerability during storms; flash flooding is likely in any creek or riverbed during the course of precipitation anywhere in that drainage. Lightning is also of concern. Though these threats can be very real, they can also be easily avoided if you are sure to maintain your awareness of the local weather patterns.

## ✳ Outfitter Services

Moab is a town with more outfitter operations than you could imagine. For services particular to your desired activity, refer to *Outdoor Activities* in the Southeastern Utah chapters.

### WATER SOURCES

For such a dry area, Moab has two extremely convenient ways to get excellent water. The first is a natural spring near the Colorado River, which is potable and available 24/7. This is a favorite for campers passing through town. When entering town from the north (along US 191), take a left onto UT 128 immediately after crossing over the Colorado River. Head down this road just a few hundred yards, looking for the first decent-sized pullout on the south (right) side of the road. Here a pipe serves as the spout for this natural, consistently flowing spring. Climbers and mountain bikers bypassing town (or arriving after business hours) find this to be a quick way to fill up en route to their destination. There is no need to use iodine or any other sanitation methods in this water.

The second option, equally good during business hours, and superior for those in town needing a stop at the gear shop, is **Gearheads** (471 South Main St.; 435-259-4327). This very extensive outdoors shop has unlimited, free filtered water. It even sells various size containers to haul it, in case you've traveled without your own.

# ✳ Special Events

*Early March:* **Skinny Tire Festival** (435-259-2698; www.skinnytirefestival .com). This event takes place at the beginning of March and lasts four days. Riders tour some of the area's best scenery, including red-rock cliffs along the shores of the Colorado River, Arches National Park, Dead Horse Point State Park, Moab Valley, and the foothills of the La Sal Mountains.

*End of March:* **Moab Half-Marathon** (435-259-4525; www.moabhalf marathon.org). This race is one of southern Utah's biggest running events, 34 years running (as of 2008), and attracts well over 1,000 partici-pants for the 5K and 13.1-mile dis-tances. The race follows the Colorado River along UT 128.

*Mid-April:* **Canyonlands Film and Video Festival** (435-259-9135). This three-day festival brings independent filmmakers together for screenings, talks, and more. Screenings generally take off at the Star Hall (159 East Cen-ter St.), and tickets can be purchased in advance or at the door. Because of the location and tradition of the festi-val, many films focus on environmental issues and other topics pertaining to the southwest desert. This festival has been a Moab tradition since 1995.

*Easter Weekend:* **Jeep Safari Week-end** (435-259-7625). This insanely popular event takes place during East-er weekend and the week preceding it. The four-wheel-drive, off-road festival, which began in 1966, attracts enthusi-asts from all around the nation. If you are ever in the vicinity that weekend, the influx of large vehicles and trailers laden with desert mobiles will be unmistakable. A few thousand vehicles participate each year on roughly 30 trails spanning the range of technical difficulty.

*Memorial Day Weekend:* **Moab Arts Festival** (435-259-2742; www.moab artsfestival.org). The end of May usual-ly brings warm, sunny conditions. A full variety of media and styles are placed on display at **Swanny City Park,** 400 North 100 West, Moab. Local food vendors and restaurants sell their wares, and musicians take the stage. Evening temperatures are incredibly pleasant, making the music all the more enjoyable.

*Mid-June:* **Canyonlands Rodeo** (www.myspace.com/moabrodeo). This is, for those unfamiliar with rodeo, a great chance to become acquainted with the sport and Western tradition brought to the area by the Professional Utah Rodeo Association. The rodeo takes place at the **Old Spanish Trail Arena** (435-259-6226; www.old spanishtrailarea.com), 3461 South US 191, Moab.

*Late August/Early September:* **Moab Music Festival** (435-259-7003; www .moabmusicfest.com). This takes advan-tage of the falling temperatures and brings chamber music to the shores of the Colorado River. While some of the shows take place at **Star Hall** (159 East Center St.), other performances are held outdoors. Guests are escorted up the Colorado River to a natural amphitheater beneath several hun-dred-foot sheer sandstone cliffs.

*First Weekend of September:* **Moab Studio Tour** (www.moabstudiotour .com). The tour lasts three days, dur-ing which local artists open their gal-leries to the public. Look for a resurrection of this event in early December.

*Late September or Early October:* **The Moab Century Tour** (435-259-2698; www.skinnytireevents.com). This is another popular athletic event that takes place over the course of three days and is open to all skill levels. The course begins alongside the Colorado River and ascends to the base of the La Sal Mountains before returning. Three ride lengths are available, from 35 miles to 100. Evening events include speakers and dinner.

*End of October:* **Moab Fat Tire Weekend** is one of the representative weekends of the area, showcasing one of Moab's best features: mountain biking. Because of the general popularity of mountain biking, and the international clout the area's slick rock brings to Utah, this is certainly among the nation's most popular weekends of its genre. Group rides of different levels, and various races and hill climbs, take place, as well as a Halloween party. The weekend is usually toward the end of the month.

*Early December:* **Moab Studio Tour** (www.moabstudiotour.com). See *First Weekend of September.*

# MOAB

The southwest expanses of Utah are comprised of vast and diverse desert, high plains, mountains, the Colorado Plateau, and the San Rafael Swell. It is rare that such diverse geologic strata collide, and Moab is located amid the intersection of all of these. Though the town itself is not necessarily located in the most scenic point of this region, its very near surroundings are beautiful and quite accessible. Venture only a short distance in any direction, whether into a national park or elsewhere, and you will find beauty. The wilderness will never cease to produce a new scene—a canyon unlike the last, a new ecology, or a lush oasis.

A huge vertical relief, from the tips of the dominating La Sal Mountains to the deep narrows of the desert canyons, the Colorado River system has slit, cleaved, and carved this area to reveal a diverse and spectacular cross section of the earth. These sights remain fairly hidden as few as 50 miles away from Moab but become rapidly more exposed with each mile. As near as Green River, the desert vistas are fairly plain and uninspiring, with dull colors and little geographic variety. However, as you travel south, these drab browns give way to deep blues of high mountains and the reds, oranges, whites, and purples of sandstone.

The Moab area also enjoys more than a fair amount of sunshine and pleasant weather. It is not a surprise then, that the combination of stunning scenery and beautiful weather has made this one of the nation's most popular spring and fall recreation destinations. River enthusiasts enjoy the state's best access to the Green River's gentle, canoe-friendly Labyrinth and Stillwater canyons, as well as the Colorado River's nationally famous, extremely powerful rapids of Cataract Canyon. Mountain bikers are in paradise on the area's slick rock trails, which are considered the best riding in the country by many. Off-road devotees enjoy a culture of their own and come together each year for the week preceding Easter for Jeep Safari Weekend. Less-popular sports also enjoy some of the best of theirs here—rock climbers are in sandstone crack climbing paradise, and skydivers are gifted with great weather and spectacular landing zones. Hikers and sightseers enjoy infinite miles of trails in the surrounding national and state parks—Arches, Canyonlands, and Dead Horse Point—as well as trails in equally spectacular, lesser-known areas. There is so much beauty hidden and tucked in and around the sandstone clefts of this region that it can almost be taken for granted. Located anywhere else in the nation, this entire corner of the state would be a national park.

All of this is available, with the eager-to-please tourist infrastructure to go with it. For such a small town, Moab has many offerings. Though the area only has

THE GREEN RIVER'S LABYRINTH CANYON IS A MELLOW, MEANDERING STRETCH OF WATER LEADING OUT OF GREEN RIVER CITY AND INTO STILLWATER CANYON. TOGETHER, THESE TWO CANYONS ARE POPULAR AMONG CANOEISTS.

roughly 5,000 residents, the town often sees as many as 20,000 guests in one busy weekend. Obviously, the town is keen on hosting these guests and is prepared to do so with restaurants of many varieties, breweries, and hotels galore. Much of the cuisine has a fresh, Southwestern affect, though some restaurants serve gourmet cuisine spanning from traditional to contemporary, Continental to Chinese. Fitness freaks are not the only crowd inspired by these surroundings; shoppers can purchase the works of local artists, each with its own take on the rich colors dominating the landscape and its natural history.

As in any other region in the world, Moab's history begins much before written records. Before Europeans had even heard of North America, these lands were occupied by many tribes. These peoples were the ancestral Anasazi, Fremont, Navajo, and Paiute tribes. Though the lands here are difficult to navigate and the climate harsh, they persisted as hunter-gatherers and small-time farmers. Surprisingly, much of the evidence of these peoples' existence was created during presumed times of stress—in the form of often incredibly small uninhabitable cliff dwellings in narrow, deep, and hidden river valleys. Other illustrative evidence of these peoples' lifestyles is in the form of the plentiful petroglyphs on sandstone walls.

Before Mormon settlement, any Europeans entering the area were transient and low in number. They were missionaries, explorers, outlaws, and trappers. During the early 1800s, this area had been recognized as a point of crossing over the Colorado River. Because this river often flows in canyons more than 1 mile deep, easy crossings were coveted in the time before large bridges. For this reason, the area had come to exist as part of the transcontinental Spanish Trail.

After Salt Lake City was founded by the Latter-day Saints, they began sending members out into the region in order to create the foundations for their would-be empire. Twelve such founding men were sent to Moab by Brigham Young and arrived in the area in 1854. Though the initial arrival required them to lower themselves by rope into the Spanish Valley off a 25-foot precipice, they already enjoyed the company of 41 more pioneering men by the following year. Their mission was to establish a Mormon settlement in this valley, and the first was first dubbed the Elk Mountain Mission.

During the first years of permanent Mormon occupation, there was Native American–settler cohabitation and trading in the valley, and tribal leaders promoted a peaceful relationship between the two groups. Despite efforts, a bout of violence in September of 1855 led to enough deaths and animosity that the initial fort was abandoned and the population dwindled for fear of further violence. The region returned again to the migrant hands of traveling tribes, traders, and cowboys.

The Mormans tried again to settle the area, arriving more than 20 years later, in 1878. This time they were able to create infrastructure around their settlement, rooting themselves more strongly in the area. They built schools, ranches, and farms. What helped their efforts this time was their location within 35 miles of the Thompson Springs railroad depot along the Rio Grande Western Railroad line between Denver and Salt Lake City.

Once reestablished, Moab began to quickly grow into its role as southern Utah's Mormon outpost. A ferry crossing the Colorado River was established by 1885, in 1903 Moab was incorporated, and by 1912 a bridge was constructed in the area to take the ferry's place. The warm, sunny climate and nearby waters of the Colorado River allowed Moab to develop into one of the state's major fruit producers. Apples, oranges, peaches, and grapes grew very well here. In addition to agriculture and transportation, Moab had certain significance for the Mormons—it was seen as a crucial ambassador on the southern border of the Latter-day Saints' kingdom.

The next major phase in the town's history would be the discovery of uranium in the surrounding hills. Because of the value of this element and the timing of its discovery (post-war 1950s), the area quickly assumed the pace and population of a booming mining town. In 1950, the population of Moab was just under 1,300; by 1960, the population had grown almost fourfold to be 6,700. Naturally, with this influx of population came a surge of hotels, restaurants, and schools. The second

THE MORE DURABLE SANDSTONE STRATA IN THE VICINITY OF CANYONLANDS NATIONAL PARK FORM TOWERING SHEER CLIFFS AND TOOTHLIKE TOWERS ALONG THE GREEN RIVER.

largest uranium mill in the United States was located here at this time. Almost
simultaneously, serious oil drilling began, and three major oil fields boosted the
economy still more during this time. Potash, a primary constituent in glass production and a fertilizer, was another mineral mined in the area. Naturally, these booms
each saw a decline, and it became time for another industry to keep the town
buoyant.

Moab's city leaders recognized its potential as a scenic destination quite early in
the 20th century. But it would be a gradual process before tourists would flock to
the area. Arches National Monument was sanctioned in 1929, and after the nation
survived the Great Depression and World War II, it became a popular destination.
Around this time, white-water boating emerged as a sport and brought adventurers
to the Colorado River beginning in the 1950s. Canyonlands National Park was designated in 1964. But it was not until the last 30 years or so that visitors really took
advantage of this invitation. The invention and popularity of such sports as mountain biking, off-roading, boating, paddling, and rock climbing married the perfect
environment and friendliness of the town to create a perfect destination. Perhaps
the most lasting identity of Moab will be as an outdoor recreation and tourist
haven, yet the evidence of all of these roles is evident today.

GUIDANCE **Moab Area Travel Counsel** and **Visitors Center** (435-259-8825
or 800-635-6622; www.discovermoab.com), Main and Center St., Moab. The
Travel Counsel is likely the primary welcoming center in town and is located in a
very obvious, central location. Phone hours for the center are 9–5 Monday–Friday.
Hours at the visitors center vary per season, but it is open daily (with the exception
of Thanksgiving, Christmas, and New Year's Day).

**www.moab-utah.com.** This Web site lists maps, photographs, accommodations,
activities, attractions, restaurants, churches, events, and transportation pertaining
to the area as a whole.

**The Moab Area Chamber of Commerce** (435-259-7814; www.moabchamber
.com), 217 East Center, Moab. The chamber's Web site offers a printable Community Guide available for download, as well as current events, weather, and community alerts.

GETTING THERE *By air:* **Salt Lake International Airport (SLC)** (801-575-
2400 or 800-595-2442; www.slcairport.com), about 5 minutes west of Salt Lake
City on I-80. This major western hub is just more than 230 miles (or three and a
half to four hours) to the northwest of Moab.

**Denver International Airport** (303-342-2000; www.flydenver.com), about 30 minutes northeast of downtown Denver. Denver is about 350 miles or four and a half
hours away (without encountering Denver traffic), almost all of which is on I-70.

**Walker Field/Grand Junction Regional Airport** (970-244-9100; www.walker
field.com), Grand Junction, Colorado. This is a small, but not tiny, airport about
120 miles away from downtown Moab. This airport services six commercial airlines. Shuttles between Grand Junction and Moab are operated by **American
Spirit Shuttle** (scheduled services, 970-523-7662 or 888-226-5031; www.gisdho
.com) and **Roadrunner Shuttle** (reservations recommended, 435-259-9402;
www.roadrunnershuttle.com). Offers airport shuttles, as well as bike, motorcycle,
hiking, and river shuttles.

**Canyonlands Field/Moab Airport** (435-259-4849; www.moabairport.com), 16 miles north of downtown Moab on US 191. This is the smallest airport, but very near, and offers air shuttle transportation to and from Denver Airport with **Great Lakes Airlines** (800-554-5111).

*By car:* Moab is located in the southeastern portion of Utah, about 30 miles south of I-70 on US 191. From Salt Lake, Moab is reached by heading south on I-15 to Spanish Fork, then southeast on US 6 (not advised during heavy winter storms), and traversing east on I-70 before taking US 191 South to Moab. This drive is about 230 miles and takes three and a half hours, if you're quick.

**SHUTTLES IN AND AROUND** If you require shuttle service to or within Moab, there are a number of options. The area has a variety of shuttle services, many of which are rooted in outdoor recreation transport: namely mountain biking and river trips. When not providing these services, these companies also double as in-town or airport chauffeurs.

**Black Dog River Runner Shuttle Service** (800-241-2591; www.rr-ss.com). This is primarily a river runner's service, but they also provide just about any other transport service in town on request, including airport, hotel, and bar runs. Call for availability and rates.

**Coyote Shuttle** (435-259-8656; www.coyoteshuttle.com). This company primarily operates mountain bike and river shuttles, but offers rides in their outdoorsy van-a-gons (and other quirky vehicles) to anyone with a reasonable plan.

**Nomad Cab Company** (435-260-9986; www.moabtaxi.com). Nomad is Moab's by-the-books taxi service, exactly as you would expect a taxi service to be. Slight discounts are given to seniors 62 years and older.

**Porcupine Shuttle** (435-260-0896; www.porcupineshuttle.com). Porcupine is another of Moab's rugged-vehicle, mountain-bike shuttle service companies that also offers custom rides to those with other needs.

**AIR TOURS** **Redtail Aviation** (435-259-7421; www.moab-utah.com/redtail) and **Slickrock Air Guides** (435-259-6216 or 866-259-1626; www.slickrockairguides .com). In addition to scenic tours, these airlines also offer backcountry access that is sometimes crucial for certain endeavors, like river trips.

**TOURS** *By river:* **Canyonlands by Night or Day** (435-394-9978). This tour consists of a 6-mile upstream jet boat trip during the fading daylight hours, accompanied by tour guide tidbits about the geological and historical features along the river. As darkness sets in, the boats turn around and spotlights come on, illuminating the sandstone walls towering 500 feet above the surface of the river. At this point, music comes on, and Native American myths and other Colorado River lore are embellished by the unique atmosphere.

*By plane:* **Moab Adventure Center** (435-259-7019 or 866-904-1163; www.moab adventurecenter.com). Scenic flight tours of the Canyonlands with the unique opportunity to visit all three regions of the park, and in just about one hour.

*By foot:* As more traditional tours go, the **Moab Walking Tour** is a self-guided jaunt that can be taken with a free brochure from the Dan O'Laurie Museum and the Grand Country Travel Council. The complete journey leads you past 23 historically significant buildings, the oldest of which is the 1881 **Balsley Log Cabin** (68 South 100 East). Brochures can be obtained at the Moab Visitors Center and the Dan O'Laurie Museum.

MEDICAL EMERGENCIES **Allen Memorial Hospital** (435-259-7191; www .amhmoab.org), 719 West 400 North, Moab. This small hospital has clinical, emergency, surgical, and even oncological services.

**Moab Regional Medical Clinic** (435-259-7425), 719 West 400 North, at Allen Memorial Hosptial, Moab. This clinic is for those who don't require full-blown ER services, but also don't want to wait for an appointment.

LOCAL PUBLICATIONS *The Moab Times* (www.moabtimes.com). The *Times* is the area's daily independent newspaper. Available for reading online, and distributed in newsstands around town, this is the quintessential small-town paper with occasional blips about the goings-on of the outside world.

*The Canyon County Zephyr* (www.canyoncountryzephyr.com). This is a free magazine that addresses local issues, features events, and advertises local businesses. It can be viewed online, or picked up at any coffee shop and at many other businesses.

## ✳ To See and Do

Moab has had an eye on the tourist industry as early as 1906, when the local newspaper of the time began promoting the area as an outdoors destination. The idea has really caught on, and Moab swells in spring and fall, drawing in motorists, mountain bikers, jeep drivers, rock climbers, casual hikers, and sight-seers. Though the tourist industry is strong, the town itself too has substance.

**Dead Horse Point State Park** (435-259-2614; www.stateparks.utah.gov), west of Moab via UT 279, Dead Horse Point Rd., and UT 313 (call for specific directions). This is one of the most scenic canyon overlooks in the desert Southwest. Onlookers

DEAD HORSE POINT, A PENINSULA OF LAND IN THE SKY ENCLOSED BY NEARLY 360 DEGREES OF PRECIPITOUS DROP-OFF, WAS NAMED SO FOR THE HORSES THAT PERISHED IN THE 1800S, CORRALLED THERE AND LEFT ALONE WITHOUT FOOD OR WATER.

Amiee Maxwell

gaze 500 feet below them at the Colorado River carving chasms into the sandstone and giving Canyonlands National Park its namesake features. This dramatic vertical relief creates spectacular vertigo that adds to the natural beauty. The overlook is on a peninsular mesa that is reached by way of an 80-foot-wide filament of land. In addition to the paved pathway that accesses overlook point, the state park has numerous other hiking trails, campgrounds, and picnic areas. $10 per day visit; $20 for camping.

The name of this park originated in cowboy history. Apparently this mesa, because of the sheer fall away on all sides and narrow access point, was a convenient and inexpensive place to corral wild horses. All that was required was a fence to block access to the main body of land. According to the story, the cowboys took only the most-fit horses and left the others, and left the area. Without water or any possible way to escape, the horses left behind perished, and their bones were left on the mesa.

**MUSEUMS Dan O'Laurie Canyon Country Museum** (435-259-7985; www .discovermoab.com/museums), 118 East Center St., Moab. Open 10–6 Monday– Friday and noon–6 Saturday–Sunday, April 1 through October 31; 10–3 Monday– Friday and noon–5 Saturday–Sunday, November 1–March 31. Closed Thanksgiving, Christmas, and New Year's Day. This museum examines the geologic, ecologic, and human history of the area through collections of artifacts, facts, replicas, photographs, and illustrations. Features include Anasazi tools, baskets, pottery, and tiles; a paleontology and geology room; and early settler items and artifacts like a player piano. Free admission; donations accepted.

**The Film Museum at Red Cliffs Ranch** (866-812-2002; www.redcliffslodge .com/museums), mile marker 14 on Scenic Byway 128, northeast of downtown. Open 8 AM–10 PM daily. This museum consists of an extensive collection of photographs depicting the movies that have been filmed in this scenic area. The photographs are generally small—usually no larger than 8½ x 11 inches—and the décor is not fancy. However, these photographs begin in the 1940s and absolutely cover the raw pine walls in this modest space. The museum is located at the Red Cliffs Ranch. Established in the late 19th century, this ranch has been running ever since and is raising cattle even today. Free admission.

## ❋ Outdoor Activities

**BIKING** Where to begin? Of course, when most people think about Moab at all, they immediately envision mountain biking. And it goes without saying that the trail riding around Moab is among some of the finest in the world. So much of the reason for excellence is, of course, the climate and the scenery . . . well, it just so happens that the paved roads of the area enjoy the same favorable weather and beautiful setting—so skinny-tire peddlers get theirs, too.

### Rentals, Shops & Tours

**Chili Pepper Bike Shop** (435-259-4688; www.chilibikes.com), 702 South Main St., Moab. In this fleet there are road and full-suspension mountain bikes, including basic full suspension, freeride, and downhill models; children's bikes; a retail selection; online trail and event information; an espresso bar; and a no-snobbery staff.

## CRYPTOBIOTIC WHAT?

One drive across town, and you will probably see dozens—if not hundreds—of off-road vehicles and plenty of other evidence of rough outdoor activities. However, you should be advised that the high-desert ecosystem everywhere around Moab is extremely delicate. The topsoil layer is very sandy and thin, and is held atop the sandstone often only by a fragile layer of (sometimes invisible) cryptobiotic soil. This living structure is a slow-growing symbiotic organic combination of cryptobacteria and micro lichen, algae, and fungi. Old growth clusters of this are recognizable as blackish, crusty-looking swells on the ground resembling the texture of broccoli heads. Patches of this bacteria take decades to develop and are destroyed by just one foot- or tire print. Continuous tracks, such as those laid by wheels, are the most harmful.

Other plants, though generally thorny, spiky, waxy, and aggressive, are also fragile and very vulnerable to human-induced destruction. Because the topsoil layer is indeed so thin, a very small amount of erosion can completely eradicate plant and animal habitat. It is a volatile political subject in the area, and heavy access restrictions will likely be imposed on the area, particularly if the area is treated carelessly. **Thus, with all of these considerations, it is imperative to keep all traffic—vehicular, foot, camping, and biking of every variety—on established trails, roads, and campsites.**

Lecture aside, this landscape has an incredible amount to offer any type of summer recreational enthusiast. Golfers, hikers, road and mountain bikers, fishers, climbers, skydivers, boaters, and anyone that enjoys sunshine will be in paradise here much of the year, particularly in spring and fall.

**Dreamride** (435-259-6419; www.dreamride.com). A custom bike builder, Dreamride offers many different vacation and tour packages, as well as a long online list of Moab area–specific cycling suggestions, including tips on sand, slick rock, equipment, and health. Primarily an outfitter service and custom bike builder; mountain bikes only.

**Moab Cyclery** (435-259-7423; www.moabcyclery.com), 391 South Main St., Moab. Moab Cyclery is an all-around shop with repair services, retail selection (including other outdoors sports), guided single-day and multiday tours, and mountain, road, and women's-specific bike rentals, as well as online trail information.

**Poison Spider Bicycles** (435-259-7882 or 800-635-1792; www.poisonspider bicycles.com), 497 North Main St., Moab. Offering full service for mountain, road, BMX, downhill, and freeride bikes, Poison Spider also leads day trips and longer tours, and rents road bikes, a spectrum of full-suspension mountain bikes, and children's bikes. Online they list events, photos, and relevant links.

**Rim Cyclery** (435-259-5333 or 800-304-8219; www.rimcyclery.com), 94 West 100 North, Moab. Rim Cyclery specializes in mountain bikes. They maintain an all full-suspension fleet, including children's bikes and child tag-a-longs, retail shop, and online trail and desert safety information.

**Slick Rock Cycles** (435-259-1134 or 800-825-9791; www.slickrockcycles.com), 427 North Main St., Moab. A cool bike shop and espresso bar, this shop offers adults' and children's mountain bikes, demo programs, retail shop and cycle sales, bike tours, and cycle service.

**Western Spirit Cycling** (435-259-8732; www.westernspirit.com), 478 Mill Creek Dr., Moab. Western Spirit is a tour-based operation that guides trips per style of cycling (road, mountain, cross-country), length, and intensity. Family rides are available, as well as custom options. World Mountain Biking Champion Alison Dunlap guides here, and a ride with her can be arranged by special appointment. Most tours last somewhere around five days.

## Mountain Biking

Moab is most famous for its slick rock riding—riding along bare sandstone plateaus. This is a huge area attraction, and people travel long distances just to ride these trails. However, not all of Moab's trails are bare sandstone. Many other flavors of riding exist, including forested and subalpine dirt trails in the La Sal Mountains and varied canyon riding. Despite the technical and strenuous nature of the famous Slickrock Trail, there are many moderate and easy trails in the area that treat riders to gorgeous desert scenery. A great collection of detailed, waterproof maps is available for purchase at the **Moab Area Visitors Center** (intersection of Center and Main St., Moab, as listed in the *Guidance* section). One of Utah's best resources for mountain bikers is www.utahmountainbiking.com, an amazingly thorough catalog of trails and events in the areas, as well as technical tips and access advisories. Designed and maintained by a passionate bunch, this site has impeccably thorough route descriptions, including photographs, maps, and even video for each ride.

THE GREEN RIVER NEAR CANYONLANDS

**Bar-M Loop** offers more of an introductory ride, with respect to fitness and skill alike. Near enough to town, the trailhead for this ride is less than 10 miles north of Moab on US 191 (an extension of Main St.). The elevation gain on this ride is only around 280 feet spread over 7 miles of riding—this is about as mellow as it gets around Moab. The riding is varied but includes Jeep trails and slick rock surfaces. A perk of the ride is a vista of the Window Arch in Arches National Park. To reach the trailhead, take US 191 north of Moab 9.5 miles, and make a right (head east), following signs for the Bar-M Chuckwagon. Take the first right (going south), which leads you into a parking lot. The trail departs from the south side of this lot.

**Slickrock Trail** is the first trail that everyone associates with Moab. This 10-mile trail is an area showpiece, as well as a test piece for fitness and skill. This loop trail requires high levels of skill and fitness. If you doubt your abilities, or want an easier entrance exam on this medium of riding, a 2-mile practice loop is a great resource. The trail is indicated on the rock by painted white dashes. Spring and fall are the most popular times to ride. Mountain bikers share access with motor-cyclists, so do not be alarmed or offended if you encounter motorbikes en route. Plan to allow several hours to complete the ride, despite the relatively short distance. A counterclockwise direction of travel is encouraged. The trailhead is located along Sand Flats Road, 2.3 miles northeast of its intersection with Mill Creek Drive (near Rotary Park).

**White Rim Trail,** at 103 miles, is considered to be Utah's best multiday loop. This trip usually takes people four or five days to complete and has vistas and overlooks enough to keep you fully entertained. A permit is required for overnight camping along this trail and can be obtained by contacting **Canyonlands National Park Reservations** (435-259-4351). Call well in advance for your site; the popularity of this trail makes the wait time on some sites as long as one year. Most riders coordinate with family and friends willing to drive a sag wagon; the length of the trail almost ensures some sort of mechanical problems. The most common access point is inside of Canyonlands National Park. You will be required to check in at the visitors center and pay the park entrance fee.

## Road Biking

Though mountain biking is center stage in Moab's recreation arena, the road biking here is also quite good. Both kinds of biking in Moab are made great by the climate and scenery. Many rides incorporate the Colorado River Gorge (running east–west, just north of Moab) in some way.

**Castle Valley/La Sal Mountain Loop** is one of the most scenic and challenging loops in the area. It can be done clockwise or counterclockwise. If you go clockwise, you will leave Moab, heading north on UT 191, and make a right on UT 128 to follow the Colorado River. After 15.5 miles, head right (south) and into Castle Valley on the La Sal Mountain Loop Road. Continue on this road until you can take a right onto (dirt) Sand Flats Road. This will eventually bring you back into Moab. This total loop is about 54 miles and has serious elevation gain as it ascends the mighty shoulder of the La Sal Mountains.

**Colorado River Gorge** is a scenic natural passageway that intersects with US 191 just north of Moab. To the west it follows by UT 279 for more than 10 miles as it snakes toward Dead Horse Point State Park and Canyonlands National Park. To the east it follows UT 128, about 10 miles before it reaches US 6 and then I-70.

**Moab Century Tour** (435-259-2698; www.skinnytireevents.com). This is another popular event that takes place at the end of September or the beginning of October each year. It lasts three days and is open to all skill levels. The course begins alongside the Colorado River and ascends to the base of the La Sal Mountains before returning. Three ride lengths are available, from 35 miles to 100 miles. Evening events include speakers and dinner.

**Skinny Tire Festival** (435-259-2698; www.skinnytirefestival.com). This event takes place in March. It is the season opener and lasts four days. Rides traverse roads sandwiched between imposing red rock cliffs and the shores of the Colorado River, toward Arches National Park, and reach the dramatic gaping-chasm vistas of Dead Horse Point State Park, before returning to Moab Valley and the foothills of the La Sal Mountains.

BOATING Moab sits near the two biggest, most popular boating rivers in Utah: the Green and the Colorado. These rivers offer both white-water and still-water trips. The best white water in the vicinity is in Cataract Canyon just beneath the confluence of the two (in the heart of Canyonlands National Park). The best flat-water trips are on the Green in Stillwater and Labyrinth canyons (just south of the town of Green River).

Permits for all trips on these rivers is required and must be booked with the governing agency of the relevant section(s) of water. To pass through Cataract Canyon without a guide, one must obtain a permit months (or years) in advance and must be able to document experience as a river *guide* on rivers of comparable difficulty. If you do not have this on your resume, call any of these guide services.

**Adrift Adventures** (435-259-8594 or 800-874-4483; www.adrift.net), 378 North Main St., Moab. This Moab-based company has been guiding on the Green and Colorado for three decades. This company not only offers raft trips, but scenic jet-boat trips, and horse packing, Jeep, and boating combination trips.

**Canyon Voyages** (435-259-6007; www.canyonvoyages.com), 211 North Main St., Moab. A variety of trips are offered here, including petroglyph hikes, horseback rides, kayak lessons, guided raft trips, biking trips, and multisport packages. This business also has a retail and rental selection.

AS STILLWATER CANYON CUTS MORE DEEPLY INTO THE SURROUNDING SANDSTONE STRATA, IT OPENS UP AND IS ADJOINED BY MANY SMALLER TRIBUTARY CANYONS.

**Navtec Expeditions** (435-259-7983; www.navtec.com), 321 North Main St., Moab. Navtec has been in Moab for a century and now offers boating trips down Westwater and Cataract canyons, as well as off-road Jeep tours.

**Sheri Griffith Expeditions** (800-332-2439; www.griffithexp.com), Moab. This was the winner of Utah Best in State for 2008. This company specializes in trips on the Green, Yampa, Delores, and Colorado rivers, with trips at destinations such as Desolation

Canyon (up river on the Green), as well as nearby Cataract Canyon. On these trips, the emphasis is on good service (including wine and cheese, if requested!) and relaxation. Specialty trips include women's only and particular watercraft.

**Western River Expeditions/Moab Adventure Center** (801-942-6669; www.westernriver.com), 225 South Main St., Moab. This company offers a long list of trips per region and length. Usually, expeditions last between two and seven days, and are on the Green River, in Cataract, Westwater, or the Grand canyons. Trips can be combined with ranch stays and other special vacation packages.

**Colorado River.** Popular sections of this famous, muddy river include the moderately choppy **Fisher Towers** section, the more serious **Westwater Canyon,** and the very famous **Cataract Canyon.** As per its name, Cataract Canyon, which sits just a few miles downstream of the Green and Colorado confluence, is where this massive body of water pumps steeply down a narrow gap between two sheer canyon walls. During spring, boulders send rooster tails of water dozens of feet skyward. In the fall, the volume falls away, but what is left behind are huge, angular, boat-munching boulders of the most dangerous variety.

Kami Hardcastle

THE MUDDY FISHER TOWERS CONTRAST WITH THE OTHERWISE HARD, SHEER SANDSTONE OF THE CASTLETON AREA EAST OF MOAB.

**Green River.** Many canoers begin in the city of Green River and head south on this river through Labyrinth and Stillwater canyons. Beginning in the suspiciously unspectacular scenery around the put-in, the river carves fairly quickly into otherwise unassuming hillsides, meandering into ever-deepening canyon walls and horseshoe bends. During the main season, the beauty and accessibility of the trip invite a large population of boaters—but during post-season, this trip can be enjoyed in complete solitude, and decent weather.

**GOLF Moab Golf Course** (435-259-6488), 2705 South East Bench Rd., Moab. Moab has but one golf course, and it is quite picturesque. This course is par 72, has 6,800 yards, 18 holes, and a driving range. Because of the limited amount of courses in the area, it is wise to call ahead for reservations (as the next nearest course is northwest about an hour away in Green River, or in Monticello, about an hour to the south). This course is very scenic and visually appealing, as its greens and fairways are surrounded by red rock buttes.

Zac Robinson

CLIMBERS CROSS THE SHOULDER BETWEEN CASTLETON AND RECTORY TOWERS AS THEY APPROACH THE ROUTE, FINE JADE, ON THE SOUTH FACE OF THE RECTORY.

**HIKING** Moab is located among some very diverse terrain, almost all of it accessible by hiking. From the carved sandstone and lush ecosystems of the Colorado River–side canyons to the sagebrush of the high desert plateaus, soaring desert towers, and subalpine landscape of the 12,500-foot La Sal Mountains, this southeastern corner of the state has a different opportunity in every season. For a more extensive consultation, it is advised that you stop in at any of the fine gear shops listed at the beginning of this section.

**Corona Arch Trail** is a relatively short out-and-back trail, about 1.5 miles each way. The trail heads up to the top of rim rock via a series of cairns and traverses sandy and slick rock ecosystems to reach a vista of this arch, whose opening is 140 by 105 feet in size. Elevation gain is minimal, at less than 500 feet. To reach the trailhead, head north out of town on US 191, taking a left (heading southwest) on UT 279, about 0.5 mile after crossing over the Colorado River. About 10 miles after this turn, park on the north side of the road at the trailhead by a small kiosk.

THE FISHER TOWERS, FAMOUS FOR THEIR FRAGILE, MUDDY APPEARANCE, ARE NONETHELESS POPULAR AMONG CLIMBERS FOR THEIR NOVELTY.

Craig Bowden

**Fisher Towers Trail** is a very moderate and flat hike leading out to these very distinctive namesake towers. This is another out-and-back hike, 2.2 miles each way, the terminus of which is marked with a humorous TRAIL END rock placard placed in the trail itself. While much of the sandstone in the area is very strong and sheer Wingate sandstone characterized by clean, vertical faces, the Fisher Towers are quite different. These towers are hundreds of feet tall yet resemble stalactites made with mud drippings. Amazingly, these are also popular among rock climbers, if only for the aesthetic quirkiness and novelty of "mud" climbing. In addition to gaining these towers, the hike offers visitors the chance to experience a beautiful valley and middle-distance views of the famous Castleton and Rectory towers to the west, as well as Fisher Mesa and the Book Cliffs. This trail is accessed by heading north of Moab on US 191, making a right (easterly) turn onto UT 128, and following the Colorado River. After 21 miles, make a right (south) turn onto an improved (sometimes unmarked) dirt road. Drive 2 miles and park. The trail departs from here. Elevation gain is less than 1,000 feet.

**Moab Rim Trail** gives hikers what could be considered a quintessential smorgasbord of Moab's grandiose and open scenery. The trail ascends slick rock to reach overlooks of the Moab Valley, skirts by Navajo sandstone domes, and reaches viewpoints above the Spanish Valley. It affords views of large sandstone fins and Hidden Valley. Three miles of hiking brings you to the intersection with the Hidden Valley Trail (which connects to US 191 just south of Moab, if you are interested in hiking just one way and arranging for a vehicular shuttle from one end of the trail to the other). The trail departs from Kane Creek Road/UT 279, just 2.5 miles west of (and 0.1 mile beyond the first cattle guard) its southwesterly departure from US 191 (just north of the Colorado River crossing).

**Negro Bill Canyon** (yes, the name is a product of insular culture) offers a distinctly different experience than many of the nearby high desert/ plateau trails. It is a very narrow canyon that enjoys the cooling and vitalizing effects of a clear stream year-round. The trail requires 2 miles of hiking to gain Morning Glory Bridge, a rock span of 243 feet (the sixth longest in the nation). The trailhead is fairly near Moab, on UT 128, just 3 miles east of its junction with US 191, on the south side of the road.

**HORSEBACK RIDING** Horseback riding is always one of the more unique and romantic ways to explore any region, but it is especially well suited to the red-rock desert setting that surrounds Moab. Whether you ride across high plains and plateaus, through lush canyons, or on subalpine, forested trails, a bad setting for this activity is hard to imagine.

JUST WEST OF MOAB, ACCESSED BY KANE CREEK ROAD, THIS SPECTACULAR CANYON TOURS THROUGH EONS OF SANDSTONE STRATA; BIRTHING ROCK IS ABOUT 2.5 MILES INTO THE CANYON, NEAR ITS JUNCTION WITH MOON FLOWER CANYON.
Amiee Maxwell

**Adrift Adventures** (435-259-8594 or 800-874-4483; www.adrift.net), 378 North Main St., Moab. This guide service has many specialties, including horseback trips and package trips (see *Boating*).

**Moab Adventure Center** (435-259-7019 or 866-904-1163; www.moab adventurecenter.com), 225 South Main St., Moab. Moab Adventure Center offers rides guided by professional wranglers in Castle Valley. Total trip time is three and a half hours, and takes place in morning and afternoon shifts. Each session begins with a lesson—so beginners are welcome. A minimum age of eight is required; for the sake of the horses, human weight is capped at 220 pounds per person. A bonus to this trip is the private access of trails; no loud motorists will startle your horses. Tours begin at the Red Cliffs Coral.

**ROCK CLIMBING** The rock climbing around Moab is, of yet, unregulated. There are no fees or rangers. However, climbing has become increasingly famous and popular of late. This very

Craig Bowden

NEGRO BILL CANYON, EAST OF MOAB. THIS NARROW CANYON IS COOLED BY A STREAM AND IS POPULAR AMONG DAY HIKERS DURING WARMER MONTHS.

fragile ecosystem is becoming inundated with a growing number of visitors. Thus it is extremely important to treat it with utmost respect. Restrict all vehicle and foot traffic exclusively to well-established trails, roads, and campsites. Remove all of your own garbage and waste. There is an outhouse at Indian Creek, but it is in high demand; it is considered standard practice to bring your own means for waste removal. The most popular method is disposable bag "toilets" that seal completely and can be purchased in most outdoors shops. Burial of waste is not acceptable. Many guidebooks to the area exist and include Falcon's *Desert Rock* series and David Bloom's *Indian Creek*.

FISHER TOWERS TRAIL END, EAST OF MOAB

Craig Bowden

**Big Bend Boulders** has no guidebook to this area; there is a good amount of bouldering concentrated at the "Big Bend," beneath riverside cliffs. Here nature has conspired to create just enough features to make the rock climbable, but not so much as to efface all challenge. This boulder field is located along the Colorado River. It is reached by taking UT 128 about 5 miles east out of Moab. You will notice an obvious parking area and cluster of boulders on the south side of the road.

Craig Bowden

CASTLETON AND RECTORY TOWERS OFFER SOME OF THE WORLD'S BEST SANDSTONE TOWER ROCK CLIMBING AND FORM THE FAMOUS LANDSCAPE SO OFTEN FEATURED IN PHOTOGRAPHS OF THE DESERT SOUTHWEST.

**Desert Towers** are as infamous among cinematographers and photographers as they are among rock climbers. Many are found in the vicinity of **Indian Creek** (see p. 258) and the southern entrance of **Canyonlands National Park** (approach as for Indian Creek) or in **Castle Valley** (east of Moab about 15.5 miles on UT 128, and then south on La Sal Loop Rd.). Indian Creek tower climbing is at the Bridger Jack Mesa, near the Bridger Jacks Campground. Though not technically a "tower," this very narrow, fin-like feature has plenty of multipitch, tower-esque climbing. The Six-Shooters are the towers nearest Canyonlands. If any towers in the vicinity have true moderate routes, these are it. However, traditional protection and solid crack skills are still a must-have. In the Castle Valley area are the world-famous Rectory, Castleton, and Fischer towers. All but the Fischer Towers offer relatively clean, if not excellent (but difficult) routes. The Fischer Towers, however, are an entirely different beast. Most climbers visit these unique, twisting towers for the novelty of climbing "mud."

THE NORTH AND SOUTH SIX-SHOOTER TOWERS ARE SO NAMED FOR THE VAGUE RESEMBLANCE THEY BEAR TO REVOLVERS; THESE, TOO, ARE POPULAR AMONG ROCK CLIMBERS.

**Indian Creek,** a unique, world-famous stash of splitter cracks, is some of the world's most solid and clean sandstone. More than a dozen main cliffs offer cracks of all sizes and shapes, though they are generally ver-

INDIAN CREEK CANYON IS HOME TO THE WORLD'S PREMIER SANDSTONE CRACK CLIMBING AREA; THE MESAS ARE COMPOSED OF VERY HARD AND SMOOTH WINGATE SANDSTONE, FRACTURED INTO PERFECT VERTICAL CRACKS OF ALL SIZES.

tical, and the rock faces are otherwise featureless. This the place to learn (or be forced to learn) pure crack climbing technique. The rock here is generally Wingate sandstone—one of the most vertical, sheer, hard, and clean varieties. To reach Indian Creek, head south from Moab on 191 for 40 miles, and turn west on UT 211. This road traverses a high plateau, and then winds down into Indian Creek Basin. Campsites and crags are at many locations. For more information, see David Blume's *Indian Creek*.

**Pagan Mountaineering** (435-259-1117; www.paganmountaineering.com), 59 South Main St., Moab. This gear shop has all of the hardware, literature, and beta that you will need to embark on a journey . . . assuming you have the prerequisite skills to do so. If you do not have the know-how, Pagan offers guide services.

SKYDIVING **Skydive Moab** (435-259-5867; www.skydivemoab.com), at the Canyonlands Field/Moab Airport, 16 miles north of Moab on US 191. Moab is full of recreational opportunities; many of these are even once-in-a-lifetime chances for some. Because the recreational energy of the area is so high, these opportunities are ultraconcentrated, very popular, in the hands of top-notch experts, and are relatively affordable. Unless you're here with your own plane and equipment, you'll be seeking the services of a guide. Jumps for novices are done tandem—that is, piggyback with an instructor. This is considered the safest and most reassuring way for a beginner to learn. As a bonus, the roughly 30-minute plane ride to elevation allows a seldom-seen viewpoint of the region. This Moab company specializes in skydiving and skydiving only. $210 for first-time jumps, tandem with an expert.

# ✳ Lodging

Almost 100 percent of visitors coming to Moab will enter town via US 191 from the north. This is really the only road connecting Moab to civilization and has the highest concentration of hotels, mostly of the basic variety, in town. These hotels can be booked up well in advance during Jeep Safari Weekend; call ahead. The US 191/Main Street list includes: **Comfort Suites** (435-259-5252; www.comfortsuites.com), 800 South Main St.; **Days Inn of Moab** (435-259-4468; www.daysinn.com), 426 North Main St.; **Holiday Inn Express Hotel & Suites** (877-863-4780; www.ichotelsgroup.com), 1515 North Main St.; **La Quinta Moab** (435-259-8700; www.laquintamoab.com), 815 South Main St.; **Ramada Inn—Moab** (435-259-7141; www.ramadainn.com), 182 South Main St.; **Sleep Inn** (435-259-4655; www.moabsleepinn.com), 1051 South Main St.; and **Super 8 Motel—Moab** (435-259-8868; www.super8.com), 889 North Main St.

HOTELS AND MOTELS **Aarchway Inn** (435-259-2599; www.aarchwayinn.com), 1551 North Main St., Moab. Simple rooms serve sleepy adventurers well by offering a variety of layout choices. Rooms range from small to large and have only the necessary furnishings. Recreation packages available. $59–$300 (top prices apply only on major tourist weekends).

**Big Horn Lodge** (435-259-6171 or 800-325-6171; www.moabbighorn.com), 550 South Main St., Moab. This huge, locally owned hotel has desert southwest décor, yet is still a simple hotel—perfect for outdoors types who might get a bit dirty. While the rooms are no fancier than those in a standard budget hotel, they are adorned with sandstone color schemes and raw pine accents. The service and quality satisfy those who know what to expect from a no-frills lodge. Rates vary greatly with the season, $70–$250.

☗ **Bowen Motel** (435-259-7132 or 800-874-5439; www.bowenmotel.com), 169 North Main St., Moab. This is one of Moab's most unadorned, inexpensive, yet cheery and locally owned motels. Rooms are very plain, yet come in a variety of sizes. Pets and mountain bikes are allowed inside for a fee. A gues thouse is also available for rent, and there is an outdoor pool. Guest rooms $80 and up; guest house $400 and up.

**Gonzo Inn** (435-259-2515; www.gonzoinn.com), 100 West 200 South, Moab. Gonzo is one of the more up-scale large hotels in town. Appropriate for the area, it still is low-key and filled with desert motifs. While the service and accommodations are still fairly basic, they one-up the competition by a notch or two. For a large establishment at relatively low cost and central location, this seems to be good compromise on quality and price. Rooms and suites are available. $100–$200.

☗ ↝ **Kokopelli Lodge** (435-259-7615 or 888-530-3134; www.kokopellilodge.com), 72 South 100 East, Moab. Just off the main drag in Moab, this allows you to see Moab beyond its billboards and outdoors shops but be within walking distance of all the downtown amenities. This unassuming little bargain offers the most simple of accommodations but has hidden perks, such as the use of earth-friendly cleaning products. $35–$80.

**Moab Valley Inn and Conference Center** (435-259-4419 or 800-831-6622; www.moabvalleyinn.com), 711 South Main St., Moab. Guest rooms are universal in their basic furnishings. However, they are spacious, plentiful, modern, and available for a fair price.

THE LAZY LIZARD, ON THE SOUTHERN END OF MAIN STREET, OFFERS $3 SHOWERS TO THOSE ROUGHING IT IN A TENT.

A major feature of the hotel for many is its large conference facilities. **Thrifty Car Rental** is located on the premises. $100 and up.

🐾 **River Canyon Lodge** (435-259-8838 or 866-486-6738; www.river canyonlodge.com), 71 West 200 North, Moab. This hotel is similar to a midlevel national chain but has overtones of rustic Rocky Mountain flavor with occasional nude timber and river cobble masonry. A variety of suites and guest rooms are available. Small details, like window seats, differentiate the rooms a bit. Pets are allowed in certain rooms. Check the Web site for links to area activities. Special area activities packages are available. $100 and up.

**Silver Sage Inn** (435-259-4420; www.silversageinn.com), 840 South Main St., Moab. Very basic and very affordable, this motel is perfect for bikers, climbers, and other gear mongers wishing to stay on the main drag.

Simple, durable rooms and storage facilities intended precisely for your equipment allow for you to have a warm bed at night without feeling like an elephant in a china shop.

**BED-AND-BREAKFASTS** **Cali Cochitta Bed & Breakfast** (435-259-4961; www.moabdreaminn.com), 110 South 200 East, Moab. This pleasant property has all of the simplistic, soulful details of the old-fashioned, toned-down lifestyle. This historic home has clean, sunshiny coats of paint, yet also has endearing quirkiness and the odd angles of 1800s Victorian architecture. Exposed brick, landscaped gardens, antique furniture, and lots of greenery seem to isolate this from the rest of main-drag Moab. This bed-and-breakfast is located in a section of town that seems less transient and more genuine. Because of the age of the actual building, rooms are small but generally feel cozier than cramped. Special touches are a shaded porch, outdoor dining table, and homemade breakfasts, fruit bowls, and baked goods. $100–$150 and up.

**Sunflower Hill Luxury Inn** (435-259-2974 or 800-662-2786; www .sunflowerhill.com), 185 North 300 East, Moab. Though the ambience of the inn is that of the countryside, the overall effect is very tasteful. Light bathes each room, and the furniture is arranged so as to leave a clean impression. The rooms offer enough softness to be comfortable but are not nearly as cluttered as those in some bed-and-breakfasts. All rooms are nonsmoking. A full, homemade breakfast is included in the rates at this four-diamond establishment. $120–$230.

**RANCHES AND OUTFITTERS** **Sorrel River Ranch Resort & Spa** (435-259-4642 or 877-359-2715; www.sorrelriver.com), mile 17 on

UT 128, east of Moab. This is one of the area's most luxurious lodging options, with a full-service spa, riverside Jacuzzi and pool, riverside dining (weather permitting), and horseback riding trips. These all complement the already unique and tasteful guest rooms and suites. For business travelers and groups, conference space is plentiful, and on-site catering is available. For adventurers, to-go lunches can be made to order. Rooms offer luxury but have Western overtones, ranging from single rooms to spa and family suites. This is a four-diamond establishment with the on-site **Sorrell River Grill,** which offers a contemporary, Southwest-influenced gourmet selection.

**Pack Creek Ranch** (435-259-5505; www.packcreekranch.com), 1075 South US 191/Main St., Moab. Just south of town, this campus of guest cabins offers relative solitude in a very pleasant, off-the-beaten-path setting. Guests enjoy views of the La Sal Mountains without having to stray too far from the creature comforts of town. Some on-site accommodations include a licensed massage therapist, hot tub, and outdoor pool. Cabins range quite a lot in size. $85–$400.

## ✳ Where to Eat

**DINING OUT** **Center Café** (435-259-4295; www.centercafemoab.com), 60 North 100 West, Moab. Open at 3:30 PM daily; call for reservations. This is recognized across the state as one of best eateries in southern Utah and has been picked up by *Zagat's* radar as one of the top restaurants in America. Whenever possible, ingredients on the menu are organic and locally grown. When not, they're brought in from the best purveyors around. Food here is classically prepared, and the menu is in constant

revision to best accommodate the season's availabilities. A "small plates" menu is available between 3:30 and 6 PM for tapas-style enjoyment. In the midst of many less refined restaurants, this elegant experience stands out. Full dinner begins at 5:30 PM. An extensive wine list is available. American Express is not accepted. Entrées $18–$30.

**Desert Bistro** (435-259-7424; www .desertbistro.com), 1266 North US 191/Main St. Open nightly for dinner during peak season; closed occasionally during the off-seasons; call to inquire. From first course through dessert, this is a fine-dining experience. This restaurant has operated since 1979 in a two-story, restored 1869 brick home constructed of locally made bricks and paint. In its hundred-and-some years, it has seen many

ANCIENT ARTS IS THE MOST FAMOUS ROCK CLIMBING ROUTE IN THE FISHER TOWERS BECAUSE OF ITS MOST PECULIAR SHAPE.

Zac Robinson

**262**

SOUTHEASTERN UTAH

things; it was the site of a seven-day standoff with the law following an inner-family murder; it has been relocated; it was visited by the infamous Butch Cassidy and his gang. Inside the building these days is a menu offering rich beef, game, and seafood entrées, including tenderloin, duck, and other cuisine of European influence, often with overtones from the Germanic and French realms. Patio dining during the warm months affords guest an enjoyable experience away from Moab's flashy main drag. A full bar and wine list are available. Reservations are recommended. $16–$32.

🌊 **The Sunset Grill Restaurant and Terrace** (435-259-7146), 900 North Main St., Moab. Opens at 5 PM Monday through Saturday. This restaurant has been serving dinner in a panoramic dining room, 200 feet above Moab, since 1993. The menu spans an eclectic, generally European-influenced range of foods that dabble in Italian, French, American, and even Norwegian cuisine. The restaurant is walled almost entirely in glass, and the views during early evening are beautiful from this perch. The grill operates from the former home of area uranium mining magnate Charles Steen. Children are welcome; a special kids' menu is available upon request. $12–$30.

**EATING OUT Eddie McStiff's** (435-259-2337; www.eddiemcstiffs.com), 57 South Main St., Moab. Open for dinner nightly at 4:30 Generally the portions are large enough to fill even a hungry belly, and include Mexican, Italian, Southwestern, and American cuisine. The menu is heavy in steaks and ribs, as well as burgers served with house-made chili sauces, blackened fish in burritos, and the like. McStiff's also has a specialty pizza menu. As Moab's oldest brewery, this place sells its own goods (including a delicious cream stout) but also confidently serves other in-state and national beers. A wine list is also available. $8–$25.

**Eklecktic Café** (435-259-6896), 352 North Main St., Moab. Open for breakfast and lunch daily. This is a great stop for a fresh, healthy breakfast on the quick. All meals are made from scratch, and the coffee is fair trade. Morning meals include notoriously delicious quiches; various plates of potatoes, cheeses, herbs, and veggies; and hot bagel sandwiches, all available starting at 7 AM. Also available are bagels with cream cheese, baked goods, and granola. Foods that become available in the afternoon include wraps, satays, quesadillas, sandwiches, salads, and melts. Hearty vegetables and whole foods, like avacados, carrots, sprouts, as well as nuts and seeds make up much of the ingredient list. Lunch continues until 2:30; limited breakfast items are available through this time. Boxed lunches are available with sandwich, fruit, drink, chips, and cookie with 48 hours' notice. $8–$14.

**La Hacienda** (435-259-6319), 574 North Main St., Moab. Open daily for lunch and dinner. A Mexican restaurant located immediately on Main Street serves a great purpose in this town. Portions are large, and the price is acceptable. Traditional fare is spiced up a bit in comparison to other similar eateries in the area. This is a surefire way to quench your appetite with simple, familiar food. $10–$15.

**Mandarin Szechwan Restaurant** (435-259-8984), 125 South Main St., Moab. Open for lunch and dinner daily; Sunday brunch. The Szechwan is Moab's representative Chinese restaurant in town. Located on the main drag, this restaurant is rarely crowded. The atmosphere and cuisine are very low-key, and prices are very reasonable. A lunch buffet is available. $8–$12.

**Milt's Stop & Eat Burger** (435-259-7424; www.moab-utah.com/milts), 356 Millcreek Dr., Moab. This local burger place has been in business since 1954. Today you can still belly up to the soda fountain–style bar, where they hand cut fries right in front of you. This has all the authenticity of a historic local burger joint, without the familiar trappings of a plastic tourist outfit. As a bonus, these savvy restaurateurs serve only locally raised, hormone-free beef. In addition to classic burgers, fries, malts, and shakes, they also serve salads, fish burgers, chicken, and Southwest-influenced melts—spanning the range from old-fashioned kid's cuisine to that of an environmentally conscious 21st-century adult. Milt's is set away from the main drag, so parking and location are easy (with a map). All seating is on fixed bar stools, and the atmosphere is very low-key. $6–$10.

**Moab Brewery** (435-259-6333; www.themoabbrewery.com), 686 South Main St., Moab. Open daily for lunch and dinner. This microbrewery's brews are served across Utah and are generally named after such desert items as scorpions, lizards, and dead horses; if it's available on your visit, try their Dead Horse Amber. Every day brings some sort of in-pub specialty, from bargain pints and pitchers to nickel wings. The menu is extensive and of the high-end pub variety, with a general Southwest overtone. Generally, the food here is better than at McStiff's (the other pub, north about 1 mile on Main Street), and the cuisine has fresh and inventive overtones. The selection spans dishes from vegetarian specialties to Mexican, chicken plates, pasta, and soup. Indeed, a selection of more formal entrées is available, mostly fea-

turing carnivorous items, but some seafood as well. This restaurant has a pleasant, wide-open seating area; patio dining is available. Beer is sold to go in a variety of containers. (But no kegs; they are illegal for public distribution in Utah.) $9–$22.

**Moab Diner and Ice Cream Shoppe** (435-259-4006; www.moabdiner.com), 189 South Main St., Moab. Open Monday–Saturday for breakfast, lunch, and dinner. This is one of the more visible restaurants on the main drag and is a Moab staple. This restaurant is a great quick fix for a big appetite and greasy spoon cravings. Breakfast is served all day, but lunch and dinner also become available when the time is appropriate. The menu includes omelets, different skillets, and vegetarian and "heart-healthy" options, as well as appetizers, deep-fried items, hot and cold sandwiches, burgers, soups, and salads in the afternoon and evening. Each day has a different special. Boxed lunches can be purchased to go.

**Mondo Café** (435-259-5551; www.mondocafe.com), 59 South Main St., Moab. Mondo Café, located

MCSTIFF'S PLAZA IS ONE OF MOAB'S MOST POPULAR HANGOUTS FOR OUTDOORSY TYPES; A ONE-STOP SHOPPING CENTER, THE PLAZA HAS A BREWPUB, COFFEE SHOP, BOOKSTORE, CLIMBING GEAR SHOP, AND MORE.

EAST OF MOAB, THIS WINERY IS LOCATED ON A SCENIC CAMPUS ALONG THE COLORADO RIVER AND OFFERS WINE TASTING IN ITS RESTAURANT.

adjacent to Eddie McStiff's and Pagan Mountaineering, is one of the major hubs for those needing a cup of joe, small snack, or wireless access on a long trip. Because of its location immediately on Main Street, the relaxed atmosphere, and its proximity to good shops, this is the most reputable meeting spot for those connecting with each other from different corners of the earth. In addition to coffee, they also serve basic confections, bagels, oatmeal, sandwiches, tea, and more.

**Slickrock Café** (435-259-8004; www .slickrockcafe.com), 5 North Main St., Moab. Open daily for breakfast, lunch, and dinner. This upscale café offers appetizers of the filling, Southwest variety, sandwiches hot and cold, spiffed-up burgers, and entrées from tilapia to New York steak, pot roast, and fettucini Alfredo. They have you covered for breakfast as well, offering hearty plates of eggs, meats, and veggies. Imagine a diner menu crossed

with pub fare. Beer, wine, liquor, and margaritas are available for those of proper age. $9–$26.

## ✳ Selective Shopping

**BOOKSTORES ABC & Beyond Used Books** (435-259-3336), 59 South Main St., Moab. This shop is located in one of the main outdoor-hipster plazas of town and is sandwiched between Eddie McStiff's and Mondo Café. A used-book selection and buy-back program set this bookstore apart from others and attract climbers and other desert residents looking for rest-day entertainment.

**Back of Beyond Books** (435-259-5154 or 800-700-2859; www.backof beyondbooks.com), 83 North Main, Moab. A good place to begin your tour, this is where you can become acquainted with the history, geography, culture, and geology of the area through the store's collection, which specializes in regional and rare volumes.

**GALLERIES The Cat's Lair Gallery** (435-259-2458; www.catslaircollection .com), 59 South Main St., Moab. Cat's Lair features one of Moab's widest varieties of handiworks and fine arts. Pieces range from wooden bowls to pottery, paintings, large-scale sculpture, and handcrafted drums.

**Framed Image Art Gallery** (435-259-4446; www.framedimagemoab .com), 59 East Center St., Moab. This gallery presents the works of a handful of local artists whose media range from sculpture to oil and watercolor paints. Much of the art is scenic; other art is influenced by more abstraction.

**Hogan Trading Company** (435-259-8118; www.hogantrading.com), 100 South Main St., Moab. This busy collection of Southwestern-influenced handicrafts and traditional Native

American images is much less serious than some of its fine-arts sisters. However, it does offer some refined works. Goods for purchase here include turquoise-embedded jewelry, brass sculpture, Southwestern metal cutouts, wind chimes, and more.

**Lema's Kokopelli Gallery** (435-259-5055; www.lemaskokopelligallery.com), 70 North Main St., Moab. Bearing some similarity to Hogan Trading Company, Kokopelli's wares range from small interior decorations to jewelry, paintings, rugs, and other Native American–influenced and –created items.

**Moab Art Works** (435-259-3010; www.moabartworks.com), 35 North Main St., Moab. Unlike many of the tourist-friendly shops around, this is one of Moab's edgier fine galleries.

Though the works featured here are typically created locally, they stray from the stereotypical red-rock scenes typical of the area. Much of the focus is still on the natural landscape, but often through a clever political lens or via another creative refraction.

**Tom Till Gallery** (435-259-9808 or 888-479-9808; www.tomtill.com), 61 North Main St., Moab. This gallery features the vibrant, colorful landscape works of photographer Tom Till. The gallery sells prints as well as note cards, calendars, photography books, and more.

**THRIFT STORES WabiSabi** (435-259-3313), 145 West 200 South #6, Moab. This small, densely packed thrift shop is known across Utah for its collection of hip vintage clothing.

# ARCHES NATIONAL PARK

Arches National Park is located on the richly diverse and geologically dramatic Colorado Plateau, just north of the Colorado River. This river and other erosive forces has cleft canyons and created the dramatic landscape that reaches from the river's surface to the peaks of the La Sal Mountains, just 20 miles south as the crow flies. Within this short distance, there is nearly 2 miles of vertical relief. Because this area sees less than 10 inches of precipitation each year, wind and streams have been allowed to act as the primary erosion agent, sweeping past rocks and scooping them with eddies. Such steepness of terrain and undulations of carved Entrada sandstone have given way to roughly 2,000 arches within the park boundaries alone. Though most of the arches have Entrada's orange-pink hue, some ivory-colored Navajo formations can be seen as well.

With so little ambient moisture, it follows that life here is of the strict desert variety—cactus, yucca, sagebrush; mule deer, kangaroo rats, porcupine, mice, squirrels, jackrabbits, snakes, and lizards—anything waxy, spiny, or clever enough to produce its internal moisture. Though environment here is overwhelmingly arid and exposed, canyons form lush pockets of reprieve. These riparian areas and ephemeral pools support much larger species, including cottonwood trees, willow, tamarisk, bighorn sheep, bobcats, and coyotes. It is also here that many birds, including large raptors, make their homes.

Casual observation would lead anyone to suspect that this massive sand sculpture must have somehow originated from the sands of an ancient beach. During the Jurassic Period, this area was covered in sea. Beaches were continuously deposited atop salt beds. Topography allowed these sand deposits to become almost 2 miles thick, and chemical lithification converted these sands to stone. As the seas receded and the Colorado Plateau saw tectonic thrust, the intrinsically fragile, underlying salt beds gave way under the burden of its thick sandstone load. Huge blocks of sandstone were broken and steeply tilted by gravity as their foundation gave way unevenly. These cracks and chasms became exaggerated and deepened by opportunistic winds carrying sands, and streams obeying gravity.

The first humans to occupy the area were thought to do so as recently as 3,000 years ago, or as long as 11,000 years ago. The most evident residents were the Anasazi, Fremont, and Pueblo peoples. The Anasazi, who resided in the area as recently as 700 years ago, left behind rock art, artifacts, and dwellings, some of which can still be seen in the park today. More recently, the Ute and Navajo tribes patrolled these lands. The Navajo had a vast territory, and it is thought Arches was on the northern fringes of it; however, little evidence of their presence exists. The Utes, however, had led a more obvious existence here and were responsible for evicting would-be European settlers in the mid-1800s.

The park, despite its location just north of the Spanish Valley (the location of present-day Moab) and the busy, 18th-century Spanish Trail, saw little interest or visitations by white settlers or explorers until quite a while after much of the adjacent area was "discovered." Only a select few, including a handful of Mormon settlers and trapper Denis Julien, were known to have entered the park's boundaries at all, and those who did enter had only a transient presence.

The Moab area was eventually settled by Mormons with permanence and fortification in the 1880s, breaking down the stronghold the native tribes had on the area. Moab residents began to hear of the beautiful natural phenomena of Arches and were prone to visit. Civil War veteran John Wolfe became the first white settler to establish a residence in Arches. He lived on Salt Creek, near Delicate Arch, from around 1898 to 1910.

National interest in the area's beauty grew. The nearby Rio Grande Railroad, which had a stop about 30 miles to the north, was invited to consider the prospect of creating a tourist destination. The National Park Service caught wind of this scheme and was quick to include Arches on its roster by 1929, under President Hoover. The park was greatly expanded nine years later, but it wasn't until 1958 that the first paved road was created.

Arches has had the good fortune of being protected through the different geological pillaging eras of the regions, most particularly the uranium mining boom of the 1950s and 1960s. Because it has been a national park since long before this, the park bypassed much of the destructive history that civilization has imparted to its surrounding landscapes. It is free of the visible damage that similar, nearby lands incurred during these decades.

Today this park sees the better part of a million visitors each year and is home to such famous attractions as Delicate Arch, petrified sand dunes, Double Arch, and Balanced Rock. Arches is a simple park, with one entrance and only one main road, though it does fork. $10 per vehicle; $25 for a year-long "Local Passport" to Arches, Canyonlands, Hovenweep, and Natural Bridges. Camping at Devil's

DELICATE ARCH IS UNDOUBTEDLY UTAH'S MOST FAMOUS ARCH, FEATURED ON THE UTAH LICENSE PLATE.

Zac Robinson

SOUTHEASTERN UTAH

Garden Campground is $15. Camp-sites and tour size are limited, so reservations are recommended as much as four weeks in advance during peak season.

**GUIDANCE Arches National Park Visitors Center** (435-719-2299; www.nps.gov/arch), park entrance. Open 8–4:30 daily November through March; 7:30–6 daily April through October; closed Christmas. Located just inside the park's only entrance, in the far southern corner of the park, this small welcome center is exactly what you would expect to find at a national park—informative and to the point.

**GETTING THERE** *By air:* Arches is just 5 miles north of Moab; see the *Getting There* section in the "Moab" chapter for specific air travel instructions.

*By car:* Arches National Park is located north of Moab, in the crook between US 191 and the Colorado River. The entrance is along US 191, just 5 miles north of Moab.

*By bus:* About 50 miles to the northwest, the town of Green River is serviced by Amtrak and Greyhound. Greyhound also services Crescent Junction. For more specific detail on this, see the *Getting There* section in the "Moab" chapter; virtually all services that apply to Moab also apply to Arches, as they nearly border on each other.

**TOURS Arches Bus Tours** (435-259-7000; www.archesbustours.com). This is the prototypical group bus tour service that offers narrated trips, as well as custom trips.

**Arches Tours** (435-658-2227 or 800-724-7767; www.archestours.com). Tours by this company are generally long and extensive, and usually combine destinations including Canyonlands, the Grand Canyon, Bryce Canyon, Lake Powell, Dead Horse Point State Park, and Zion National Park. Some trips have a set itinerary; others are custom. One package originates in Salt Lake City, so if that is the primary location of your visit, you may want to look into this option as a convenient, relaxing way to take in desert scenery.

**Moab Adventure Center** (866-904-1163; www.moabadventurecenter.com). This megatour center guides tours of many varieties, including river trips (on the Colorado River), hiking trips, and scenic flights. Their bus tour of Arches is conducted at sunset for maximum visual drama.

---

## PETS IN UTAH'S NATIONAL PARKS

Though pets are allowed in the parks, it is with severe restrictions. Most pet owners would agree that pets are best left at home when possible, especially if owners intend to engage in any activities away from pavement. No pets are allowed on any hiking trails. Pets are never allowed off-leash, and they may only be outside the vehicle in campgrounds and on paved overlooks and pullouts. Leaving pets inside a vehicle unattended is not a solution, as they are not allowed to cause disturbance—but most importantly because heat can quickly become severe in a closed vehicle and will kill your pet.

**MEDICAL EMERGENCY** Though the park is staffed with rangers who are trained to assist in case of emergency, there are no medical establishments in the park. For a listing of medical treatment options, see the *Medical Emergency* section in the "Moab" chapter. Cell service is not to be expected in the park but is generally fair to good on US 191, so in case of emergency, reaching this highway is crucial for assistance with evacuation.

## ✳ To See and Do

**LANDMARKS** The most famous landmarks in the park will be very well documented and clearly demarcated. However, you still should know ahead of time what exactly you want to look for.

**Delicate Arch** is probably the most famous arch in the park and is on the frontispiece of many Utah memorabilia items, including Utah's license plate. This arch is located in the far eastern portion of the park.

**Double Arch** is another of the park's more spectacular and most photographed arches with a few cameo appearances to its name, including that in *Indiana Jones and the Last Crusade*. Double Arch is located near the end of the southwestern fork of the park road.

**Devil's Garden** is a collection of features that can be accessed by various hiking trails. Landscape Arch is among this collection and is the largest arch in the entire park, with a span of roughly 290 feet. The hike to this arch is 1.5 miles out and back, and is listed in *Hiking*.

**Petrified Dunes** are less a singular object and more a brief landscape that can be viewed from the roadside. The overlook is located between the Windows trailhead area and the Courthouse Overlook.

LOCATED IN THE WINDOWS REGION, IN THE EAST-CENTRAL PORTION OF THE PARK, DOUBLE ARCH IS A PAIR OF TWO CONJOINED ARCHES THAT IS UNIQUE IN ITS TOP-DOWN EROSION FORMATION, AS OPPOSED TO THE SIDE EROSION THAT IS RESPONSIBLE FOR THE CREATION OF MOST OF THE PARK'S OTHER ARCHES.

Zac Robinson

# ✳ Outdoor Activities

**CAMPING** The park has no lodging per se. However, camping at the **Devil's Garden Campground** is a great option for those prepared and willing to do so. Sites cost $15 per night. Campsites are limited, so reservations are recommended as much as four weeks (or longer) in advance during peak season. This can be arranged for a $9 dollar booking fee online at www.reservations.gov, or by telephone by calling 877-444-6777 or 877-833-6777.

**HIKING** Hiking is probably the most accessible, most practical way to become acquainted with the natural beauty of the park outside of your vehicle. Generally speaking, the shorter trails in the park will be well worn and immaculately maintained. Longer trails will typically be less groomed, which is usually preferred for those seeking wilderness. For exact location of the trailheads, consult the map provided with your entry fee. Regardless of your fitness level or perceived level of ruggedness, you should be sure to never leave the car without a generous amount of water and sunscreen. It is not unreasonable to bring at least one liter of water per person per hour. Be advised that backpackers and anyone else sleeping in the backcountry must obtain a permit to do so.

**Delicate Arch,** the infamous arch seen on Utah's license plates, can be accessed by three separate access points. The first requires virtually no hiking but provides an overlook only; this is found at the Delicate Arch parking area in the northeastern side of the park. From this same parking area is another trail that is only 0.4 mile each way. The second is 3 miles round-trip and begins from the **John Wesley Wolfe Ranch,** the first homestead in the area, settled in 1898. For the distance, this trail is very mellow, as it gains less than 500 feet of elevation. The Wolfe Ranch is located northeast of the Double Arch.

**Double Arch.** Because of its short distance, flat profile, and unique vista of conjoined natural arches, this is one of the classic hikes of the park. The round-trip journey is only 1 mile. Just beyond Double Arch along the same trail is the **Cove of Caves,** worth the slight extension. The trailhead for this feature is located at the tip of the park road's southeast fork.

**Fiery Furnace,** one of the park's unique and more famous natural attractions, is a deep and narrow maze that winds through the narrows between richly colored sandstone fins. It is accessed exclusively via ranger-guided tours but is a great itinerary goal nonetheless. Because of the attractive nature of the hike, these limited-capacity adventures sell out. Reservations can be obtained in person only. There is a booking fee, which is worth it if the desired experience is important to your trip. $10 for adults, $5 for children ages 6–12, $5 for Golden Pass holders.

**Landscape Arch** requires only a 1-mile trip each way and is the park's largest arch, with an opening of roughly 290 feet. Parking for this hike is at Devil's Garden trailhead, at the northern tip of the park's pavement, where a brochure is also available.

**Park Avenue,** in the southern part of the park near the entrance, requires some distance and has elevation change. Park Avenue descends for 1 mile into a wash where hikers see the **Courthouse Towers.**

**Skyline Arch** requires only 0.2 mile of hiking to reach one-way. This arch, in the northern end of the park, was doubled in size before 1940 when a massive chunk of stone broke loose and fell from its underbelly. Located in the northwestern corner of the park.

**Tower Arch Trail** ascends through a variety of geology in its 1.7-mile course to the arch. The trail is a nontechnical ascension up a rock wall, sand dunes, and fins.

**Windows Trail** shares a trailhead with that of Double Arch is almost exactly 1 mile round-trip. Along the way, it passes the **North and South Windows** and **Turret Arches.**

ROCK CLIMBING Rock climbing in Arches is a matter of controversy. Though it is generally not practiced here, some issues have come to national attention of late. Professional rock climber Dean Potter free-soloed (ascended without protection of a rope or any equipment) Delicate Arch in May 2006. This was thought to be illegal by park officials, though it turned out the laws of those times were unenforceable because of language issues. Since then, the books have been amended to specifically outlaw any rock climbing (or similar activities) on any natural bridge or arch within the park.

The good news is that climbing is allowed on other features within the park, with a few restrictions. One does not need to obtain a permit for climbing unless the trip will involve an overnight stay in the backcountry (whether camping at the base of a climb or on a bivy ledge). Also, it is important to note that white climbing chalk is no longer allowed. Red chalk can be purchased at Moab climbing shops. **Pagan Mountaineering** (59 South Main St., Moab; 435-259-1117; www.paganmountaineering.com) of Moab sells exactly this type of rather uncommon chalk.

The routes in Arches are generally categorized as desert crack and are usually on good, though often sandy, stone. The park has a mix of single- and multipitch (clean only), aid, and tower lines. One of the area's most classic lines, **Owl Rock,** is a single-pitch 5.8 that is a good introduction to the area's style of climbing. As desert rock often offers pure-crack climbing, it requires a very specific set of skills and fitness much different than face climbing. The guidebook most useful for this park is Eric Bjornstad's *Desert Rock*, also available at Pagan Mountaineering.

# CANYONLANDS NATIONAL PARK

Canyonlands National Park, southwest of Moab, is yet another desert sandstone phenomenon created by a miracle of geology. Though in close proximity, this park is somehow radically distinct from Arches National Park or any nearby canyon. The park is centered around the V-shaped junction of the Colorado and Green rivers and occupies 530 square miles. The overwhelmingly flat and horizontal strata of this sandstone have been worn into complex and deep fissures by the tributaries of these two rivers. Deep into these planar masses of sandstone, these waters and dry desert winds have carved mesas, pillars, spires, and arches. The deep walls of these canyons display cross sections of millions of years of preserved geologic history and invite viewers to imagine the eons of geologic activity that have transpired since the formation of the planet.

This national park was designated as such by the National Park Service in 1964 and, unlike Yosemite, has remained a rather rugged and undeveloped park whose roads do little to dent the wild interior. The park has two main entrances: one in the northeast and one in the southeast. The northern entrance accesses the Island in the Sky, a fossil-rich region that occupies the northern cleft between the Green and Colorado rivers. This region is characterized by flat, broad plateaus deeply rift by serpentine river canyons. Island in the Sky is the tallest portion of the park, and

A HIKER ENJOYS THE FINAL MINUTES OF DAYLIGHT IN THE NEEDLES DISTRICT OF
CANYONLANDS NATIONAL PARK.

Amiee Maxwell

most people enjoy this particular part of the park for its gaping scenic viewpoints. Developed camping here is available at Willow Flat Campground.

The southern entrance intrudes into the Needles region of the park, just to the southeast of the Colorado River. This region of the park sits much lower than the Island in the Sky and gets its name from the white and red elongated spires that dominate the skyline. This part of the park has deep canyons and varied topography, and contains petroglyphs, ruins, hiking trails, arches, and more. These paved roads bring visitors only slightly into the park, but most of this region is accessed by hiking trails only. Camping in this region is at the Squaw Flat Campground (the location of the park's only group sites).

The third distinct region of the park is The Maze, which has no easy vehicular access or improved infrastructure. A network of unimproved and unmarked roads departs from UT 25 (to the north of Hanksville) and from UT 95 (to the south of Hanksville and to the north of Lake Powell). Though inconvenient and often restricted to four-wheel-drive vehicles, this unimproved road system has preserved the rugged wilderness of this remote and harsh desert environment for those who are willing and able to earn this experience. As its name might suggest, this was in fact one of the best hideouts for outlaws, including Butch Cassidy and the Sundance Kid.

Oldest evidence of inhabitants in these lands dates back about 10 millennia. For the same reasons that render the area impractical to settle today, the peoples of the past likewise treaded lightly and seasonally through the area. Most evidence of these ancient visitors is in the form of tools left behind: points, arrows, and the like. However, it seems that more permanent residents created homes here roughly 5,000 years ago. These cultures were small in breadth, as their size and complexity was severely restricted by the constrained resources. Hunter-gatherer lifestyles allowed these peoples to subsist on the land in small populations only.

Historians assume that the peoples of this area must have, at some point, come into contact with, and learned the agricultural ways of, the Mesoamerican peoples. Archaeologists have uncovered maize storage bins carved into the rock. This newly learned horticultural lifestyle must have outgrown its home here, for it seems the people migrated away. Likely they relocated to broader fields capable of being watered by more sweeping flood irrigation techniques.

More recently, the ancestors of modern-day Utes, Paiutes, and Navajos came to occupy the area. Though they lived here as recently as 700 years ago, their lifestyle here was nomadic. They traveled to follow the most ideal climate and healthiest animal herds—and left with severe temperatures and lack of food.

The first Europeans to encroach into these lands, as in much of the rest of Utah, were of the Dominguez-Escalante Expedition. These Franciscan Friars and explorer-missionaries came through the area from the south. Theirs was a mission to establish a passable route from present-day Santa Fe, New Mexico, to Monterey, California. This route took them through a good portion Utah. Harsh weather and lethal aridity turned the expeditions around somewhere near today's Utah Valley, of which Provo is the county seat. Other passersby were equally nomadic, including mostly trappers, later traders and outlaws, and sometimes explorers like John Wesley Powell. These men passed quietly over the most readily traversed routes and made themselves scantly known. They were generally alone, unthreatening, and on good terms with the indigenous folk. They left occasional markings in the river canyons and published various volumes on Western adventure and exploration.

Today, this region is still, for the most part, untamed. True, this is a national park; however, the vast majority of it is isolated backcountry. It is extremely important when visiting Canyonlands to be prepared for some kind of beating by the climate. Though average summer highs are typically in the 90s, temperatures in this area can easily reach and surpass 110°F, with nighttime lows being as much as 60 degrees (or more) cooler. Winter brings highs in the 30s and lows in the teens or cooler. The air is extremely dry, and there is almost no shelter from the sun. Sunscreen and seemingly excessive amounts of water are a must. People engaging in physical activities should consider bringing along as much as one liter of water per person per hour. Bringing more would not be excessive, especially on strenuous hikes during warm months. Other means for beating the heat include light-colored, lightweight clothing and electrolyte supplements. The cooler evenings and cold winter temperatures require insulating clothing, and sometimes rain- and wind-resistant gear. $5 admission for individuals for seven consecutive days, $10 per vehicle. $25 for "Local Passport" pass to Arches, Canyonlands, Hovenweep, and Natural Bridges. For more information, visit www.nps.gov/cany.

GUIDANCE **Hans Flat/Maze Ranger Station** is open daily 8–4:30, with extended hours from March through October. The ranger station is reached by taking UT 24 south 24 miles from I-70. Take a left just past the Goblin Valley State Park turnoff, and continue southeast on this improved dirt road for 46 miles to the ranger station.

**Island in the Sky Visitors Center** is open daily 9–4:30, with extended hours from March through October. The center is located just beyond the Island in the Sky entrance.

**Needles Visitors Center** is also open daily 9–4:30, with extended hours from March through October. This center is located just beyond the Needles entrance.

GETTING THERE *By car:* Canyonlands has three distinct regions, divided by very unnavigable geography: the Green and Colorado rivers and their deep canyons. Of the three, the northern portion (Island in the Sky) and the southeastern portion (Needles) are popular; the western side (Maze) entrance requires long-distance travel on unimproved and poorly mapped roads. There are no civilized improvements on this side, making it less appealing to some and more appealing to others.

**The northern entrance/Island in the Sky** can be reached via US 191, just 9 miles north of Moab and 20 miles south of I-70. This region is most known for its broad buttes, plateaus, and meandering river canyons that expose horizontal rainbows of red. This part of the park has the highest elevation and some of the best viewpoints accessible by automobile. **Willow Flat Campground** is this portion of the park's developed camping.

**The southern entrance/Needles** can be reached by departing from US 191, 39 miles south of Moab (14 miles north of Monticello). Take UT 211 west into the park, which lies to the southeast of the Colorado River. On this route, you begin on high-desert plateau but, after about 15 miles of driving, dip steeply down a few switchbacks into what is known as Indian Creek Basin, a world-famous Wingate sandstone crack climbing area, and a very beautiful one at that.

**The Maze,** which is the western and third entrance of the park, is separated from the northern and eastern portions by the Green and Colorado rivers. This has no entrance station and no main highway—or any paved roads at all. This is reached by a number of unimproved, crudely mapped dirt roads departing from UT 95 to the south of Hanksville, or from UT 25 to the north of Hanksville. Because of the remoteness of this road, the harshness of the climate, and the ruggedness of the roads, this is recommended only for those with solid navigation skills, proper experience, and sufficient vehicle and equipment. There is no fee to use this portion of the park, as there are absolutely no services here. Camping inside The Maze is forbidden, though there is plenty of camping just outside the park on Bureau of Land Mangement land.

TOURS **Canyonlands by Night or Day** (435-259-2628 or 800-394-9978 www .canyonlandsbynight.com). This tour company offers quite a selection of ways to see Canyonlands, and the Moab region in general. Included are raft, small plane, Hummer, ATV, 4x4, jet boat, and nighttime boat tours.

**Moab Adventure Center** (435-259-7019 or 866-904-1163; www.moabadventure center.com). This megatour company offers scenic flight tours of the Canyonlands. This means of tour gives you the unique opportunity to visit all three regions of the park in just about one hour.

**Zion Tours** (435-658-2227 or 800-724-7767; www.ziontours.com). This company offers private and group tours from Las Vegas and Salt Lake City. True private tours can be arranged from anywhere in the region. The fleet of vehicles includes SUVs, minibuses, and coach buses.

MEDICAL EMERGENCY Cell service in Canyonlands is usually nonexistent and spotty at best. Do not expect to be able to make mobile calls. Cell service is generally okay on US 191, so in case of emergency, reaching this highway is crucial if you need assistance. Otherwise, no medical services exist in Canyonlands, so you're on your own. Be prepared.

## ✳ Outdoor Activities

BIKING **White Rim Road Trail** is a very popular multiday biking route, offering 103 miles and three or four days of enjoyment. This route is technically casual, as it follows Jeep roads and is mostly flat. However, there are a handful of stiff climbs and roughly 6,000 feet total of elevation gain, all told. This trail traverses the geographical boundary of the Island in the Sky, has an elevation usually around 4,800 feet, and enjoys overlooks that peer 1,000 feet down to the Green and Colorado rivers. For a number of factors, most riders prefer to ride clockwise, departing south from Schafer Trail, the trailhead for which is on UT 313, just west of the Island in the Sky Entrance Station. There is a selection of campgrounds along the route, but they cannot be taken at random; they must be booked through the National Park Service. Because of the popularity of the route, they are sometimes booked more than a year in advance. No pets allowed. Riders must pay the $10 entrance fee but will likely have already reserved and paid in advance for their campsite.

CAMPING **Island in the Sky** developed campsites are at **Willow Flat Campground** and cost $10 per night. No reservations are accepted for these sites, as

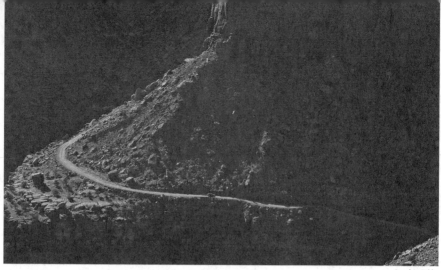

WHITE RIM ROAD IS A 103-MILE JEEP ROAD THAT FORMS A LOOP NESTLED IN THE V-SHAPED JUNCTION OF THE COLORADO AND GREEN RIVERS. THIS ROAD IS PERHAPS MOST POPULAR FOR MULTIDAY MOUNTAIN BIKE TRIPS.

they are taken on a first-come, first-served basis. Permits are required for backcountry camping, and reservations are accepted for this, regardless of region in the park. All reservations must be made by completing an application available at www.nps.org/cany. For more information regarding reservations, contact the ranger's office (435-259-4351) Monday–Friday, 8:30–12:30 (or sometimes until 4 PM, if a ranger is available).

**Needles** developed campsites are at **Squaw Flat Campground** and cost $15 per night. Only group sites can be reserved. This is done by calling the park (as listed for Island in the Sky, above).

MESA ARCH IS LOCATED ON THE EDGE OF A PLATEAU IN THE ISLAND IN THE SKY DISTRICT OF CANYONLANDS NATIONAL PARK; THROUGH THE ARCH ARE SWEEPING VIEWS OF DEEP CANYONS BELOW.

## HIKING

### Island in the Sky

This portion of the park is comprised of the Island in the Sky Mesa, an incredibly flat portion of land that ends in cliffs up to 1,000 feet tall, carved into winding walls by the Colorado River. The dozen hikes here tend to either be short (accessing the rim of the canyons) or long (descending into the canyons).

**Grandview Overlook** requires an easy 1-mile, low-profile hike to be reached. At about 6,700 feet elevation, it offers a panoramic view of the high desert plateau at your feet, and several very similar layers beneath you. To get here, drive west from the visitors center, staying left at the Y in the road. Continue about 6 miles and look for the obvious pullout.

**Lathrop Trail** is the only developed trail that descends from the top of the mesa to the banks of the Colorado River. The trail is just more than 8 miles each way and usually requires more than one day to accomplish, as it has more than 2,000 feet of elevation change. After about 5 miles it crosses the White Rim Road, and then continues downward for just more than 3 miles. The trailhead is 1.8 miles south of the visitors center.

**Mesa Arch Loop Trail** is a 0.5-mile hike that gains this enormous, broad, flat arch through which you see views of the La Sal Mountains. The trailhead for this is located 7 miles southwest of the visitors center, just before a three-way junction in the road.

**Neck Spring Loop Trail** is a 6-mile loop that begins at the visitors center and passes two small springs that were quite important for Native Americans and cowboys as recently as the 1960s, as cowboy artifacts found left behind will testify. There is little more than 250 feet of elevation change, making this a reasonably casual hike, despite the distance.

**Neck Springs Overlook** is a popular, middle-distance trail. Five miles of hiking take you in and around the tributaries to Taylor Canyon and past old ranch ruins. The trailhead for this hike is just south of the visitors center.

**Syncline Loop** is a loop that encircles the unexplained and enormous Upheaval Dome. This trail changes about 1,400 feet in elevation over 8 miles and is fairly strenuous. As there is one campsite along the way, this can be done as a backpacking trip with the necessary permits. On the northern portion of the trail, the Syncline Valley, there is usually some amount of shade and often water.

**Upheaval Dome** is nearly 3 miles across and 1,500 feet deep. Because it grossly upsets the otherwise consistent flatness of the area's rock strata, it is thought to

LAYERS OF SANDSTONE STRATA ERODE AND FORM CONES OF DEBRIS, UNINTERRUPTED BY VEGETATION AND UNDISTURBED BY PRECIPITATION ALONG US 163.

Jonathan Echlin

Amiee Maxwell

CHESLER PARK, IN THE NEEDLES DISTRICT OF CANYONLANDS NATIONAL PARK, IS
CHARACTERIZED BY PALE YELLOW AND CLAY ORANGE DOMES.

have been created by a meteorite impact crater or collapsed salt dome. This hike
requires 1 mile of walking to the first overlook and an extra mile to the second. To
reach the Upheaval Dome parking area, head southwest from the visitors center,
staying right at two consecutive Y-intersections. About 5 miles after the second Y,
look for parking at the terminus of this road.

THE GLOBULAR ROCK FORMATIONS AND
RELATIVE FLAT TOPOGRAPHY OF THIS
PORTION OF CANYONLANDS' NEEDLES
DISTRICT MAKE THE AREA POPULAR FOR
CASUAL SCENIC HIKING.

Amiee Maxwell

## Needles

This southern region of Canyonlands
was named after its profusion of colorful and tall rock spires. Though beautiful, it is largely only accessible by
hiking, as roads are fairly minimal. This
is a boon for some and a deterrent for
others.

**Cave Spring Trail** is named for a natural spring flowing from a cave. At the
site of this spring is the remains of a
cattle ranching operation, here because
of the fresh water source and the natural shelter the cave afforded these cowboys. There is a 0.6-mile hike to this
site, departing from a dirt road a mile
south of the Needles Visitors Center.

**Chesler Park** is a nearly 1,000-acre
meadow encircled and dwarfed by
some of Needles' most quintessential
red and white spires. Squaw Flat
Campground offers the trailhead of the
shortest approach trail. There is quite a
network of trails departing from this

point, so be sure to carry a map with you as you hike. To reach Squaw Flat Campground, travel southwest from the Needles Visitors Center, staying left whenever possible. The trailhead is about 6 miles from the center and is the same trailhead used by four-wheel-drive vehicles on the Elephant Hill Road.

**Confluence Overlook Trail** is 5.5 miles each way and of moderate difficulty. This trail is exposed to the sun and does not have any water along the way (nor at the confluence, where you are 1,000 vertical feet above the rivers below). At the terminus, you'll be able to see the Green and Colorado. The Green River comes from the west, but you'll be able to tell which it is just by its color. The trailhead is at the Big Spring Canyon Overlook.

**Druid Arch** is a moderate hike, 5.1 miles each way, with only 800 feet of elevation change. This arch is strangely geometric and, some say, reminiscent of Stonehenge. The trail crosses over slick rock and through Elephant Canyon. The trailhead is at Elephant Hill Trailhead.

## The Maze

The Maze is one of the most rugged and isolated portions of the lower 48, as it receives very little human traffic. Visitors here must come prepared with plenty of water, gear, and a good spare tire or two. Here the rock is red, orange, yellow, and white, and there are valleys, spires, and dunes. The dominant formations here are thin, rounded fins that partition the area below into chaotic canyons. Because of its remoteness and hectic layout, this area was frequented by Butch Cassidy and other outlaws when they needed a really good place to get lost.

FROM THE CONFLUENCE TRAIL IN CANYONLANDS NATIONAL PARK, IT IS POSSIBLE TO SEE THE GREEN AND COLORADO RIVERS JOIN BEFORE THEY ARE FUNNELED INTO THE WORLD-FAMOUS WHITE WATER OF CATARACT CANYON BEFORE FINALLY ARRIVING IN LAKE POWELL.

Amiee Maxwell

Amiee Maxwell

IN THE NEEDLES SECTION OF
CANYONLANDS NATIONAL PARK, THE
JOINT TRAIL WINDS THROUGH NARROW
SANDSTONE PASSAGEWAYS ALONG ITS
ROUTE.

**Horseshoe Canyon** has many different access roads, none of which are easily passable or require less than 30 miles of dirt road driving. However, this canyon includes the Great Gallery, a world-famous pictograph wall with life-sized (and larger than life-sized) figures. Other rock art is also present in the canyon and dates back as far as 2,000 years. Camping is allowed on BLM lands only (at the canyon rim) and not anywhere within the canyon itself. Inquire with the Park Service for specific recommendations.

**Spanish Bottoms Trail** is only 2.75 miles long, but it is steep. It departs from the Standing Rocks area to the shores of the Colorado River at Cataract Canyon. This canyon is one of the most famous canyons in the Southwest—even in the United States. Cataract includes two of North America's biggest drops (rapids called Big Drop One and Big Drop Two). The river was recorded in 1984 as reaching volumes of more than 115,000 cubic feet per second. This section of river is a spectacular site, as it is forced into an incredibly narrow and steep rock chute. It is a very popular white-water rafting destination. Though the water level decreases dramatically in the late summer and fall, the river remains incredibly challenging to navigate, as sharp boulders scattered throughout send spectacularly high roostertails of water into the air and create lethal obstacles and churning holes.

**HORSEBACK RIDING** Horseback riding is a popular way to explore many parts of this park because its remoteness means the inherent need to travel on trails. For horse packers in the area, visit the *Horseback Riding* section of the "Moab" chapter.

# THE FAR SOUTHEAST CORNER: HOVENWEEP, NATURAL BRIDGES, AND LAKE POWELL

## HOVENWEEP NATIONAL MONUMENT

**Hovenweep National Monument** (970-562-4282; www.nps.gov/hove). The vast majority of this national monument is on the other side of the Colorado/Utah border. However, a small island of the monument called the Square Tower is within Utah just west of the border, at the park's "base camp." (There is another site in Utah called Cajon. These ruins are not part of the national monument and are on Navajo reservation land.) The sites in Colorado are Holly, Horseshoe & Hackberry, and Cutthroat Castle. This national monument contains the preserved ruins of six villages dating to the Pueblo era that span roughly 20 miles and are all atop mesas. Some of these structures have multiple floors. Migratory habitation in the area dates back as far as 10,000 years. Permanent residence here began around 1,100 years ago, and so these towers were born.

Utah's **Square Tower Monument** is the park's central area to which all road signs point. From here a 1.5-mile hiking loop departs from this center and tours Little Ruin Canyon. This canyon is where all of the ruins are located; it contains roughly 10 more ruins, the most famous of which are the namesake Hovenweep Castle and Square Tower, and the twin towers. The other ruins are sometimes almost entirely unexcavated and are less frequently visited. The park is open year-round, and the visitors center (located in Colorado) is open 8–6 April through September, 8–5 during the rest of the year.

To get there from most anywhere in Utah, head south on US 191 from I-70, through Moab and Monticellow. About 20 miles after passing Blanding (but just before Bluff), head east on UT 262/Hovenweep Road for about 20 miles to reach the monument. Paved roads exist up to the Square Tower parking, but otherwise the roads are dirt. Some of the noncentral roads can get pretty gnarly, so call ahead for current road conditions. $3 admission for individuals for seven consecutive days, $6 per vehicle. $25 for "Local Passport" pass to Arches, Canyonlands, Hovenweep, and Natural Bridges.

## NATURAL BRIDGES NATIONAL MONUMENT

**Natural Bridges National Monument** (435-692-1234; www.nps.gov/nabr). This is the site of some of the world's best and most well-preserved cliff dwellings. These dwellings are perched on sandstone ledges in the White Canyon. Additionally, there are three natural bridges in the area: Kachina, Sipapu, and Owachomo (from which the park gets its name). A bridge is different from an arch in that it spans a stream or river; an arch does not. Kachina is the newest and most hardy, Sipapu is somewhere in the middle, and the Owachomo is quite a filament in its twilight. A one-way, 9-mile driving loop inside the park tours the bridges: first Sipapu, then Kachina and Owachomo. While no biking is permitted off road at any time, there are three different hiking options. One is an 8-mile loop that connects all three bridges as it tours the canyon bottom. The other two are shorter (about 6 miles each) and tour only two bridges each (Sipapu/Kachina and Kachina/Owachomo). Shorter overlook trails exist, and each is less than 1 mile each way. The most famous dwellings here are at the **Horsecollar Ruin,** which has several structures, some quite large and fairly intact.

There is no backcountry camping allowed in the monument, but a 13-site campground is located just west of the visitors center. Sites are $10 per evening. No reservations are accepted. If the campsite is full, there is infinite primitive camping in the Bureau of Land Management land surrounding the park, with the exception of a 1-mile strip immediately at the park's entrance. The visitors center is open 8–6 April through September, 8–5 during the rest of the year. $6 entrance fee per vehicle.

Natural Bridges can be reached by heading south on US 191 though Moab. In Blanding, head east on UT 95. (If coming from Capitol Reef National Park, Hanksville, or Lake Powell, head south on UT 95.) The park is off UT 95 via Natural Bridges Road (about 40 miles southeast of Lake Powell's northernmost marina, Hite, which is now out of commission due to dropping water levels) and 38 miles west of Blanding. If traveling via UT 261 through the Mexican Hat region, be advised that this road contains a unpaved stretch with grades up to 10 percent. This is quite difficult to pass with RVs and the like.

## LAKE POWELL

**Lake Powell** (www.nps.gov/glca and www.lakepowell.com). This is Utah's largest reservoir, with capacity for up to nearly 63 cubic kilometers of water and a length of 186 miles at capacity. The current 30 cubic kilometers of water sit in Glen Canyon and are contained by the Glen Canyon Dam, at the southwestern tip of the lake. This body of water supplies residents in Colorado, Utah, Wyoming, New Mexico, Arizona, Nevada, and California with water, but it is also the main attraction of the **Glen Canyon National Recreation Area.**

Lake Powell and was named after Major John Wesley Powell. This was the first man of European descent to ever penetrate and document this entire region of North America, beginning in Green River, Wyoming, in May 1869 and reaching the Virgin River on August 30 of the same year. Powell had a deep passion for this land and its native people. He was well known and respected by the Native Americans he encountered along his journeys. He made as second trip in 1871 and 1872 with a set of photographers and cartographers. After these expeditions, he pursued a career of conservation and ethnology.

A vast desert, steep sandstone cliff walls, and almost no towns surround this reservoir. Don't expect shoreside villages or dozens of ways in. In fact, access points are quite limited, and Page, Arizona (at the southwestern tip, along US 89), is the only town on the lake. **Glen Canyon Dam Visitors Center** (928-608-6200; www.nps.gov/glca) is located at the Glen Canyon Dam and has information on the area, as well as views down the 583-foot-tall, 2,280-megawatt dam. This structure was 10 years in the making and was completed in 1966. Water entering from the north does not exit the reservoir for more than seven years. As of the summer of 2008, there was a white "bathtub ring" painting the cliffs 114 feet above the surface of the water. This is caused by reservoir evaporation more rapid than the Colorado River can replenish. The northern portion of the lake can be reached by UT 95, and the middle sections can be reached from the north and south by UT 276, which is connected across the lake by the John Atlantic Burr Ferry (as described below). The trailer-unfriendly Burr Trail Road, a very scenic dirt road with a very steep switchback section, from the north, also connects to this ferry from the northwest and Capitol Reef National Park.

**Lake Powell Resorts and Marinas** (888-896-3829; www.lakepowell.com). This centralized recreation company coordinates rentals and reservations. Many people arrive in Page, Arizona, as it is the largest, closest town to any part of this lake. The Wahweap Marina is the largest such facility and rents all kinds of watercraft. Lake Powell Resorts and Marinas operate shuttles between Wahweap Marina and various locations in Page, Arizona, such as Wal-Mart, Safeway Grocery Store, and the Glen Canyon Visitors Center. Beware: Arizona does not observe daylight savings time. Call for times and to request a ride. No pets allowed on shuttles.

**Individual Marinas and Ferries** are in **Wahweap** (928-645-2433), north of Page, Arizona, on US 89. **Halls Crossing** (435-684-7000) is on the southern shore on UT 276, and **Bullfrog** (435-684-3000) is just northeast of Halls Crossing on the northern shore, on UT 276. Another, **Dangling Rope Marina,** is located on the north shore between Wahweap and Hall's Crossing, but it has no land access. This is a refueling center for those already on the water. The **John Atlantic Burr Ferry** (operated by Kane County: 435-644-5923) connects the two legs of UT 276, split in twain by the reservoir.

AS LAKE POWELL EVAPORATES, IT LEAVES BEHIND A "BATHTUB RING" OF WHITE ON ITS NAVAJO SANDSTONE BASIN; AT TIMES THIS IS MORE THAN 200 FEET ABOVE THE SURFACE OF THE RESERVOIR.

# South-Central Utah

BOULDER AND ESCALANTE

GRAND STAIRCASE–ESCALANTE
NATIONAL MONUMENT

CAPITOL REEF NATIONAL PARK

BRYCE CANYON NATIONAL PARK

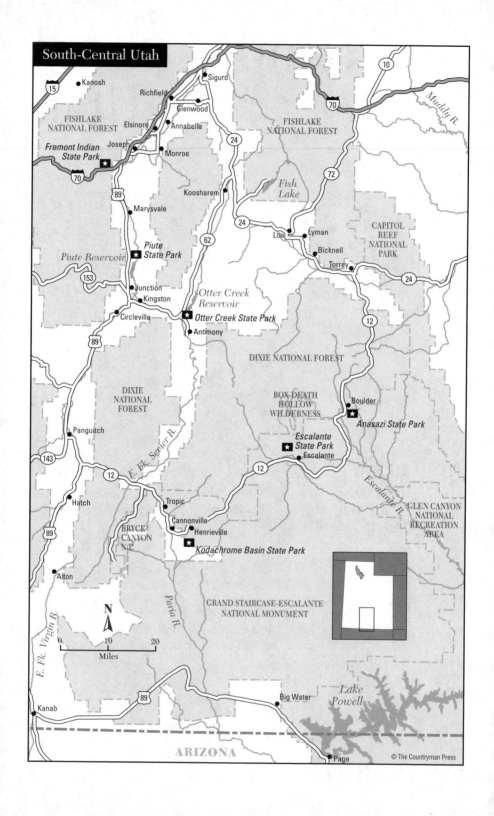

South-Central Utah

© The Countryman Press

# BOULDER AND ESCALANTE

**B**oulder and Escalante are located in Garfield County and are separated by 27 miles of the very picturesque UT 12. These towns are located in one of Utah's most scenic regions and enjoy a large number of visitors for such small settlements. As of the 2000 census, Boulder had a population of just 180, and Escalante had 818 residents. To the northeast is Capitol Reef National Monument; to the southwest is Bryce Canyon National Park. UT 12 connects these two parks and forms the northern border of Grand Staircase–Escalante National Monument. Just a notch farther away is Zion National Park to the northwest, and Lake Powell to the southeast. Also within a day's drive to the east are Moab, Canyonlands National Park, Hovenweep National Monument, and Arches National Park. Boulder and Escalante are right in the center of this dense concentration of national parks, and many people come here simply to relax and enjoy the sights.

GUIDANCE **Interagency Visitors Center in Escalante** (435-826-5499), 755 West Main St., Escalante. This visitors center is a smart cooperative effort of all the area's parks and is a centralized way to obtain information or permits.

**Escalante & Boulder Chamber of Commerce** (435-826-4810; www.escalante -cc.com). This two-town chamber maintains a Web site explaining nearby attractions, area history, and even suggested trip itineraries.

**The Boulder Business Group** (www.boulderutah.com). This Web site was designed specifically to list lodging, dining, and recreation in a visitor-friendly format.

**Garfield County Travel Council** (435-676-1160 or 800-444-6689; www.bryce canyoncountry.com). Garfield County contains most of Grand Staircase–Escalante National Monument, Bryce Canyon National Park and Capitol Reef National Park, as well as a tiny portion of Canyonlands. This Web site has information on all of the national parks and monuments in this region, as well as the lands and towns surrounding them.

**Dixie National Forest Supervisor's Office** (435-865-3200), 1789 North Wedgewood Ln., Cedar City. The Dixie National Forest occupies a huge amount of land in southern Utah, and this office should be able to assist you with specific questions regarding these lands.

ODD ROCK FORMATIONS JUST NORTH OF I-70 ON US 89

**GETTING THERE** *By car:* Boulder and Escalante are located on UT 12, the very scenic highway connecting Bryce Canyon National Park, Grand Staircase–Escalante National Monument, and Capitol Reef National Park. It is east of I-15 about 80 miles, and south of I-70 about 60 miles, as the crow flies. However, this region is accessed on all accounts by winding scenic drives only and is not quickly or directly reached by vehicle.

*By air:* The nearest airports of any reasonable size are in the town of St. George and Salt Lake City. See the *Getting There* sections for the "Salt Lake City" and "St. George" chapters for information on air travel.

**OUTFITTER SERVICES** **Escalante Outfitters** (435-455-0041; www.escalante outfitters.com), 350 Main St., Escalante. This company offers fly-fishing guide services, camping and RV parking, guest cabins, a small store with camping and other adventure gear, sports bars, and some clothing, as well as hard-tail mountain bike rentals, and Esca-latte, a café inside of the store.

**TOURS** **Earth Tours** (435-691-1241; www.earth-tours.com). Guided tours of the region's canyons through this company include hikes and scenic drives. Trips last anywhere from a few hours to multiple days.

**Red Rock & Llamas Tours** (877-955-2627; www.redrocknllamas.com). This unique tour group offers Jeep tours in addition to their namesake llama treks in the Escalante and Glen Canyon areas. Llamas are utilized on the treks to tote gear while you hike without a load. Meals and campsites are prepared for you.

**MEDICAL EMERGENCY** **Richfield's Sevier Valley Medical Center** (435-893-4100), 1000 North Main, Richfield. This facility is only 100 miles away, but it requires more than two and a half hours to reach. Cell service in this region is quite spotty, so be careful and treat your body kindly whilst out and about.

# ✳ To See and Do

**SCENIC BYWAY 12** This is one of the more beautiful highways outside of a national park in all of the United States. The stretch of UT 12 between Escalante and Boulder is called the "Million Dollar Road to Boulder" and was built in 1935 by the CCC. The attractions below are listed in order from south to north and described according to their location relative to the towns of Escalante and Boulder.

### 60 Miles West of Escalante

**Red Canyon,** though not part of Bryce Canyon National Park, could fool you if you didn't know otherwise. This is where UT 12 departs from US 89 and the scenic highway begins. This canyon has deep red colors, cliffs, and hoodoo rock formations, as well as a visitors center (open Memorial Day through Labor Day), hiking and biking trails, viewpoints, and campgrounds. Hiking trails here include the 0.75-mile Arches Trail that passes 15 natural arches, 3-mile Pink Ledges Loop, 8-mile Thunder Mountain Trail, and the 78-mile Grand View Trail. (See the *Hiking and Mountain Biking* section later for more information on the Thunder Mountain and Grand View trails.)

### 50 Miles West of Escalante

**East Fork of the Sevier River** departs from UT 12 and heads south. It runs parallel to (but outside of) Bryce Canyon National Park. This region is what Bryce Canyon would look like had it not eroded away to show its brilliant subterranean layers. This canyon's innards have remained covered with evergreen forests, grass, mountain biking trails, and hiking trails. Dozens of tributaries drain the Paunsaugunt Plateau as they head toward the East Fork. Though not as spectacular as Bryce, the Dixie National Forest has plenty of fishing and camping opportunities, as well as being in the vicinity of the Tropic Reservoir.

### 46 Miles West of Escalante

**Bryce Canyon National Park** (see the "Bryce Canyon National Park" chapter).

### 34 Miles West of Escalante

**Kodachrome Basin State Park** (435-679-8562; www.stateparks.utah.gov). Kodachrome Basin State Park is one of the first attractions along this scenic byway. Inside the park is a network of seven main hiking trails (that can be linked for more variations) and two campgrounds. The sandstone chimneys and smooth cliffs of this park range from gray to red and orange. These formations formed as tectonic activity created pressure that injected liquid sand into fissures whose surroundings have since eroded away. Features are sometimes quite peculiar and include the more famous **Grosvenor Arch,** a gothic-looking gray double arch with two openings

CASTO CANYON IS YET ANOTHER TRAIL OFF UT 12 AND US 89, SHARED BY MOUNTAIN BIKERS, HIKERS, AND ATV USERS, WITH VIEWS OF GLOBULAR ROCK FORMATIONS CALLED HOODOOS.

Kami Hardcastle

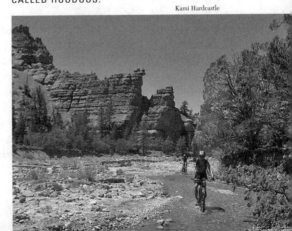

surrounded by more white Navajo sandstone cliffs. The entrance to **Cottonwood Narrows** is 4 miles after Grosvernor Arch. Cottonwood Narrows is a tight canyon that is of interest for about a mile's walk downstream. Do not attempt to travel the dirt roads in the park if there is looming precipitation. The park is 9 miles south of UT 12. $6 per vehicle; $16 for camping. Open daily 6 AM–10 PM.

## Western Escalante

**Escalante Petrified Forest State Park** (435-826-4466 or 800-322-3770; www .stateparks.utah.gov), 710 North Reservoir Rd. This park contains, in addition to a petrified forest, 1,000-year-old artifacts left behind by Fremont Indians, two short hiking trails, Wild Hollow Reservoir with canoe rentals, and a visitors center with dinosaur fossils and petrified wood samples. Many of the pieces are actually quite camping.

## Central Escalante

**Posey Lake Scenic Byway** starts in Escalante as 300 East/Pine Creek Road and heads north out of town, terminating in Bicknell after 40 miles of dirt driving. Along the way is Posey Lake and access to Hell's Backbone Road (see the description below in *3 Miles West of Boulder*). Posey Lake is an acre of natural mountain lake surrounded by evergreen and aspen trees about 16 miles north of town. Camping at this lake is spread across 22 sites ($8 per site; call for reservations: 877-444-6777) on the southern side of the lake. Trout fishing is popular here, but motorboats are prohibited. An elevation of 8,600 feet makes the water a bit cooler in temperature than you would expect.

**Smoky Mountain Scenic Byway** is a 78-mile dirt road that gains excellent views of Lake Powell, Kaiparowits Plateau, Bryce Canyon, and Navajo Mountain. The most peculiar feature of this road is the smoke that sometimes rises from the ground as subterranean coalfields smolder, just as they have for more than 100 years. This road, which heads south from Escalante, is only recommended for high-clearance vehicles and dry conditions. To access this drive, turn south from Main Street onto 500 West, and continue on along this street as it curves out of town.

## 5.5 Miles East of Escalante

**Devil's Garden/Hole in the Rock Road** is a series of globular rock formations sometimes with thin, drippy filaments that form arches. The sandstone takes on many appearances: Sometimes it is buffed smooth, other times it is swirled and patterned. There are no trails here, so visitors have the freedom to wander around among the formations.

Devil's Garden is a stop along Hole in the Rock Road, a historically significant lane dating back to 1879. This road, almost 60 miles of dirt, was the path a group of Mormons took in 1879 as they sought to find a shorter route to the San Juan Mission. Travel toward that region was otherwise completely blocked by the very sheer walls of the Glen Canyon. Though this passageway helped them avoid the typical 1,200-foot drop to the Colorado River below, they still had to navigate a 40-foot vertical drop. To solve this problem, they constructed an elaborate road that would help them pass. The last 300 vertical feet of this road are now underneath Lake Powell, but the majority of this historic route remains.

To get to Devil's Garden and Hole in the Rock Road, head north 5.5 miles from Escalante (south 22 miles of Boulder) on UT 12 and head southeast on Hole in the

Rock Road. Travel for just less than 13 miles on this dirt road, where you turn right (south) onto Devil's Garden Road. If you wish to check out the Hole in the Rock Road, continue straight. The road stays acceptable for passenger vehicles until around mile 40, at which point it steepens; at around mile 50, high clearance is required.

### 14.5 Miles East of Esclante/11.5 Miles West of Boulder

**Calf Creek Recreation Area** is another naturally beautiful area in the Grand Staircase–Escalante National Monument accessed by UT 12. A trail just less than 3 miles long that descends to the Lower Calf Creek Falls, a 125-foot-tall veil of water terminating in a broad and clear pool. This nature trail has a brochure, which illustrates flora, fauna, ancient ruins, and pictographs on the way. Don't be alarmed by scantily clad people sunning themselves in this pool underneath the falls. The creek has created a lush little ecosystem that is quite pleasant. (As this trail is fairly sandy, gaiters or high socks are recommended.) There is an upper falls 3 miles upstream that has a much more challenging hike to reach. $3 day-fee for parking.

Kami Hardcastle

THE 130-FOOT CALF CREEK FALLS IS A POPULAR HIKING DESTINATION WHOSE TRAILHEAD IS ALONG UT 12, ROUGHLY HALFWAY BETWEEN BOULDER AND ESCALANTE. THE POOL BENEATH THE FALLS IS PLEASANT, SHOULD YOU CHOOSE TO TAKE A DIP.

### 3 Miles West of Boulder

**Hell's Backbone Road** (Forest Service Rd. 153) is one of the state's most preposterous roads. This little strip of asphalt winds its way along the very ridge of a small mountain as it descends into the distance. Farther off the shoulder of this mountain, steep canyons cut even more deeply into the hillsides, making the road seem even more precarious. Though it is perfectly safe for sober drivers, it has a huge amount of exposure, as there are dizzying drops immediately off the road. The road is in great condition, and unless you're a terrible driver, there is no danger involved. The vertigo just adds a bit of excitement to the drive. This road is not recommended in winter or during bad weather.

### Boulder

**Anasazi State Park** (435-335-7308), 460 North UT 12, Boulder. This park is located right outside Boulder and is the site of one of the largest prehistoric Anasazi villages in the country today. Experts believe the village was occupied 800 to 950 years ago. In the state park there are partially excavated buildings and a small museum. Park admission is $5.

**Boulder Mountain/Aquarius Plateau** is the very elevated area roughly between UT 12, UT 24, and Forest Service Road 154/Pine Creek Road, and the towns of Grover, Teasdale, Escalante, and Boulder. The 50,000-some acres of this uplift are the highest timbered plateau in North America. The peak of Boulder Mountain itself is the highest in the Dixie National Forest, at 11,322 feet. Similar to the Uintas, this region is a significantly large, high-elevation area with many lakes. **Blind Lake** is the largest of roughly 75 lakes in this plateau, at 50 surface acres. From the tops and eastern slopes of this mountain are great views of the wild and remote **Henry Mountains** to the east (described in the "Bryce Canyon National Park" chapter). They are greatly higher than its surroundings, topping out at 11,370 feet. Other views include **Circle Cliffs** to the southeast, **Navajo Mountain** beyond these cliffs, **50-mile Mountain,** and the **Waterpocket Fold** of **Capitol Reef National Park** to the east. This area is managed by the **Dixie National Forest** (435-865-3700). Boulder Mountain is penetrated by dozens of interconnected dirt roads of varying quality. Because of the height of this range, the recreation season here is abbreviated. Snow makes access all but impossible except between late June and October during most years.

**Burr Trail** is a scenic back road connecting the Bullfrog Marina to Boulder. Though this road is only 74 miles, it takes at least two or three hours to traverse. This historic road is generally dirt (for historic purposes), though an ownership issue rendered some of it paved, to the chagrin of many. This pavement is hardly noticeable, though, and travelers along this road enjoy scenery uninterrupted by civilization. The Muley Twist section, "so narrow it could twist a mule," actually in Capitol Reef National Park, is the famous section for which this road is named. This section contains an incredibly steep section of road that switches back and forth up the walls of an improbably steep and narrow canyon. This is where John Burr used to drive his cattle from summer grazing above to warmer winter grounds below. The Burr Trail connects to Boulder directly as UT 1668.

## ✳ Outdoor Activities

**CANYONEERING** **Neon Canyon** has some good fun to offer, including lots of swimming, many rappels, pools, and quirky corkscrew-type tunnels. **The Golden**

THE HENRY MOUNTAINS, LOCATED SOUTH OF HANKSVILLE AND NORTH OF LAKE POWELL, IS ONE OF UTAH'S REMOTEST MOUNTAIN RANGES AND IS HOME TO A FREE-ROAMING HERD OF BISON.

**Cathedral** is a famous room with three ceiling holes. This is located 17 miles south of UT 12 on Hole in the Rock Road. Take a left turn onto a dirt road, following signs for Egypt. Just 10 miles down this road is the well-marked trailhead. Carefully study detailed topographic maps before entering.

**Peek-a-boo and Spooky Gulch** are part of a network of slot canyons very near to each other. Spooky is a very, very narrow passageway through which you can wiggle completely. Peak-a-boo is an easy walk through pleasantly winding passages that is reached by a challenging drive. Neither is technical, but both are fun. (There is more information listed under *Hiking and Mountain Biking*, below.)

**FISHING Alpine Anglers** (801-425-3660 or 888-484-3331; www.fly-fishing-utah .net). Trips hosted by this company take place all over south-central Utah, from Capitol Reef to Boulder Mountain. They do hunting and horse packing trips as well.

**Boulder Mountain,** part of the Aquarius Plateau, is high and remote enough to support healthy trout populations in its streams and lakes. Because of its elevation, these waters stay cool enough for this variety of fish. In this area there are roughly 80 lakes, half of which are regularly stocked. Small streams here are also numerous. The highest concentration of fishable bodies of water is along the eastern slope of this uplift, near UT 12. Forest Service roads 149, 153, 165, 179, and 521 access the most streams and lakes.

**Boulder Mountain Fly-Fishing** (435-335-7306; www.bouldermountainflyfish ing.com). This is one of the area's most recommended fly shops, with an extensive Web site that has in-depth information on local streams, lakes, history, and species.

**East Fork of the Sevier** is to the west of, and parallel to, the western edge of Bryce Canyon National Park. Because many visitors in the area are drawn to the more famous national parks, this canyon sees significantly reduced traffic. There are many tributaries feeding this fairly straight river, and the Tropic Reservoir is right in the center of the valley. The most common fish here are cutthroat, brown, and rainbow trout.

**Pine Lake** has excellent fishing and a Forest Service campground. This is on the southwestern end of the remote Boulder Mountain area but is one of its more developed lakes, with a boat ramp, official campsites, and a fish cleaning station. At junction of UT 12 and 63, head north for 11 miles and follow Forest Service Road 132 to Pine Lake for 6 more miles.

**Posey Lake** is a picturesque mountain lake located 15 miles northwest of Escalante. The lake is popular for trout fishing and has a Forest Service campground. Dirt roads that connect to other lakes, reservoirs, and campgrounds in the surrounding Dixie National Forest make for excellent mountain bike rides. Motorboats are forbidden at Posey. From here is access to the Great Western Trail. This is also a short hike away from Tule Lake. Another hiking trail leads to a lookout on the mountainside. The road to Posey Lake is closed in winter.

**HIKING AND MOUNTAIN BIKING Box–Death Hollow Wilderness,** through which the Hell's Backbone Road/Forest Service Road 153 runs, has two canyons that are frequently hiked. Box Canyon has been carved by Pine Creek and is a very narrow canyon accessible only from the lower end. Death Hollow is the

Craig Bowden

THE HENRY MOUNTAINS ARE ACCESSED ONLY BY UNMARKED DIRT ROADS. HIGH
CLEARANCE IS ADVISABLE, AS ROAD CONDITIONS CAN BE VERY MARGINAL.

canyon formed by Death Hollow Creek—known as such because of a herd of cattle that died attempting to cross during high water decades ago. Both canyons
should be avoided if any rain is in the region; they fill rapidly and violently.

**Canyons of the Escalante** is the catchall phrase locals use to describe the many
tributary canyons in the Escalante River system. These vary in size and character
from one to the next. Each cuts through standstone, but some have tall and sheer
walls, while others have short and rounded walls; some are open and filled with
vegetation; others are incredibly narrow. Depending on the season, many of these
canyons might have a fair amount of water running through them, but they are
generally passable (except in cases of active precipitation). Because the canyons
themselves are the trails, there is no actual development of the pathways; rather,
you simply follow and explore these riverbeds. There are a number of different
places to access these rivers. You can access the Escalante River in the town of
Escalante, from the UT 12 Bridge (14 miles east of Escalante), Calf Creek Falls
area (14.5 miles east of Escalante), as well as along the Burr Trail, Hole in the
Rock Road, and the Egypt Bench Road, among others. During peak season, you
can recognize popular hiking canyons by cars parked alongside roads at access
points.

The **Grand View Trail** is serious business. This trail shares the same trailhead
(just west of the Red Canyon Visitors Center) as Thunder Mountain and heads
generally south for 75 miles. Because of its length and scenery, it is popular for
mountain bikers, horse packers, and backpackers. This trail trends due south for
about half of its length before curving east, and then north toward Bryce Canyon
National Park. Along the way it intersects with several trails, such as Badger Creek,
Skunk Creek, and the Paunsaugunt OHV trail system. Bring a detailed trail map if
you intend to tour much of this trail.

**Peak-a-boo and Spooky Gulch** is a short but interesting and moderately challenging hike through a slot canyon. The recommended route is clockwise: north

through Peek-a-boo, east on connecting flatlands, and down and back through Spooky Gulch and Dry Fork to the start. Peek-a-boo is recognized by steps carved into the stone at the beginning of the route. The entire loop is just less than 4 miles and is a great half-day activity. Some water can exist in these canyons even during dry spells, so be prepared to get wet. To get there, head 5.5 miles east of Escalante (22 miles west of Boulder) on UT 12 and go south on Hole in the Rock Road for 26 miles. Turn northeast (left) onto Dry Fork Road, staying left at the first branch (which comes up quickly). The trailhead is signed.

**Posey Lake,** just 15 miles north of Boulder in the Dixie National Forest. This area has a lot of opportunities for hiking. Just above the campground is the old fire lookout tower, which has great views of the surrounding area for little effort.

**Red Canyon,** 60 miles west of Escalante on UT 12. The Red has a few different options for longer hikes and rides. **Thunder Mountain** is a steep, 8-mile trail that requires skill and cool under pressure. This trail has great views of the nearby canyon country and mountains but also a lot of vertigo-inducing exposure. Part of the reason for the expansive views is the sparse vegetation; keep this in mind with respect to sun exposure and heat. You can make a loop by taking the **Red Canyon Trail** (paved, running parallel to UT 12) and Fremont Trail up, and saving Thunder Mountain for the downhill for a total of 14.5 miles. This trail traverses some interesting terrain with red, orange, and white soils; Bryce Canyon–like rock formations; and bald ridges. To do this loop, start at the **Thunder Mountain Trailhead,** but take the Red Canyon Trail east, then turn south onto the Fremont Trail, and finally loop south to do Thunder Mountain as a downhill. (Another option, good for families, is to take the paved Red Canyon Trail only. Its total length is 5.5 miles, and it climbs only 1,000 feet, a very gradual elevation gain.)

THE THUNDER MOUNTAIN TRAIL IN RED CANYON CAN BE RIDDEN AS A LOOP; ITS TRAILHEAD IS ON UT 12 ABOUT 3 MILES EAST OF US 89.

Kami Hardcastle

# ✳ Lodging

Though this region of Utah is among its least populated, it has grown accustomed to hosting people from around the world. The lodging and dining options reflect this—though there are not many fine establishments, those that are here have good style. There are also scattered mom-and-pop motel-type joints in Boulder and Escalante, as well as in the other small towns—some much nicer than others. Though these towns are small, their guest beds are limited, so advanced reservations are highly recommended.

**LODGES** ⌁ **Boulder Mountain Lodge** (800-556-3446; www.boulder-utah.com), 20 North UT 12, Boulder. This eco-friendly lodge is located on its own private plot, set back from traffic. This lodge has a pleasantly rustic exterior true to its Western ranch location, but it has fully modernized rooms and guesthouses that have been redone to complement the original structure. The property also contains a 15-acre lake with bird sanctuary, around which this campus of lodging is clustered. There is one main building with a few satellite options. Each has a very tasteful and modern interior, and a natural feel with muted colors and quality stonework and timber. With **Hell's Backbone Grill** on the grounds, this lodge shares space with what some consider to be southern Utah's best restaurant. This serially award-winning restaurant takes greens from its own gardens on the property. $75–$175.

**BED-AND-BREAKFASTS Canyons Bed & Breakfast** (866-526-9667; www.canyonsbnb.com), 120 East Main St., Escalante. This bed-and-breakfast is a cozy lodging option right in town. Though it is located on Main Street, this town is so small that the hubbub is generally nonthreatening. The building is a 1905 wood-sided farmhouse, and there are only three guest rooms in this establishment. Because of this, there is no crowding, and there is a reduced potential for loud neighbors and wedding parties. $115–$125.

**Escalante's Grand Staircase Bed & Breakfast Inn** (435-826-4890; www.escalantebnb.com). This motel/bed-and-breakfast hybrid is the perfect solution for those who want modern, clean, and attractive accommodations without trying to stay in the nicest or priciest option. One of the high points of this establishment are the changing "cook's choice" breakfasts that feature fresh fruit, eggs, griddle items with homemade fruit sauces, teas, and coffee. The other high point is that, despite the name "bed-and-breakfast," your door opens to the outside, and you need not walk through a lobby or past a desk coming and going. Rooms have new, Western-style, thick pine furniture and Southwestern color schemes. $135 and up.

**Slot Canyons Inn Bed and Breakfast** (866-889-8375; www.slotcanyonsinn.com), 3680 West UT 12, 4 miles west of Escalante. This modern pair of buildings, constructed in 2006, is located on 160-acre lot at which North Creek flows into the Escalante River. There are two buildings that make up this inn: a private cabin and the main inn itself. The inn is a modern facility with plenty of light and clean lines, but décor to complement its Southwest environs. This cabin is built into the hillside in the most aesthetic way possible, among a hill littered with plate-shaped boulders, and against a backdrop of evergreen-covered, red-soil hills. The cabin actually dates back to 1899, but it was fully restored and moved across the property in 1999. It has 1,600 square feet of living space in addition to its sitting porch. The cabin is now completely modern with plumbing, electricity, and tasteful, mountain-style décor. Near the inn is a Brigham Young University archaeological dig in which artifacts of Anasazi, Fremont, Paleoaxchaic, Numic, and Archaic peoples are being uncovered. $150 and up.

HOTELS AND MOTELS **Circle D Motel** (435-826-4297; www.escalante circledmotel.com), 475 West Main St., Escalante. This is a super basic motel with very cheap rates. However, for such an inexpensive option in an otherwise tourist-priced region, this simple hotel is quite appealing. $45 and up.

**Pole's Place Motel** (800-730-7422; www.boulderutah.com/polesplace), 465 North UT 12, Boulder. This 12-room motel is owned by a family that has been in the area since the 1880s. Low-key, relatively inexpensive lodging just across from Anasazi State Park. The Western-themed building also includes a gift shop and **Pole's Place Eatery** (see *Eating Out*). $80–$120.

**Prospector Inn** (435-826-4653; www .prospectorinn.com), 380 East Main St., Escalante. This hotel is one of the biggest in the area, with 50 guest rooms and an on-site, small-town café-style restaurant. Locally owned, this has some small-town quirkiness and mountain-man flair to its style. In the hotel is a taxidermied bear and endless pine planks. Lodging here is very no-frills, though, and "deluxe rooms" will not be what you had imagined. However, the hotel is clean and quite affordable. $50 and up.

**Red River Ranch** (435-425-3322 or 800-205-6343), 2900 West UT 24, Teasdale. This is certainly one of the area's finest lodging options, located just north of Boulder and near the intersection of UT 12 and UT 24. In fact, *Travel + Leisure* called this one of the country's best 25 lodges. This lodge is rustic Western, but in a most attractive, elegant style, with deluxe bedding, fine stonework, and buffed-out wood. Their on-site restaurant, the **Cliffstone Restaurant** (see *Dining Out*), serves breakfast, lunch, and dinner. $175–$250.

## ✳ Where to Eat

All restaurants' hours are susceptible to change during the tourist season. Particularly if you are visiting during winter, be sure to call ahead to verify that you can be seated. Most restaurants open daily from mid-April through mid-October.

DINING OUT **Burr Trail Grill** (435-335-7503; www.burrtrailgrill.com). This restaurant serves casual fare, but in the atmosphere of local art. The menu includes burgers, sandwiches, and salads, as well as espresso drinks, wine, and beer. The grill is annexed to the Outpost, which sells jewelry, books, and the like. $9 and up.

**Café Diablo** (435-425-3070; www .cafediablo.net), 599 West Main St., Torrey. Dinner is served seven days a week. This restaurant combines contemporary cooking styles with South-western flair to produce dishes such as

BARREL CACTUS BLOOMS IN THE SPRING IN THE ESCALANTE AREA.

Kami Hardcastle

fire-roasted pork tenderloin, pumpkin seed trout, turkey relleno, and medallions of New York strip steak with squash. The entrées are a bit pricy, but considering the location and ingredients, not egregious. Patio dining is available when the weather allows. Entrées $21–$29.

**Cliffstone Restaurant** (435-425-3322 or 800-205-6343), 2900 West UT 24, Teasdale. This is located at the Red River Ranch (see *Hotels and Motels*) and serves breakfast, lunch, and dinner. (Weddings and large events sometimes interrupt this otherwise consistent schedule, so call ahead to be sure there will be a meal during your visit.) Dinner is really for the carnivores, with offerings from stuffed chicken to baby back ribs. Do not expect the choices to be numerous, as this area is very remote; until the 1940s, all of Boulder's mail was still delivered by mule, and it was not until 1985 that the road over Boulder Mountain was actually paved. Dinner is worth the trip; lunch, though good, is not on the same level as dinner. $20 and up.

↬ **Hell's Backbone Grill** (435-335-7464; www.hellsbackbonegrill.com), 20 North UT 12, Boulder. This is far and away the region's most acclaimed restaurant, whose reputation has permeated the state and, to some extent, the region. The food here is all fresh and local when possible. You might wonder: How do they get a constant supply of fresh, heirloom vegetables so far out in the desert? In fact, whenever possible, all of the herbs and vegetables—used as ingredients, sides, or for

sauces—have been grown organically on the property. The menu changes regularly to accommodate the changing seasons and has Pueblo, Southwestern, Western, and faint contemporary American influences. Beers are from Utah, and the wine list contains organic selections. This ecosensitivity highlights the fragility of the area, and the respect required to keep it beautiful. Filet mignon, trout, buffalo, and pork are some of the main-course staples. $13–$30.

**Mesa Grill** (435-335-7447; www .bouldermesa.com), 155 East Burr Trail, Boulder. You would never guess it from the outside, but this restaurant has one of nicer menus in town, with seafood including lobster, jumbo shrimp, and clams all prepared in contemporary American style. The menu, though good, is severely reduced in the off-season because of lack of ingredient flow. Lunch includes sandwiches and burgers, some with a twist: marinated turkey burger and Polish sandwich on rye. The atmosphere is elegant but without snobbery, and the food, though delicious, has been prepared to showcase the fresh ingredients—not to add 3,000 calories to your day. Breakfasts are prepared with the same style and touch as dinners. $13–$25.

**EATING OUT Pole's Place Eatery** (800-730-7422; www.boulderutah .com), 465 North UT 12, Boulder. This small restaurant offers a quick bite to eat, with burgers (beef and veggie), milk shakes, and salads. Cuisine is simple. $7–$15.

# GRAND STAIRCASE–ESCALANTE NATIONAL MONUMENT

The Grand Staircase is part of the Colorado Plateau, a region that occupies 130,000 square miles and spans the four-corners area of Utah, Colorado, Arizona, and New Mexico. This incredibly dramatic uplift is a result of major tectonic activity along Hurricane Fault (running east–west just south of Cedar City) and Sevier Fault (running east–west just north of Kanab). In this region there is more than a vertical mile of exposed sandstone strata, eroded and torn to the surface. Deposited over hundreds of millions of years, this sandstone belongs to many different epochs and has a huge spectrum of colors and qualities resulting in a few distinct series of major cliff bands, as well as many extremely beautiful and distinct mini ecosystems.

Starting from the southern and lowest point on the staircase, the major cliff systems that compose the Grand Staircase as it rises from Kanab to Lake Powell are the Chocolate, Vermilion, White, Gray, and Pink cliffs. Each sandstone erodes in its own way, and the region has much more diversity than one could imagine. Atop the Vermilion Cliffs is the Kaiparowits Plateau to the east and Coral Pink Sand Dunes to the west. Zion Canyon (of Zion National Park) cuts deeply into the plateau atop the White Cliffs. Bryce Canyon itself has eroded into the highest plateau of them all, the Paunsaugunt Plateau. The northernmost edge of this uplift ends in a dramatic step down; fault activity and erosion have shorn these strata, resulting in a 6,000-foot quick drop from Brian Head down to Cedar City.

Fremont and Kayenta Anasazi cultures lived in this region roughly 1,000 years ago and left behind evidence of their existence in the form of pictographs and artifacts. Later the Southern Paiute people visited the region nomadically, but they left behind little to illustrate their existence here. As you hike through the canyons, much more hospitable than the high desert plateaus above, you will see many examples of the old petroglyphs, dwellings, granaries, and more. It is highly illegal and selfish to disturb any artifacts, so don't touch.

Though Mormons had begun to settle in Utah's southwestern region in the 1850s and 1860s, this region remained long untouched. In 1866 there is record of European contact by James Andrus, a military captain. He had entered the Paria River drainage as he chased Paiutes but did not document the region with any seriousness. Powell, despite his tremendous observation skills, had failed to recognize the Escalante River as a significant tributary, and so bypassed it altogether on

Amiee Maxwell

PETRIFIED SAND DUNES AT SUNSET IN GRAND STAIRCASE–ESCALANTE NATIONAL MONUMENT

his first expedition in 1869. However, on his second expedition, Powell sent an exploratory party out on a mission to recover a missing boat. Once on land, they realized that they stood above an entirely new river system and named it the Escalante River after Friar Silvester Valez Escalante, an explorer from 100 years prior.

Because of its mazelike, steep-walled canyons, this region has historically been a major impediment to travelers. For this reason, the Hole in the Rock Expedition (see *To See and Do* in the "Boulder and Escalante" chapter) went to discover an accessible route across the Colorado River. They ended up doing some major stone carving and had to lower their wagons several dozen feet with ropes. Even still, the road is still dirt, and the last bit is now covered by Lake Powell.

Today Grand Staircase–Escalante National Monument contains more than 1.9 million acres. It is bounded by the Utah-Arizona border to the south and Glen Canyon National Recreation Area and Lake Powell to the east. It reaches almost to Kanab and touches Bryce Canyon on its western edge, and follows Scenic Byway 12 all the way to Capitol Reef National Park, its northeastern border. Administered by the Bureau of Land Management (BLM), it contains the Circle Cliffs, Kaiparowits Plateau, the Escalante River and its tributaries, Vermilion Cliffs, Paria River, and many, many more features.

Most of the monument is accessed from dirt roads along UT 12, though US 89 provides some access into the southern portion. Both of these highways are popular, as UT 12 is one of the nation's most scenic highways, and US 89 is the access road for the Grand Canyon's northern rim.

The monument is divided into three roughly equal parts (from west to east): Grand Staircase, Kaiparowits Plateau, and Escalante Canyons. The central **Kaiparowits Plateau** has mixed sage, grasslands, and canyons. The eastern portion of the monument is characterized by narrow sandstone canyons as drained by the **Escalante River** system. This region as a whole has historically been more rugged and remote that most of Utah, and the Escalante River itself was the final river to be fully documented and mapped in the lower 48. Its slot canyons, because of their unique beauty and nearness to scenic UT 12, are quite popular. The **Stair-**

case region is in the southern portion, near US 89 and Kanab, and because of its wild and colorful beauty, is popular for sightseeing motorists. Some hiking and mountain biking take place here as well (though mountain bikers are bound to stay on the dirt roads), as this portion of the park enjoys many vistas of Lake Powell and its canyons. The Paria River has slot canyons similar to those of the Escalante River, but this area's more severe remoteness makes this less popular for safety and convenience reasons.

Though there is no fee to enter the monument, backcountry permits (also usually free) are required for any overnight trips and can be obtained at any of the visitors centers, listed below in the *Guidance* section. Hiking in the Calf Creek area or the Paria Wilderness is not free, and permits must be purchased at the visitors centers.

GUIDANCE For such a massive landmass, there is a correspondingly substantial number of visitors centers. This is great because there is quite an amount of ground to cover to get from one end of the monument to the other.

**Anasazi State Park Museum** (435-335-7382), 460 North UT 12, Boulder. This state park is immediately in Boulder. For more information, see the *To See and Do* section in the "Boulder and Escalante" chapter. *Scenic Byway 12*, page XX.

**Big Water Visitors Center** (435-675-3200), 100 Upper Revolution Way, Big Water. Open 9–6 during peak season; open 9–5 November through March. The focus of this center is on paleontology, with fossils and a mural interpreting what life may have been like in the region millions of years ago.

**Bureau of Land Management Grand Staircase–Escalante National Monument Visitors Center** (435-644-4680), 745 East US 89, Kanab. Open daily 8–5. This visitors center is located near the southwestern edge of the monument and has some displays illustrating the geologic history, including a three-dimensional topographic model of the monument.

**Cannonville Visitors Center** (435-826-5640), 10 Center St., Cannonville. Open 8–4:30 daily; closed mid-March through mid-November. This BLM center focuses on human history and its impact on the region, as well as the region's impact on it. This has yet another topographic model of the region.

**Garfield County Travel Council** (435-676-1160 or 800-444-6689; www.bryce canyoncountry.com). Check this Web site or call for information on all of the national parks and monuments in the "South-Central Utah" section of the book, as well as the lands and towns surrounding them.

**Interagency Visitors Center** (435-826-5499), 755 West Main St., Escalante. This center also has a topographic model of the monument, and displays and exhibits dedicated to the biology and ecology of the area.

GETTING THERE Grand Staircase–Escalante National Monument is reasonably near I-15 and I-70, if you were to draw a straight line, but still at least 100 miles away along winding roads. UT 12 runs between Escalante and Boulder (as described above) and is one of the most famous and beautiful roads in Utah. It bends and weaves quite a bit, but its general trend is from southwest to northwest. This road serves as the most common access point to the monument and forms its northern border. In the southern part of the region, US 89 departs from Kanab and comes into the region's western half. The southeastern portion of the monument is bounded by Lake Powell, and access here is limited.

MEDICAL EMERGENCY See the *Medical Emergency* section in the "Boulder and Escalante" chapter.

## ✳ Outdoor Activities

BIKING & BIKE RENTALS Grand Staircase-Escalante National Monument is not necessarily suited to biking; it has very little pavement for road biking and very few trails for mountain biking. Rather, its slot canyons are perfect for hikers, and dirt roads great for cars. If you're willing to bike on dirt roads, **Cottonwood Road, Circle Cliffs/Wolverine Loop, 50-Mile Bench Road,** and **Paria Breaks/Sand Gulch Loop** are some of the more scenic journeys. But if you're looking for single track, this is not your bread and butter; even if you found a passable trail, bikes are not allowed off-road.

**Egypt Road** begins about 16.5 miles south of UT 12 on Hole in the Rock Road. Along this road are good vistas of the Escalante River system. Though you will bypass a trailhead en route, do not leave the road; mountain bikers are not allowed off-road.

**Escalante Outfitters** (435-455-0041; www.escalanteoutfitters.com), 350 Main St., Escalante. This store rents hard-tail mountain bikes, in addition to their retail selection that includes fly-fishing, camping, and other adventure gear. They also offer camping and RV parking, and the Esca-latte, a café, is inside the store.

**Nipple Creek Loop** starts at the eastern end of the town of Big Water, just north of Lake Powell on US 89. This is a dirt road loop, so mileage will tick by fairly quickly—but the loops are quite big regardless. Nipple Creek is the shortest loop. Head north along Nipple Creek Wash. After 14 miles, you will reach Nipple Butte. From here, you can return to the car in 12 miles via Tibet Canyon. If you want to do a longer loop in the same area, check out the Smoky Mountain Loop (below). This ride provides great views of Lake Powell and Smoky Mountain, which derives its name from its smoldering subterranean coalfields. Though these roads form a simple system, it would still be a good idea to bring a detailed map with you.

**Smoky Mountain Loop** also begins in Big Water. Locate Warm Creek Road (which becomes Smoky Hollow Road) and head east; this will bring you into the Glen Canyon National Recreation Area. After about 15 miles, you will come to a junction with Smoky Mountain Road. If you continue along Warm Creek/Smoky Hollow Road, you will enjoy especially good views of Lake Powell.

BOATING **Escalante River.** This river is not often run, though it is possible. The window of time when the river is passable is short, usually from the middle of May through the middle of June, depending on the year's snowpack and rate of spring thaw. Consensus is that 50 cubic feet per second is the best flow—enough to be able to make it through, but not so much as to be particularly hazardous. Permits are required and can be obtained at any visitors center listed in *Guidance*, above (with the exception of the Anasazi State Park visitors center). The put-in is on the northern end of the monument, 14.5 miles east of Escalante on UT 12, and the take-out is at Bullfrog Marina on Lake Powell. Be sure to have arranged for a shuttle to get off the lake.

**HIKING** Rain is troublesome for hikers in this region, whether in a canyon or atop slick rock. In canyons flash flooding is a very real and lethal threat. Even if rain is not falling in the immediate vicinity, rain anywhere in a river system can lead to a sudden surge in water flow; check the forecast before you go. On slick rock, rain changes the friction and strength of rock.

**Hackberry Canyon** is a 21-mile trip in total, usually done in multiple days as a backpacking excursion. However, this canyon, cooled by the stream and shaded by its walls, can also offer a good short hike, as you can turn around at any point on the way. Many side canyons present excursions along the way as well. Take US 89 east from Kanab. At mile marker 18, go north on Cottonwood Road/BLM Road 400. After 14.5 miles of northward travel, park at the trailhead.

**Lick Wash** is a bit more secluded than Hackberry Canyon if only because you must drive a bit farther along dirt roads to reach it. Either way, the extra driving might be worth it during peak season in order to avoid frequent human encounters. This canyon has just more than 5 miles of hiking each way and is usually dry. Along the way are arches, an old cabin, and other points of interest. To approach this canyon, get to Glendale on US 89, near the western portion of the monument. Head east on Bench Road/300 North. Continue 15 miles to a junction, at which point there is an informational kiosk. Keep going northeast on the road now called Skutumpah Road/BLM Road 500; this is not passable when wet. In 14.8 more miles, head south on BLM Road 554, and park. (A flash-flood warning sign should be your indicator to watch for this difficult-to-see road.)

**Sheep Creek Canyon** offers a few options. The first is an out-and-back hike that can be as long as 7 miles each way, if you hike it all the way to the Paria River. It can also be a 1.6-mile segment that, with Willis Creek Canyon and Skutumpah Road, forms a triangle-shaped loop hiked clockwise. To get there, approach as for Willis Creek (below), only stop after just 3 miles on Skutumpah Road. The trail departs due south from the trailhead parking.

**Willis Creek.** This is an easy hike in an often very narrow canyon. After just 2 miles, this trail meets Sheep Canyon. There is usually some amount of water flow, but only a few inches and not enough to get into your shoes. Sheep Canyon can be looped with Willis Creek to make a longer hike. (If you turn into Sheep Creek Canyon, it will bring you back to the road in 1.6 miles, along which you will return to your car.) To reach this trailhead, drive just less than 3 miles south out of Cannonville on Cottonwood Road/BLM Road 400, and turn right (west) on Skutumpah Road/BLM Road 500 (not passable when wet). After 6 miles, you will reach Willis Creek and the parking for this hike.

# CAPITOL REEF NATIONAL PARK

Capitol Reef National Park is yet another of Utah's unique national parks with a distinctive variation on sandstone, with its own specialty. While Bryce has its muddy-looking warbly canyons, and Arches has . . . arches, Capitol Reef has its own flavor. The main feature of this park is a 75-mile section of the Waterpocket Fold, composed of striking horizontal white and red bands, and proud bluffs topped by huge sandstone monuments.

The Waterpocket Fold is a feature of white Navajo sandstone that runs 100 miles from Lake Powell in the south to Thousand Lake Mountain (just west of the Capitol Reef's northern tip) in the north. This was so named for the actual basins of water trapped in the stone at the time of its original formation, sometimes creating arches and bizarre canyon formations. This rare type of folding occurs in the presence of a fault and is the result of recent geological activity. In fact, the current surface of this fold was only brought to light as recently as 15 million years ago, at the time the Colorado Plateau was lifted. The canyons in this feature were only carved into the rock in the last 5 million years; many are as new as 1 million years young. The park contains the most spectacular portion of this formation and is named Capitol Reef for two reasons. One is the way in which its Capitol Dome looks somewhat like the Capitol Building in Washington, D.C. The other is for the way the structure is like a barrier reef in that it presents a significant obstacle to passersby. Within the visible layers of sandstone are 200 million years of geologic history in a 10,000-foot cross-sectional strata.

Human history in the park belongs to the Fremont and Anasazi, and later to hiding outlaws and the Mormon settlers and of the 19th century, and finally to the uranium miners of the mid-20th century. Wildlife in this corner of the world is often limited to small creatures suited to withstand desert heat and small enough to fit into small pockets of shade. However, in this park, there are occasional reports of black bears, mountain lions (also known as catamounts), and bobcats. These animals are to be respected, and it is important to not bait them into a conflict by approaching too closely or by leaving food out at campsites.

Today UT 24 runs west–east through the northern third of the park from Torrey to Caineville, parallel to the Fremont River. This river cuts one of only five canyons across this long and imposing rock formation. This is the most popular road, as it is paved and has origins nearest civilization. Another paved road, Burr Trail/Notom

Road, originates at Lake Powell's Bullfrog Marina and travels north for about 70 miles to reach UT 24. This road is almost entirely dirt and begins as part of the very scenic Burr Trail (see *To See and Do* in the "Boulder and Escalante" chapter). As the Burr Trail turns northwest at Muley Twist Canyon (about halfway up this route), this road stays due north and dips in and out of the park as it parallels the eastern border and the Waterpocket Fold. In the northernmost region of the park is Cathedral Valley, much different than the Waterpocket Fold region; instead, freestanding "cathedrals" (sandstone monoliths) dot the land, in addition to gypsum deposits and occasional sinkholes. Gypsum and volcanic plugs also exist here. This area is best accessed with rugged vehicles or on foot. $5 per vehicle. Any overnight trip requires a free permit, obtained at the **Capitol Reef National Park Visitors Center** in person (See *Guidance* below).

GUIDANCE **Capitol Reef National Park Visitors Center** (435-425-3791; www.nps.gov/care). Open 8–7 daily Memorial Day through Labor Day, 8–4:30 otherwise. This center is located on UT 24 at the junction with the park's Scenic Drive, which departs to the south. This is where backcountry permits are obtained, as well as park information, guided hiking trips, maps, and the like. There is also a brief slideshow here that describes the history, geology, and present state of the park in brief. Native American artifacts, rock and mineral samples, and a topographical map of the park's entirety illustrate some of the park's highlights.

**Garfield County Travel Council** (435-676-1160 or 800-444-6689; www.bryce canyoncountry.com). This countywide information source can help you with questions on any of the national parks and monuments in the "South-Central Utah" section of the book, as well as the lands and towns surrounding them.

GETTING THERE The park is most easily and commonly accessed via UT 24, which runs through Torrey in the west and through Caineville toward the east. UT 24 is also popular for the reason that, as it travels west, it intersects with UT 12, the scenic highway that runs through Boulder, Grand Staircase–Escalante National Monument, Escalante, and Bryce Canyon National Park. Furthermore, this road is also popular for the reason that it is the only paved road that enters the park, is connected to civilization, and is guaranteed to be open year-round. The **Burr Trail/Notom Road** runs north–west on the eastern edge of the park. It originates at Bullfrog Marina on Lake Powell and travels north for about 70 miles until it meets UT 24. This road is mostly dirt and is susceptible to inclement weather conditions. Additionally, not many people take this road because it really doesn't access any major towns—or any towns at all, for that matter.

## ✳ To See and Do

UT 24 Listed below are the main attractions on UT 24 as you pass through the park from west to east. As you first enter, there are a few rock formations signed. Though they aren't necessarily spectacular, they are peculiar and worth a look. **Twin Rocks** are two very similar round sandstone formations perched on a rise that look quite like each other. **Chimney Rock** is one of the first prominent prows of golden orange rock perched atop a base of angled, yet smoothly eroded Moenkopi sandstone. **The Castle** formation is a similarly large prow of red sandstone atop a base. However, this more blunt formation is composed of many individual pillars of various heights atop a base of sandstone talus that is still atop many varying layers of white and red sandstone.

**Behunin Cabin** is a teeny testament to the living standards of the 19th-century Western frontier. This rectangular cabin, an eastern outpost of Historic Fruita, is neatly constructed of redstone. It is so small that it's a wonder that there is even room for a door, fireplace, and glass window–let alone a family of 12. This dirt-floor home was built in 1882 by Elijah Behunin and his family, in which there were 10 children. He, his wife, and youngest few children slept inside, while the older children slept outside. This Mormon family was among the first of white settlers in the entire region. This cabin is on the south side of UT 24, about 6 miles east of the visitors center.

**Capitol Dome.** Little is left to the imagination as to why this dome might have earned its name. This large, golden cupola stands out high on the skyline. Though other knobs of the same sandstone layer are in the vicinity, this particular landmark has the most distinct shape. The much darker reds and distinct textures of strata beneath this dome do a lot to differentiate it by contrast. This can be seen to the north of UT 24, just less than 3 miles east of the visitors center.

**Fruita Historic District.** This town dates back to the 1880s and is now located at the junction of UT 24 and the Scenic Drive. The town was based in Mormonism and agriculture. There are many points of interest in this town, including a schoolhouse, sorghum processing site, old barns, black boulder stone fences, historic orchards, and the private residence called the **Gifford Farmhouse.** The last resident in this town left in 1968. The buildings are located in the vicinity of this junction, with the school being just east of the junction on the northern side of the road. School was first held in the **Fruita Schoolhouse** in 1900 and was conducted by Nettie Behunin, then just 14 years old. At the time there were eight families in this town with 22 children.

**Goosenecks** requires continuing south on this road for less than a mile after it turns to dirt. Sulphur Creek, a meandering creek in prehistory, continued along its path as the Waterpocket Fold was gradually lifted. It continued cutting its winding path into the slowly rising rock, creating what today is called the Goosenecks. There is an overlook just before the road plunges steeply down. It offers views 800 vertical feet to the bottom of this creek; you must hike 200 yards to reach this point. The Sulphur Creek bed is also hikeable; see *Hiking.*

**Hickman Bridge.** This natural bridge is reached by a 1.25-mile hike. The trailhead for this Navajo sandstone feature is located about 2 miles east of the visitors center. The Park Service publishes a brochure on this hike detailing nearly 20 points of interest that you will encounter on this short walk (available at the visitors center). The bridge at the end of the trail sits above the banks of the Fremont River and is very broad. Though both a natural arch and a natural bridge are spans of rock, a natural bridge must be threaded by a body of moving water; a natural arch has been eroded by wind.

**Panorama Point, Goosenecks Overlook, and Sunset Point.** This point is the first stand-alone point of significance as you travel east into the park. You must depart from the main road and drive an eighth of a mile south. At Panorama Point are views of Boulder Mountain and the Henry Mountains perched atop the sweeping and distinct sandstone strata and canyons of the park. Both formations are massive, lone uprisings and are often covered in snow well into the summer. (Boulder Mountain is described in the *Outdoor Activities* section of the "Boulder and Escalante" chapter and the Henrys are described in the *Henry Mountains* sidebar in the "Bryce Canyon National Park" chapter.)

**Petroglyphs.** These illustrative etchings left by the Fremont people, in residence in the area roughly 1,000 years ago (with a 200-year span on either side of this point), can be seen 1.25 miles past the visitors center on the northern side of the road along the Fremont River. A trail traverses these, exposing more than one panel to view. Keep all foot traffic on the trail.

**Sunset Point** is a short, casual trail that is only about .25 mile long and gains a more private view of the Henry Mountains and national park below. From this point you can see the gently inclined, yet perfectly parallel strata of rock that display the region's variation of color, thickness, solidity, and erosion and fracture patterns.

**Capitol Reef National Park Visitors Center.** As described in the *Guidance* section earlier, this center is next on the route. Located at the junction of UT 24 and the Scenic Drive, this is amid the historic Fruita Village.

**CAPITOL REEF NATIONAL PARK SCENIC DRIVE** This drive begins at the visitors center and heads south from UT 24 for a total of 10 miles of pavement. Brochures are available at the entrance station and are complimentary with the park entrance fee. Along the way are many dirt roads that lead to hikes and other points of interest, including Grand Wash and Capitol Gorge. As these are dirt roads, they are highly susceptible to weather and can become impassible with significant precipitation. Multiple stops along this drive showcase the hundreds of millions of years of sedimentary and metamorphosed geology. Green shale; red, white, and orange sandstone; and petrified wood all represent various histories of this region. Variations in color are accounted for by the varying mineral compositions of the rock, as well as the former geographies of the regions and the plant and animal life there.

Because these rock layers are of such diverse backgrounds—volcanic ash, river beds, sand dunes, and the like—they have quite different physical properties, which leads to artistic erosion patterns. Harder Wingate sandstone layers exhibit very smooth erosion patterns, often forming sheer, very planar cliffs multiple hundreds of feet tall. Navajo sandstone tends to be much softer than Wingate, and its white surfaces are generally eroded into curving domelike features. Moenkopi sandstone, a very soft variety, seems to have the best ability to capture and preserve history; in this you can see very clear ripple marks of ancient seas (much as you would see on a beach), very clear layering of ancient sand deposits, and

A STREAM RUNNING THROUGH THE BOTTOM OF DARK CANYON MAKES BACKPACKING IN THIS REMOTE REGION MUCH MORE ENJOYABLE.

Craig Bowden

the cracks that formed as ancient mud planes dried—sometimes even with dinosaur footprints preserved.

**Grand Wash** is your first option to depart from the main road and is reached less than 2 miles south of the visitors center on the Scenic Drive. This dirt road follows the wash that heads northeast from the main road into a cataract of golden, orange, and red sheer Wingate sandstone cliffs. This road has a length of about a mile before access is by trail only. This is one of many canyons in which Butch Cassidy hid out to evade law enforcement. Cassidy Arch has been named as such in honor of him. The caverns created for a uranium mine in 1904 still exist here and are occasionally noticeable in yellow rock strata.

**Capitol Gorge Road** is the second spur and lasts only about 2 miles. (For a few decades, it was a through road, leaving the park to the west. Because of the old road scar, it is quite possible to hike for quite a while along this trajectory.) As with Grand Wash, you will enter through a slender canyon of Wingate sandstone. The depth and steepness of the surrounding walls seem implausible, as it is hard to imagine such a passageway through such imposing walls. But in fact, the river has quite effectively cut through these massive sandstone formations, and it has historically been a route across the land. Wagon trains and prehistoric peoples alike have used this route, and pictographs evidence this fact. Pleasant Creek is along this road and is aptly named, as it is the only creek that consistently runs in the area.

## ✳ Outdoor Activities

BIKING This sport is not especially popular in the park. Though the area is gorgeous, bike travel is restricted to roads. Bikes may not travel on any kind of trail or in any wash. However, if you are in the area with your bicycle, you may as well check out the park under your own leg power.

**Cathedral Valley Loop,** though only partially inside the park, is a nearly 65-mile mountain-bike loop that can be done in one extended day, but it is generally done in at least two days. (A no-fee, primitive campground exists at the northwestern-most part of this route, at about the halfway point.) The ride begins outside of the park. To do the ride in counterclockwise fashion, head north from Hartnet Road, just 11.5 miles east of the visitors center on UT 24. This road eventually curves northwest and meets Cainville Wash Road, which heads west and curves south to reconnect with UT 24, 7 miles east of the Hartnet Road intersection. The ride presents virtually no water along the way (except at spring river crossings, and in this case, the water must be treated to be potable). It has strenuous passes through switchbacks and up significant topography. This journey is extremely beautiful, though, and because of the ruggedness of the road, is avoided by most motorists. Avoid this ride during the summer and winter.

**Scenic Drive,** a somewhat inclined, 10-mile stretch of road, can be ridden. However, be aware that this road is extremely popular with motorists, and it has virtually no shoulders. This road is paved and is best for road bikers. (Other side roads like the South Draw Road and **Capitol Gorge Road,** as discussed in the *Capitol Reef National Park Scenic Drive* section, above, offer riding alongside slower traffic for those with mountain bikes.)

HIKING Many hiking trails exist right off UT 24 and the Scenic Drive Road. At the visitors center you can pick up a guide to these hikes, or visit www.nps.gov/

care for an abbreviated guide. Trips range from 0.5 mile to more than 10 miles, so there is a wide range of difficulty for everyone. Points of interest include historic wagon pathways, pictographs, and plain old scenery.

**Chimney Rock Loop** is a steep 3.5-mile loop that an accesses views of the park's otherwise difficult-to-access Chimney Rock region. This trail departs from the north side of the road, just 6 miles east of Torrey (and slightly west of Goosenecks Overlook), and passes through switchbacks en route. This loop enjoys pleasant, small-canyon scenery.

**Goosenecks of Sulphur Creek.** Scramble through a beautiful (and overlooked) 5.4-mile slot canyon filled with pools and waterfalls. Expect wet feet and perhaps some swimming.

**Rim Overlook/Navajo Knobs Trail** begins as for the Hickman Bridge trail (see *To See and Do*) but takes a right-handed fork after less than 0.5 mile. It continues about another 1.75 miles, passing Navajo Dome and The Castle before reaching Navajo Knobs.

**HORSEBACK RIDING** This backcountry activity, unlike mountain biking, is allowed on the park's trails but is restricted to certain areas. A list of these restricted areas is kept at the visitors center or at www.nps.gov/care. Because of the harshness and general barrenness of the park, horse travel can be taxing for animals, even on trails where riding is permitted. The Park Service specifically recommends riding on **Halls Creek, the Old Wagon Trail, South Draw,** and the **Old South Desert.**

**Alpine Anglers** (435-425-3660; www.fly-fishing-utah.net), 310 West Main St., Torrey. As listed in the *Fishing* section of the "Boulder and Escalante" chapter, this service offers horseback riding trips across southern Utah.

**ROCK CLIMBING** Climbing in the park has not been particularly heavy during the park's history. However, in recent times there has been increased activity here. No permit is required to climb in the park unless you plan to spend the night at a bivy or on a ledge. If this is the case, you must obtain a free backcountry permit at the visitors center before embarking on the climb. As it is a national park, the preservation of the natural state of the area is of utmost importance, and certain restrictions apply here that may be a surprise. For example, white chalk is prohibited; red or orange must be used. Other obvious restrictions apply, such as no power drilling, and no replacement of webbing with any but the most camouflaged of materials. Specific area closures exist where rock art is present; see the park for exact closures and rules. Finally, sandstone becomes extremely fragile when wet, meaning the rock will not hold protection in case of a fall and will suffer advanced wear under hand and foot traffic. Respect the rock and yourself, and refrain from climbing after rain. For more information on specific routes here, see Stewart Green's *Rock Climbing Utah* or Eric Bjornstad's *Desert Rock*. Both of these books can usually be purchased at the store inside the visitors center.

# BRYCE CANYON NATIONAL PARK

Bryce Canyon, the namesake attribute of the park, is one of the most unmatched and striking geologic phenomena in Utah, even among vast regions of national-park-worthy red-rock terrain. All of the other parks in the state—Zion, Arches, Canyonlands, and Capitol Reef—have incredible natural scenery, including deep Wingate sandstone canyons, slick rock domes, arches, and soaring towers. However, none are so peculiarly eroded and so dramatically contrasted by their surroundings as Bryce.

Surrounding this "canyon" are high desert plains, deep green evergreen trees, and brush on rather flat topography. Yet, seemingly from nowhere, Bryce Canyon cuts deeply into the subcutaneous soil of this plateau, exposing wild hues of oranges, reds, and whites, which are made even more dramatic by their gentle green surroundings. Interestingly, Bryce Canyon is technically not a "canyon" as the definition goes; its erosion did not come from the top down as done by a stream. Instead its erosion came from below as waters ate into the earth above, creating what is called the amphitheaters of the park. The rock in Bryce is a very soft type of sandstone that gives itself easily to erosion. As erosion gently removed the majority of the region's stone, the remaining rock was left as a forest of sand castles, within which original horizontal stripes remain preserved from one tower to the next.

Bryce Canyon sits atop the Grand Staircase (as described at the beginning of the "Grand Staircase–Escalante National Monument" chapter), which is part of the Colorado Plateau. Bryce Canyon itself cuts into some of the highest plateaus of this region, the Paunsaugunt and Kaiparowits. In the northeastern portion of this large uplift, Bryce Canyon's rim is between 8,000 and 9,000 feet, much higher than the nearby national parks.

Various tribes are believed to have existed in the region for around 10,000 years. These belonged to the Fremont and Anasazi groups, and their presence is evidenced by various artifacts they left behind, including baskets, stonework, pictographs, and more. The Paiute tribe was the most recent Native American group to have lived in the area, in somewhat of a settled fashion. Though they were primarily hunter-gatherers, they supplemented their diets with modest crops. The peculiar "hoodoo" formations of the park, formed by a larger, more solid capstone resting on a thin pillar of softer sandstone, were part of the spiritual belief system of these tribes.

Mormons were the first people to ever establish widespread settlements in Utah, and they did not arrive in Salt Lake City until 1848. However, in fewer than

Craig Bowden

CRYPTOBIOTIC SOIL IS A VERY FRAGILE AND IMPORTANT "SKIN" THAT IS OFTEN THE ONLY
ANTIEROSION AGENT AND IS EASILY DESTROYED BY FOOTPRINTS AND TIRE TRACKS.

10 years they had created satellite communities across present-day Utah. In the late 1850s people had already begun to settle what is now southern Utah. As soon as 1873, the lands in and around this park were used for cattle grazing. The canyon itself was homesteaded in 1875 by Mormon settler Ebenezer Bryce. Soon more would follow. The fragile landscape could not simultaneously support the indigenous populations and newly introduced livestock, and by 1880, the Paiutes and Ebenezer Bryce had vacated the premises. At this point a few remaining settlers were able to prolong their stay there by diverting water from the Sevier River to the immediate area.

Despite its remoteness, Bryce was such an attraction that very soon after the initial (and difficult) settling of southern Utah, the area became a popular tourist destination. By the early 1900s, the area's first hotels had been constructed, and promotional exposés were written and distributed nationally. By 1924, enough attention had been generated that motions in Washington were being made to classify the area as a national park or monument. The park went through a few different designations and ownership transfers, but it was eventually called Bryce Canyon National Park on February 25, 1928, under Calvin Coolidge.

Today the park contains 36,000 acres and a scenic drive, an extension of UT 63 roughly 18 miles long with 13 scenic overlooks along the way. Eight day-hiking and two backpacking trails, a visitors center, two campgrounds, and 10 miles of ungroomed Nordic skiing paths (connecting to 20 miles of groomed trails in Dixie National Forest and Ruby's Inn) lend the park many uses for its 1.5 million annual guests. Nordic skiing here a special treat for those who enjoy the sport because of the awesome visual contrast between the white snow and red sandstones. Photography is particularly first-rate here, not only because of the park's intense beauty, but also because of the area's consistently pristine air quality. $12 per vehicle.

GUIDANCE **Garfield County Travel Council** (435-676-1160 or 800-444-6689; www.brycecanyoncountry.com). Visit this Web site for information on all of the national parks and monuments in this region, as well as the lands and towns surrounding them.

**Bryce Canyon National Park Visitors Center** (435-834-5322; www.nps.gov/brca), 4.5 miles south of the UT 63/UT 12 junction. Open 8–8 May through September; 8–6 October and April; 8–4:30 November through March. This is a classic National Park Service visitors center, staffed with park employees and filled with free brochures and relevant books for purchase.

GETTING THERE AND GETTING AROUND Bryce Canyon National Park is just south of the junction of UT 63 and UT 12. UT 12 is the scenic "Million Dollar Highway" that connects Bryce to Grand Staircase–Escalante National Monument, Escalante, Boulder, and Capitol Reef National Park. During the summer there is free, unlimited use of shuttle buses inside the park. This public transportation system alleviates congestion within the park and allows visitors to enjoy the views without worrying about staying on the road. Because of the elevation of the park, summer is actually a good time to visit, as it does not bake in the same way that nearby parks do. This elongated park is stretched north–south, and the visitors center is toward the northern end of the park where UT 63 enters the boundary, just south of its junction with UT 12.

## ✳ Outdoor Activities

BIKING There is no biking off-road in the park, and so the only biking done here is road biking. However, because of heavy traffic during comfortable temperatures, it is not necessarily a recommended ride. If you do decide to ride, you should consider riding early in the morning before the crowds arrive. This is great in summer, because you simultaneously beat the heat and traffic of the day.

HIKING Bryce Canyon has eight day-hiking trails, including two backpacking options. Permits are required for overnight hikes. They are obtained at the visitors center, in the northern end of the park, and range in price depending on the number of people in the group. Many of these trails intersect at the bottoms of the amphitheaters, and these often-short trails can be linked to expand the experience. Pick up a park map at the visitors center for portable guidance on your hike.

**Bristlecone Loop** is a short hike, just 1 mile in total, and is a good hike for warm and sunny days, as it travels through an evergreen forest before breaking out over an expansive cliff-side viewpoint. Ancient, yet living, bristlecone pines along the route reach ages of roughly 1,700 years. This trail is at the highest and southern-most part of the park. The trailhead is at Yovimpa Point/Rainbow Point, at the southern terminus of the park's main road.

**Hat Shop** is a short and steep trail that loses nearly 900 feet of elevation in just 2 miles to reach some of the park's funniest hoodoos—epitomal dolomite-capped towers. Thin, muddy-looking sandstone is capped by huge boulders of gray dolomite that appear like oversize river cobbles. Many of the hoodoos have plate-shaped dolomite chunks in their stalks, with some cantilevered out to the side. Because of the dolomite's chemistry, it is much less soluble in water than sandstone, and so has avoided much of the erosion that has affected the red rock beneath (and formerly above) it.

**Mossy Cave** is just less than 0.5 mile one way and is a good hike for warm weather, as it follows a man-made stream to a waterfall. This stream was created in the late 1870s by Mormon settlers in order to channel water from the Sevier River to their

Craig Bowden

DESCENDING HUNDREDS OF FEET BENEATH THE DESERT SURFACE, HIKERS IN THE DARK
CANYON ENJOY AN OASIS-LIKE ENVIRONMENT FED BY THE RESIDENT STREAMS.

homes and crops. This trail has two forks, each of which reaches a special feature.
The left fork of the trail leads to the namesake cave that was formed by an underground spring. The right fork of the trail leads to a small waterfall that has persisted
in this streambed because of the dolomite's resistance to erosion. This dolomite has
different solubility and hardness than the sandstone strata nearby, and it is what
often forms the capstone on peculiar looking hoodoos that can be seen along this
hike. These and other distinct features have eroded as such because Bryce is not a
canyon formed by stream erosion; instead, gentler headward erosion forces have
allowed the fragile rock to endure in this precarious formation. This man-made
canyon has already destroyed many of these hoodoos with its foreign erosive
strength, washing them away at their base. It will continue to do so and will eventually change the entire canyon. This trail departs from UT 12, 4 miles east of its junction with UT 63, and is fairly steep, gaining roughly 300 feet in its short journey.

**Navajo Loop** is just 1.25 miles in total and tours the jugular of Bryce Amphitheater, the largest of the park. Along the way are two of the park's more famous features, Wall Street and Thor's Hammer. **Thor's Hammer** is an especially large,
roughly cubic hoodoo perched high on a rock pillar of especially dubious quality.
**Wall Street** is a special canyon, parts of which are so overhung by roofs that it
appears almost to be a meandering tunnel. The citrus orange of the rock gives it a
particular glow that casts a coppery tone on everything inside—from the people to
the tall trunks of the occasional evergreen tree. On May 23, 2006, there was quite
a substantial rockslide directly into Wall Street. When all was said and done, the
debris pile occupied a volume approximately 15 feet wide, 15 feet deep, and 60
feet long—approximately 500 tons of rock. The Park Service decided to reopen the
path by redirecting the trail up and over the rubble. As it was a natural matter of
course that the rocks fell, the park will leave the pile as is. The trailhead for the
Navajo Loop is at Sunset Point, a little more than 3 miles south of the park's
entrance.

**Queen's Garden Trail** is just less than 1 mile each way but is often done in combination with the **Navajo Loop** for a total of just less than 3 miles. This popular

Craig Bowden

THE HENRY MOUNTAINS, AS SEEN FROM NEAR THE NORTHERN TIP OF LAKE POWELL

## HENRY MOUNTAINS

The Henry Mountains were the among the very last explored and surveyed ranges in the lower 48. They are located in one of Utah's most remote places. South of Hanksville, but north of Lake Powell, these mountains really have no direct means of approach from the east or the west. Located east of the 100-mile-long, barrier-like Waterpocket Fold, west of Canyonlands, in an area of enormous geologic turmoil and deeply cut canyons, these mountains rise enormously from their surroundings to a maximum height of 11,615 feet and really dominate this skyline.

The Henrys, which contrast enormously with their surroundings, have two major rises. The northern portion is the tallest, with Mount Ellen being

trail is among the least-strenuous options for descending into Bryce Amphitheater and has a very smooth, wide surface. Along the way you pass hoodoos of different sizes and proportions, sand dunes, and through a few man-made tunnels. This trail tours Bryce Amphitheater and starts and ends at Sunrise Point.

**Peek-a-boo Loop** is 5.5 miles round-trip. This trail is shared with horses and travels through Bryce Amphitheater. The Bryce Connector, a steep trail that leads from Bryce Point to Peek-a-boo, was washed out and buried with debris during heavy rains. Though it is currently closed for repairs, it is anticipated to reopen in 2009. Current access to the loop is via the Queen's Garden Trail or Navajo Loop, both described above.

**Riggs Spring Loop** is about 8.5 miles long and can be done as a day hike or as a backpacking trip, as there are four designated campsites along the trail. Evergreen forests and occasional aspen stands are the norm here, and the namesake spring is

the tallest peak at 11,615 feet. Also in the north, Mount Penell soars to 11,371 feet and Mount Hillers to 10,723 feet. The southern portion, with Mount Ellsworth at 8,235 feet and Mount Holmes at 8,000 feet, is about 3,000 feet shorter.

The Henry Mountains were formed as a result of tectonic and volcanic activity, hence its characteristic pluglike shape and that of its features. The rock found on this mountain, porphyritic diorite, is quite distinct because it is volcanic; it does roughly resemble granite. However, the texture and density of this rock is much different than granite: It has many more spongelike holes and much glossier surfaces. These mountains have a similar age, origin, and characteristics to its sister range, the La Sals (just east of Moab). Visually they are quite alike.

The Henrys are home to one of only four genetically pure herds of wild American bison. This herd, which is not native to this range, was established in the area when 18 animals were taken from Yellowstone National Park and re-released southeast of Hanksville in 1941. These animals have survived well and now live elevated in the range, usually around 10,000 feet or higher.

The Henry Mountains are indeed remote, and as such do not have the mountain biking trail networks characteristic of other Utah ranges. They do see some recreational use, but not much for their size. There is some very difficult, undocumented rock climbing and plenty of free space for camping (almost 2 million acres in all). There is some hiking in the mountains, the most popular route being from Bull Creek Pass to the summit of Mount Ellen. Most other hiking must be done off-trail. Because of a recent forest fire, this is actually quite easy near the horn. This wildfire, part of a natural cycle, has destroyed huge patches of vegetation, but in so doing has opened up many great views. The best access to this range is along UT 276, which departs south of Hanksville and runs along the eastern flanks the range.

located about halfway into the hike. This trail descends about 2,250 feet, so it is quite strenuous. The trailhead is at Yovimpa Point, at the southern end of the park.

**Rim Trail** is a very popular trail, 11 miles round-trip. It follows the top rim of a cliff band between Fairlyland Point and Bryce Point. There are many signed overlooks along the way, and part of the trail is even paved (between Sunset and Sunrise points). Though most people do not walk the entire length of this trail, many people walk at least a portion of it. As of 2008, sections of this trail were under construction; these parts of the trail needed to be relocated in order to allow for the natural process of erosion to take place at the cliff's edge.

**Swamp Canyon Loop** is just less than 4.5 miles in total, and follows the Under-the-Rim Trail for part of the way. This area is so named because, fed by two very small streams, it is the wettest part of the park. This departure from the gaping views otherwise typical of Bryce gives hikers a chance to witness its details up close, and not just as part of thousands in a huge landscape. This trail originates at the Swamp Canyon Overlook, just more than 6 miles south of the park entrance.

**Tower Bridge** is 1.5 miles each way and is yet another trail that originates at Sunrise Point. This takes the Fairyland Loop counterclockwise and down nearly 1,000 vertical feet to gain this very distinctive natural arch. Aptly named, Tower Bridge appears quite like a road bridge with two sizable towers on each end. The trail does not end at the bridge, however, and the hike can be made longer by remaining on the **Fairyland Loop.** This 8-mile loop takes a fairly extensive tour of Bryce Amphitheater before returning to its trailhead.

**Under-the-Rim** is the longest single trail in the park and stretches from Bryce Point to Rainbow Point. Because of its length, most people hiking the majority or entirety of the trail do so as backpackers, camping at any of the eight sites along the way. There are many access points throughout the park.

HORSEBACK RIDING This activity in the park is restricted to select trails. Many of these share access with hikers, which is generally not problematic, as there are no pets or mountain bikes allowed anywhere off-road in the park. **Canyon Trail Rides** (435-679-8665 or 435-834-5500; www.canyonrides.com) guide service is based out of Tropic, Utah. They offer horse and mule trips of different lengths along the Peek-a-boo Trail.

# Southwestern Utah

ST. GEORGE

CEDAR CITY

CEDAR BREAKS NATIONAL
MONUMENT

ZION NATIONAL PARK

Craig Bowden

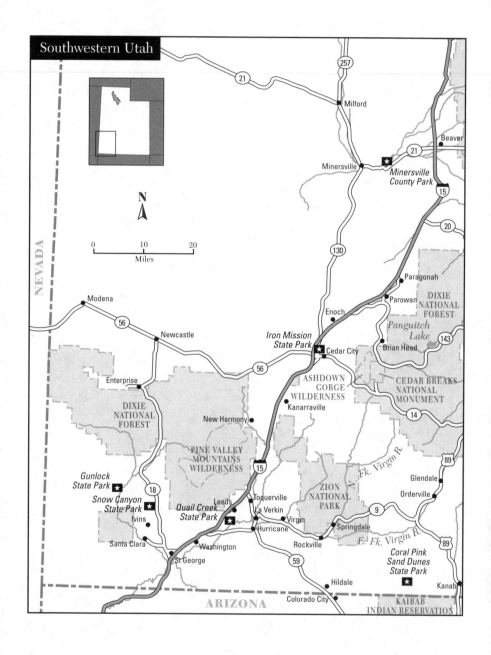

Southwestern Utah

# SOUTHWESTERN UTAH IN BRIEF

Southwestern Utah, called "Utah's Dixie," is today Utah's vacation and retirement land, replete with sunny golf courses, outdoor opportunities, and rapidly growing communities. However, before its settlement, this was *not* the case; the Rocky Mountain West is one of the most hostile regions in the country for unsupported human life. It is thoroughly dry and has wicked temperature swings throughout each day, as well as across the seasons. Correspondingly, prior to agriculture, the region has always provided a short supply of indigenous fruits, fatty animals, and building supplies. Thus most of Utah's human history has been comprised by small groups of lightly treading tribes—most of which were migratory. This southwest corner of Utah was traditionally inhabited by the Fremont, Anasazi, and Southern Paiute tribes. Though little evidence of their occupancy exists, there are petroglyphs scattered throughout the area, namely near Parowan Gap, just north of Cedar City.

European descendents prior to the late 1800s in this region were few and far between, and were just as isolated and flighty as the indigenous peoples. Many were outlaws, traders, trappers, or missionaries. None had the crutch of Western civilization necessary to stay long, and they drifted through seasonally, often without leaving a trace. The first known such men were of the Dominguez-Escalante expedition. Two friars had intended to find a route from Santa Fe, New Mexico, to Monterey, California. The not-so-friendly reputation of Utah's tribes encouraged them to take a roundabout route through Utah, and unfortunately they encountered brutal weather conditions along the way. They made it as far as Utah Valley, recognizing these lands of the Timpanogot Tribe as a likely settlement site, but were forced to turn around shortly afterward. In 1826 another religious devotee, Methodist Jedediah Smith, passed through the area en route to California. He was able to complete his journey, and it was the aggregate effort of these and other parties that "paved the way" for the Spanish Trail.

As with Salt Lake City and the rest of the Great Basin settlements, it would take a special group of people before southern Utah could be settled. Discipline, unity, cleverness with resources, and the desire to be left alone were the ingredients that allowed the Mormons to settle these areas first. Because of their atypical slant on Christianity and their fondness of polygamy, Mormons had been persecuted wherever they lived among society, from New York to Illinois. Brigham Young and other prominent followers decided upon the Great Basin as a perfect colonization location for their sect precisely because of its extreme isolation and difficulty to settle. So on July 24, 1848, after more than 1,000 miles of lethal trekking, Brigham Young and a spearhead group of pioneers landed in Salt Lake Valley and declared it "The Place."

The trip had rendered the group mangled and starving. But after surviving the first brutal winter, the settlers vigorously recovered and moved forward with their colonization efforts. By the following year, they had solidified their home base enough to receive more pioneers and send colonizing groups out into the vast surrounds.

Quickly, plans were put in place to establish various missions in "Dixie." The first settlement in the area was the Iron Mission (at present-day Parowan) in 1851, settled by Parley Pratt and 120 men, 30 women, and 18 children. Next, Harmony was settled in 1852, then Santa Clara in 1854, and Washington in 1857. The development of this area was calculated and efficient. Agricultural and water-management plans were first met, followed by industrial development. Each successful settlement provided easier establishment of the next. In 1861, 309 families were selected by Apostle George Smith (the namesake of the future city), and left Salt Lake City to establish what then would become the Cotton Mission that is now St. George. This area is often referred to as "Utah's Dixie" because of its original function as the Cotton Mission.

It was the intention of the Mormons that they would create a sovereign nation of their own, the State of Deseret. It would have occupied almost all of most of the desert Southwest: virtually all of present-day Nevada, Utah, and Arizona, as well as good portions of Idaho, California, New Mexico, Wyoming, and Colorado. This intention actually worried leading U.S. politicians during the Civil War. They believed that the Mormons would side with—and fight with—the Confederacy in order to be granted their wish of sovereignty.

Though the cotton industry would prove vulnerable to economic depression, the Mormon faith would remain the community's glue. This southernmost LDS outpost was viewed as one of the most important of all, as it was valued for its opportunity to attract new members from California and other southern neighbors. The St. George Temple was actually the first completed in Utah, in 1877, and was the only one finished before the death of Brigham Young. Dixie College, originally St. George Academy, was established in 1933. Since the 1950s, southern Utah has been one of the most rapidly growing populations in the state because of its reputation for warm weather, great golf, LDS spirituality, and retirement opportunities.

## ✳ Weather

The southwest corner of Utah is classic desert environment. Low elevations and latitudes combine forces to produce the warmest, most sun-drenched area in the state. Valley elevations for Cedar City and St. George are just under 3,000 feet above sea level; this is almost 1,400 feet lower than Salt Lake City, and just a bit more than 300 miles more southern. During a "typical" January day, Salt Lake City will be around 35°F, Park City will be around 25°F, and even Moab (also in southern Utah, but higher in elevation) will often be in the low 30s. St. George, however, will be as warm as the mid- to upper 50s. Naturally, the summer months bring much warmer temperatures to the area, on average about 10 degrees warmer than along the Wasatch Front. July's average high is almost 102°F. Many people consider this area too hot, but others consider it perfectly tolerable; it is simply a matter of perspective. In any case, you should remember that it is still cooler than Las Vegas, Austin, and Los Angeles, and has virtually no humidity.

The most pleasant months are March, April, October, and November, when highs are in the 60s and 70s. The climate is bone dry, with an annual precipitation accumulation of just more than 8 inches. The "wettest" months are during the winter, with around 1 inch each month. June is the driest, with an average of less than 0.2 inch.

Though southern Utah's weather is generally pleasant, travelers should be advised that desert climates are extremely unkind to watery creatures such as humans. Such copious amounts of sunshine require water, electrolytes, and sunscreen to maintain health. Dry air and environment do not hold heat well; an increase in elevation, or the disappearance of the sun behind clouds, will result in a drastic temperature drop. Drink water, bring along extra clothing, apply sunscreen with great frequency, and enjoy.

## ✳ Special Events

*January 13:* **Parowan's Birthday.** This 13th day of the month marks the anniversary of the 1851 founding of this LDS town and is replete with wholesome townwide, family-friendly events.

*End of January:* **St. George Winter Bird Festival** (Red Cliffs Audubon Society: 435-673-0996). Held the last Friday through Sunday at Tonaquint Park and Nature Center (1851 South Dixie Dr.), this festival invites the community to learn about the many aspects of southern Utah's native bird species, habitats, bird-watching opportunities, and to learn about the nature center itself. This event includes kids' workshops, presentations, exhibits, field trips, and banquets.

*Easter Weekend:* **St. George Art Festival** (435-634-5850). This festival has been taking place on Friday and Saturday of this weekend since 1978. For southwest Utah, it is the largest festival of its kind, with food, music, entertainment, and more than 100 booths. Entertainment is varied and includes dance and pageantry representing many different continents and regions of this country.

*Summerlong:* **Tuacahn Summer Season of Theater** (435-652-3200; box office: 435-652-3300; www.tuacahn.org), held in the Tuacahn Ampitheater, Snow Canyon State Park, just northwest of St. George. This immaculately well-kept, clean state park is a beautiful place to enjoy the arts on a warm summer night.

*June:* **Utah Summer Games** (sports director: 435-865-9223; www.utah summergames.org). This statewide athletic event lasts three weeks, and Cedar City is one of its athletic venues. Though the fame of this event is mostly contained within Utah's borders, it is quite popular indeed, attracting more than 8,000 participants each year. Competitions began in 1986 and include almost 30 disciplines, including swimming, running, triathlon, soccer, marksmanship, weight lifting, and more. This is manned by thousands of volunteers and is reminiscent of the summer Olympic Games.

*Second Week of June:* **Paiute Restoration Gathering** (435-586-1112), Cedar City. In 1950, the Paiutes lost their official status as a tribe in the eyes of the U.S. government. Thirty years later, this status was reinstated and is now celebrated during this event. Festivities include a powwow, dinner, parade, and more cultural expositions.

ZION NATIONAL PARK IS KNOWN FOR ITS VERY NARROW CANYONS AND INCREDIBLY TALL, SHEER SANDSTONE WALLS. THIS VIEW IS FROM THE ROCK-CLIMBING ROUTE MOONLIGHT BUTTRESS ACROSS TO ANGEL'S LANDING.

*July 24:* **Pioneer Day.** For those completely unfamiliar with Mormon traditions, prepare to be surprised. This LDS holiday is their equivalent of Independence Day. This day is the anniversary of the 1847 arrival of Brigham Young and followers in the Salt Lake Valley. Because the Mormons of that era had hoped and lobbied for a sovereign nation of their own (and had always thought of themselves as a separate society), this is still celebrated today as their own Independence Day. Yet because of the close ties of this faith-based community, this holiday is celebrated with much more enthusiasm and home-team pride than Fourth of July celebrations across the United States.

*Early August:* **Washington County Fair** (St. George; www.washcofair.net), at the Washington County Fairgrounds, 197 East Tabernacle St., Hurricane. This fair takes place just outside of St. George and is a quintessential summer fair, showcasing local crops, handiwork, and music.

*Mid-August:* **Jedediah Smith High Mountain Rendezvous** (435-586-5124). This is a family-friendly throwback to the days of mountain men, trappers, traders, and cowboys. Costumes, period fare, and reenactments take place in Cedar City during the middle of August each year.

*Week before Labor Day:* **Iron County Fair** (435-590-8185; www.ironcounty.net), at the Iron County Fairgrounds, 68 South 100 East, Parowan. This is much more than a typical fair. It includes all the Western traditional entertainment options like rodeo, dances, a beauty pageant, as well as many other entertaining options, like helicopter rides, hot dog and watermelon eating contests, a mud pit, automobile show, trail rides, and bicycle and running races.

*Second Weekend of September:* **Lions Dixie Roundup** (435-628-2898). This professional rodeo lasts three days and is held at St. George's Sun Bowl (435-652-1330), 2450 East 130 North, St. George.

*End of September:* **Santa Clara Swiss Days** (435-673-6712). This occasion is a refreshing departure from Utah's (appropriate) obsession with Mormon pioneer heritage. Though the town was indeed founded by Mormons, they were largely Swiss converts, and this event, which takes place on the last Friday and Saturday each September, is a tribute to Santa Clara's European roots. Sample the crafts, dances, cuisine, and history of this town and Switzerland.

*Early October:* **St. George Marathon** (435-627-4500; www.stgeorgemarathon .com) is one of Utah's favorite athletic events, with more than 4,000 participants each fall. The beautiful weather and the scenic course begins roughly 1,600 feet higher in the Pine Valley and winds into St. George, giving runners a top-ranked experience for scenery and speed.

*Mid-October:* **Huntsman World Senior Games** (800-562-1268; www .hwsg.com). This event is quite substantial and includes dozens of sports, from golf to cycling, horseshoes, basketball, running, swimming, volleyball, pickleball, and even square dancing. Each year, the world's most elite 50+ athletes gather in the Southwest corner to compete.

*End of November:* **Christmas in the Country** (435-477-3331). This is Parowan's holiday season initiation, with a torch-lit parade, Santa Claus interactions with the children, dances, and other festivities.

*Thanksgiving Week:* **Jubilee of Trees** (www.jubileeoftrees.org). This marks the commencement of St. George's Christmas season each year. It takes place at the Dixie Convention Center (just southeast of exit 6 on I-15) and is fairly extensive, with Christmas wonderland/gingerbread house–type general admission offerings as well as special events that include dinners, shows, and more.

# ST. GEORGE

St. George is Utah's southwesternmost city and the primary township of the entire region. It is located off I-15, about a dozen miles north of Utah's southern border and about 100 miles north of Las Vegas. It is located at the northern edge of the Mojave Desert and is on the shores of the Virgin River. This river, which carved Zion Canyon, runs through town, and then steeply down the Virgin River Gorge on its way into Arizona and Nevada, and eventually the Colorado River.

St. George is in Washington County, which had an estimated population of 140,000 in 2007. This county is the fastest growing in all of Utah; each month it gains more than 1,000 residents. Experts project that by 2050, this corner of Utah could easily contain almost 750,000 people. What's bringing all of these people here? This is the corner of the state that truly begins to resemble Nevada and Arizona, where the reds of sandstone deepen, and vegetation all but disappears. Where the daytime temperatures never average lower than 50°F.

**GUIDANCE City of St. George Chamber of Commerce** (435-628-1658; www.stgeorgechamber.com), 97 East St. George Blvd., St. George. Though not strictly a tourist bureau, it does offer a fairly good selection of items that would be of interest to visitors.

THE GEM TRAIL TOURS A RIM ABOVE THE VIRGIN RIVER OUTSIDE OF HURRICANE.

Kami Hardcastle

**St. George/Zion Utah** (800-869-6635; www.utahstgeorge.com). This group exists expressly to provide visitors with information, beginning with a basic town-by-town introduction, and offering categories of data like accommodations, recreation, dining, national and state parks, and an events calendar.

**Utah Arts Council and the Washington County Travel & Convention Bureau** (435-634-5942; www.utahsdixie.com). This is the area's ultimate umbrella resource, and outlines the area in terms of Washington County and individual cities and towns, with special emphasis on history.

GETTING THERE *By car:* Southwestern Utah is conveniently located along I-15 just more than 100 miles north of Las Vegas and just under 300 miles south of Salt Lake City. (www.aztecshuttle.com, stops between Salt Lake City and St. George)

*By air:* **Cedar City Regional Airport (CDC)** (435-867-9408), 2560 Aviation Way, Cedar City. This is a small, public airport that is roughly just 50 miles north of St. George via I-15.

**McCarran International Airport (LAS)** (702-261-5211; www.mccarran.com), 5757 Wayne Newton Blvd., Las Vegas, Nevada. Located outside of Utah, this airport has perks beyond the obvious 100-mile proximity to St. George. The biggest is the proximity to inexpensive, accessible liquor—very unlike liquor shopping in southern or rural Utah. (Note: It is illegal to transport alcohol into Utah across state lines, especially if it's visible to the police.)

**St. George Shuttle** (435-628-8320 or 800-933-8320; www.stgshuttle.com). This company is perfect for those flying into Salt Lake City or Las Vegas; it picks guests up at these two major airports and arrives in St. George at (and departs from) the America's Best Value Inn at 915 South Bluff Street; costs $20 each way.

**St. George Municipal Airport (SGU)** (435-634-5822), 444 South River Rd., St. George. Most people arriving in the area would choose a larger airport, but enough business exists to keep this small operation in business.

**Salt Lake International Airport (SLC)** (801-575-2400 or 800-595-2442; www.slcairport.com) is less than 10 minutes from downtown on I-80. This airport, like that in Las Vegas, is also a major hub, but it is 300 miles north of St. George.

*By bus:* **Greyhound Bus Lines** (www.greyhound.com) has stations in St. George (435-673-2933), inside McDonald's, 1235 South Bluff St.; Cedar City (435-586-7400), 1495 West 200 North; Las Vegas (702-384-9561), 200 South Main St.; and Salt Lake City (801-355-9579), 300 South 600 West.

GETTING AROUND AND TOURS **St. George Historic Walking Tour,** at the St. George Chamber of Commerce, 97 East St. George Blvd. If you prefer a free, self-guided tour enhanced by an informative brochure, pick up a copy of this brochure.

**Suntran** (435-673-8726; www.sgcity.org/suntran). This is the primary local public transportation in St. George, a bus in the fleet that runs along four routes Monday–Saturday 6 AM–8 PM. The route nexus is on Dixie State College at the Transit Center, 100 South 1000 East. These buses do not operate on Memorial Day, Independence Day, Pioneer Day, Labor Day, Thanksgiving, Christmas, or New Year's Day. A day pass costs only $2.50 and is good for the entire day; a single ride costs $1. Cash and exact fare are required. Buses visit each stop every 40 minutes.

MEDICAL EMERGENCY **Dixie Regional Medical Center** (435-251-1000; www.intermountainhealthcare.org), 1380 East Medical Center Dr., St. George. This is the region's major hospital, complete with emergency room in case you need to go straight there.

**Intermountain Hurricane Valley Clinic** (435-635-7227; www.intermountain healthcare.org), 75 North 2260 West, Hurricane. Hurricane is northeast of St. George on UT 9, just northeast of St. George and Washington, and very near Sand Hollow State Park. For minor emergencies and illness in this area, this is much better than an expensive visit to the emergency room.

**Intermountain River Road Clinic** (435-688-6000; www.intermountainhealth care.org), 577 South River Rd., St. George. This is one of St. George's two instant-care-type clinics. This particular facility is just east of Dixie State College and slightly east of I-15.

**Intermountain Sunset Clinic** (435-634-6000; www.intermountainhealthcare .org), 1739 West Sunset Blvd., St. George. This is St. George's other instant-care facility, a bit northwest of the center of town. This clinic is just north of Sunbrook Golf Club and east of Santa Clara.

NEWSPAPERS *The Spectrum* (www.thespectrum.com). This paper functions as southern Utah's regional news center and covers all of the surrounding towns up to and beyond Cedar City. Aside from news, this paper publishes movie theater listings, local sporting events, weather, and other useful tidbits.

## ✳ To See and Do

The **Cinder Cone Trail,** about 1 mile south of the park's northern entrance, gains the base of a cinder cone active as recent as 1,000 years ago. **Johnson Arch Trail,** whose trailhead is near the park's southern entrance, is a 1-mile trail that brings hikers to a sandstone arch. With this trail, it is worth inquiring about current accessibility, as land ownership issues have been occasionally problematic in the past. Many other trails in the park take you past petrified sand dunes, lava flows and tubes, deep and narrow canyons, arches, nonpetrified sand, and on self-guided flora tours.

**Joshua Tree National Landmark** (St. George BLM: 435-688-3200; www.blm .gov). This 1970s natural area marks the northernmost point of the natural growing region for these plants and the Mojave Desert. To get there, take US 91 just 2 miles west of Gunlock, and turn south. This road cuts through the Shivwits Paiute Reservation, climbs Witwer Canyon, and traverses the base of Jarvis Peak before climbing a ridge to gain a view of the Joshua trees before looping back to US 91 after 16 miles.

**Matheson Preserve** (435-259-4629), entrance is on Kane Creek Rd., along the Colorado River, Moab. This 890-acre preserve has a critical place in this desert. It provides habitat for reptiles, amphibians, and migratory and local birds including raptors, waterfowl, and shorebirds.

**Snow Canyon State Park** (435-628-2255; www.stateparks.utah.gov), west of St. George on Bluff Street, then west on Snow Canyon Pkwy., and in 3.5 miles, take a right onto Snow Canyon Dr. Open year-round 6 AM–10 PM, no holiday closures. Admission $5. Snow Canyon is one of Utah's most accessible, beautiful, and well-maintained state parks. This scenic red-rock-esque park has about 18 miles of trails (3 miles of which are paved) that wind through the bold reds and oranges of Kayenta and Navajo sandstone. Atop this sandstone is a layer of basalt (very dark, geologically recent volcanic rock) that contributes to the aesthetic of the area. The 7,400 acres of this park are just a small portion of the 62,000 acres of the Red Cliffs Desert Reserve. This park is popular for hiking, photography, road cycling, and wildlife viewing. Desert species include roadrunners, tree frogs, desert tortoises, and leopard lizards.

Craig Bowden

THE AUTHOR'S SILHOUETTE AGAINST THE BACKDROP OF ST. GEORGE FROM HIGH ON THE SANDSTONE CLIFFS IN SNOW CANYON STATE PARK

**MUSEUMS Daughters of Utah Pioneer Museum** (435-628-7274; www.dupinternational.org), 145 North 100 East, St. George. Open Monday–Saturday 10–5. The Daughters of Utah is a longstanding pillar of Utah tradition, its museum paying tribute to the women and men of Utah's history. Throughout the history of the Mormon religion, women have ideally served a highly domestic and thrifty role. This museum examines the household workings, period clothing, and domestic industries of the pioneer days. Free admission.

**Rosenbruch Wildlife Museum** (435-656-0033; www.rosenbruch.org), 1835 Convention Center Dr., St. George. Open Monday noon–9, Tuesday–Saturday 10–6. This museum is a new, 25,000-square-foot space with educational exhibits and dioramas featuring 300 species of animals from the earth's far corners. $8 for adults, $6 for seniors ages 55 and up, $4 for children ages 3–12, free for children under two.

**St. George Art Museum** (435-627-4525; www.sgcity.org/artmuseum), 47 East 200 North, St. George. Open Monday–Saturday 10–5. The building that houses the museum is one of the few remaining early buildings of St. George's earlier days. Built in 1934 for the Utah-Idaho Sugar Company, it was originally a sugar beet seed storage shed and could hold about 2 million pounds of seed. After falling into disrepair, it was purchased and revitalized in 1997 to become the St. George Art Museum. Today, the museum allows guests to absorb art in open space lit by skylights. $2 for adults, $1 for children ages 3–11, and free for children under 3.

**LANDMARKS Anasazi Ridge Petroglyphs,** west of St. George. On the capstone about 250 feet above the valley are several hundred petroglyphs. These were made by the Virgin Anasazi (named so because of the Virgin River). Brigham Young University excavations have discovered potential ruins of pueblos on the ridge as well. A wide variety of figures, symbols, and items (such as blankets and tools) have been etched into the dark brown varnish. This trailhead is located just south of UT 8, toward the southern end of Leeds, off South 3 Mile Lane (which is just west of 800 West St.).

**Brigham Young Winter Home** (Temple Visitors Center: 435-673-5181; www.lds .org/placestovisit), 67 West 200 North, St. George. Because of his important role as spiritual leader and director of the burgeoning 19th-century Mormon empire, Brigham Young had almost as many homes across Utah as wives. This home was finished and occupied by Young in 1873, four years prior to his death. A telegraph line allowed him to stay connected to Salt Lake City while he oversaw the construction of the St. George Temple, whilst the warm "Dixie" climate soothed his aches and pains throughout the winter. The interior has been diligently preserved and restored, and is adorned with period furniture and Young's personal effects. Mulberry trees in the front yard commemorate the pioneer days when working silkworms were fed the mulberries produced by these trees.

**Fort Pearce** (www.blm.gov), 11.5 miles southeast of Washington; reached by following 400 South Street in Washington across the Virgin River and into the Warner Valley. Access is regulated only by road conditions, which are sometimes bad during winter. It wasn't that long ago that Utah was the frontier—a time when Native American and Mormon relations were uncertain at best. Fort Peace is a small fortification from this era that still stands as a reminder of these times no longer than 150 years ago. This was built during the 1865–1870 Black Hawk War.

THE GEM TRAIL TOURS A RIM ABOVE THE VIRGIN RIVER OUTSIDE OF HURRICANE.

Kami Hardcastle

Though not actually a war, it was a period of raids committed on the Mormons by the Ute and sometimes the Navajo tribes. Only ruins of this outpost remain, but they are interesting to see nonetheless. Free admission.

**Grafton Ghost Town** was originally founded in 1859 and never meant to endure. Just more than two years after its settlement, it was completely demolished by catastrophic flooding. After a relocation to higher ground, it continued to endure abuse from the Virgin River and attacks from Indian tribes during the Blackhawk War. This ghost town is impressively expansive and well preserved, with some reconstruction. This was a filming site for *Butch Cassidy and the Sundance Kid* during the late 1960s. Grafton is accessed by taking Bridge Lane south out of St. George across the Virgin River, then turning immediately right and heading west for about 2.5 miles.

**Green Gate Village Historic Inn** (435-628-6999 or 800-350-6999; www.green gatevillageinn.com), 76 West Tabernacle, St. George. This campus is a collection of 14 historical St. George Victorian-style homes. Now a high-end inn complex near downtown St. George, these were once the homes of the city's first gentry, including Orson Pratt and William Bentley, and were built as early as 1862. Some of the homes have been at these exact locations since their erection; others were moved and rebuilt piece by piece to save them from "the March of Progress." Naturally, these have been updated to function as hotels, but their original style remains. Other homes include the 1864 Christmas Cottage, 1872 Thomas Judd Home, 1879 Orpha Morris Home, and the 1881 William Tolley House.

The name "Green Gate" has a comical place in history. As the St. George was being completed, Brigham Young put in an order for white paint. Upon the delivery of the paint, Young was disappointed to discover that the paint was in fact green. UPS wasn't around yet to return this item, so Young donated the paint to members of the community to paint their homes. Some of this remains on the gate in front of Green Hedge (on 200 East). Self-guided tours of the campus are allowed every day from dawn to dusk; a guided tour can be arranged with a docent (by appointment only) Wednesday at noon.

**Jacob Hamblin Home** (call the St. George Visitors Center: 435-673-5181; www .lds.org/placestovisit), intersection of Santa Clara Blvd. and Hamblin Dr., Santa Clara. Open 9–5 in winter, 9–6 in summer. Jacob Hamblin, one of the earliest settlers of the St. George area and a prominent church leader, was best known for his gift of peace negotiations in potentially hostile Native American situations. Fittingly, this church leader was also the head of a very large family that lived in this home in the late 1800s. Today you can get a visual impression of domestic life in these times and walk the on-site orchards. Free admission.

**Mountain Meadows Massacre Site,** reached by taking UT 18 north from St. George through Veyo and Central for a total of about 30 miles; signs indicate a parking lot on Dan San Hill, about 5 miles past Central. This site is one of early Utah's most sensitive topics. During the summer of 1857, a pioneer wagon train was crossing through Utah. En route from Arkansas to California, they had set up camp here and were attacked during the early morning hours of September 7. During these hours, they were inexplicably besieged by local Mormon militia and accompanying Native Americans. Through a series of brutal and calculated events over the course of five days, almost every member of this pioneer group was murdered. Of roughly 120 travelers, only 17 children were spared. This event is sorrowfully remembered by the descendants of the victims and by the LDS church.

Indeed, Utah's Mormons felt harassed and threatened by the U.S. government during the Utah War, and there was general animosity between Mormons and non-Mormons. Though this suggests a motive behind the slayings, a justifiable or compelling reason for such a horrific act has never been discovered.

**St. George Tabernacle** (435-673-5181; www.lds.org/placestovisit), intersection of Main St. and Tabernacle Ave., St. George. Open 9–5 in winter, 9–6 in summer. Unlike many of the modern, peculiar Mormon buildings, this tabernacle is more reminiscent of a historic New England church than its western sisters. Construction of this building began almost immediately after the founding of St. George, in early June of 1863. This structure took 13 years to complete, and today it bears the etchings and stonework of its original construction. Materials range from sandstone quarried locally to original glass brought from New England at the time of construction. Free admission.

**St. George Temple** (435-673-3533; www.ldschurchtemples.com), 250 East 400 South, St. George. The temple's interior is closed to all but qualified Mormons; the visitors center (on the lawn) is open 9–9 daily. This temple was the first Utah temple to be finished and the only one that was completed before Brigham Young's passing. Ground was broken in 1871, and the dedication took place in April of 1877. This temple, because of its early completion and potential for ambassadorship to southern, non-Mormon settlements, has always been considered one of (if not *the*) most significant and special temple in the religion, and it is the world's oldest functioning LDS temple. Though it is stunningly white, it is actually built of sandstone coated in white stucco.

**Silver Reef Ghost Town,** reached by taking I-15 north from St. George about 15 miles to Leeds; in this town, head to the northeast end of town on UT 228, and you will see signs for Silver Reef. Another in Washington County, this town has a most interesting place in modest history. In an area of Caucasian settlers that were otherwise virtually 100 percent Mormon, this mining town was full of Catholic and Protestant miners excavating the only silver vein ever to be found in sandstone. Through a quirky and unlikely series of geologic events, silver had prehistorically been deposited in abundant supply in petrified driftwood that was found plentifully scattered throughout the area. The town grew rapidly in population and wealth from the 1870s to the 1880s. In stark contrast to St. George and the other nearby towns and missions, this town had almost 40 mines and thrived on saloons, brothels, and gambling. Beyond this was the conservative infrastructure of schools, churches, food suppliers, clothiers, and even a newspaper. At one time it was suggested that this town should even become the territorial capital, but the surrounding Mormon majority would have none of it. As with many other boomtowns, the "boom" ended with a bang around 1893 when a series of events would cause people to demolish many buildings seeking hidden coin. A renovated Wells Fargo building, originally built in 1877, contains the **Silver Reef Museum** (435-876-2254) and **Jerry Anderson Studio and Gallery.**

AMUSEMENT PARKS ♂ **Fiesta Family Fun Center** (435-628-1818; www .fiestafuncenter.com), 171 East 1160 South, St. George. Open 10–10 Monday–Thursday, 10 AM–11 PM Friday–Saturday, and 11–7 Sunday. This amusement center is a good option for families. Kids might gravitate toward the arcade, children's go-karts, and the extensive jungle-gym-type complex, while adults and teens prefer bumper tubes in the pool, adult go-karts, the batting cage, and mini golf. Prices are à la carte; package deals are available. Access to certain rides is height dependent.

✦ **Laser Mania** (435-656-5832; www.laser-mania.com), 67 East St. George Blvd., St. George. Open 4–10 Monday–Thursday, 4–11 Friday, 11–11 Saturday; closed Sunday. Here you can choose between two main tag rooms. One is a multilevel, 3,600-square-foot room with a celestial theme. The other is a maze with neon murals that pop to three dimensions with the use of 3D glasses. Other attractions are an arcade and an army tank room where participants control miniature tanks equipped with laser tag technology via remote control.

## ✳ Outdoor Activities

Early spring and late fall are the best times to play outside in St. George. However, winters are quite pleasant by comparison to many places, and high mountains, like Brian Head Resort, enjoy reasonable temperatures in the summer. The area's most famous outdoor attraction is its 12 beautiful golf courses. In addition to the activities listed below, do not forget that Zion National Park, Cedar Breaks National Monument, and other national parks are nearby (and listed in this book).

BIKING Biking in and around St. George is greatly benefited by the open land, scenic desert landscape, and sunny, warm climate. As with the other outdoor activities, biking in St. George is best done in the spring and fall. Winter is usually a bit too cool for most people's taste, and summer is much too hot. Both road biking and mountain biking here are quite good; for mountain biking information, check www.utahmountainbiking.com. This is an outstanding database with dozens and dozens of rides listed according to location (roughly 40 in the St. George area alone), each with a complete approach and route description, trail notes, comments on technical and physical difficulty, and illustrative photos—many descriptions are even accompanied by video.

THE TOASTED FOREST NEAR BRIAN HEAD FEATURES MANY OF UTAH'S OLD AND GNARLED BRISTLECONE PINES.

Kami Hardcastle

## Bike Rentals & Shops

**Bicycles Unlimited** (435-673-4492 or 888-673-4492; www.bicyclesunlimited .com), 90 South 100 East, St. George. This shop has a retail selection, as well as rentals of road and mountain bikes (full and front suspension), children's bikes, children's trailer bikes, children's trailers, and car racks.

**Moke Sports** (435-652-4499; www.mokeoutdoors.com), 205 West St. George Blvd., St. George. Moke offers a variety of outdoor sports, including camping, hiking, biking, and related apparel. Bike rentals are available by reservation. Call ahead, or download, complete, and mail a rental form to the store.

### Mountain Biking

**Anasazi Trail** is a small network of trails with multiple access points. This trail stays atop the rim above the Santa Clara River. Because rapid city growth in the area means the speedy rise of housing developments, roads in the area are constantly changing and being added. Call any of the shops listed at the beginning of this section to verify access. The Anasazi Trailhead is located in the Santa Clara River Preserve, the location of the very condensed petroglyphs site (mentioned in *To See and Do,* earlier). This trailhead is located just south of UT 8, toward the southern end of Leeds, off South 3 Mile Lane (which is just west of 800 West St.).

**Green Valley Trail/Bear Claw Poppy** is a very built-up, highly technical, and thrilling BMX-like trail whose 6 miles are packed with entertaining terrain—rolling jumps, banked turns, and sections with names like "Clavical Hill." All of this gravity-powered fun is attained by way of a respectable mile-long climb at the very beginning of the ride. Before dropping in, you can check out the view where you can see Snow Canyon State Park and, more remotely, Zion National Park to the east. To get there, head west of I-15 on Bluff Street. Take a left to head south on Tonaquint Drive. Follow this road as it bends west, and then south again. This will "T" into Bloomington Drive, at which point you take a right to head west on this road. After it curves to travel south, make a right onto Navajo Drive, and continue on this road as it turns to dirt. The ride begins at the cattle guard.

**Gooseberry Mesa** is the nearest off-road riding to Zion National Park that you can do. A 5-mile dirt road has been the main trail for years. However, a system of single-track trails has recently been developed here that features sections of slick rock as well as single track. Along the ride are views of Zion National Park's monuments and overlooks of the Virgin River. The trailhead is along Bridge Road; this is a dirt road accessed either by heading south from UT 9 in Rockville, or by heading north from UT 57 to the southeast of Hurricane.

### Road Biking

**Snow Canyon Loop** is one of the area's most accessible and scenic rides. To do this ride, take Bluff Street northwest out of St. George and turn onto the Snow Canyon Parkway. At this point, you have two options: one is a true road ride; the other follows along a bike path. The road option heads through Snow Canyon along UT 8 and returns downhill to St. George on UT 18. The other option is to take the Snow Canyon Paved Loop. This essentially traces the same route as that of the state highways, but it is set away from motorized vehicles. To take this loop, look for the trail just after you've made a left onto Snow Canyon Drive. You will be forced to ride a short distance on UT 8 at the top of the park. The loop around the

Kami Hardcastle

THE GOOSEBERRY MESA TRAIL IS LOCATED JUST WEST OF THE ZION NATIONAL PARK ENTRANCE AND, PACKED WITH UTAH'S FAMOUS SANDSTONE SLICK-ROCK RIDING, IS ONE OF THE MOST POPULAR MOUNTAIN BIKING TRAILS IN SOUTHWEST UTAH.

park is 18 miles long, with an elevation from 2,910 to 3,960 feet. $5 admission to Snow Canyon State Park.

**FISHING AND BOATING** The St. George area is certainly no fishing and boating destination, but for those already living or visiting the area, some fishing does exist. Most bodies of water in the vicinity used for this type of recreation are reservoirs.

**Fremont River Outfitters** (435-491-0242; www.flyfishingsouthernutah.com). Based in the Fremont Valley, this is the only full-service fly-fishing guide service and fly shop in Utah's southwestern corner. Clients enjoy private access to hidden lakes and 6 miles of river for fly-fishing small-stream style. Set amid the Markagunt Plateau in the Fremont Valley to the north of Thousand Lakes Mountain and beneath the Boulder Mountains, this company offers trips to all skill levels. Fish species include brown, cutthroat, rainbow, brook, and tiger trout.

**Hurst Sports Center** (435-673-6141; www.hurststores.com), 160 North Bluff St., St. George. This sportsman's shop has been in business since 1946 and is a good place to stop for gear, permits, and recommendations.

**The Sportsman's Warehouse** (435-634-7300; www.sportsmanswarehouse.com), 2957 East 850 North, St. George. This large store is a multifaceted, very traditional outdoors/hunting superstore with fishing department.

**Gunlock Reservoir State Park,** located 21 miles northwest of St. George (and just south of Gunlock City); take Sunset Boulevard/UT 8 northwest out of St. George, then Old US 91, and make a right on North Gunlock Road just a few miles after leaving the outskirts of Ivins. This is one of the more popular and accessible fisheries in the area. It is a fairly small reservoir set in stark, low-vegetation desert hills. There are just 250 surface acres, but its boat ramp, free access, camping availability, and bluegill, catfish, crappie, and largemouth bass are attractive.

**Baker Reservoir** is about 23 miles northwest of St. George; from Veyo, take UT 18 about 5 miles north, and turn east onto Baker Lake Drive. This offers brown trout, crappie, and rainbow trout fishing, but has no boat ramp.

**Quail Creek Reservoir,** 10 miles northeast of St. George via I-15 exit 16 and UT 9. This state park has a boat ramp, red-rock surroundings, a picnic area, beach, and developed campground.

**Sand Hollow State Park,** also accessible by I-15 exit 16 and UT 9. Open 6 AM–10 PM daily. Utah's newest state park features a slightly larger reservoir than Quail Creek and is at the base of Sand Mountain. This reservoir is quite distinctive, with its clean waters lapping rounded, deep orange sandstone. $10 for boat launches, $13 for primitive camping, $25 for developed campsites.

**GOLF St. George** (435-652-4653), 2190 South 1400 East, St. George. This very open, public course has a maximum of 7,192 yards and 18 holes. Built in 1975, the greens of this course are fairly straightforward, and hole 9 is one of the best in the state, with views of Bloomington Hills and the city. $33 October through May, $19 June through September.

**Coral Canyon Golf Course** (435-688-1700; www.coralcanyongolf.com), 1925 North Canyon Greens Dr., St. George. Coral Canyon, an 18-hole, par-72, 7,029-yard public course, is beautifully laid out and tucked very pleasingly into surrounding red-rock peninsulas. $103 October through May, $78 June through September; discounts for Washington County residents.

**SunRiver Golf Course** (435-986-0001; www.sunriver.com), 4210 South Bluegrass Way, St. George. This course has a challenging desert layout, yet is considered good for all skill levels, with often wide fairways and reasonable prices. This 18-hole, 6,704-yard course has a very open layout and rolling topography. $46 October through May, $26 June through September.

**HIKING** Because of the desert climate and general lack of canopy around southwest Utah, hiking in the St. George area is best done from late fall through early spring, unless hiking at very high elevations. Because of the very dry and exposed nature of this environment, you should prepare yourself by bringing several liters of water per person per day, high-rating sunscreen, and plenty of warm clothing to protect from wind and rain.

**Anasazi Trail/Petroglyphs.** See *To See and Do* and *Mountain Biking*.

**Red Cliffs Nature Trail,** trailhead at the Red Cliffs Campground, 15 miles north of St. George in Leeds; take the Frontage Road south to Quail Lake and follow signs for the Red Cliffs. This popular campground and hiking trail is administered by the BLM and is very well marked on all accounts. Along the trail are small placards identifying various flora, fauna, and other natural phenomena. This trail follows along a stream in an intimate canyon; the main route ends at a waterfall (sometimes dry in late summer), but a trail leads up, over, and miles beyond the waterfall.

**Signal Peak (from Oak Grove Campground),** 8.5 miles north of Leeds; from Leeds, head north on Silver Reef Road as it turns to Oak Grove Road This trail is 7.5 miles round-trip and ascends the flanks of the highest peak in the Pine Valley Mountains. At a junction along the way, follow signs for FURTHER WATER. Though the trail comes just shy of the actual summit, expansive views of Zion National Park and the surrounding Beaver Dam and Pine Valley mountains are more than sufficient.

**Snow Canyon State Park** (435-628-2255; www.stateparks.utah.gov). As described in *To See and Do*, this is a very popular hiking place, with trails leading through very diverse geology and flora, rewarding hikers with discoveries of lava tubes, Joshua trees, high mountain peaks, and narrow sandstone canyons. Many of the hikes are quite short but gain interesting viewpoints, including the **Butterfly Trail, Cinder Cone Trail, Johnson Canyon,** and **Hidden Pinyon Trail. Jenny's Canyon,** near the mouth of Snow Canyon, is a short, nontechnical slot canyon. By nature of it being a state park, there is staff at the entrance station who can advise you based on your needs.

ROCK CLIMBING The St. George area is one of Utah's more popular rock climbing destinations during early spring and late fall, as well as on warm winter weekends. Though it is generally considered too hot to climb proficiently here in the summer months, some dead-north-facing cliffs and caves (in canyons or at high enough elevations) are considered somewhat climbable in the hot season. Most of the climbing around St. George is limestone and sandstone sport climbing, but there are also some traditional sandstone routes, basalt sport climbs, and sandstone boulder problems. The Web sites www.rockclimbing.com and www.mountain project.com offer general, community-fed information on the area. Also available at www.drtopo.com are free mini guides to Las Vegas–area roped climbs and St. George–area climbs.

**Outdoor Outlet** (435-628-3611; www.outdooroutlet.com), 1062 East Tabernacle. This shop has a climbing selection, as well as staff who can help point you in the right direction, crag-wise. Moe's Valley is reached only by a complicated set of directions and through a rapidly developing neighborhood. Be sure to inquire here if you wish to boulder there.

**Red Rocks, Nevada.** This is a vast complex of climbing (sport, traditional, and bouldering) just west of Las Vegas. The most popular areas at Red Rocks are the single-pitch sport routes along the scenic loop. However, excellent multipitch climbing exists in the near vicinity. The very tall walls of **Ice Box Canyon** and **Black Velvet Canyon,** both primarily traditional sandstone walls west of Las Vegas, are two of these. Many books exist for Las Vegas–area rock climbing. Three books that cover essentially the same areas at or near the Red Rock Scenic Loop are *Red Rock Canyon: A Climbing Guide* by Roxanna Brock, *The Red Rocks of Southern Nevada* by Joanne Urioste (with many climbs not covered by any other book), and *Rock Climbing Red Rocks* by Todd Swain. Another book that covers the mostly limestone climbing mainly to the north of Las Vegas is *Las Vegas Limestone* by Roxanna Brock, and Nevada's entire selection of limestone is covered by *Islands in the Sky,* by Dan McQuade, Randy Leavitt, and Mick Ryan.

**St. George Crags.** Closest to St. George is **Moe's Valley** sandstone bouldering, **Chuckawalla Wall** and other sandstone sport climbing, and **Snow Canyon State Park** traditional sandstone climbing. The next nearest areas, all within 30 minutes of driving, are limestone **Utah Hills, Welcome Springs,** and **Woodbury Road Crags** sport climbs, and the very difficult sport routes in the limestone **Virgin River Gorge.** Farther still (in the general vicinity) are the conglomerate sport

Craig Bowden

THE SUN SETS ON THE UTAH HILLS, JUST WEST OF ST. GEORGE.

crags of **Parowan Gap** and **Shiobe,** and limestone sport climbs at **West Cedar Crags,** and Basalt and Welded Tuff at **Brianhead.** The driving directions and approaches for all of these areas is quite lengthy, but the authority on all of these crags is the book by Todd Goss, *Rock Climbs of Southwest Utah & the Arizona Strip.*

SKIING See the *Skiing* section in the "Cedar City" chapter.

## ✳ Lodging

St. George has more than 2,800 hotel and motel rooms, and that number is rapidly growing. However, these hotel rooms are exclusively divided among many familiar modest hotels. Though these are familiar chain names, it is good to have a selection, as lack of vacancy can sometimes be an issue here. These include **Hilton Garden Inn** (435-673-8440; www.hiltongarden inn1.hilton.com), 1731 South Convention Center Dr., St. George; **Hampton Inn** (435-652-1200; www.hampton inn.com), 53 North River Rd., St. George; **Holiday Inn** (435-628-4235 or 877-863-4780; www.ichotelsgroup .com), 850 Bluff St., St. George; **Crys-** **tal Inn** (435-688-7477; www.crystal inns.com), 1450 Hilton Dr., St. George; **St. George Howard Johnson** (435-628-8000; www.hojo.com), 1040 South Main St., St. George; **Best Western Coral Hills** (435-673-4844; www.coral hills.com), 125 East St. George Blvd., St. George; **Best Western Travel Inn** (435-673-3541; www.book.bestwestern .com), 316 East St. George Blvd., St. George; **Fairfield Inn** (435-669-4338; www.marriott.com), 1660 South Convention Center Dr., St. George; and **Best Western Abbey Inn** (435-652-1234), 1129 South Bluff St., St. George.

**The Coyote Inn at the Green Valley Spa** (435-628-8060 or 800-237-

1068), 1871 West Canyon View Dr., St. George. This is St. George's all-in-one vacation, accommodations, spa, and fitness center. This campus has a style marked by greenery and stucco, and is accented with a 45,000-rose garden. Here there are facilities for tennis, racquetball, and golf, as well as a 20,000-square-foot spa, six pools, full fitness center with weights, and guided outdoor trips. All of this is supported by fitness, wellness, and spiritual programs; four-star accommodations; and on-site dining. Their fitness activities include rock climbing, yoga, Pilates, golf, mountain biking, tennis, and desert hiking. The cuisine at the spa has a focus on elegantly prepared whole foods; the selections add to the healthy environment rather than detract from it with opulence. All rooms and suites have four-diamond status, private balcony, and a neat, bright Southwest design that adds to the cleansing experience. Prices vary dependent on the package.

**Green Gate Village Historic Inn** (435-628-6999 or 800-350-6999; www.greengatevillageinn.com), 76 West Tabernacle, St. George. The Green Gate Village is one of St. George's most historic sections of town. (See the *Landmarks* section of this chapter.) These homes are among some of the oldest homes in the area and were built by some of the most significant founding fathers. Their history is the pride of this village, and so is featured wherever possible. Plaques, restoration, appropriate furniture, and décor do as much as possible to leave this sentiment intact. Because this village is a private campus, you feel encapsulated by the time period, as you are completely surrounded by the brickwork and style of the 19th century. Naturally, the era of construction does not lend itself to spacious quarters, but

the lack of clutter gives the rooms cozy simplicity. $99–$350.

**Red Mountain Spa** (435-673-4905; www.redmountainspa.com), 1275 Red Mountain Circle, Ivins. The Red Mountain Spa features a full resort, as well as overnight accommodations. Guests can choose between rooms and suites. Both varieties are designed and decorated with modern, artsy Southwestern themes, though they avoid the stereotypical stucco and woven blanket look, instead integrating curves, art, and desert color themes, avoiding the kitsch. The rooms and the villas have been designed to flow aesthetically into the surrounding natural landscape. The spa exists to saturate its guests with natural health and living, and the restaurant continues along this theme. Not only is the gourmet food wholesome, of the earth, and fresh, but the spa also offers culinary education so that the experience and goodness here can be blended into life back at home. Additionally, there is extensive physical education, integrated fitness programs, detoxification programs, and outdoor recreation trips and information. This is meant to create an all-inclusive fine experience that accentuates and is accentuated by an already beautiful environment and climate. Rates depend on the package.

**Seven Wives Inn** (800-600-3737; www.sevenwivesinn.com), 217 North 400 West, St. George. This is a historic bed-and-breakfast located squarely in the old section of town, adjacent to the old Brigham Young House and within walking distance of local galleries and restaurants. The Seven Wives is a conglomerate of two homes and one small cottage. Rooms vary in size and décor, but the common thread is elegant compliance with the historic nature of the homes. Breakfast is prepared each morning from scratch and is served in the dining room. A variety of massage service is available upon request. An outdoor pool is located in the center of this small property. $99–$215.

## ✴ Where to Eat

St. George, like many midsize Utah towns, is heavy on familiar, cheap-and-easy restaurants that cater to families and are light on the wallet. There are very few restaurants in the middle range; the vast majority are quite generic and inexpensive, and there is a giant leap to an elite class of rare fine-dining establishments. Be aware that food service is very difficult to find much later than 8 or 9 PM (other than the high-end establishments) and is next to impossible to locate on a Sunday.

**Painted Pony** (435-634-1700; www.painted-pony.com), northwestern corner of St. George Blvd. and Main St. Open for lunch and dinner Monday–Sunday. This is one of St. George's best dining options, serving inventive, fresh American cuisine with slight hints of Japanese, European, and Western American menus. There is a heavy emphasis on seafood and fine beef and poultry. A wine list, which is not available everywhere in this part of the state, *is* here. Entrées $22–$32.

**Scaldoni's** (435-674-1300), intersection of Sunset Blvd. and Valley View Dr. (just west of Bluff St.). This is St. George's best Italian restaurant, and a contender for its best all-around dining establishment. The presentation of the plates, service, quality, and creative pairing of ingredients allows you to take a detour from heavy plates laden with generic pasta. Surf and turf, seared ahi, fresh-herb sauces, and creative appetizers give this a very contemporary flavor. Classic salads, poultry, and pastas stay true to the Italian roots. The dining room is very handsome and bathed in soft, but warm, light. Entrées $11–$35.

## ✴ Entertainment

MUSIC **Celebrity Concert Series** (435-652-7994; www.dixie.edu), Cox Auditorium, Dixie State College campus (along 700 South, just south of the intersection of 700 East and 300 South), St. George. Though St. George is neither a major city nor a cultural hub, its residents adore the arts, and the city provides them accordingly with a high-density concentration of top-notch theatrical, dance, opera, symphonic, modern, and ethnic experiences for the most affordable prices possible. While most events take place in the Cox Auditorium, a few artists perform in the Browning Auditorium, in the north-center of campus, just south of the intersection of 900 East and 100 South. Parking for both auditoriums is on the northeast corner of 700 East and 300 South.

**Southern Utah Heritage Choir** (435-628-1658). This home-grown choral group, a very dedicated amateur bunch that is in part sponsored by the National Endowment for the Arts, puts on nearly 20 concerts each year. The choir originated from the idea that southern Utah holds a special place in the region's heritage and should be commemorated through music. Thus it is a cornerstone of festivity and the arts throughout the holidays, heritage events, and town celebrations. While performances are held all over, perhaps the most can be seen in the St. George Tabernacle.

**Southwest Symphony** (information: 435-688-8183, tickets: 435-652-7800; www.southwestsymphony.org). This symphonic orchestra is composed of 85 members and has been playing for the St. George area since 1982. This well-honed group puts on somewhere around 20 concerts each year. Under the same umbrella is the **Southwest Chorale** and the **Zion Youth Symphony**. The home stage for these organizations is Dixie College's Cox Auditorium.

**VENUES O. C. Tanner Amphitheater** (435-652-7994; www.dixie.edu/tanner), on Lion Ave., north of UT 9 (en route to Zion National Park, Springdale). Owned and operated by Dixie State College, this outdoor amphitheater is one of the best places to spend a summer evening enjoying an installment of a concert series that fills the stands May through September each year. Musicians of many varieties, from bluegrass to classical and jazz, grace the stage while a film featuring Zion is projected onto a mammoth-sized screen. Just miles west of the towering, sheer sandstone walls of Zion National Park, this amphitheater has a surrounding as fine as any theater in the world. Check the Web site or call for event schedules and pricing.

**St. George Tabernacle** (435-673-5181), 18 South Main St., St. George. The St. George Tabernacle has been at the physical and community center of the town since its completion in 1876, after 13 years of construction. Aesthetically, it resembles a historic New England church and is considered one of the more beautiful pieces of LDS architectures. Most of the ingredients of this tabernacle were quarried or harvested locally. The upper walls are made of sandstone, and 3-foot-thick basement walls are made of limestone. The two spiral staircases here were hand carved with full balustrades. The on-site clock was brought across the country from New York and was considered quite a grand addition by the early townspeople, as it was thought to have given the town legitimacy and

prestige. This building was painstakingly restored in 1993 to emulate its original condition, and today it seats 1,200 people. Free recitals are generally given daily, as well as church services, and the weekly Dixie History and Music Series.

**THEATER The Utah Shakespearean Festival** (general information: 435-586-7880, tickets: 435-586-7878 or 800-752-9849; www.bard.org), Cedar City. This is a major event with hundreds of performances of 10 or so dramas from June through September each year, complete with extras including backstage tours, symposiums, and other bonuses. See *To See and Do* in the "Cedar City" chapter.

**St. George Musical Theater** (435-628-8755; www.sgmt.org), 200 North 1000 East, St. George. The St. George Musical Theater uses deluxe staging, believable costuming, and well-rehearsed music to share the joy of musical theater with the community. The theater emphasizes fun and historic presentations. The theater was the brainchild and life's work of the late Mark Ogden and continues to put on around five or six different productions each season.

**Tuacahn Amphitheater** (435-652-3300 or 800-746-9882; www.tuacahn.org), 1100 Tuacahn Dr., Ivins. Tuacahn is a large, state-of-the-art campus that takes advantage of the beautiful southern Utah landscape and climate to create a beautifully integrated campus for the arts. The name itself means "canyon of the gods," and the facility includes a high school, 2,000-seat outdoor amphitheater, indoor auditorium (inside the Hafen Theater), and gift shop. All of this is nestled among boulders and desert plants beneath 1,500-foot sandstone cliffs. This modern facility attracts hundreds of thousands

## COYOTE ART VILLAGE

**Coyote Gulch Art Village** (435-674-9595; www.coyotegulchartvillage.com), 875 Coyote Gulch Ct., Ivins. Coyote Gulch is an actual art village with galleries, dining, art classes, and even film screenings. At the heart of this community is a very condensed and vivid scene of creativity encased in thoughtful modern architecture and integrated into its natural surroundings. Views of the spectacular desert surrounding the compound leave little guessing as to what exactly the inspiration for these artists is. Outside are the **Desert Rose Labyrinth,** a stone-garden-type installation outside, and the **Xetava Desert Arboretum** (435-673-6628), a colorful and artistic living bouquet of desert plants.

Be sure to look at the Web site's events calendar during your visit.

**Datura Gallery** (435-674-9595), 845 Coyote Gulch Ct., Ivins. Open 10–5 daily. This gallery is largely a jewelry gallery, its works ranging from carved wood to brass, silver, bronze, and stained glass. Most of the pieces here, whether jewelry or not, were created locally by Native American artists, some of whom live in the village.

**Blue Raven Studio** (435-627-2361), 807 Coyote Gulch Ct., Ivins. This is another community space whose focus is on painting. The studio is available to the public through classes and monthly rentals.

**Gallery 873** (435-673-6628), 873 Coyote Gulch Ct., Ivins. This is the metal

each year and is completely handicapped accessible.

**SPORTS Dixie State College Rebels** (www.dixieathletics.com). Dixie State athletics is the home of St. George's most popular and advanced sports teams. This NCAA member has basketball, softball, baseball, men's golf, football, tennis, cross country, volleyball, and soccer teams.

## ✳ Selective Shopping

**MALLS The Outlets at Zion** (435-674-9800; www.theoutletsatzion.com), 250 Red Cliffs Dr., St. George. Located just east of I-15, this bargain center offers a variety of high-quality goods in

high concentration at reduced prices. Here you'll see plenty of familiar names, like Eddie Bauer, Van Heusen, Gap, Levi, Polo Ralph Lauren, and Urban Wear.

**Red Cliffs Mall** (435-251-9970; www.redcliffsmall.com), 1770 Red Cliffs Dr., St. George. This classic mall houses Barnes and Noble, Hollister, Coach, Dillard's, JCPenney, and Sears, as well as a food court, movie theaters, and the like.

**GALLERIES The Artist's Gallery** (435-628-9293; www.theartists gallery.com), 95 East Telegraph Rd., Washington. The Artist's Gallery is a community-wide co-op showcasing the

arts gallery on the Coyote campus. Sculpture includes indoor, wall, jewelry, and other functional or decorative items.

**Juniper Sky Art Gallery** (435-674-2306), 851 Coyote Gulch Ct., Ivins. Open 10–5 daily. This is a simple, clean space with spacious windows ushering in sunlight. Its walls' subdued desert coloring allows the colors of the paintings and the textures of the sculptures to pop. The fine art here is often local but ranges from painting to sculpture, furniture, and blown glass.

**Xetava Gardens** (435-656-0165; www.xetavagardenscafe.com). This is a desert arboretum with art displays, a reading room, café, and tapas-style dining. Each Friday a film is screened at the open-air patio. Delicious Mediterranean-influenced breakfast and lunch served seven days a week, and dinner is available Thursday through Saturday. Beer and wine are available. This restaurant is full of vitality, with fresh produce, sunshine, tasteful desert furnishings, and special events that range from belly dancers to tea tastings.

**Zia Pottery Studio** (435-688-8300), 833 Coyote Gulch Ct., Ivins. This high-ceilinged work space is filled with light, creativity, clay, wheels, kilns, and glazes. Better yet, this studio is open to the public—open to novices through classes, and open to experienced potters through membership. Workshops include wheel-thrown, hand-building, tile-making, and mask-making techniques. Call or look online for a detailed schedule.

works of as many as 20 artists at once. It is made possible only by the volunteer work of these artists and volunteers. Because of the diversity of the artists, the works are varied and include fine arts, small gifts, greeting cards, and art and keepsakes of other media.

# CEDAR CITY

Cedar City is one of Utah's biggest small towns. Though it is located less than an hour north of St. George along I-15, it retains its own style and old-town charm. From the outside, it does not appear to be anything more than an interstate town, but its historic downtown is home to many local businesses, old brick buildings, and Utah's famous Shakespearean Festival. Additionally, this town is a great base camp for nearby Zion National Park, Brian Head Ski Resort, Parowan Gap rock climbing and petroglyphs, and Cedar Breaks National Monument.

**GUIDANCE** **Cedar City and Brian Head Tourism Bureau** (435-586-5124 or 800-354-4849; www.scenicsouthernutah.com). This office operates a Web site with recreational opportunities as well as lodging and dining suggestions, and live help (which operates during business hours only). The Web site hosts an interactive map that allows you to zoom in on specific features and link to information about them.

**Brianhead Chamber of Commerce** (435-677-2810), 56 North Hwy. 143, Brian Head. This small organization is the source of information for the high-elevation summer and winter recreation haven east of Cedar City.

**Cedar City Chamber of Commerce** (435-586-4484; www.chambercedarcity .org), 581 North Main St., Cedar City. One of Cedar City's most major attractions is its events calendar, especially its thespian calendar. This Web site maintains listings on the goings-on.

**GETTING THERE** *By car:* Cedar City is located right along I-15 and is serviced by exits 57 and 59. The heart of town is on Main Street between 200 North and Center Street, which is just about a mile east of exit 59.

*By air:* Cedar City is about 60 miles north of the Utah/Nevada border; within three and a half hours of Salt Lake City and one and a half hours of Las Vegas. See the *Getting There* section of the "St. George" chapter.

*By bus:* **Greyhound Bus Lines** (www.greyhound.com) operates stations in Cedar City (435-586-7400), 1495 West 200 North; St. George (435-673-2933), inside McDonald's, 1235 South Bluff St.; Salt Lake City (801-355-9579), 300 South 600 West; and Las Vegas (702-384-9561), 200 South Main St.

**MEDICAL EMERGENCY** **Intermountain Health Care Cedar City** (435-868-5500; www.intermountainhealthcare.org), 1303 North Main St., Cedar City. This is

Cedar City's regional hospital, with a walk-in clinic and a variety of physician groups.

## ✳ To See and Do

**Adams Shakespearean Theatre** (Southern Utah University Department of Theater Arts & Dance: 435-586-7746; www.suu.edu), southwest of the Center St. and 300 West intersection, Southern Utah University Campus, Cedar City. This 1977 building was designed by local artistic production directors in conjunction with the Utah building heads to emulate 16th-century Tudor-style stages, and it is unmistakably reminiscent of the old Globe Theater. Because of this, Shakespearean films and series have been filmed there. This theater is surrounded by large evergreens and is a perfect place to spend a warm midsummer's night.

**Auditorium Theater** (Southern Utah University Department of Theater Arts & Dance: 435-586-7746; www.suu.edu), on the southwest corner of University Blvd. and 300 West St. This 1954 indoor theater has recently been renovated with fully modern aesthetics and sound technology. The main stage is a proscenium theater and has seating for about 850 people in three tiers. Though a university stage, this is one of the region's most used.

**Randall L. Jones Theatre** (Southern Utah University Department of Theater Arts & Dance: 435-586-7746; www.suu.edu), just northeast of the Center St./300 West intersection, Southern Utah University campus, Cedar City. The work of several architectural firms went into the creation of this building, with the result being a favorite of architectural magazines and arts connoisseurs. This theater seats almost 800 and hosts large groups of performance-arts fans.

**The Utah Shakespearean Festival** (general information: 435-586-7880, tickets: 435-586-7878 or 800-752-9849; www.bard.org). This festival begins in June and lasts through September. It packs the summer full of events, usually with two performance times each day (one in the morning and one in the afternoon). During the beginning of the summer, you can expect four daily performances on two separate stages: **Randall L. Jones Theater,** northeast of the Center St./300 West intersection, at the Southern Utah University campus in Cedar City; and the **Adams Shakespearean Theater,** southwest of the Center St./300 West intersection, also on Southern Utah University campus, Cedar City. The festival brings life and depth to the plays with curtain call lunches, stage tours, symposiums, and online study guides per play available. Matinees begin 2, and evening performances take place at 8 PM. Though the festival concentrates heavily on its namesake playwright, dramas by other playwrights are performed as well.

## ✳ Outdoor Activities

### BIKING

### *Bike Rentals & Shop*

**Cedar Cycle** (435-586-5210; www.cedarcyle.com), 38 East 200 South, Cedar City. This is the consummate bike shop, offering repairs, servicing, road and mountain bike rentals, and an all-around retail shop.

### *Mountain Biking*

**Navajo Lake Trail** does an 11-mile loop around this namesake (natural) lake. For its length, it is a very easy ride or hike. This is approached by leaving Cedar City as for the Cascade Falls Trail (as in *Hiking*); head 25.5 miles east on UT 14 and turn right. Stay on this road as it curves right (to the west) just before the Te-Ah Campground. Be aware that you will be sharing this trail with cyclists, hikers, and horses.

## Road Biking

**Coal Creek Parkway Trail** is a paved trail shared by walkers, runners, Rollerbladers, and cyclists. This trail is extremely short at only 3 miles round-trip, but the city intends to expand this trail in the immediate future. Access points are at the Cedar City Veterans Park, 200 North 200 East, and Canyon Bridge, on the eastern end of Cedar Canyon Road.

GOLF **Cedar Ridge Golf Course** (435-586-2970), 100 East 800 North, Cedar City. This public par-72 course has 18 holes over 6,650 yards. Designed by one John Evans, this is considered one of Utah's finer courses and enjoys the backdrop afforded by the red sandstone hills of Cedar City.

HIKING **Cascade Falls** is a moderately easy hike that is just than 1 mile each way with modest elevation gain. The namesake falls of the hike spurt out from within walls of a cliff, after flowing 2 miles in an underground lava tube from Navajo Lake. The falls cascade down the walls of the Virgin River Rim. Were the lava tube not closed due to safety hazards, it is large enough that it could actually be explored during times of low flow. Though none of the individual cliffs are this tall, the plateau on which the trail is located drops a total of 6,000 feet as it descends in pink and white sandstone formations to Zion National Park. This trail links to a portion of the Virgin River Rim Trail, as described in the *Mountain Biking* section. This particular trail is only designated for foot traffic. To get there, take UT 14 for 25.5 miles east out of Cedar City through Cedar Canyon; turn south as for Navajo

### BRIAN HEAD RESORT MOUNTAIN BIKING

**Brian Head Resort** (435-677-2035; www.brianhead.com), 329 South UT 143, Brian Head. This resort is considered to have southwestern Utah's best mountain biking. With more than 100 miles of single track, summer lift rides and shuttle services, cross-country and downhill trails, this mountain and nearby Cedar Breaks National Monument pair to make quite a scenic outing. Because of the high elevation of this ski area, the mountain bike season does not usually begin until the end of June and does not continue past the end of September. Within the ski area itself is quite a number of trails that vary in difficulty from moderate to advanced, trick-style trails, anywhere from a few miles long to 11 miles long. A map of these is available online, free to download. In addition, the trails immediately serviced by the resort are a number of connecting, often longer distance trails. These start at the 10-mile length and are as long as 33 miles. The **Virgin Rim Trail** is the longest of these, at 33 miles. Often done in multiple days, this trail enjoys views down onto the Virgin River and Zion National Park.

Lake, followed by an immediate left (turn to the east). At this point, you can follow signs to the Cascade Falls trailhead.

**Bristlecone Pine Trail** is a pleasant and very short loop that, like the Cascade Falls Trail (above), gains views of Zion National Park, the Virgin River, and southern Utah to the south. Bristlecone pine is a special species; these trees live to be several thousand years old. Some such trees in the area are believed to be roughly 3,000 years old. This particular brand is characterized by thick, knobby stumps that split into tapered, singular branches. To arrive at the trailhead, go east out of Cedar City on UT 14 (as you would for the Cascade Falls Trail), but turn south after only 17 miles, just past a Zion overlook pullout. The trail is only 0.6 mile long.

**Navajo Lake Trail** is a longer, yet easy trail with pleasant wooded surroundings. For information on this trail, see the *Mountain Biking* section.

ROCK CLIMBING See the *Rock Climbing* section in the "St. George" chapter.

SKIING **Brian Head Resort** (435-586-2478; www.brianhead.com), 329 South UT 143, Brian Head. This is Utah's southernmost downhill ski area. Because of its relative southern location, snow cover here is made possible only by the elevation of the mountain; the base area is at 9,600 feet, and its topmost point is at 11,307 feet. The resort receives an average of 400 inches of snowfall and has a vertical drop of just more than 1,700 feet over 640 skiable acres. Brian Head is known for its family-friendly services and terrain, and is popular among St. George and Las Vegas skiers. There are two main base areas: Navajo Lodge (beneath Navajo Peak) and Giant Steps Lodge (beneath Brian Head Peak). The most challenging terrain is on the slopes of Brian Head Peak; the shoulders of Navajo Peak are almost exclusively easy and moderate terrain. As of 2008, Brian Head was undergoing a massive expansion project to add two new lifts and 35 percent more terrain. By summer, mountain biking and disc golf (435-677-3101) are offered, as well as scenic lift rides and hiking. A full-day adult ticket is only $45 ($52 on holidays), and a child or senior ticket is only $29 ($32 on holidays).

**Ruby's Inn Nordic Skiing** (www.rubysinn.com) is located just outside of the **Best Western Ruby's Inn** (866-866-6616), 1000 South UT 63, Ruby's Inn. This groomed trail system offers 30 kilometers of free skiing that connects to Bryce Canyon National Park's ungroomed (but marked) trails. The trails travel through evergreen forests and gain overlooks of Bryce Canyon, particularly spectacular in winter as the white snow contrasts the reds and oranges of the park. Most trails are gently rolling, but they are challenging due to the high elevation of the area. A trail map of this system is available at the Web site.

## ✳ Lodging

Most of Cedar City's lodging is located around the intersection of Center Street/UT 56 and Main Street, with the highest concentration being along Center Street. There is a high number of budget and moderate chain hotels here, and it is rare that the beds ever fill. The Shakespearean Festival each summer presents the major exception to this case, during which you'll want to be able to have a few backup options, including: **Days Inn** (435-867-8877; www.daysinn.com), 1204 South Main St., Cedar City; **Best Western Inn**

(435-586-9900; www.bestwesternutah
.com), 189 North Main St., Cedar City;
**Holiday Inn Express** (877-449-2332;
www.hiexpress.com), 1555 South Old
Hwy. 91, Cedar City; **Quality Inn**
(435-586-2082; www.qualityinn.com),
250 North 1100 West, Cedar City; and
the **Econolodge** (435-867-4700;
www.econolodge.com), 333 North
1100 West, Cedar City.

**The Garden Cottage** (435-586-4919
or 866-586-4919; www.thegarden
cottagebnb.com), 16 North 200 West,
Cedar City. This bed-and-breakfast is
unabashedly Victorian in its style, with
antique furniture, quilt chests, hardwood floors, angled ceilings, doilies,
and floral designs. The home is surrounded by dense floral gardens, and
each morning a breakfast of fruit,
quiche, homemade bread, and more is
served at 8:30. $115–$130.

**Cherished Memories Bed & Break-
fast** (435-867-6498 or 866-867-6498;
www.cherishedmemoriesbnb.com),
170 North 400 West, Cedar City. This
historic home has been transformed
into a cozy, yet fairly reserved bed-and-
breakfast. The 1906 building itself is a
handsome brick house with sitting
porches, and its guest rooms are cozily
outfitted with tall beds, quilts, and various mismatched wooden and stuffed
furniture. $105–$115.

## ✻ Where to Eat

Cedar City's dining, like its lodging, is
most appropriately characterized as
budget chain restaurants and fast-food
establishments. These too can be
found along Center and Main streets,
as well as near interstate exits.

✐ **Cedar Creek Restaurant** (435-
536-6311; www.cedarcreekrestaurant
.net), 86 South Main St. Open daily for
breakfast, lunch, and dinner. This restaurant walks the fine line between
high-quality, even contemporary American cuisine and family-friendly comfort food. Entrées range from chicken
to tilapia, rack of lamb, snapper, and
sirloin. Other items are listed on the
menu specifically for seniors and
healthy eaters. Less-formal items and
salads round out the menu. This is a
rarity in Cedar City, as it is a non-fast-
food joint open on Sunday. $11–$20.

**Milt's Stage Stop** (435-586-9344), 5
miles east of Cedar City, 3560 East
UT 14, Cedar City. This canyon restaurant serves American cuisine with a
heavy surf-and-turf theme. The menu
is very classic, sticking to prime rib,
top sirloin, shrimp cocktail, a salad bar,
and various appetizers.

# CEDAR BREAKS NATIONAL MONUMENT

C edar Breaks National Monument is located at the top of the Grand Staircase–Escalante National Monument. The rim of this canyon has an elevation of over 10,000 feet, and its canyons are more than 2,000 feet deep. The top of this plateau is exactly what you would expect of a high, subalpine table: flat, covered in light evergreen forests, and occasional high-altitude parks and fields. However, a canyon cuts suddenly and deeply into this shelf, exposing a bowl of brightly colored cliffs. These canyon walls are immediately similar to those of Bryce Canyon. Though not as expansive as Bryce, this monument has equally impressive colors.

If you want to learn more about the monument, stop by the **Cedar Breaks Visitors Center** (435-586-9451; www.nps.gov/cebr) just inside the park from the southern entrance station, on UT 148. Open 8–6 from the end of May through mid-October. Two hiking trails are available during the summer; each is 2 miles long. The Ramparts Trail is in the southern portion of the park, departing from the visitors center. The other is the Alpine Pond Trail, which leaves from the Chessman Ridge Overlook. By winter, this monument is a favorite of Nordic skiers and snowmobilers; because of its high elevation, it has reliable snowpack, and because of its deep orange and red soils, it is considerably more beautiful than many other places. Though roads are closed during the winter (because of excessive snowfall), the park is accessible by way of Brian Head Resort. Call ahead to check access issues; it is not unheard of for the park to receive prohibitive amounts of snow during its summer season. $5 admission.

# ZION NATIONAL PARK

Zion National Park is Utah's oldest national park. Though each part of Utah's desert has its own characteristics, this might be among the most humbling. Here the two rivers (the Virgin River and Taylor Creek) have eroded the Navajo sandstone of the Colorado Plateau so deeply and steeply as to create sheer vertical walls and monuments as tall as 2,000 feet. In Zion Canyon, which most consider the "main" part of the park, the North Fork of the Virgin River has created these walls; in the northern portion, the South Fork of Taylor Creek is responsible for Kolob Canyon.

As you approach the park from the entrance, these cliffs and monuments slowly become larger and closer together, so that by the time you are inside of the park, the walls dominate the surroundings and make you fee quite dwarfed. As the rivers wind through the park, they create many different features. Some of the most famous are The Narrows and the Subway slot canyons, Angels Landing peninsula, and the Three Patriarchs monoliths.

Zion is part of the enormous region known as the Colorado Plateau, which spans a region at the four corners of Utah, Colorado, Arizona, and New Mexico that is about as large as any of these states (130,000 square miles). This area was a major seabed as recently as 240 million years ago. At that time, it was a flat area submerged in water. The weight of these seas caused the area to become a depressed natural depository for many thousand vertical feet of sand. The more sediment that was loaded onto it, the more it sank. Changing climate and tectonics would remove the sea from this area, leaving it to receive yet more deposits in the form of sands blown in from desert winds. By the end of this accumulation period, the area had nearly 2 vertical miles of amassed sediments that would eventually become lithified. Each layer of deposits was of different origin—mud, sand, etc.— and each would eventually become its own type of rock.

About 20 million years ago, very slow but persuasive subterranean activity began to heft this region. The lift was slow and nonviolent enough that the plateau was able, for the most part, to remain as one block. As it lifted these layers, the rivers of the area persisted in their paths, carving today's dramatic canyons. The Virgin created Zion Canyon, Taylor Creek created Kolob, and the Colorado created the Grand. The plateau was lifted as high as 10,000 feet above sea level. To the west, the Great Basin could not maintain as part of this unit and broke off, falling more than half the distance of this uplift. The Hurricane Fault near Brian Head is an

AFTER A NIGHT ON A PORTALEDGE, A CLIMBER RESUMES THE JOURNEY ON MOONLIGHT BUTTRESS, ZION NATIONAL PARK.

example of this. Zion is on the western edge of this uplift, where the natural gradient is the steepest. Because of this, the waters of these rivers flowed swiftly over the bedrock, able to erode steeply into the ground.

Humans have been living in the park for at least 8,000 years. Early peoples here subsisted on very humble and basic diets of forged game, berries, nuts, seeds, and the like—whatever the desert environment could offer them. Very little is left behind from these times, except scattered stone tools and plant fiber artifacts that were preserved in protected cave stashes from weather. About 2,500 years ago, the lifestyle subtly shifted to include small amounts of supplementary agriculture. Within a few hundred years, this would give way to more outright farming as performed by the Fremont and Anasazi. Because agriculture required people stay put to maintain their crops, permanent communities developed around these areas. The Anasazi and Fremont left behind many complex instances of pueblo communities in the canyons around the Virgin River and other streams. However, 700 years ago, these people apparently vacated the lands, perhaps because of persistent drought conditions. As these civilizations collapsed, they were replaced with flightier communities similar to older, flightier lifestyles.

The Virgin River came into contact with Europeans for the first time during the time of the Spanish Trail in the 1700s. Fur trappers also had a fleeting presence in the area—but there would be no systematic study of the region until John Wesley Powell came through the area during two expeditions in 1869 and 1872. During the second pass, he explored and charted Zion Canyon, and his reports provided that in fact the area could be used for major wagon traffic.

After the Mormon arrival in Salt Lake City in 1847, they began to colonize their society all across Utah. The southern portion of Utah was used as a fruit-producing region for this people. Though Zion was not as accessible as the areas to its west, Isaac Behunin had already erected a cabin here by 1863. Once his cabin was

VIEW NORTH INTO ZION CANYON FROM BIG BEND. MOONLIGHT BUTTRESS, THE ROCK CLIMBING ROUTE, IS VISIBLE ON THE LEFT; IT IS THE MOST PROMINENT PILLAR.

established, others would quickly follow. These communities would never grow, and some would never last long, for the natural surroundings would prohibit it. The narrow canyon provided very little farmable land and would often mercilessly flood, wiping out any crops and many homes.

However, by the early 1900s, the federal government had taken interest in Utah as an area of natural beauty that should be preserved and promoted. In 1909 Zion Canyon was named Mukuntuweap National Monument. The necessary roadways and tourist infrastructure would not become sufficient for nearly a decade, at which point roadways and rail access improved, and the area was redesignated as Zion National Park. Amazingly, Mount Caramel Highway was completed in 1930. This road would allow people to enter this region from the east via a sandstone tunnel 333 feet *longer* than a mile.

Today Zion has two major regions, Kolob and Zion canyons. Kolob is the more northern of the two, accessible from exit 40 on I-15. It is also the more remote of the two canyons, with its main attractions being overlooks and wilderness hikes. (The upper portion of this road closes in the winter.) Zion Canyon is accessible via UT 17 and UT 9 (exit 27) on I-15, if traveling from the north, or UT (exit 16), if traveling from the south. This canyon is the more heavily visited of the two and is outfitted with a new peak-season bus service (implemented in 2000). Here you'll find the Human History Museum as well as Zion Lodge, the famous Angels Landing, and the Zion–Mount Caramel Highway. Though Zion is quite beautiful, its natural environment (deep and narrow canyons) prohibits lengthy or numerous hiking trails that many other national parks have. Entrance is $25 per vehicle; this pass is good for seven days.

**GUIDANCE** **Kolob Canyon Visitors Center** (435-772-3256; www.nps.gov/zion), Kolob Canyon entrance. Open daily (closed on Christmas), 8–5 in the spring and summer, 8–4:30 in the fall and winter. This visitors center is not nearly as large as Zion Canyon's, but it does provide permits, informational brochures, and books.

✢ **Zion Canyon Visitors Center** (435-772-3256; www.nps.gov/zion), Zion Canyon entrance. Open daily (closed on Christmas), 8–6 spring and fall, 8–8 summer, 8–5 winter. This visitors center is quite contemporary, strongly rooted in green infrastructure. Everything in this building was designed to be powered by natural resources when possible; walls were designed to have heat-catching capabilities when necessary, and energy-free cooling towers go into effect in summer months. Solar panels provide almost one-third of the building's electricity, and natural light provides 80 percent of its lighting. This amounts to an estimated savings of nearly 75 percent of total energy use and over 310,000 pounds of carbon dioxide emission each year.

**GETTING THERE** *By car:* Zion has two distinct areas: Kolob Canyon and Zion Canyon. If you are traveling from the north on I-15, **Zion Canyon** is reached by taking UT 17, then UT 9 east from exit 27. If you are traveling from the south, take exit 16 and head east on UT 9. This area of the park can also be reached from the east along UT 9/Zion–Mount Caramel Highway. This way passes through the famous tunnel (more than 1 mile long). Though it accesses no major towns to the east, it joins with US 89, a north–south running road that is roughly parallel to I-15.

**Kolob Canyon** is the more northern of the two areas and is reached via exit 40 on I-15. This is the more remote of the two canyons, and the upper portion of its road is closed in winter.

*By air:* If arriving by air, see the *Getting There* section in the "St. George" chapter.

**GETTING AROUND** While Zion is a fairly small park with limited roadways, it is the most visited national park in Utah, so in 2000 the Park Service devised and implemented a free Zion Canyon shuttle bus system that would resolve this crunch. Shuttles originate in the town of Springdale, to the west of the park. Stops

THE HIDDEN CANYON DEPARTS IN A SOUTHERLY DIRECTION FROM BIG BEND IN ZION CANYON; ALONG THE WAY ARE VIEWS OF A 20-FOOT ARCH, SMALL SANDSTONE CAVES, AND SOME OF THE PARK'S FAMOUS NATURAL FEATURES, SUCH AS ANGELS LANDING AND THE GREAT WHITE THRONE.

Kami Hardcastle

are located throughout this town. There is shuttle parking inside the park at the visitors center; however, parking there is fairly limited and will almost always fill before the morning is through. The radio station 1610 AM broadcasts information pertaining to this. All buses are free and handicapped accessible.

**MEDICAL EMERGENCY** In Zion, you should not expect cell phones to work. For hospitals, the nearest resources are in St. George and Cedar City (as listed in the *Medical Emergency* sections for those chapters). If you can get to a public phone (or get your cell phone to work), Zion does operate a 911 system.

**Zion Medical Clinic** (435-772-3226), 120 Lion Blvd., Springdale. This is an urgent-care facility just west of Zion.

## ✳ To See and Do

**O.C. Tanner Amphitheater** (see the *Entertainment* section in the "St. George" chapter). This 2,000-seat outdoor amphitheater is one of the best venues and events centers in southern Utah.

**Zion Human History Museum** (435-772-3256; www.nps.gov/zion), Zion Canyon entrance. Open daily (closed on Christmas), 10–6 in the spring, 9–7 in the summer, 10–5 in the fall, irregular in winter; call to be sure they will be open when you visit. This small museum has a concise collection of artifacts, voice recordings, photographs, and information on the region's history. A small selection of park-related literature is available for purchase inside the museum.

**Zion Park Theatre** (888-256-3456; www.zionparktheatre.com), 145 Zion Park Blvd., Springdale. Open daily. This is a giant-screen theater; in fact, it's the largest in Utah. It's accompanied by a major sound system and is set up to have many special screenings.

VIEW OF THE TOWERING WALLS IN ZION CANYON NORTH OF ANGELS LANDING. TO REDUCE TRAFFIC, CARS ARE PROHIBITED IN THE ZION CANYON PORTION OF THE PARK FROM MARCH THROUGH OCTOBER; CONVENIENT AND FREE SHUTTLE BUSES OPERATE DURING THIS TIME.

## ✳ Outdoor Activities

### HIKING

#### Zion Canyon

**Angels Landing,** less than 5 miles northeast of the Zion Canyon entrance; at Big Bend. This is one of the park's most famous, interesting, and challenging hikes. This is one of the only ways gain a looking down from atop these fantastic cliffs; otherwise, you're pretty much destined to remain on the valley floor. This narrow peninsula of incredibly tall sandstone is accessed by a thoroughly constructed trail that begins across from the Grotto Picnic Grounds. Along the way are "Walter's Wiggles," a series of 21 rimmed and fortified switchbacks that are virtually on top of each other. From the top of Angels

THE EMERALD POOLS TRAIL COMPLEX ACCESSES A SERIES OF THREE POOLS WITH HIKES OF VARYING LENGTHS.

Landing, you can look north to Moonlight Buttress, a prow of rock that is one of Zion's most popular and best technical rock climbs.

**Riverside Walk/Zion Narrows** is one of the park's most accessible and popular trails. It can offer more than 15 miles of hiking or a much shorter trek, if that is what you seek.

It begins with a paved, 1-mile hike starting at the Temple of Sinawava (at the terminus of Zion Canyon Rd.) and travels in a northerly direction. This is a popular hike, as it follows the Virgin River beyond the road's end and remains relatively cool because of the stream refrigeration and narrow canyons. After the pavement ends, the Virgin River assumes the role of trail.

**Emerald Pools** is a small system of trails that connect a series of pools. These pools almost always contain water, though there is reliably more in spring than in fall. A number of paths exist, as well as a few options for reaching the lower, middle, and upper pools. The lower pools are reached after a 0.6-mile hike from the trailhead. Here a paved trail passes under an overhang off which water from a higher pool pours. The next pool comes very quickly after this pool. The uppermost pool is reached after another short, but slightly steeper jaunt, depending on the trail you take. You can return to the trailhead directly, or via a loop.

**Canyon Overlook** is only 1 mile round-trip and gains but 100 feet of elevation en route to this very scenic vista. Parking is on the south side of UT 9, at the east entrance of the Caramel Tunnel.

### Kolob Canyon

**Kolob Arch** is the second-largest arch in the world (second to Landscape Arch, in Arches National Park), at 287 feet wide. Two trails, each 7 miles one way, gain the arch; one starts from Hop Valley Trailhead, and the other starts from Lees Pass.

**Middle Fork of Taylor Creek** offers one of the most pleasant, middle-distant hikes in the park. This 2.5-mile trail follows Taylor Creek's Middle Fork, its main fork, and gains 500 feet of elevation over the course of the entire journey. The trail terminates at the Double Arch Alcove. Not actually an arch, this deep cave is topped with another such cave, which will someday likely form an arch. This is a very popular hike and will often be heavily trafficked.

**North Fork of Taylor Creek** is just more than 3 miles each way. This trail offers a better workout, with nearly 1,000 feet of elevation gain and somewhat proactive trail navigation. Though the trail is not hard to follow, it traverses some varied terrain and is not a wide, groomed footpath. The trail shares the same parking lot as the Middle Fork trail.

**South Fork of Taylor Creek** is a shorter, steeper hike than either of the other two Taylor Creek trails. Though it only just more than 1 mile each way, it gains nearly as much elevation as the North Fork trail. This very scenic trail terminates in a large boulder field. The trailhead is located 1.25 miles up canyon from that of the North and Middle Fork.

**The Subway** is Zion's most famous canyoneering route. It is 9.5 miles in length, begins at Kolob Terraces, and requires skill, a rope and harnesses, and a full day's worth of time and nourishment. As always, flash-flood hazards should be observed (i.e., do not enter the canyon if bad weather is anywhere in the region), and a shuttle should be arranged. Permits are required, which can be obtained at the Kolob Canyon Visitors Center when you gather other information for your adventures here. There is a limit of 50 day-hikers in this canyon at any time.

ROCK CLIMBING Climbing in both Zion and Kolob canyons is quite popular. However, this is no entry-level style of climbing; routes here are generally at least 10 pitches long (though there are some shorter) and often require expert free- and aid-climbing proficiency. Likely the most famous, and probably the most popular, route is Zion Canyon's **Moonlight Buttress.** This route takes a very scenic and direct line up a prominent attached pillar that is visible, and to the north of Angels Landing, on the west side of the Virgin River. This route is particularly popular because it is at once an easy and noncommitting aid line (A1 with fixed anchors and the ability to rappel from any pitch on the route), and a compelling and challenging free line (5.12 d, mostly splitter crack climbing). The Web site www.bigwall.com has good topographic maps and route descriptions for selected climbs in the park.

## ✳ Lodging

**Zion Lodge** (435-772-7700 or 888-297-2757; www.zionlodge.com), 3 miles north of the Zion Canyon entrance, on Zion Canyon Scenic Dr. This is the park's only in-bounds lodging and is open year-round. Guests here can choose between 75 hotel-style rooms, 6 suites, and 40 cabins; dine at the on-site restaurant; or peruse the gift shop. Rooms tend to be somewhat basic, though the lobby and the overarching impression of the lodge are above that. $150 and up.

# West-Central Utah

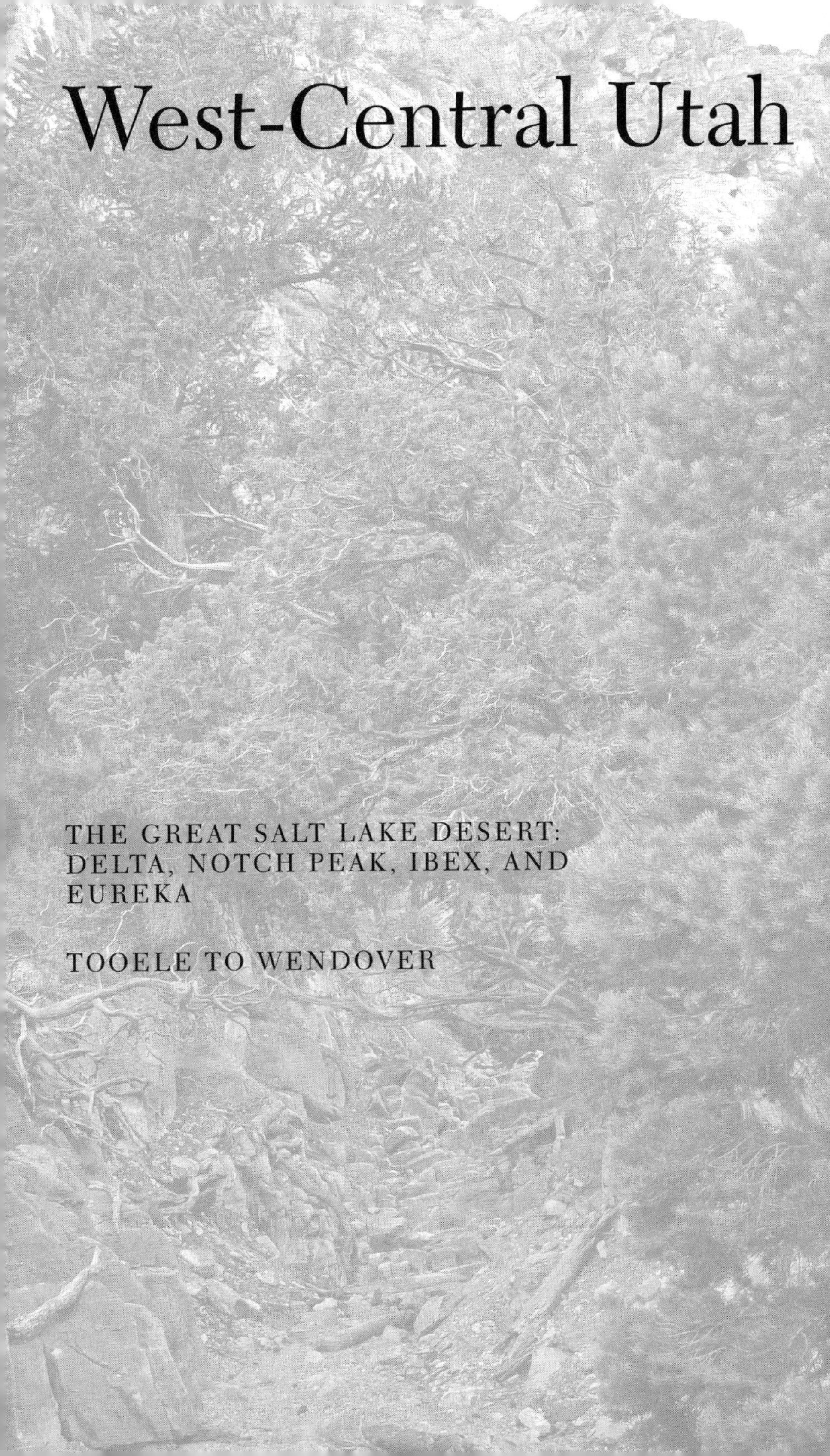

THE GREAT SALT LAKE DESERT:
DELTA, NOTCH PEAK, IBEX, AND
EUREKA

TOOELE TO WENDOVER

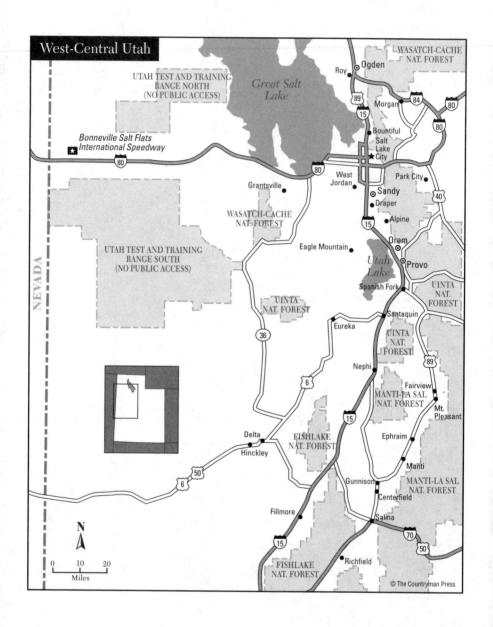

# West-Central Utah

UTAH TEST AND TRAINING
RANGE NORTH
(NO PUBLIC ACCESS)

*Great Salt Lake*

WASATCH-CACHE
NAT. FOREST

Roy

Ogden

89

Morgan

84

80

15

80

Bonneville Salt Flats
International Speedway

80

Bountiful

Salt
Lake
City

West
Jordan

Park City

80

40

Grantsville

Sandy

Draper

WASATCH-CACHE
NAT. FOREST

Alpine

Eagle Mountain

15

Orem

UTAH TEST AND TRAINING
RANGE SOUTH
(NO PUBLIC ACCESS)

*Utah Lake*

Provo

UINTA
NAT.
FOREST

NEVADA

Spanish Fork

UINTA
NAT. FOREST

Santaquin

36

Eureka

UINTA
NAT.
FOREST

89

Nephi

Fairview

6

MANTI-LA SAL
NAT. FOREST

Mt.
Pleasant

15

Delta

Ephraim

Hinckley

FISHLAKE
NAT. FOREST

Manti

50

Gunnison

MANTI-LA SAL
NAT. FOREST

6

Centerfield

Fillmore

Salina

70

N

15

50

0    10    20

Miles

FISHLAKE
NAT. FOREST

Richfield

© The Countryman Press

# WEST-CENTRAL UTAH IN BRIEF

West-central Utah is of the most desolate lands in the country; it contains a portion of the "loneliest highway" in the United States (US 50) and a similarly desolate stretch of I-80 between Wendover and Tooele, as well as military testing grounds, long-evaporated lake beds (now hardpan desert), high mountain ranges, lunar landscapes, and virtually no water. Even with modern highways, a reliable vehicle, plumbing, and electricity, it would be hard to imagine living in this region today. However, people have been living here as true hermits since the early 20th century. Today this area of the state is still virtually as untouched as it was thousands of years ago—small farming communities and occasional military testing grounds are the only interruption of the emptiness.

The main throughway in the southern end of this region, US 50, is used by a surprising number of travelers. It is a good route from central Utah through Nevada and into the Bishop and Mammoth Mountain area of Southern California. However, after leaving Delta, the road is devoid of services for about 90 miles. Farther north, I-80 brings many travelers from Salt Lake City past the Bonneville Speedway, and to the gambling border town of Wendover, Nevada, and beyond to Reno.

The environment here is classified as "basin and range" and is arid with extreme temperatures: bitter cold in winter and scorching hot in summer. Delta is one of the most major towns along US 50 west of I-15. It is quite an isolated and conservative town whose staples are religion and agriculture. Moving west from Delta, US 50 crosses to the north of the San Francisco and Wah Wah mountains, through the House and then Confusion ranges just before entering Nevada.

The San Francisco Mountains were the site of many late-19th-century mines and now are littered with ghost towns. Bristlecone pines between 3,000 and 4,000 years old are found in the canyons of the House Range, a range loved by rock climbers. Notch Peak, about 9,600 feet above sea level, is completely sheer; its north face is the highest limestone cliff in the lower 48. With a 3,000-foot vertical rise and 4,500 feet of total exposure, this is comparable to El Capitan. Climbers also love the quartzite just south of US 50 in this range called Ibex Wells. Unfortunately, these rich quartz stores are being strip-mined.

Along I-80, the most major town is Tooele, a town of significant magnitude, with more than 40,000 residents. Tooele is a pleasant town tucked on the northwestern slopes of the Oquirrh Mountains. These mountains have many trails suited for mountain biking and hiking. Some rock climbing is here as well. This is the home of the Miller Motorsports Park, a world-class speedway.

This part of the state, very much untouched by civilization, is one of the easier places to envision Utah's physical history. Because of the absolute dryness of the region, vegetation amounts to little more than sagebrush and the Mormon tea plant in the hills. There are virtually no trees except high in the mountain ranges or in canyons, and the pale valley floors are as flat as they could be and mark the old footprint of ancient Lake Bonneville. This lake, which filled and drained a number of times over the millennia, last held water about 12,000 years ago and was about half the size of modern Utah. This is the same lake that created the nearly perfect plane of the Bonneville Salt Flats and left a number of residual lakes. Lake Sevier, almost always dry, is the most visible of these from US 50 and is just west of Delta.

## ✳ Weather

This part of the state has perhaps the harshest weather of Utah. Because of its utter lack of water, it has wild temperature swings and no plant life that would provide shelter. Wind here can sail at constant speeds greater than 50 miles per hour, with nothing to interrupt its path in the wide-open hardpan valleys. During the winter, Delta sees lows that near 10°F and daytime highs of only 38°F. During July and August, its daytime highs average 94°F. Generally the valleys in the area are just a bit higher than 5,000 feet and receive less than 8 inches of precipitation each year.

# THE GREAT SALT LAKE DESERT: DELTA, NOTCH PEAK, IBEX WELLS, AND EUREKA

**GUIDANCE** **Delta City** (435-864-4316; www.deltautah.com). There isn't a lot to tell about with respect to the town, but this Web site lists public resources such as the library and businesses.

**Fillmore North Park Tourism Booth** (435-743-6714), 460 North Main St., Fillmore. Fillmore is on I-15 just south of Delta. This booth is a useful place to obtain information on area points of interest such as ghost towns and hikes.

**Millard County Tourism** (435-864-1400; www.millardcountytravel.com). This Web site is the most informative site on the region, with activity and accommodations suggestions.

**GETTING THERE** Delta is at the junction of many state and national highways, just 30 miles west of I-15 as the crow flies. The two most major highways connecting Delta to this interstate are UT 132 (which heads northeast out of Delta to Nephi) and US 50 (which heads southwest to Fillmore). US 6 and 50 merge in Delta and run concurrent, passing quickly through Hinckley before entering the truly desolate stretch containing the Confusion and House Range, and reaching the Nevada border and the Great Basin National Monument after about 90 miles.

**MEDICAL EMERGENCY** **Delta Community Medical Center** (435-864-5591; www.intermountainhealthcare.org), 126 White Sage Ave., Delta. This is the nearest hospital to the region's interior and offers round-the-clock emergency and surgical services.

**Fillmore Community Medical Center** (435-743-5591; www.intermountain healthcare.org), 674 South UT 99, Fillmore. This hospital is farther east than the Delta facility but is located very near to I-15 and may thus have the most convenient access.

## ✳ To See and Do

**Dividend Ghost Town,** on Dividend Rd.; head east out of Eureka on US 6 and south on Dividend Rd. just outside of town. This is the location of an old mining town, in operation from 1907 to 1949. Over these decades, almost $20 million of silver and lead ore were extracted from shafts more than 1,000 feet deep. Strangely, this was one of the first towns in the state to have indoor plumbing.

**Fish Springs National Wildlife Refuge** (435-831-5353; www.fws.gov/fish springs), about 65 miles southwest of Vernal and about 70 miles northwest of Delta; see the Web site for specific directions. This refuge contains almost 18,000 acres in the center of the Great Basin Desert, with more than half of its total acreage lush wetlands fed by natural springs. This is a total anomaly in this vast desert and so is absolutely crucial to the region's migratory birds. The birds here span 280 species represented by more than 20,000 individuals each year. This was designated a refuge in 1959 but has long been a stopover for migratory birds and people in its history. As many as 10,000 years ago, ancestors of the Ute Tribe left evidence of their presence—and mail carriers in the Pony Express, in operation between 1860 and 1861, operated a stage here.

**Great Basin Museum** (435-864-5013; www.millardcounty.com/gbmuseum), 328 West 100 North, Delta. Open 10–4 Monday–Saturday. This is a small, no-frills museum that provides a summary of this region's mining, farming, Native American, and natural history. Collections include fossils, rock samples, Native American and pioneer artifacts, old photographs and records, a Topaz Camp display (see **Topaz National Historic Landmark,** below), and new space technologies equipment created from the area's ore. Free admission.

**Little Sahara Recreation Area,** just west of the intersection of US 6 and UT 148; access points from either highway. Just called "the Dunes" by some, Little Saraha is a 125-square-mile collection of ever-moving sand dunes. It is a popular recreation area for locals, particularly those with ATVs. The plentiful dunes here were formed by sand sediments of Sevier River, which as recently as 12,000 years ago fed Lake Bonneville. Prevailing winds have swept the pale sand into these dunes, which collectively move somewhere around 7 feet northeast each year. Also in the area are three established campgrounds and the **Rockwell Natural Area,** a natural preserve where vehicles are forbidden.

**Topaz National Historic Landmark,** 10000 West 4500 South, 16 miles northwest of Delta. Topaz is something not frequently discussed today. During World War II, Utah was the site of multiple prisoner of war camps and internment camps. When the U.S. government took thousands of Japanese citizens from their homes, they were placed in these camps. Topaz was a Japanese internment camp in operation from 1942 to Halloween of 1945. During that time 9,000 were sent to Topaz, making it the eighth-largest city in the state at the time. More information can be obtained at the Topaz Museum (www.topazmuseum.org).

## ✳ Outdoor Activities

GOLF **Canyon Hills Park Golf Course** (435-623-9930), 1264 North 325 East, Nephi. This nine-hole, 3,452-yard, par-36 course is extremely open, flat, and allows for a speedy game or a session at the driving range. $20 weekdays, $24 weekends.

**Paradise Resort Golf Course** (435-743-4439; www.golfparadiseatfillmore.com), 905 North Main St., Fillmore. This 18-hole, 85-acre course was opened in 1998, is very scenic and well designed, and includes a driving range. Also at the resort are a swimming pool, pedestrian and bicycle paths, motel, and restaurant. $24.

**Sunset View Golf Course** (435-864-2508), 3000 East 1500 North, Delta. This par-72 course has 18 holes, 6,932 yards, driving range, little crowding, and some of the state's more pristine greens and fairways. A very open and flat course.

**HIKING** Hiking in this area is very possible and rewarding, though not as popular as in other areas because of the region's remoteness and harsh climate. However, spring and fall usually can offer very pleasant hiking conditions. You must wait only until the snow has melted out of the higher elevations, but before daytime temperatures are not yet too high. Many of the mountains in the ranges here have peaks at or above 10,000 feet and so are much cooler than in the valleys. However, the climate here is so arid that there are rarely any trees to provide any shelter from the sun.

In this area alone are four major ranges, the **San Francisco Mountains,** between Milford and Delta; the **Wah Wah Mountains,** west of Milford and bisected by UT 21; the **House Range,** about 50 miles west of Delta; and the **Confusion Range,** west of the House Range near the Nevada-Utah border. House and Confusion ranges are the most commonly hiked, as they enjoy relatively easy access via US 6 and 50.

Roads departing from the main highways will always be dirt, though they are usually very well maintained. It is advised that plenty of research be done for driving directions, being sure to cross-reference with many sources, as the roads are unmarked and often part of a complicated web of roads. Directions that seem simple at home can be irritatingly confusing in the desert. A gazetteer is helpful, though not foolproof, and a compass or GPS unit would not be a bad idea.

**Crystal Peak** is a distinctive mountain whose pyramid-shaped rocky pinnacle is completely barren of trees. The peak is composed of volcanic rock rich with fossils. Its white rock sticks out very clearly against its desert backdrop and is entirely pocked with wind-created huecos. To get there, take Crystal Peak Road northwest

THE MANY CANYONS IN THE HOUSE RANGE CONTAIN A VARIETY OF GEOLOGY, FROM PINK TO WHITE GRANITE, TO LIMESTONE AND QUARTZITE. UNMARKED DIRT ROAD ACCESS MAKES THIS MAZE A DREAM FOR SOME, BUT A NIGHTMARE FOR OTHERS.

A VIEW FROM THE TOP OF NOTCH PEAK, LOOKING SOUTH TOWARD THE DRIED-UP LAKE BED AT IBEX WELLS, AN AREA POPULAR FOR QUARTZITE ROCK CLIMBING AND BOULDERING.

about 20 miles from UT 257 (near Milford) or southeast about 15 miles from US 6 and 50, 10 miles east of the Utah-Nevada border.

**Notch Peak** is a very worthwhile hike. This peak's name is appropriate for two reasons. The first is the very distinctive, north-facing vertical wall and thus "notch" it makes on the horizon as you approach the House Range from Delta. The second reason is because of its bird's-eye view. If you were to view it from above, there would be a wedge, like a piece of pie, removed from its northwest side. This notch has a 4,500-foot nearly sheer drop, and the north-facing cliff of this notch is the sheerest, with a perfect 3,000-foot limestone cliff. This cliff is the largest limestone cliff in the lower 48 and is just a few hundred feet shorter than El Capitan in Yosemite National Park. Technical rock climbing routes exist on this face (see the *Rock Climbing* section of this chapter) and are approached from the southeast side of the mountain.

The nontechnical hike to reach the summit (and gain this overlook) is via the east-southeastern shoulder of this mountain. The parking area is in Sawtooth Canyon, visible on many topographical maps. Many dirt roads reach the area, but you want to depart from US 6 and 50 at around milepost 46. After roughly 5 miles, make a left to follow Miller Canyon Road (often unmarked). You know you've reached the trailhead when you see an abandoned brownstone cabin. Walk up the dirt road, bearing left about 0.5 mile up the road and continue in a westerly direction up a wash. You will follow this wash until reaching the mountain's shoulder, just below the summit (which will be visible at this point). On the way you can expect to see huge, ancient bristlecone pines. These trees are estimated to be between 3,000–4,000 years old. This hike is 3.5 miles each way, and given the view it gains, is not too strenuous at all.

**Swasey Peak** is the highest peak in the House Range, at 9,678 feet, and offers quite remarkable views of the surrounding desert: Notch Peak (to the south), salt flats and dried-up lake beds, the Confusion Range, Ibex, and the almost complete lack of civilization. It takes 1,700 feet of vertical gain to reach this summit. Swasey Peak is 32.5 miles west of Hinckley on US 6 and 50; turn north and follow signs for Death Valley and Long Ridge Reservoir. Continue straight for just more than 6 miles, passing a reservoir, and avoiding turns to Notch Peak Road, Marjum Pass, Swasey Spring, and Death Canyon. You will travel about 21 miles on this dirt road to the parking area. There are several routes to the top, but if you travel via the easiest nontechnical route, the southeast ridge, you will see the remains of a helicopter crash. This route is about 4 miles round-trip.

ROCK CLIMBING **Ibex** is about 50 miles west of Delta on US 6 and 50, south of the highway and marked by signs for Ibex Well. Ibex is one of the state's more famous bouldering areas, perhaps because of its lunar landscape. The valley floor is totally flat and barren hardpan, and is surrounded by peculiar, splotchy red quartzite cliffs and occasional abandoned ranch structures and shot-up old cars. Though the bouldering is what makes the area famous, the multipitch sport and traditional routes can also be quite good. There are several dozen sport and mixed routes that ascend the cliffs and towers on the western end of this area. The ratings here are generally quite stiff. For information on bouldering, use Jeff Baldwin and Mike Beck's *Utah Bouldering* guidebook, or visit www.drtopo.com. For information on roped routes, use James Garrett's guidebook *Ibex and Selected Climbs of Utah's West Desert.*

**North Face of Notch Peak,** about 55 miles west of Delta on US 6 and 50; north of the highway via many unmarked dirt roads; aim for the notch on the southeastern part of this mountain. A 3,000-foot dead-vertical limestone face, this is the largest of its kind in the lower 48. The face is divided into an upper and lower face, and is separated by a large ledge. The lower face is slightly farther south from the

THE IBEX WELL AREA IS A STARKLY BEAUTIFUL, LUNAR LANDSCAPE. BEWARE: DO NOT ATTEMPT TO CROSS THE OLD LAKE BED IF IT HAS RAINED RECENTLY; YOUR VEHICLE WILL BECOME IMPOSSIBLY STUCK.

LOOKING DOWN AT THE 3,000+ FOOT
SHEER VERTICAL FACE OF NOTCH PEAK.

summit and is about 1,000 feet tall. The upper face is 2,000 feet tall and directly beneath the summit. The rock on this face, though sometimes solid, is notoriously flaky and chossy. This means holds, and sometimes protection, cannot be trusted, and rock fall danger is extremely high. Though natural protection is supplemented with bolts, many sections of the climb are unprotectable, and run-outs of 30 to 40 feet are common, hence the R rating on many of the routes. For all of these reasons, there is only about a half dozen technical routes on this peak, and probably not much more than 100 people have summited.

ROCKHOUNDING Utah, because of its wildly varied geology and sparse vegetation, is one of the best spots for this fairly obscure hobby. Millard County is one of the more popular spots in the state. Minerals often found in this region are red beryl (a pinkish red crystal found in the Wah Wah Mountains), sunstones (yellowish-green crystals found at Sunstone Knoll), and topaz, found at Topaz Mountain. More information on this activity in Millard County can be obtained at the Web site www.millardcounty.com. If you prefer to have more of a sure bet, or want to give the kids a chance to find something cool, visit **U-Dig Fossils** (435-864-3638), 350 East 300 South.

THE LIMESTONE FACE OF NOTCH PEAK AS SEEN FROM THE SOUTHWEST, WITH PINK
GRANITE DOMES IN THE FOREGROUND

## ✴ Lodging

**Best Western Paradise Inn** (435-743-6895; www.bestwestern.com), 905 North Main St., Fillmore. This hotel is located right at the Paradise Golf Resort. Though not a luxury hotel, it is tidy, affordable, and comfortable. $80 and up.

**Budget Motel** (435-864-4533), 75 South 350 East, Delta. As its name indicates, this hotel doesn't claim to be anything fancy. A series of recent improvements have increased the quality of this hotel, and now it is a respectable, basic hotel. $35 and up.

## ✴ Where to Eat

In addition to the restaurants listed below, Delta has two grocery stores and several fast-food establishments and convenience stores on Main Street (UT 6 and 50). In Fillmore, there are two grocery stores and numerous hole-in-the-wall restaurants and fast-food joints on Main Street (UT 99). Delta and Fillmore, both small towns with strong religious foundations, see most of their businesses closed on Sunday.

**Curly's Lounge** (435-979-1496), 294 West Main St., Delta. Open Monday–Saturday, closed Sunday. Curly's is Delta's watering hole. This is the classic small-town bar with dimmed lights, opaque windows, pool, beer, and finger food. After a day of hiking or climbing, a stop here can really hit the spot. Though many would call it dingy, this lounge has a special place in the hearts of many for being exactly what it is. Curly's runs specials each day, and often has great prices on pitchers and free billiards.

✐ **Leo's Loft Steakhouse** (435-864-4790; www.theloftsteakhouse.com), 411 East Main St., Delta. Serving dinner Monday–Saturday. This restaurant specializes in beef, though seafood and chicken are available as well. Portions are hearty, and sides include a salad bar, garden vegetables, and many different preparations of potato. A wine and beer menu is available, as well as a children's menu. $12–$30.

**Mi Rancherita Mexican Restaurant** (435-864-4245), 540 Topaz Blvd., Delta. Open for lunch and dinner Monday–Saturday. This is a fairly large eatery right off Main Street on the eastern side of town. Though the restaurant is not gourmet, it has a predictable selection of large-portioned Mexican and Mexican American dishes that are unquestionably superior to fast food.

# TOOELE TO WENDOVER

This region of Utah, just west of Salt Lake City, is one of Utah's more peculiar and most ignored. I-80 beelines directly through it without curving at all. Many people view this as a tedious stretch of boring highway and bomb across it as quickly as possible; others are fascinated by the desolation of the landscape and try to catch glimpses of the Bonneville Speedway.

Tooele (pronounced "too-WILL-ah") is on the eastern end of this region, just 35 miles southwest of Salt Lake City. South of I-80 and the Great Salt Lake, it sits on the western slope of the Oquirrh Mountains (pronounced "OH-kerr") in much the same way that Salt Lake City sits against the Wasatch. Tooele is much smaller than Salt Lake City, but it still has roughly 40,000 residents of its own and is home to the Miller Motorsports Park, Utah's largest motorcycle and automobile racing track. The Oquirrh Mountains have some great recreational opportunities, including rock climbing, mountain biking, hiking, and even backcountry skiing.

The peculiar landscape beyond Tooele has *Twilight Zone* overtones—out there, it feels as if you should expect to see UFOs, a nuclear bomb, or some sort of NASA project. In fact, this land does have a history of military testing. This area was of major importance during World War II. The Dugway Proving Grounds, to the south of I-80 (and, oddly, immediately adjacent to the Fish Springs National Wildlife Refuge), contains over 800,000 acres and was designated as a testing facility in 1941 when the government decided it needed a most remote location. It is here that biological and chemical weapons, flame throwers, toxic agents, and safety clothing were tested. This is also the crash-landing site of the spaceship *Genesis*.

LOOKING ACROSS THE SALT FLATS FROM THE ENTRANCE TO THE FAMOUS BONNEVILLE SPEEDWAY

The Utah Test and Training Range (formerly the Wendover Army Air Field) is made of two parts bisected by I-80. The nearly 2-million-acre testing range came into being in the early 1940s as an outpost of Fort Douglas (where today's University of Utah campus is located). As early as March 1842, it was a bombing practice center for B-17 and B-24 aircraft. During the development of the atom bomb, a series of Little Boy tests, and later a highly explosive prototype of Fat Boy, was tested here in 1945.

Just to the east of the two testing facilities is the Skull Valley Indian Reservation. This reservation is one of the smallest in the state, at just under 30 square miles. As of the 2000 census, it was home to only 31 Goshute tribespeople. This was the site of the Dugway Sheep Incident of 1968, during which the U.S. Army was allegedly responsible for the nerve gas (VX) illness and resulting death of more than 6,000 sheep. This is also the proposed location of a much-debated federal nuclear waste disposal.

Wendover is the westernmost town in this region. Though Wendover, Utah, is all but bust, its neighbor in Nevada, West Wendover, is doing quite well for an isolated, small town. It does so by enticing people to experience Nevada's relaxed liquor laws and legalized gambling. Though it is no Vegas, people definitely consider it a good time for a night out with friends.

GUIDANCE **Be Active in Tooele** (www.beactivetooele.com). This Web site is a nice resource that has collected and organized information on most of the recreational opportunities in the Tooele area.

**Tooele Chamber of Commerce** (435-882-0960 or 800-378-0960; www.2wheelah .com), 86 South Main St., Tooele. Tooele's chamber offers a listing of area points of interest and has a section for discounted prices on certain services.

GETTING THERE *By car:* Getting to this region by car is about as simple as it gets, and I-80 slices right through the heart of it. Anything in this region worth seeing (and legally accessible to civilians) is near to this roadway.

PLACARD AT THE I-80 REST STOP EAST OF WENDOVER WITH VIEWS OF BONNEVILLE SPEEDWAY

*By air:* **Salt Lake International Airport (SLC)** (801-575-2400 or 800-595-2442; www.slcairport.com). This airport is right along I-80, just 5 miles west of Salt Lake City and about 20 minutes east of the Tooele exit.

MEDICAL EMERGENCY **Mountain West Medical Center** (435-843-3600; www.mountainwestmc.com), 2055 North Main St., Tooele. This is Tooele Valley's own hospital, complete with emergency and surgical facilities.

## ✳ To See and Do

**Aragonite Ghost Town** is an old mining town from the early 20th century that mined . . . aragonite! This mine was only in operation for a few years, but today the mineshafts are still open, and a few bunkhouses remain, as well as an old truck. Aragonite is also near the Hastings Cutoff, part of the famous Donner Party route of the 1840s. Take exit 56 off I-80 and head south just less than 3 miles. Turn right and head west on a dirt road into the mountains. After about 3.5 miles you will see these old buildings.

**Iosepa** was a peculiar vignette in history that is known by very few. This is the town to which a number of Hawaiian Mormons were relocated in 1889. These converts came to the United States to build a town in honor of their religion. They worked hard to forge a life in Zion, and the town briefly flourished. At its maximum population, the town had almost 230 residents and grew to include Portuguese, Samoans, Maoris, Britons, and Scots. Joseph Smith, early president of the Mormon church, declared this one of the most successful colonizing efforts he had seen. However, they discovered frontier life in Utah to be much harsher than expected. Food production and mine labor proved difficult and often lethal. Death rates outnumbered birth rates. Finally, an LDS church was opened in Hawaii, and though the colonizers were encouraged not to leave Utah, most did. By 1917, the town was virtually vacant. Today a monument stands to commemorate this town, though nothing of the original town remains but a graveyard.

## ✳ Outdoor Activities

**Desert Peak Complex** (435-843-4000; www.desertpeakcomplex.com), 2930 West UT 112, Tooele. This is indeed a complex, with facilities for equestrian riders; motocross and BMX athletes; lap and recreational swimmers; softball, baseball, and soccer players; archers; and putt-putt golfers. There are even two museums: one dedicated to the history of mining in the Oquirrh Mountains, and the other to Utah firefighting history. In addition to being a place to recreate, this is also a place to watch races, tournaments, and rodeos, as well as go to the fair. Prices vary per activity but are generally quite reasonable, ranging from a $4 fee for putt-putt golf (with $2 rentals) to a $10 fee for using the archery range.

### BIKING

*Mountain Biking*

**Copper Pit Overlook/White Pine Loop** comprise a set of rides that offer views of the area's natural environment, as well as a great way to see the spectacle that is the **Kennecott Copper Mine** (see the *Museums and Galleries* section in the "Salt Lake City" chapter of this book; 801-252-3234; www.kennecott.com), the world's largest open pit mine. Though some think it dubious that this scar is something to brag about, it is certainly something to behold at 0.75 mile deep and 2.5 miles wide. There are two riding options. The first is technically easier as it is on paved and dirt roads, but it's aerobically challenging. This ride is 19 miles round-trip and has an elevation gain of almost 4,000 feet. It begins at the Tooele County Museum (35 North Broadway, Tooele), climbs through the Oquirrhs' Middle Canyon, over Butterfield Pass, and up to the West Mountain Summit.

The second loop is the White Pine Loop. Though it gains only 900 feet of elevation and is just less than 4 miles total, it is technically much more challenging. This ride begins at the White Pine Canyon and heads toward the Butterfield Pass Summit. The start of this ride is reached by taking Vine Street east out of Tooele. This leads directly into White Pine Canyon and to the campground and trailhead.

VIEW FROM I-80 LOOKING SOUTHEAST AT TOOELE AND THE OQUIRRH MOUNTAINS

**Stansbury Island Loop** is a 9-mile loop with just more than 600 feet of elevation gain, and it's an excellent manner of seeing the Great Salt Lake and its unique environs. If ridden clockwise, all of the climbing will be done at the beginning of the ride, leaving the majority of the ride (a remaining nearly 8 miles) as downhill or flat. This peninsula was once surrounded by the waters of ancient Lake Bonneville, whose former shoreline the trail follows for much of the ride. The trail ascends to this former shoreline, traverses three canyons on the southwestern slopes of this island, and turns back to return to the trailhead. To get there, take exit 84 off I-80. The ramp merges with the access road, and heads first west, then north. Follow BLM signs to the trailhead.

## Road Biking

**Oquirrh Mountain Loop Ride** is a perfect century ride for those new to the distance. It has no major climbs and gains only about 2,500 feet of elevation for the entirety of the ride. This loop connects Tooele to Salt Lake City and does a loop around the Oquirrh Mountains. Depending on where you go in Salt Lake City, the ride can be almost exactly 100 miles, or a bit longer. The basic loop starts in Tooele, heads south on UT 36, southeast and then east on UT 73, north on UT 68, through the Salt Lake metro area, and west toward Tooele.

**GOLF Oquirrh Hills Golf Course** (435-882-4220; www.tehillsgolf.com or www.tooelecity.org), 1255 East Vine St., Tooele. This nine-hole, 3,200-yard, par-35 course has but a few water hazards, with many long, narrow, subtly curving fairways, but just as many that are open. The course varies between hills and flats, with the Oquirrh Mountains as a scenic backdrop, and trees sometimes occluding the view of city. $8 on weekdays, $9 on weekends.

**Overlake Golf Course** (435-882-8802; www.overlakegolf.com), 2947 North 680 West, Tooele. This is a wide-open, 18-hole, par-72, 7,248-yard, American-style links course with 11 water hazards, mostly concentrated in the back half of the course. $16 on weekdays, $20 on weekends.

**HIKING** **Deseret Peak** is the tallest mountain in the Stansbury Range and Tooele County, at 11,031 feet. Above the tree line, its upper flanks are bare but for a few cedar and juniper bushes speckling its sides, and its peaks are jagged. From the summit are expansive views of the vastly barren Great Basin Desert and the Great Salt Lake to the north. The southwest limestone face of this mountain has a sheer drop of 1,500 feet. To get there, begin in Grantsville (about 10 miles west of Tooele) and head south and out of town on South Cooley Street as it turns into the Mormon Trail Road. Roughly 5 miles south of Grantsville, head right into Willow Canyon and drive just more than 7 miles to its terminus. This is the trailhead. Two possible routes exist from this trailhead, and the shortest route is done by staying on the left fork in the trail, less than a mile into the hike. (This route should be about 3.5 miles each way.) Taking the right fork will also lead you to the peak, but it adds a slight amount of distance. The approach road is usually well maintained by the Forest Service and should be fine in any vehicle. There are many somewhat developed campsites along the road. Camping $5.

**Ibapah Peak,** at 12,087 feet tall, is certainly a respectable peak. The trailhead elevation is 6,890 feet, which means you will gain almost exactly 1 vertical mile on this hike in the Deep Creek Mountains. Though few people have heard of this peak, it

A REST STOP ALONG I-80 JUST EAST OF WENDOVER FEATURES VIEWING PLATFORMS FROM WHICH TRAVELERS CAN OBSERVE THE FAMOUS BONNEVILLE SALT FLATS AND BONNEVILLE SPEEDWAY, JUST NORTH OF THE REST STOP.

is taller than some of the more famous Utah peaks like Mount Olympus and Mount Timpanogos. The trail is only about 7 miles each way and is fairly steep. This is a great hike for the fit crowd wanting to be away from people. To get there, head south-southwest out of Wendover on US 93. After just less than 30 miles, turn southeast (left) toward Callao and Ibapah. Follow signs to Callow. At a Y-intersection about a mile before Callow, stay right and continue straight, until you reach Granite Creek Road, at which point you turn right. Stay left at the next intersection, and park at the trailhead.

## ✴ Lodging

Chain hotels are the name of the game in this region. Most lodging options are in Tooele, or just over the Nevada border in West Wendover. In Tooele, all you must do is drive the length of Main Street, and you will see the vast majority of your options. In West Wendover, your choices will be obvious as the casinos are not shy about advertising their location.

**American Inn & Suites** (435-882-6100; www.americaninnandsuites.net),

491 South Main St., Tooele. This building's exterior is somewhat uncharacteristic for a hotel, though its rooms are clean and completely normal. Accommodations range in size from single guest rooms to suites. $70 and up.

**Best Western** (435-882-5010 or 877-863-4780; www.ihchotelsgroup.com), 365 North Main St., Tooele. This hotel is very new and clean, and though it is part of a rather basic chain, it has visually appealing stone and woodwork in the lobby, and rooms with stylish simplicity. $65 and up.

**Hampton Inn** (435-843-7700 or 800-426-7866; www.tooele.hamptoninn .com), 461 South Main St., Tooele. This is one of the nicer of Tooele's many chain hotels, with a safely stylized and spacious modern lobby. The rooms are a bit dated but well kept. $80 and up.

## ✴ Where to Eat

Dining in this area is best achieved by heading to Main Street in Tooele and Wendover. There will be many fast-food chain establishments, national sit-downs like Denny's and Pizza Hut, as well as chuckwagon-type joints.

# INDEX